It is not necessary to accept everything as true,
one must only accept it as necessary."

FRANZ KAFKA, THE TRIAL

IMAGE COMICS, INC.

chief operating officer : **Robert Kirkman**
chief financial officer : **Erik Larsen**
president : **Todd McFarlane**
chief executive officer : **Marc Silvestri**
vice-president : **Jim Valentino**
publisher : **Eric Stephenson**
director of business development : **Ron Richards**
pr & marketing director : **Jennifer De Guzman**
accounts manager : **Branwyn Bigglestone**
accounting assistant : **Emily Miller**
marketing assistant : **Jamie Parreno**
administrative assistant : **Jenna Savage**
digital rights coordinator : **Kevin Yuen**
production manager : **Jonathan Chan**
art director : **Drew Gill**
print manager : **Tyler Shainline**
production artist : **Monica Garcia**
production artist : **Vincent Kukua**
production artist : **Jana Cook**

www.imagecomics.com

KAFKA
by STEVEN T. SEAGLE & STEFANO GAUDIANO

WWW.MANOFACTION.TV

ISBN: 978-1-60706-763-4
KAFKA. First Printing. July 2013

Published by Image Comics, Inc.
Office of publication:
2001 Center Street, Sixth Floor,
Berkeley, California 94704, U.S.A.

International Rights / Foreign Licensing:
foreignlicensing@imagecomics.com

THANKS TO
Deni for publishing us the first time;
Gary for publishing us the second time;
Richard for publishing us the third time;
Eric for publishing us this time;
Dayton for introducing me to Stefano;
and integral supporters Sir Ken, Bob, Diana, Marco and Liesel.
Steve

THANKS TO
Deni Loubert , Steve and Liesel, Dayton Taylor, Frank Albanese,
Steve Csutoras, Kirk Bath, Craig Gassen, and Il Gruppo Saltelli.
Stefano

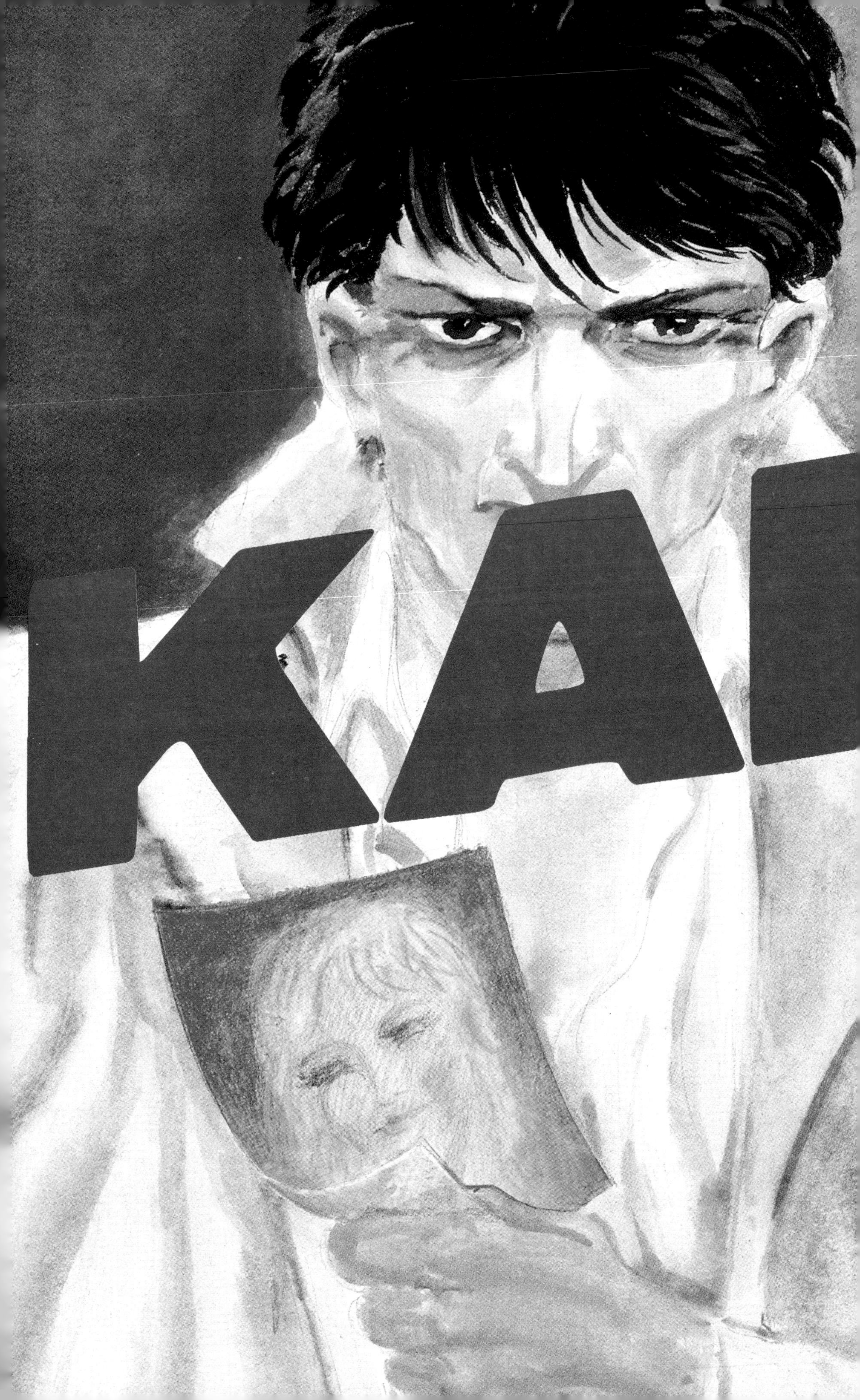
KA

KA

CREATED BY
STEVEN T. SEAGLE
STEFANO GAUDIANO

COLOR & DIGITAL REMASTER BY
MARCO CINELLO

LETTERING BY
RICHARD STARKINGS & MARCO CINELLO

BOOK DESIGN BY
MARCO CINELLO & STEVEN T. SEAGLE

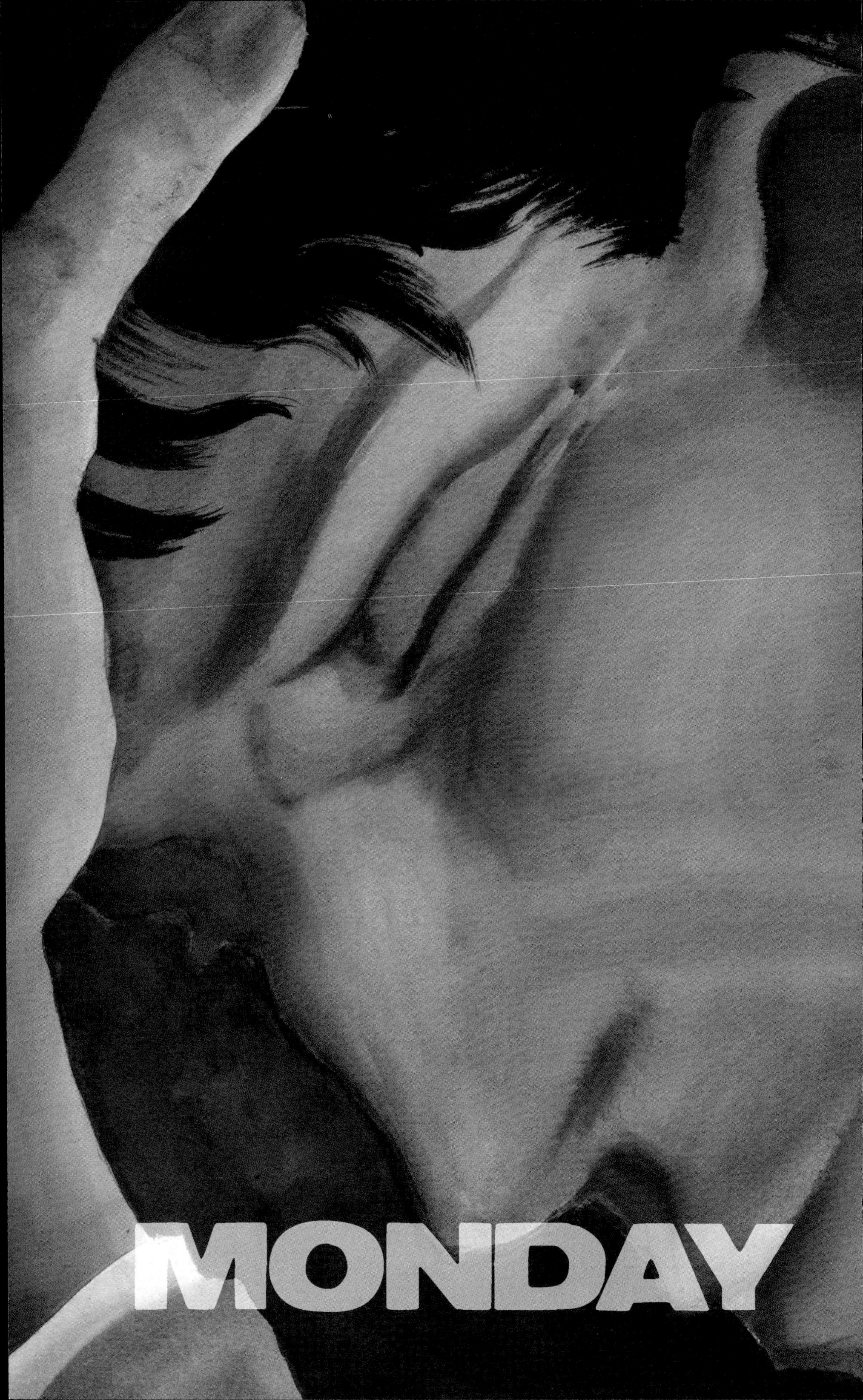
MONDAY

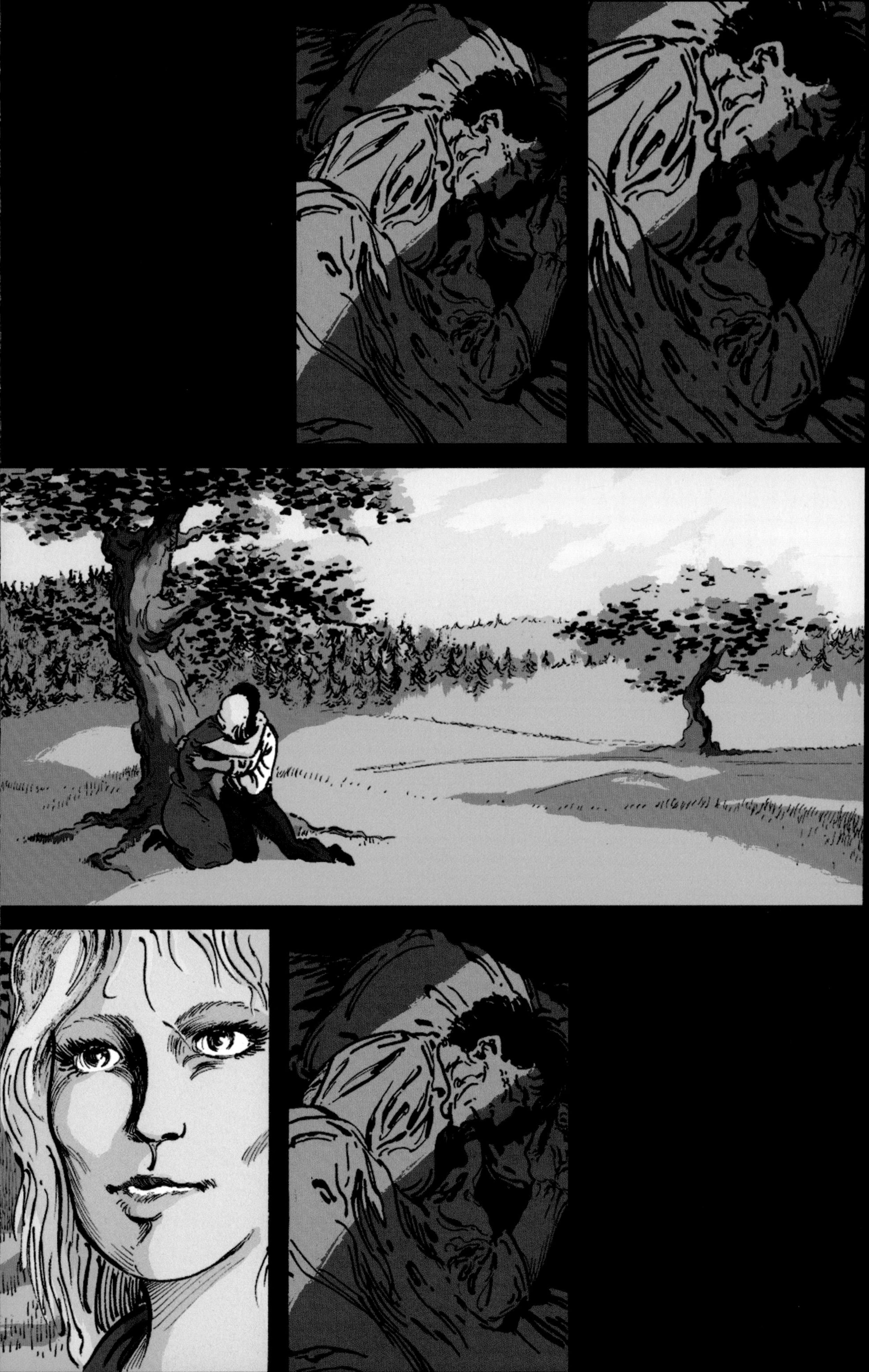

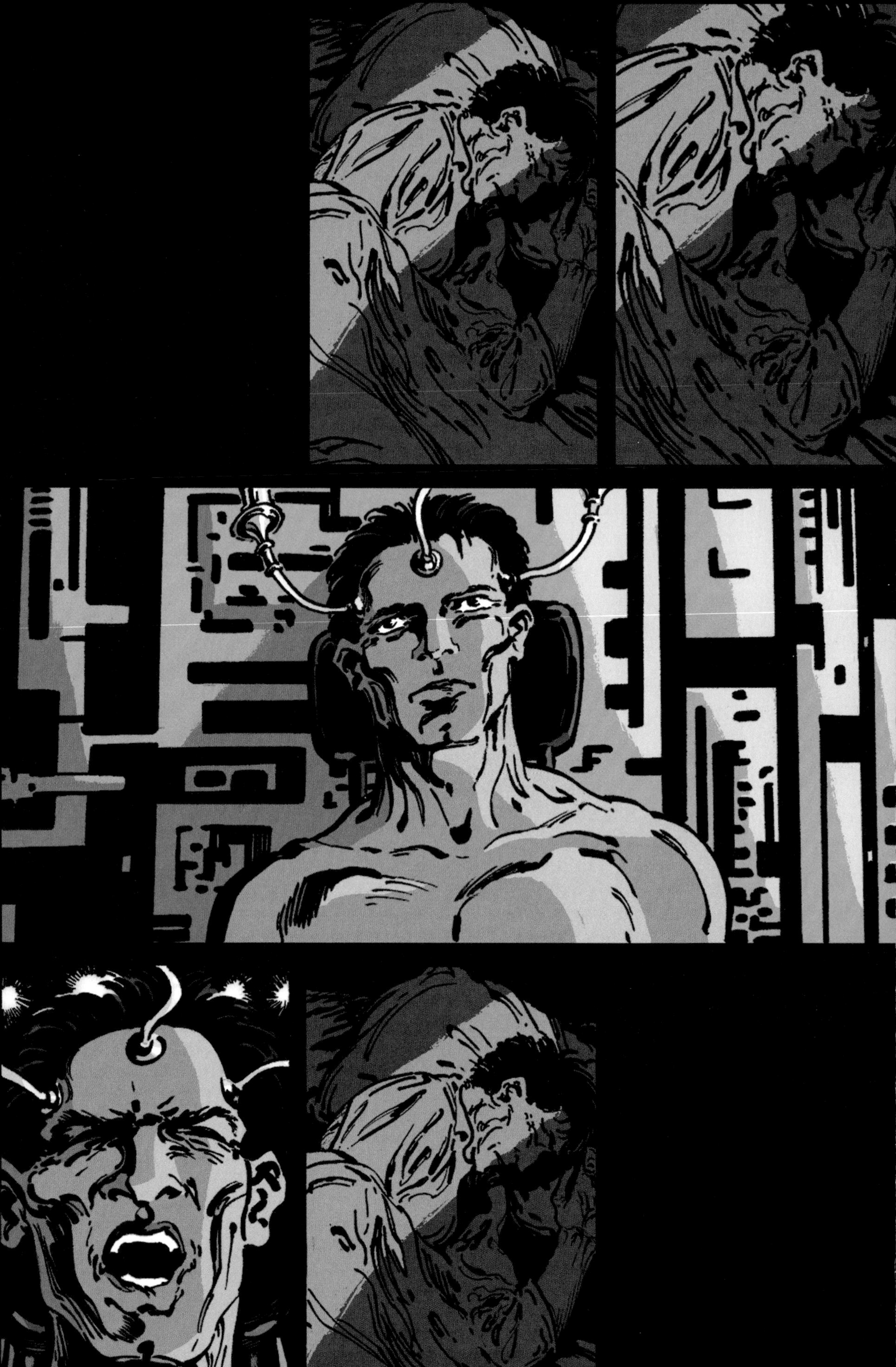

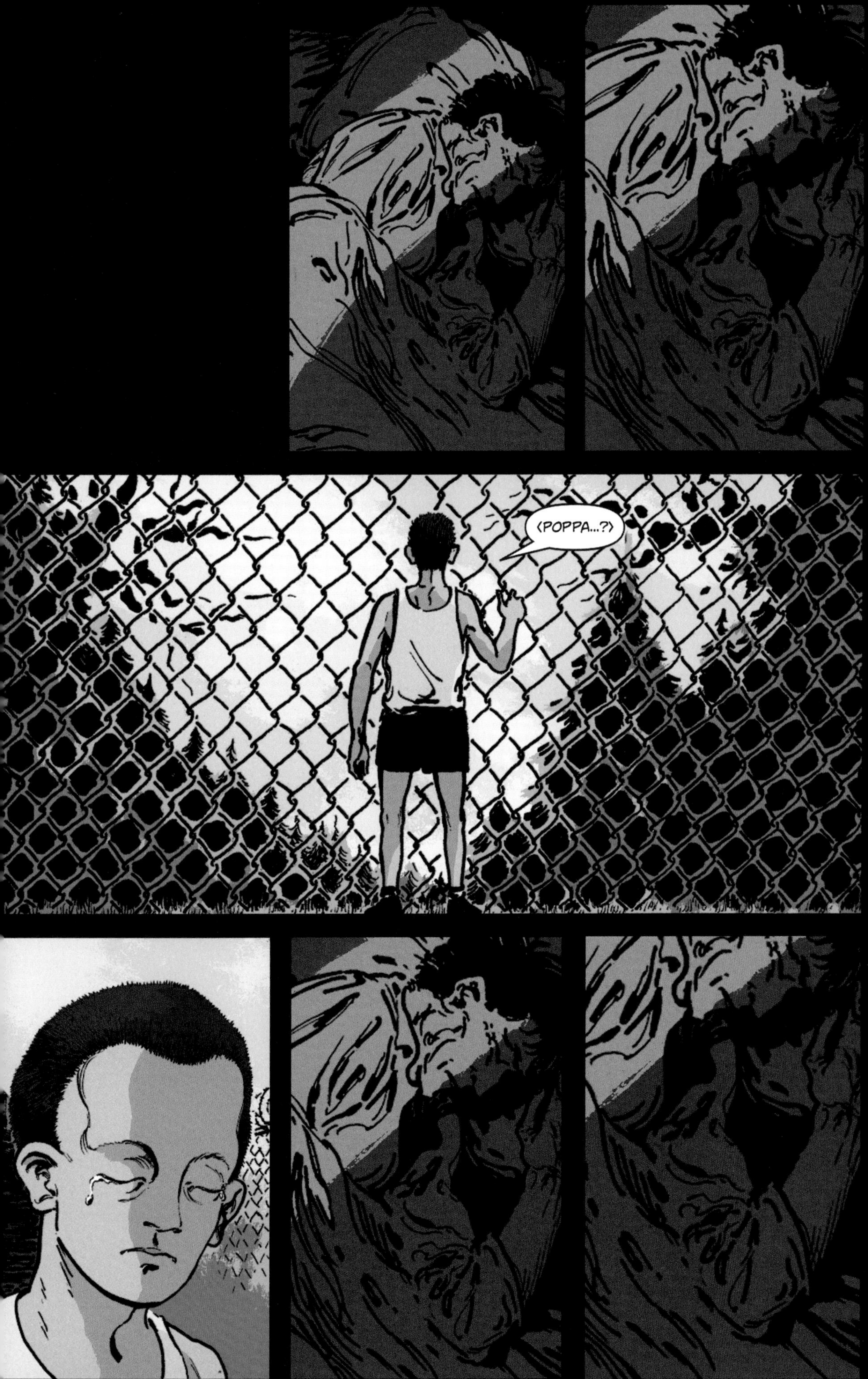
‹POPPA...?›

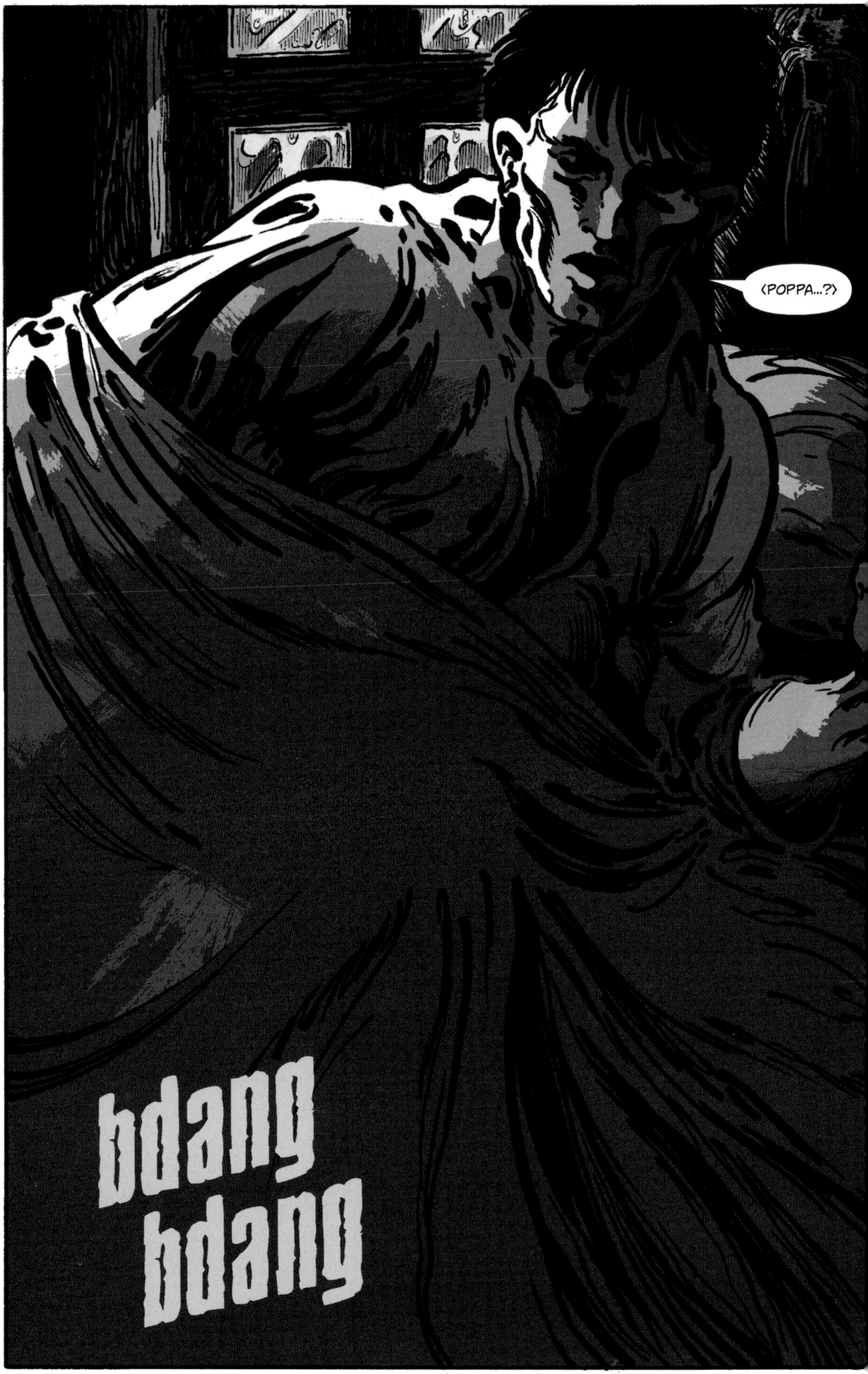
‹POPPA...?›
bdang
bdang

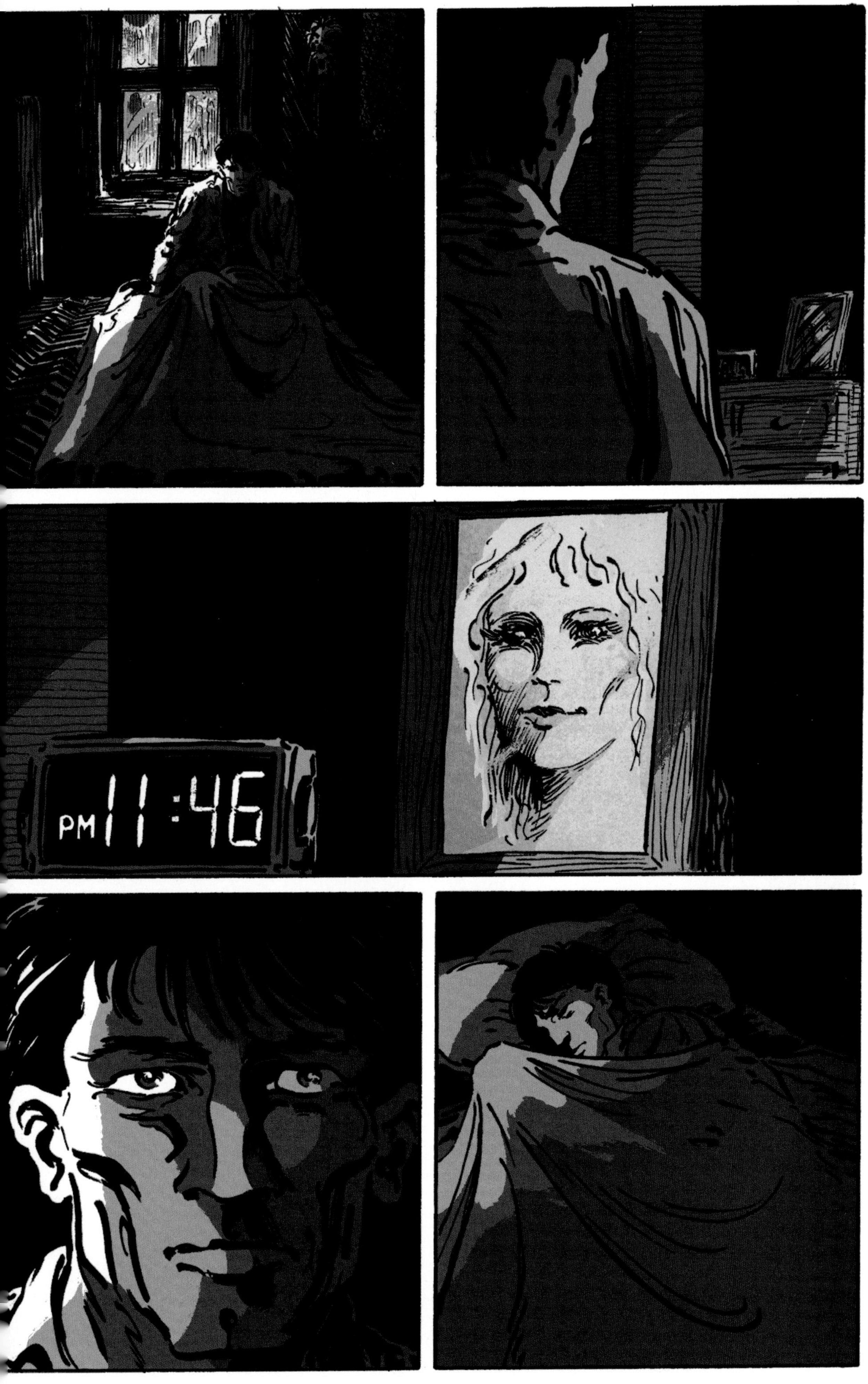
PM 11:46

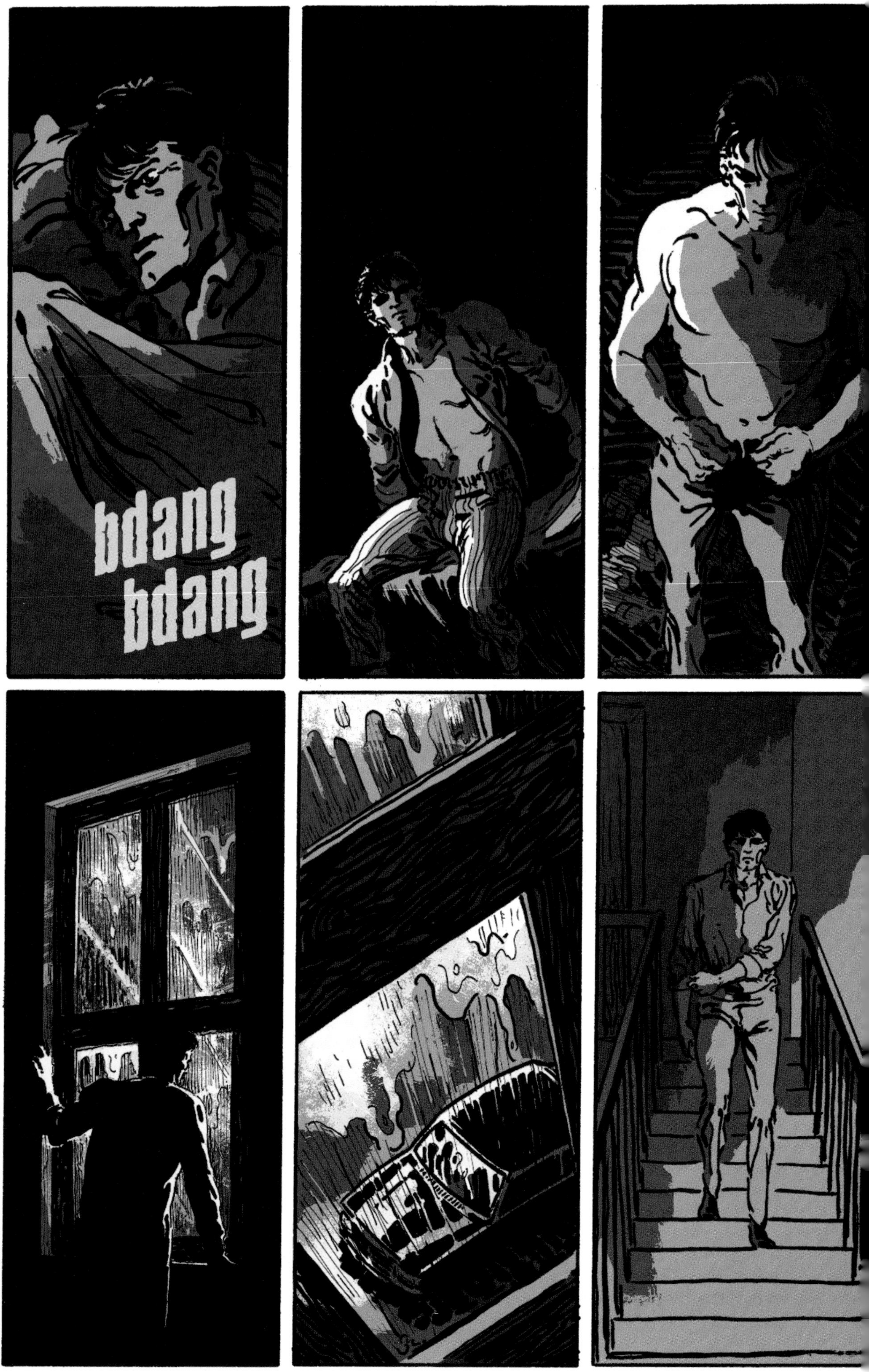
bdang
bdang

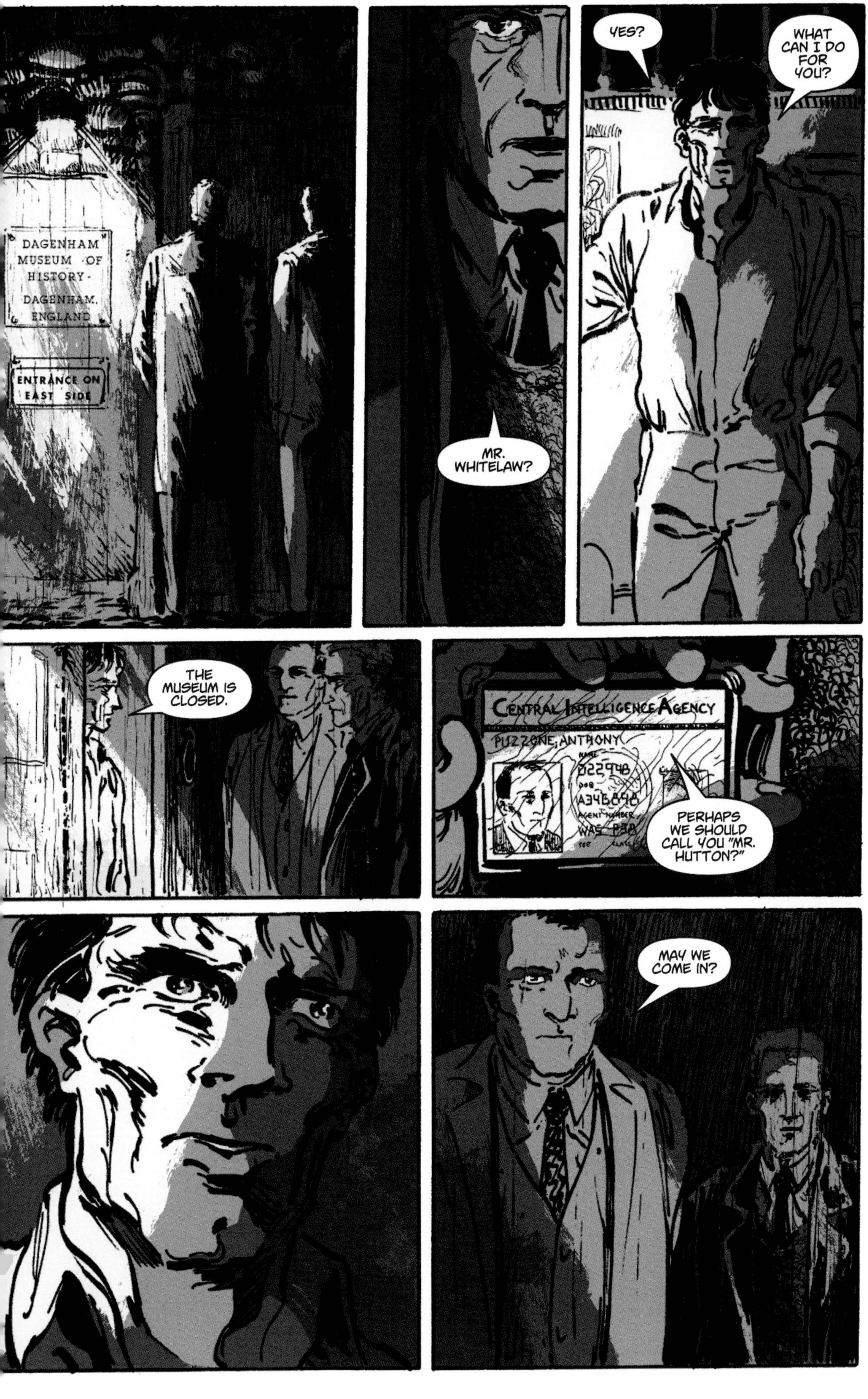
DAGENHAM MUSEUM OF HISTORY - DAGENHAM, ENGLAND
ENTRANCE ON EAST SIDE
MR. WHITELAW?
YES?
WHAT CAN I DO FOR YOU?
THE MUSEUM IS CLOSED.
CENTRAL INTELLIGENCE AGENCY
PUZZONE, ANTHONY
PERHAPS WE SHOULD CALL YOU "MR. HUTTON?"
MAY WE COME IN?

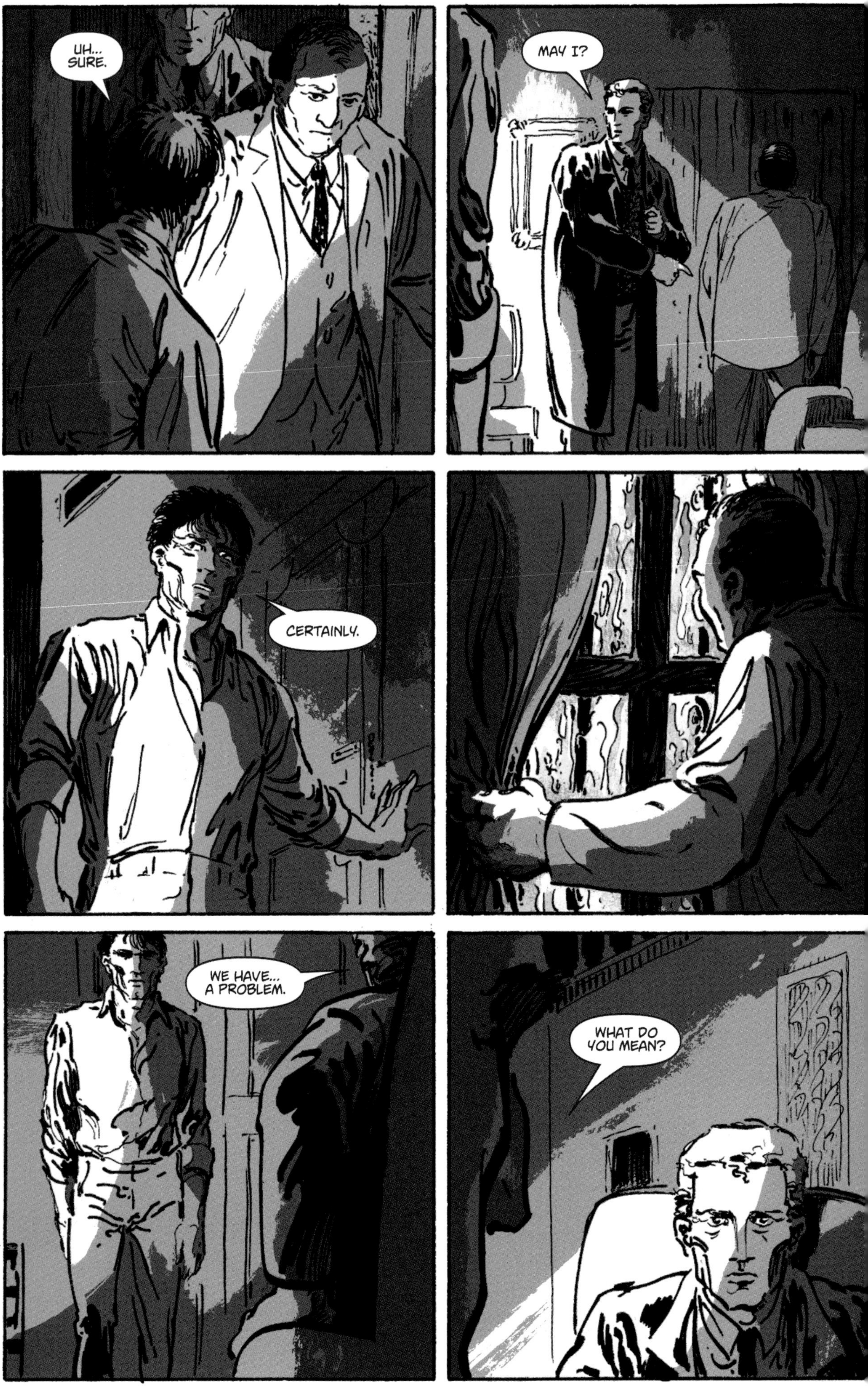
UH... SURE.
MAY I?
CERTAINLY.
WE HAVE... A PROBLEM.
WHAT DO YOU MEAN?

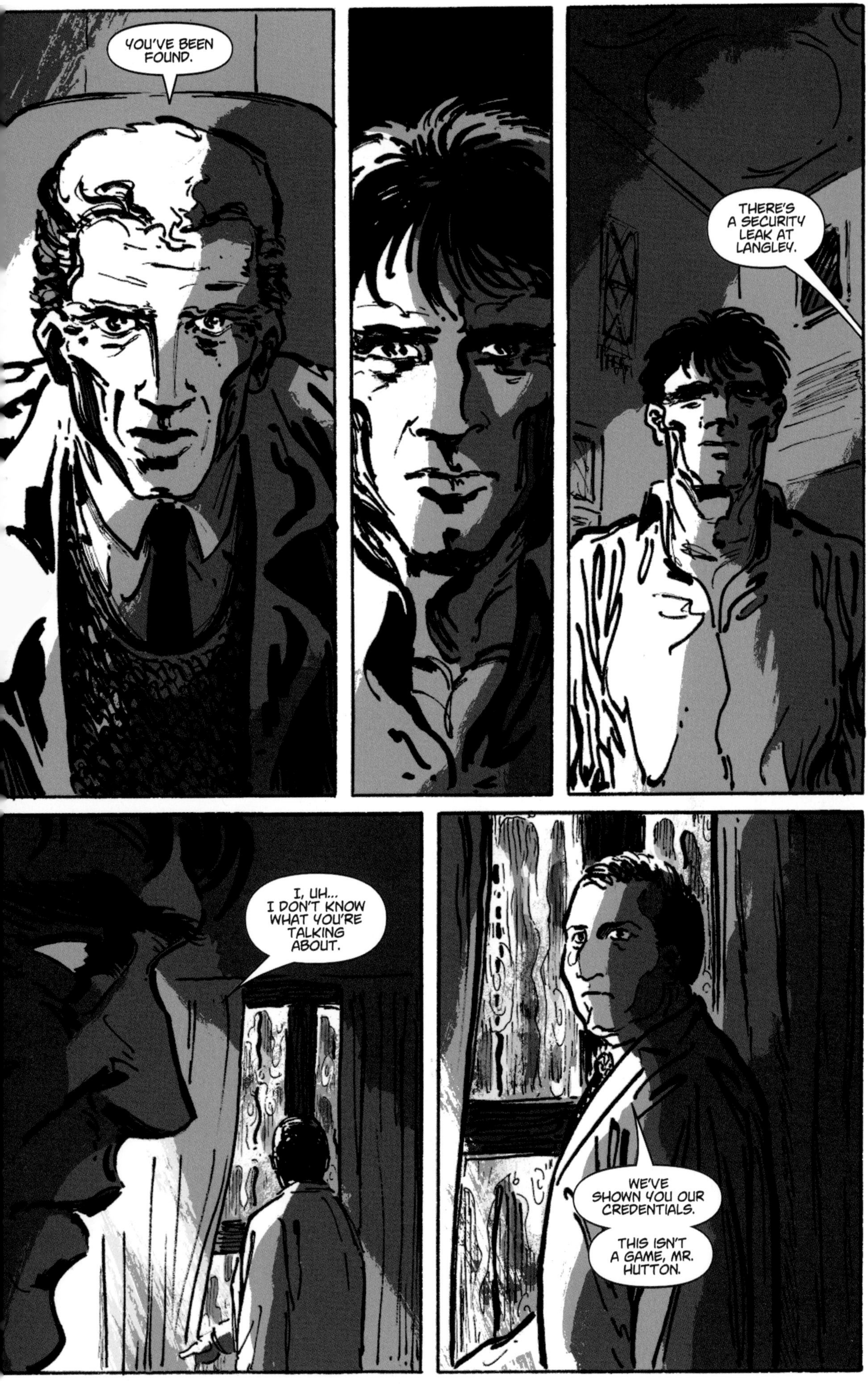

YOU'VE BEEN FOUND.
THERE'S A SECURITY LEAK AT LANGLEY.
I, UH... I DON'T KNOW WHAT YOU'RE TALKING ABOUT.
WE'VE SHOWN YOU OUR CREDENTIALS.
THIS ISN'T A GAME, MR. HUTTON.

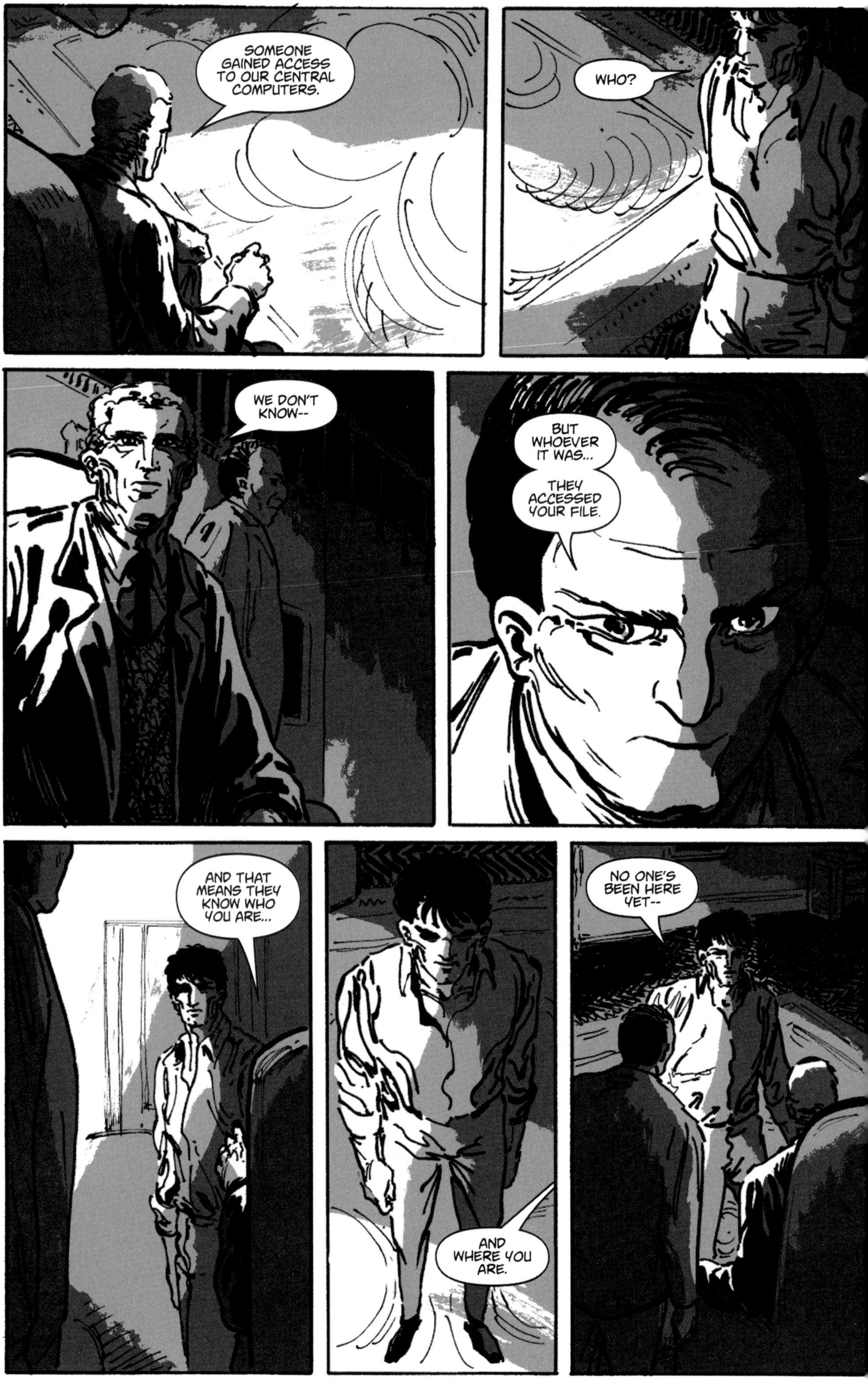
SOMEONE GAINED ACCESS TO OUR CENTRAL COMPUTERS.
WHO?
WE DON'T KNOW--
BUT WHOEVER IT WAS...
THEY ACCESSED YOUR FILE.
AND THAT MEANS THEY KNOW WHO YOU ARE...
AND WHERE YOU ARE.
NO ONE'S BEEN HERE YET--

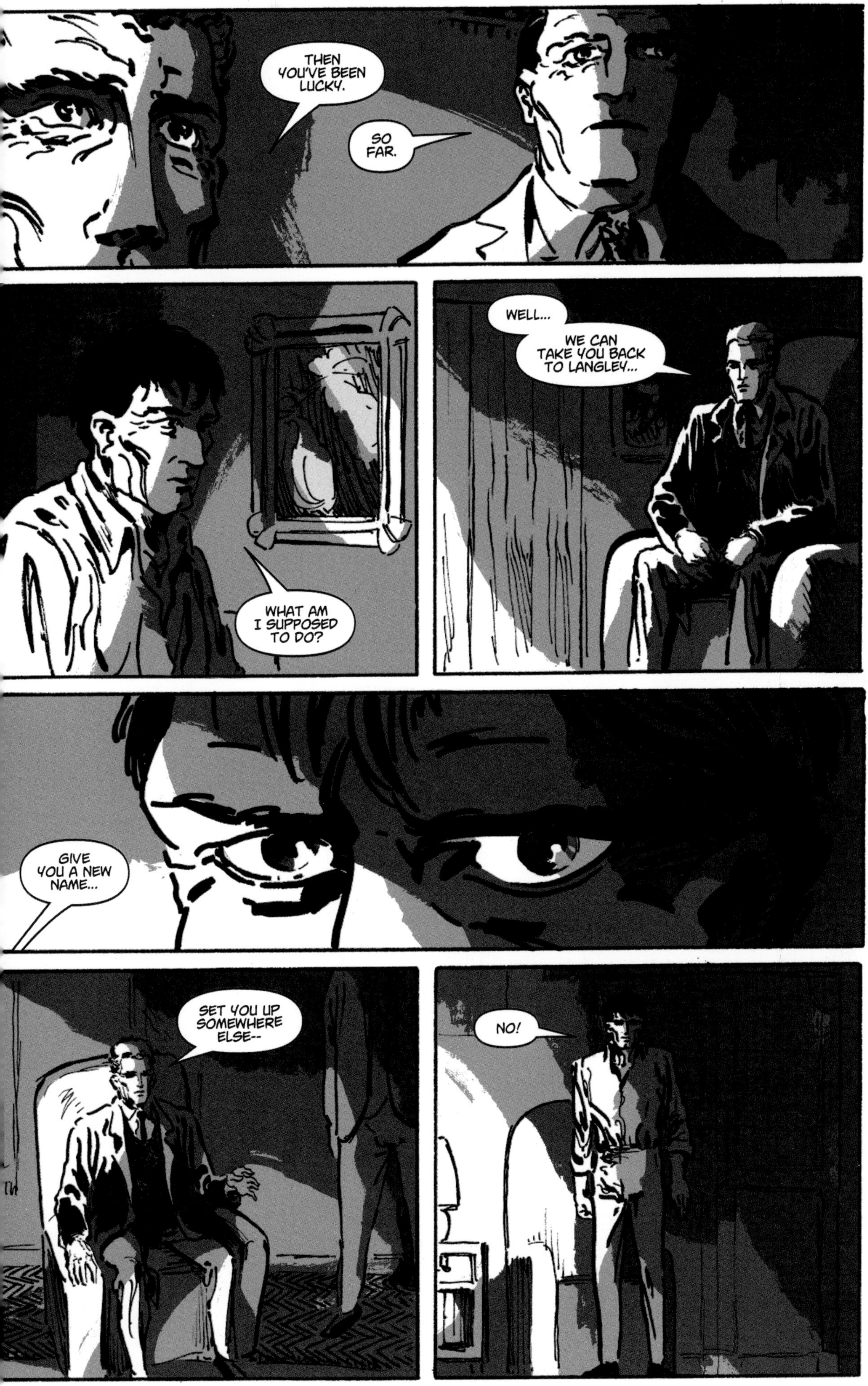
THEN YOU'VE BEEN LUCKY.
SO FAR.
WHAT AM I SUPPOSED TO DO?
WELL...
WE CAN TAKE YOU BACK TO LANGLEY...
GIVE YOU A NEW NAME...
SET YOU UP SOMEWHERE ELSE--
NO!

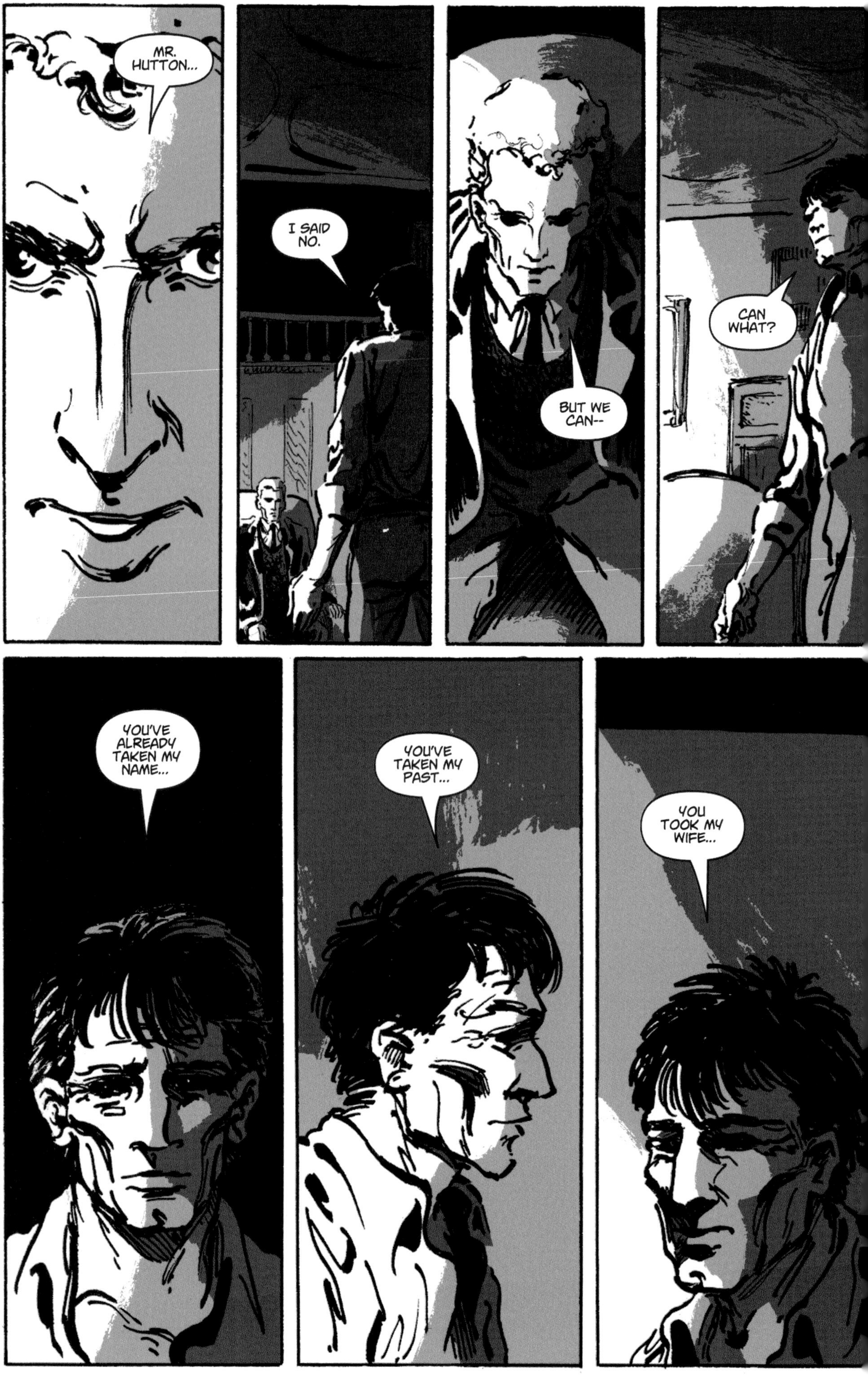
MR. HUTTON...
I SAID NO.
BUT WE CAN--
CAN WHAT?
YOU'VE ALREADY TAKEN MY NAME...
YOU'VE TAKEN MY PAST...
YOU TOOK MY WIFE...

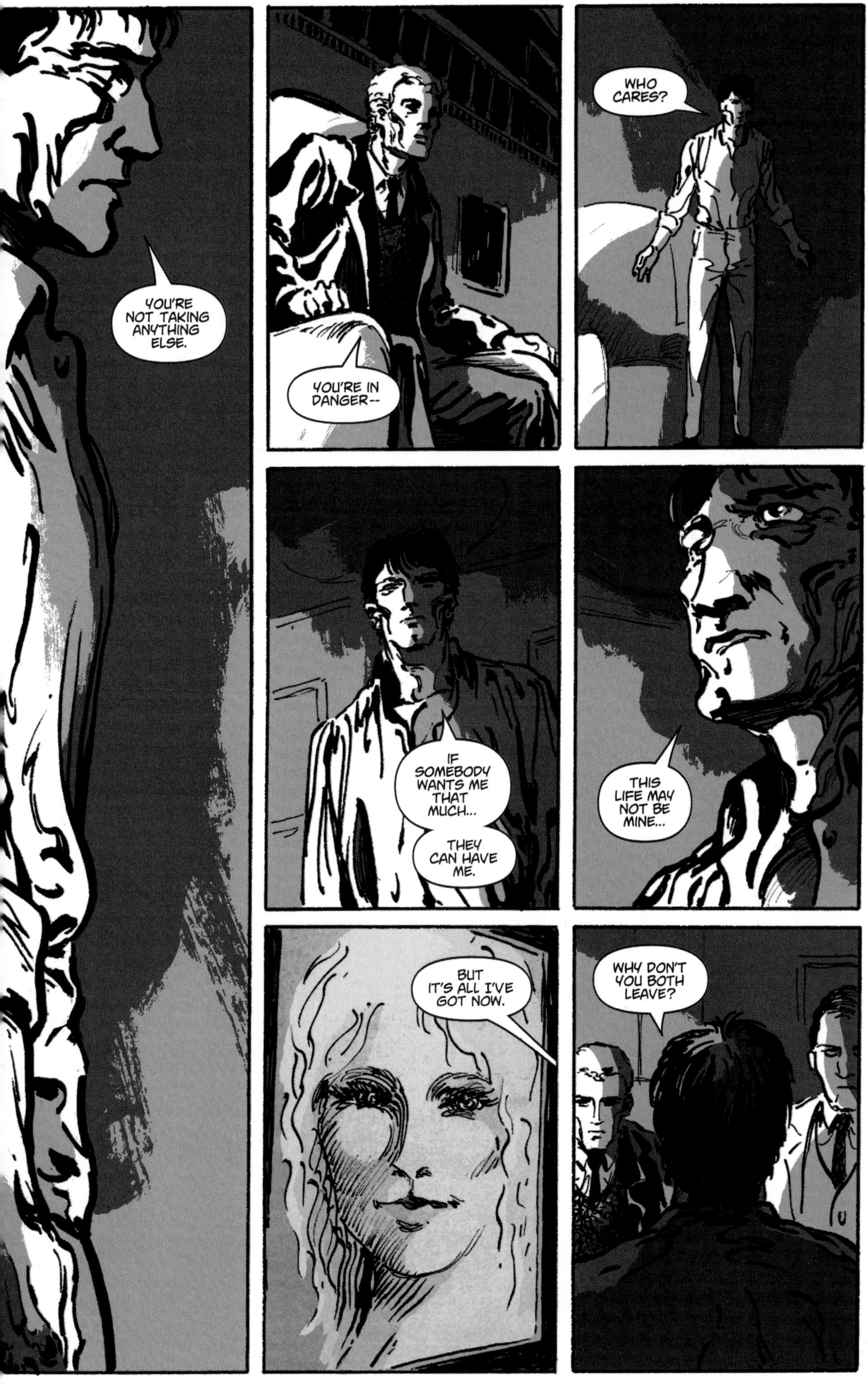
YOU'RE NOT TAKING ANYTHING ELSE.
YOU'RE IN DANGER--
WHO CARES?
IF SOMEBODY WANTS ME THAT MUCH...
THEY CAN HAVE ME.
THIS LIFE MAY NOT BE MINE...
BUT IT'S ALL I'VE GOT NOW.
WHY DON'T YOU BOTH LEAVE?

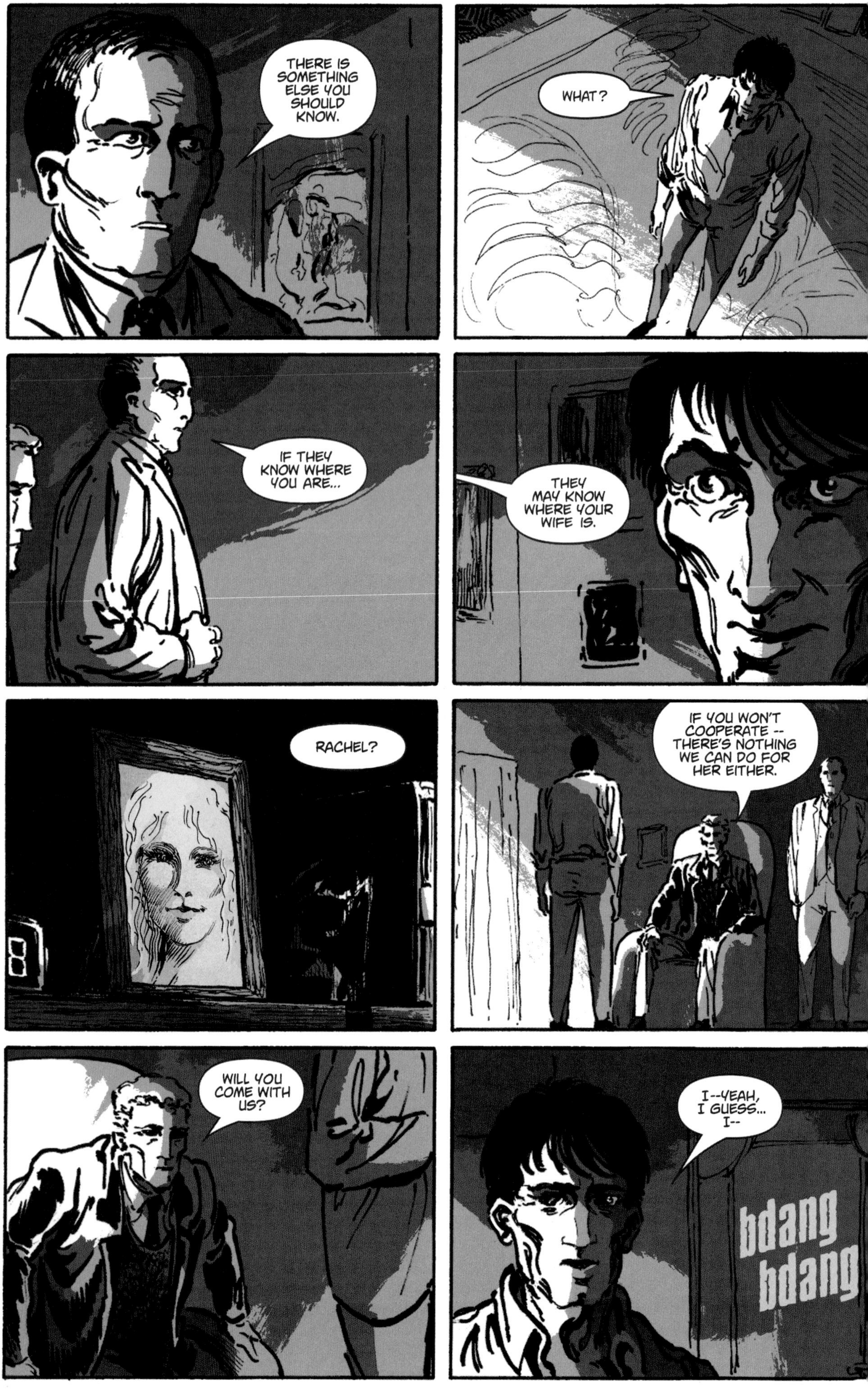
THERE IS SOMETHING ELSE YOU SHOULD KNOW.
WHAT?
IF THEY KNOW WHERE YOU ARE...
THEY MAY KNOW WHERE YOUR WIFE IS.
RACHEL?
IF YOU WON'T COOPERATE -- THERE'S NOTHING WE CAN DO FOR HER EITHER.
WILL YOU COME WITH US?
I--YEAH, I GUESS... I--
bdang
bdang

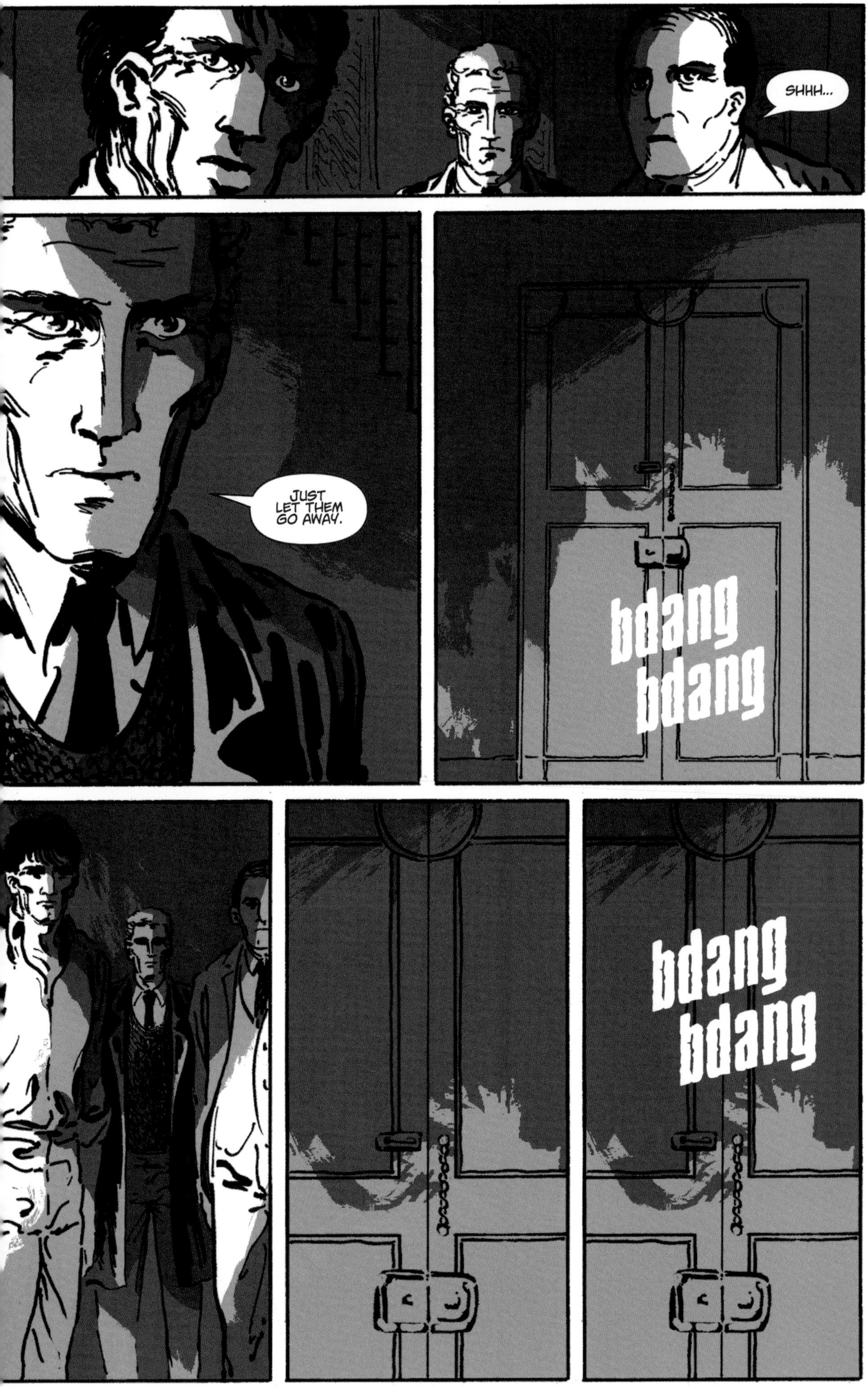
SHHH...
JUST LET THEM GO AWAY.
bdang bdang
bdang bdang

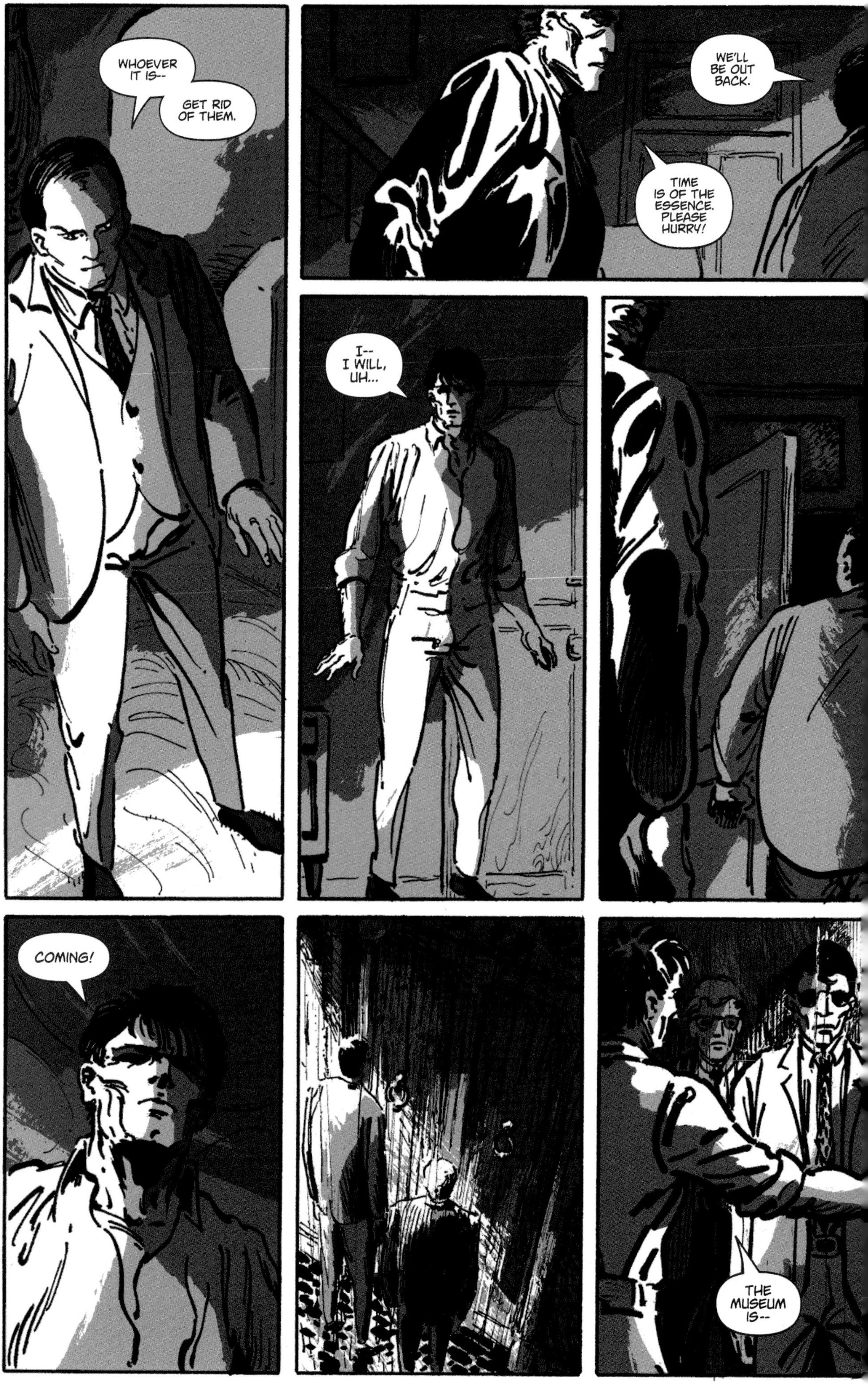
WHOEVER IT IS--
GET RID OF THEM.
WE'LL BE OUT BACK.
TIME IS OF THE ESSENCE. PLEASE HURRY!
I-- I WILL, UH...
COMING!
THE MUSEUM IS--

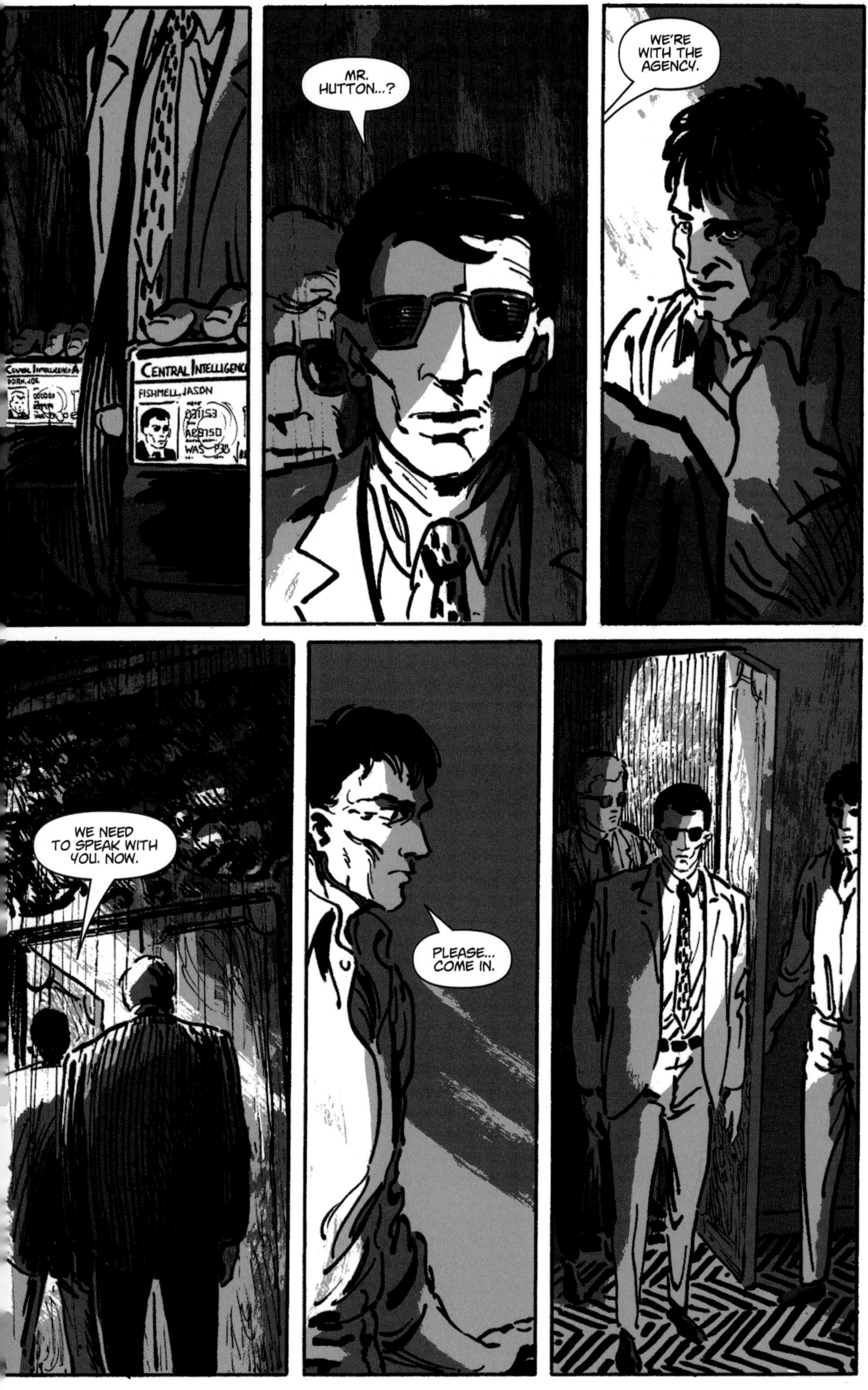
CENTRAL INTELLIGENCE
FISHMELL, JASON
MR. HUTTON...?
WE'RE WITH THE AGENCY.
WE NEED TO SPEAK WITH YOU. NOW.
PLEASE... COME IN.

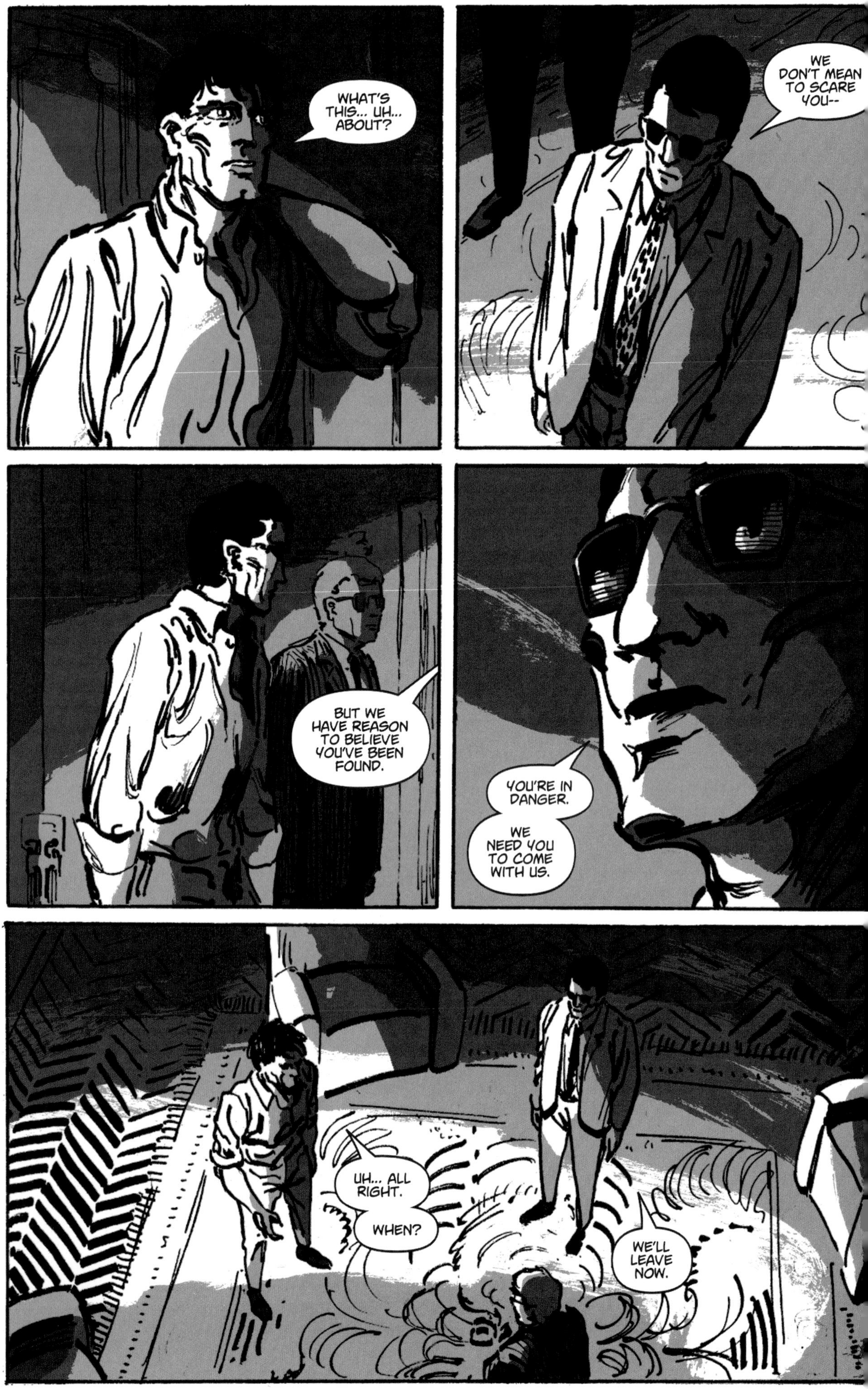
WHAT'S THIS... UH... ABOUT?
WE DON'T MEAN TO SCARE YOU--
BUT WE HAVE REASON TO BELIEVE YOU'VE BEEN FOUND.
YOU'RE IN DANGER.
WE NEED YOU TO COME WITH US.
UH... ALL RIGHT.
WHEN?
WE'LL LEAVE NOW.

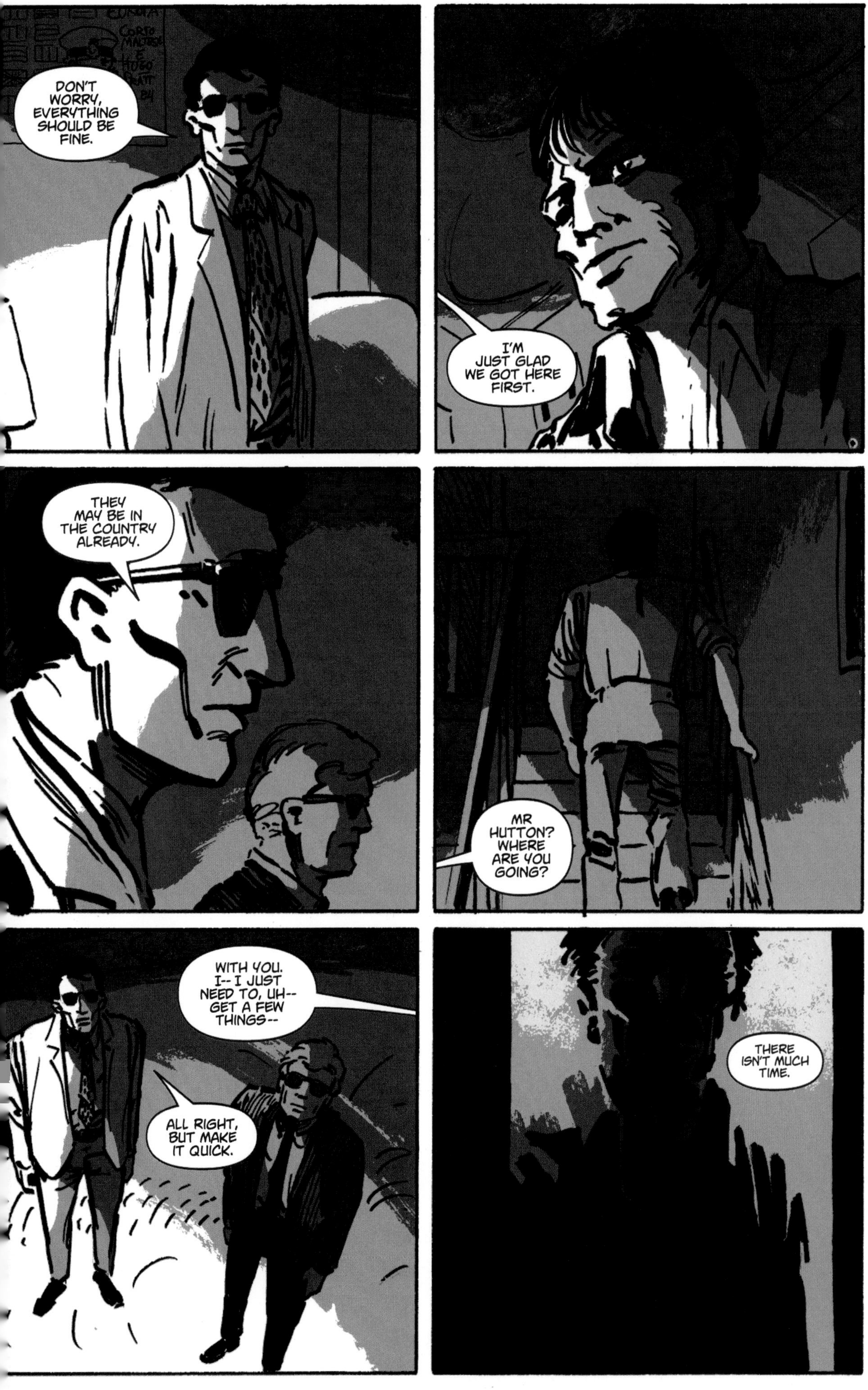
CORTO MALTESE E HUGO PRATT
DON'T WORRY, EVERYTHING SHOULD BE FINE.
I'M JUST GLAD WE GOT HERE FIRST.
THEY MAY BE IN THE COUNTRY ALREADY.
MR HUTTON? WHERE ARE YOU GOING?
WITH YOU. I-- I JUST NEED TO, UH-- GET A FEW THINGS--
ALL RIGHT, BUT MAKE IT QUICK.
THERE ISN'T MUCH TIME.

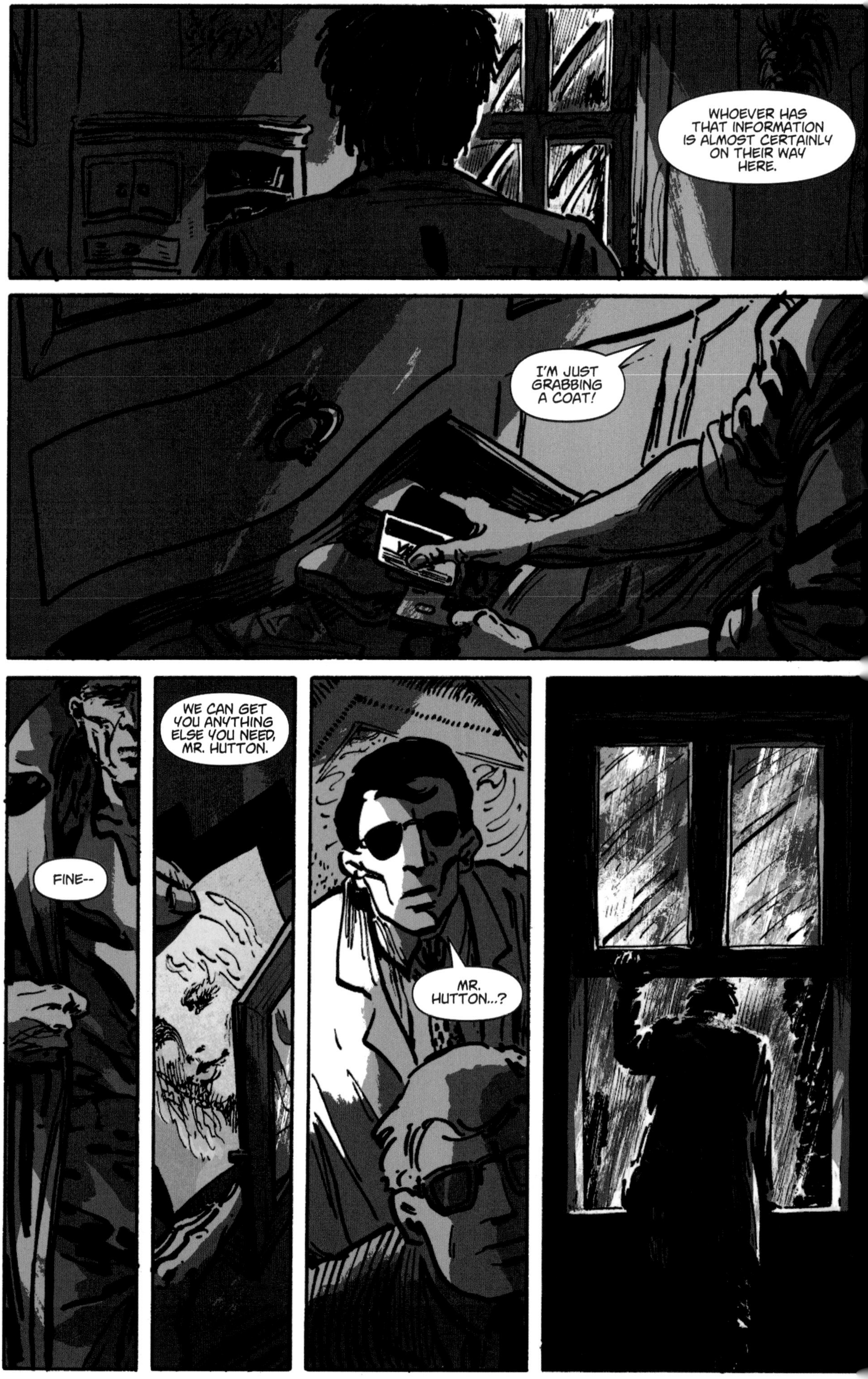
WHOEVER HAS THAT INFORMATION IS ALMOST CERTAINLY ON THEIR WAY HERE.
I'M JUST GRABBING A COAT!
FINE--
WE CAN GET YOU ANYTHING ELSE YOU NEED, MR. HUTTON.
MR. HUTTON...?

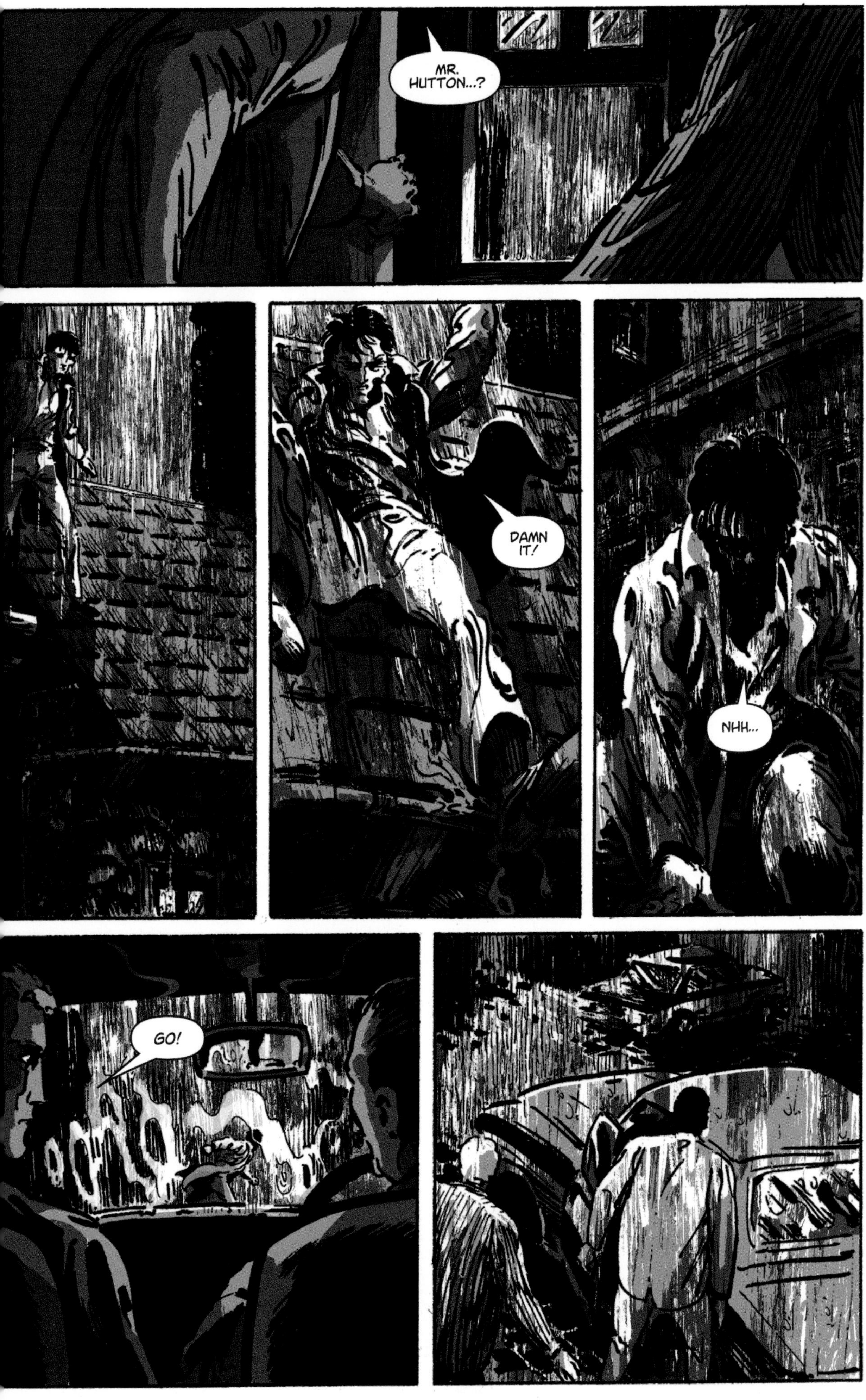
MR. HUTTON...?
DAMN IT!
NHH...
GO!

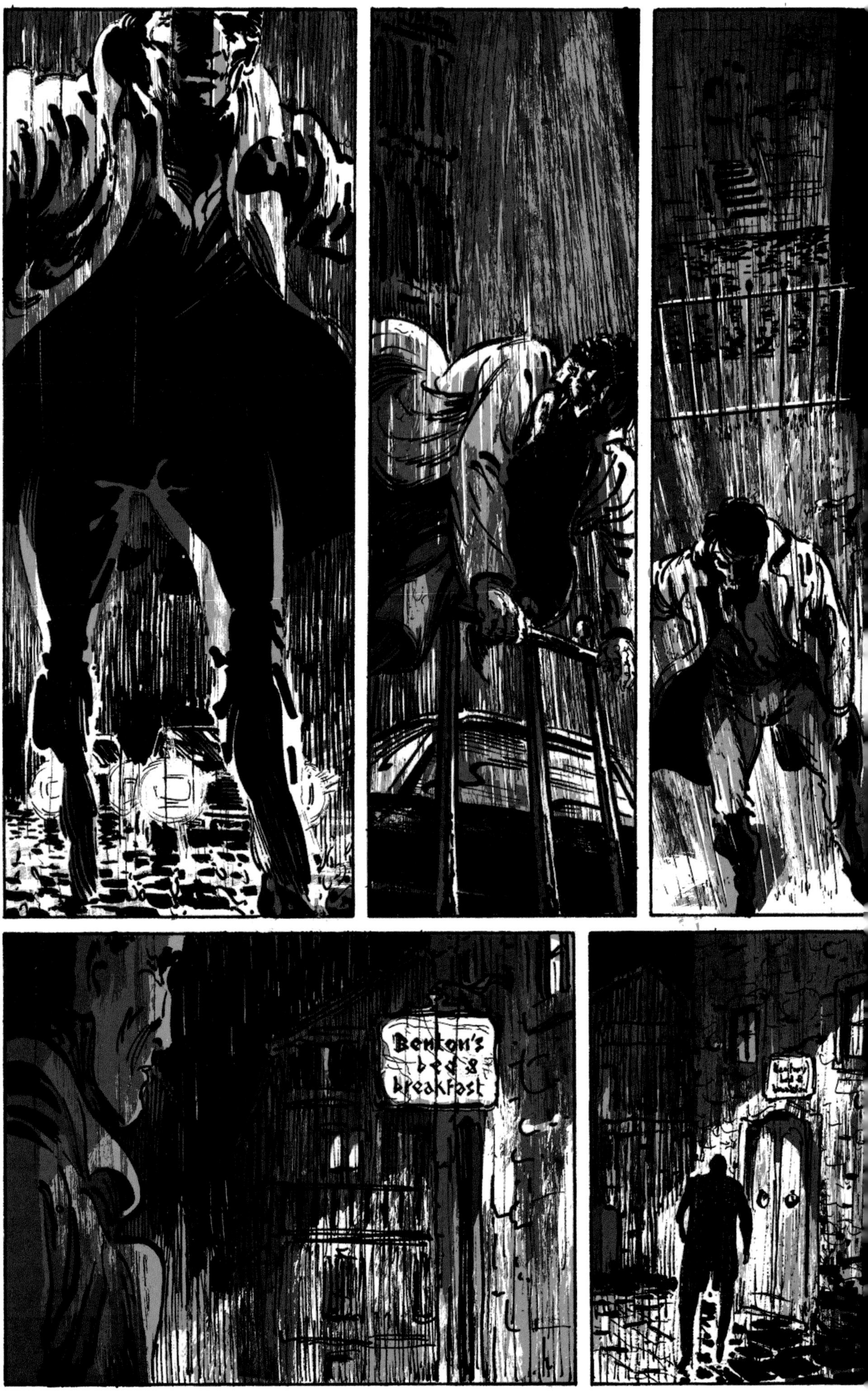
Benton's
bed &
breakfast

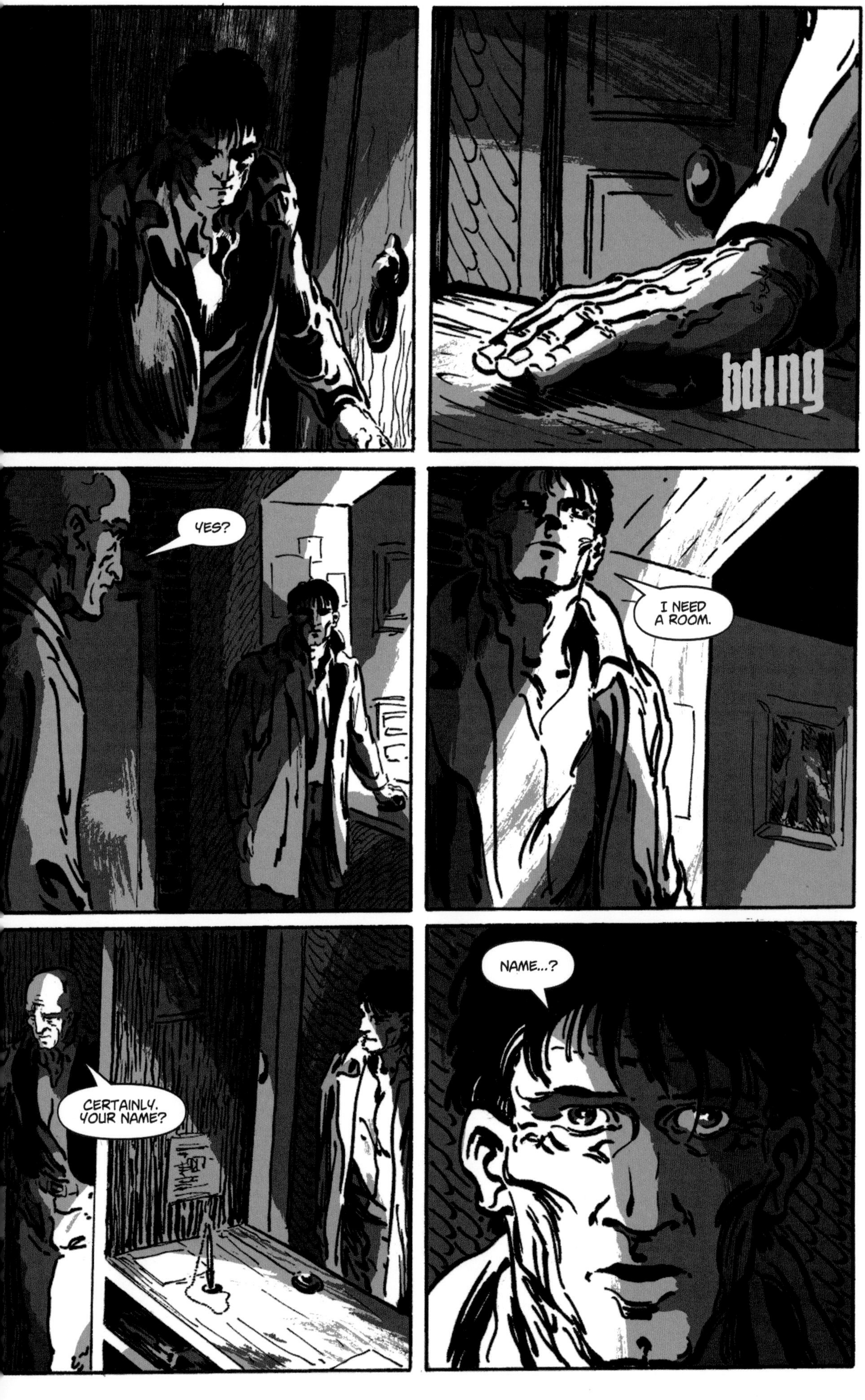
bding
YES?
I NEED A ROOM.
CERTAINLY. YOUR NAME?
NAME...?

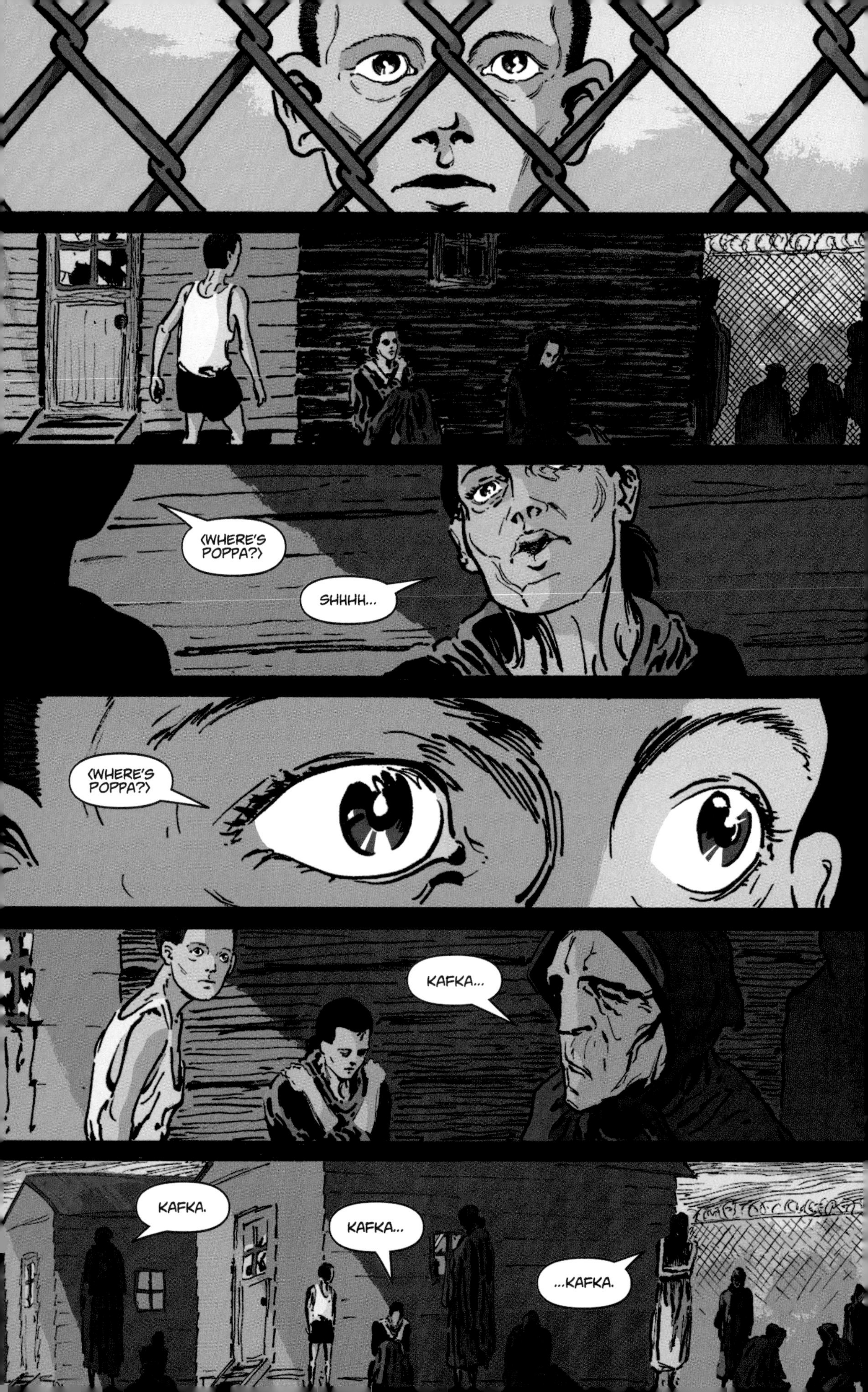
(WHERE'S POPPA?)
SHHHH...
(WHERE'S POPPA?)
KAFKA...
KAFKA.
KAFKA...
...KAFKA.

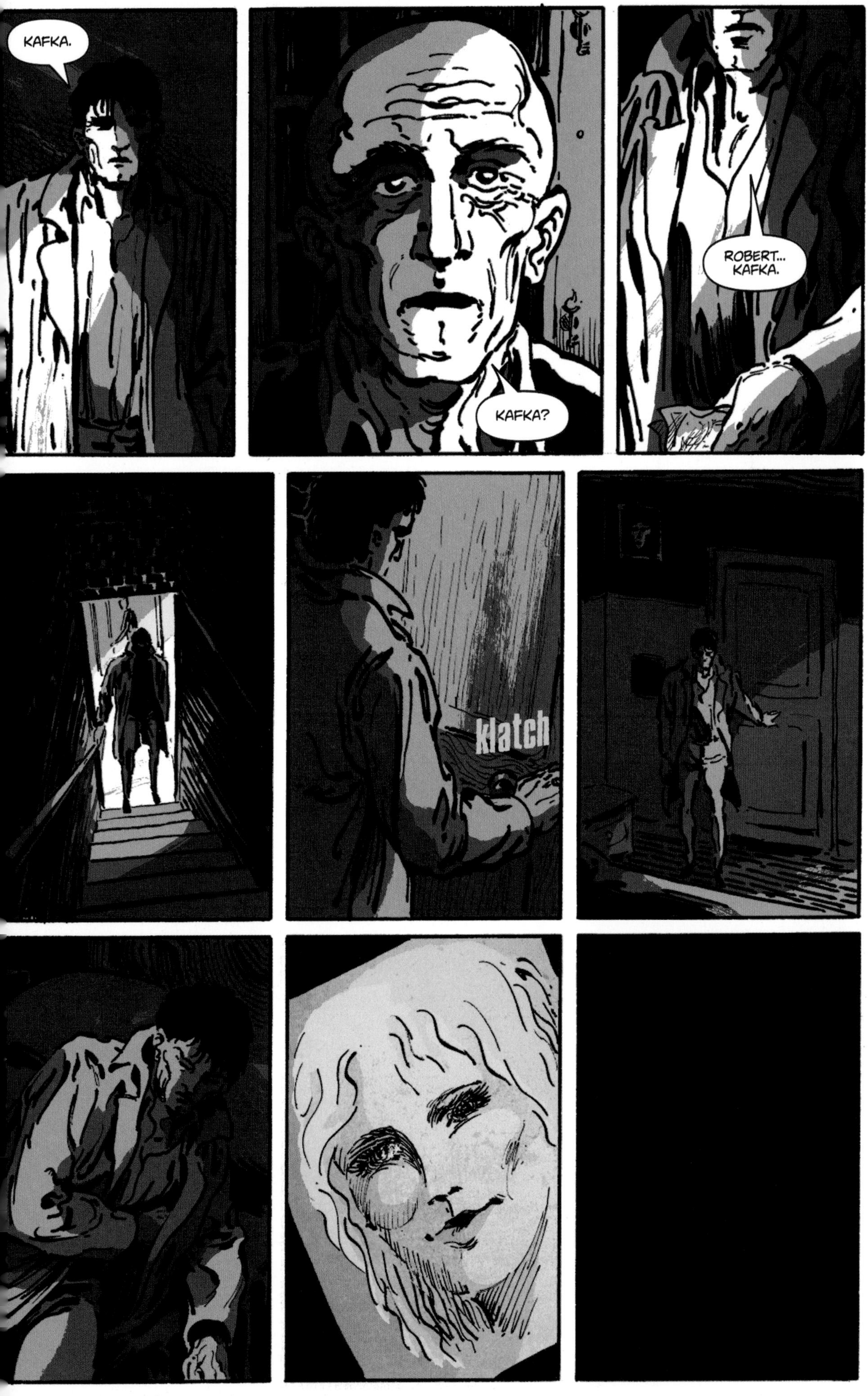
KAFKA.
KAFKA?
ROBERT... KAFKA.
klatch

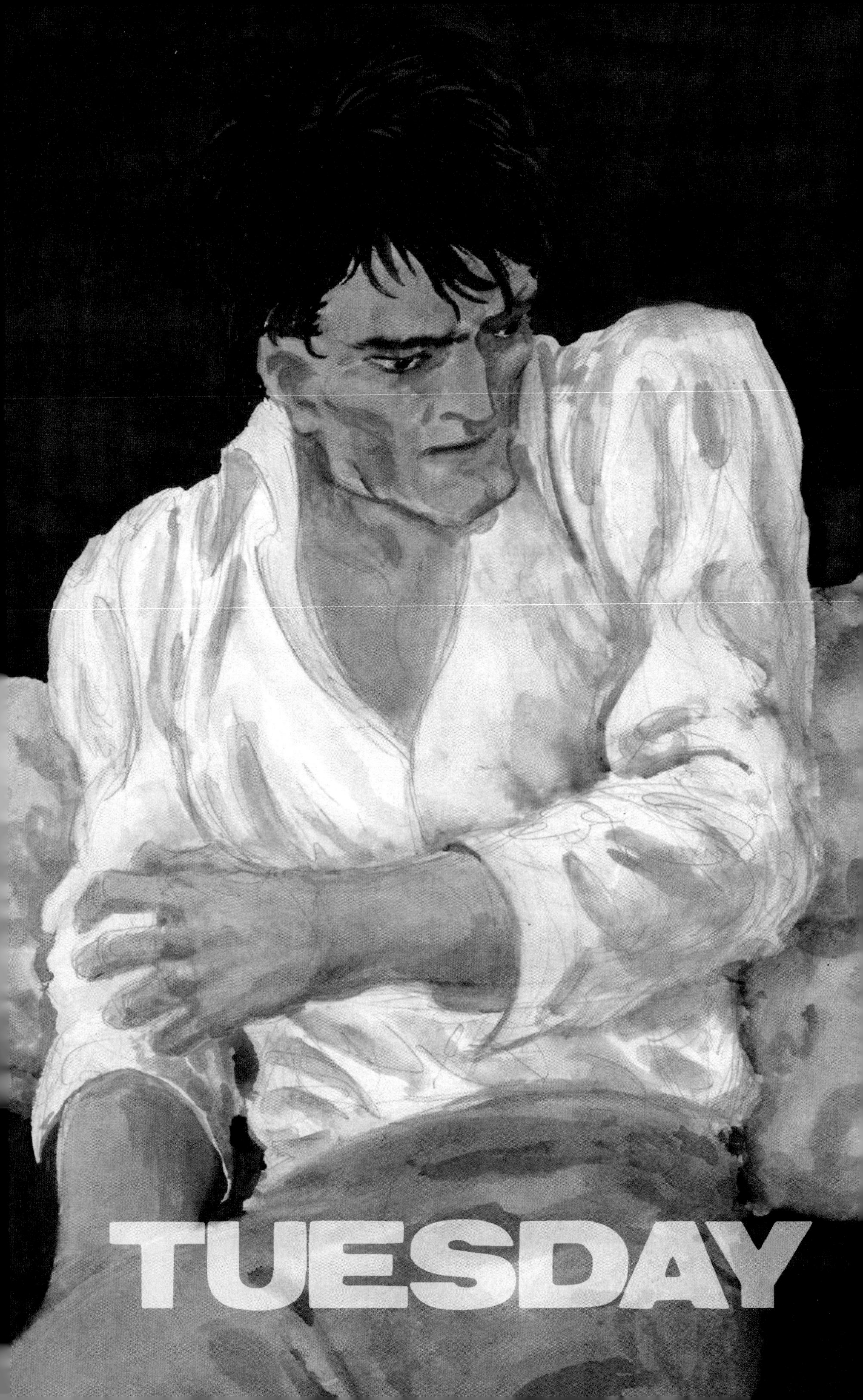

TUESDAY

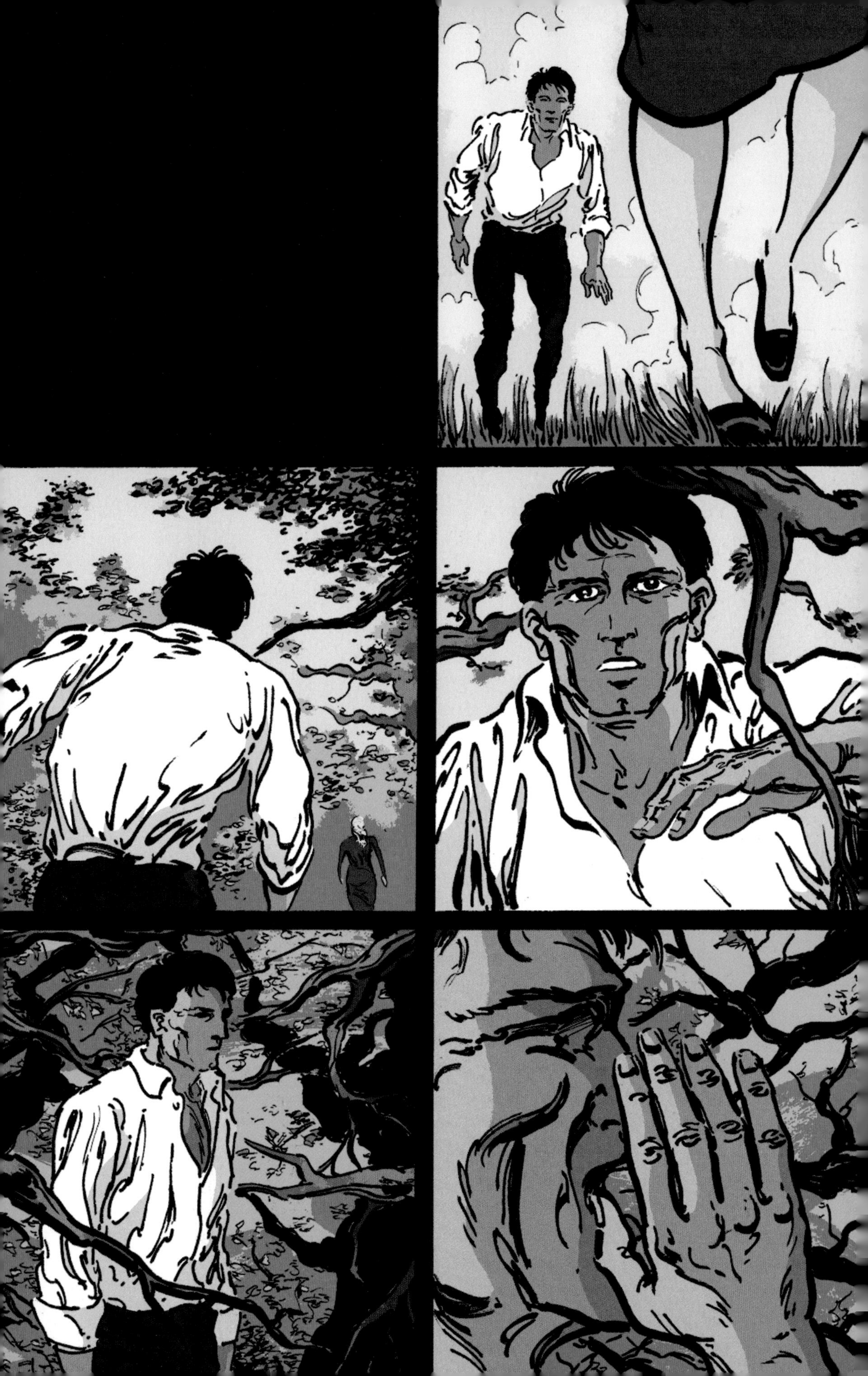

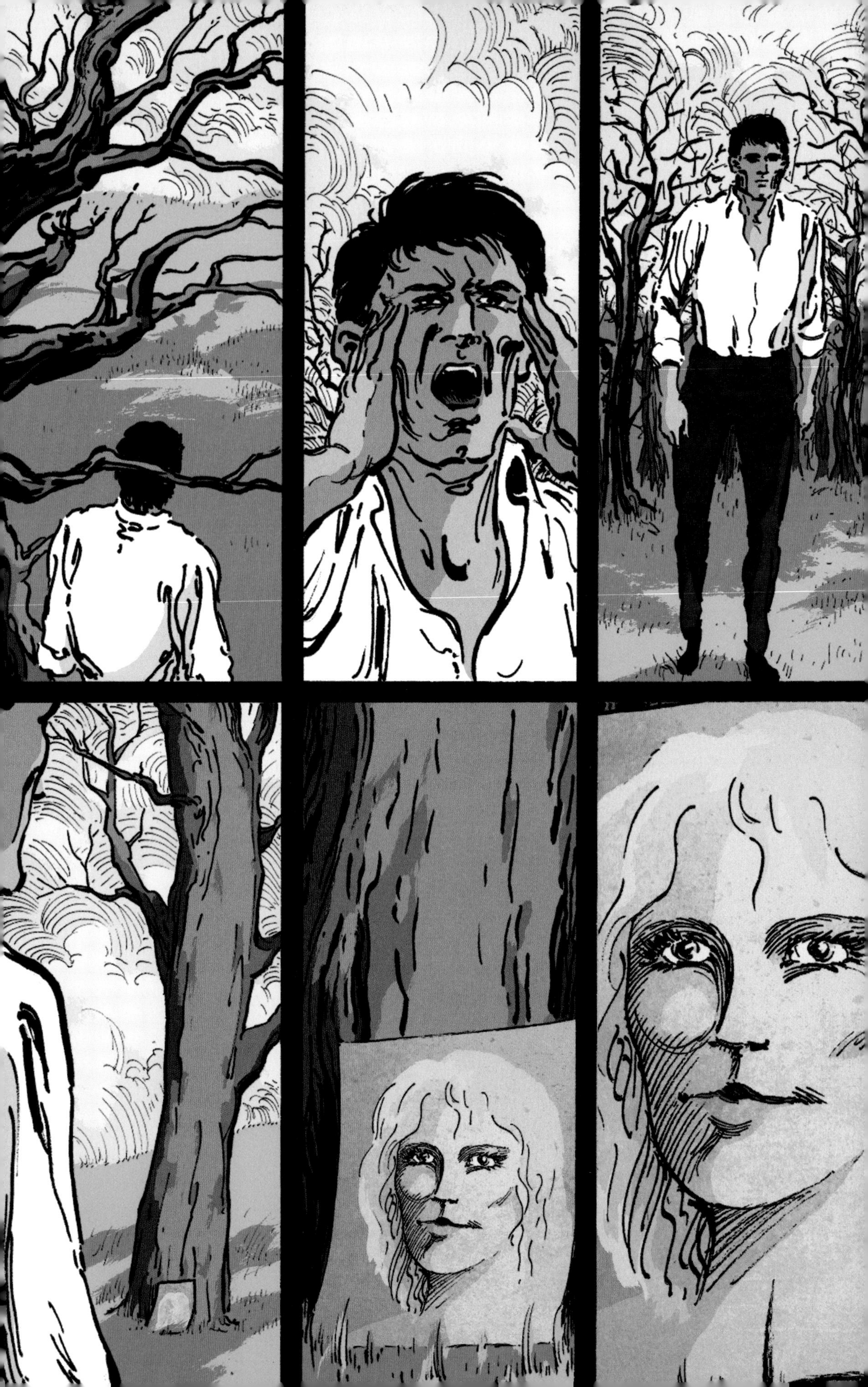

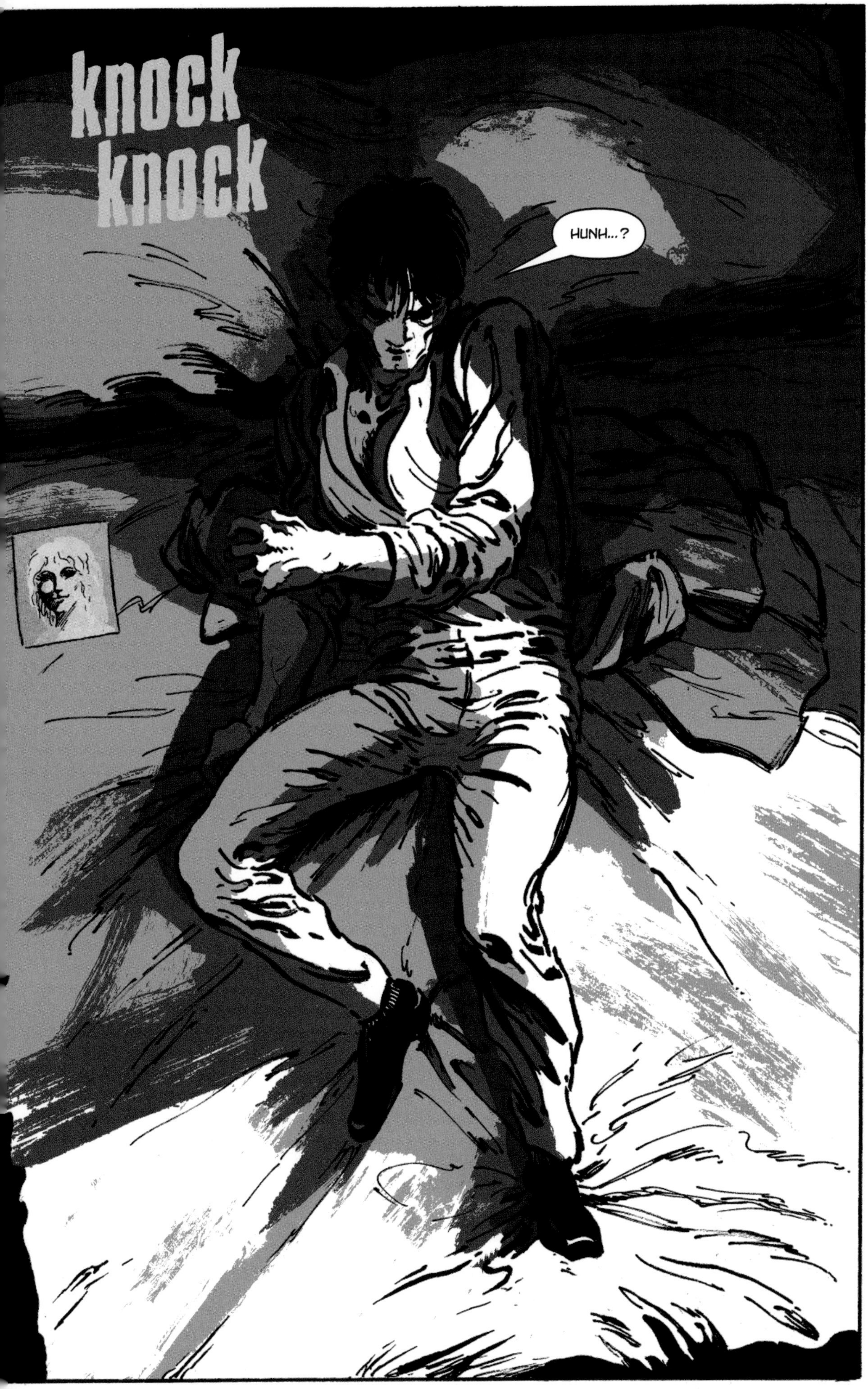
knock knock
HUNH...?

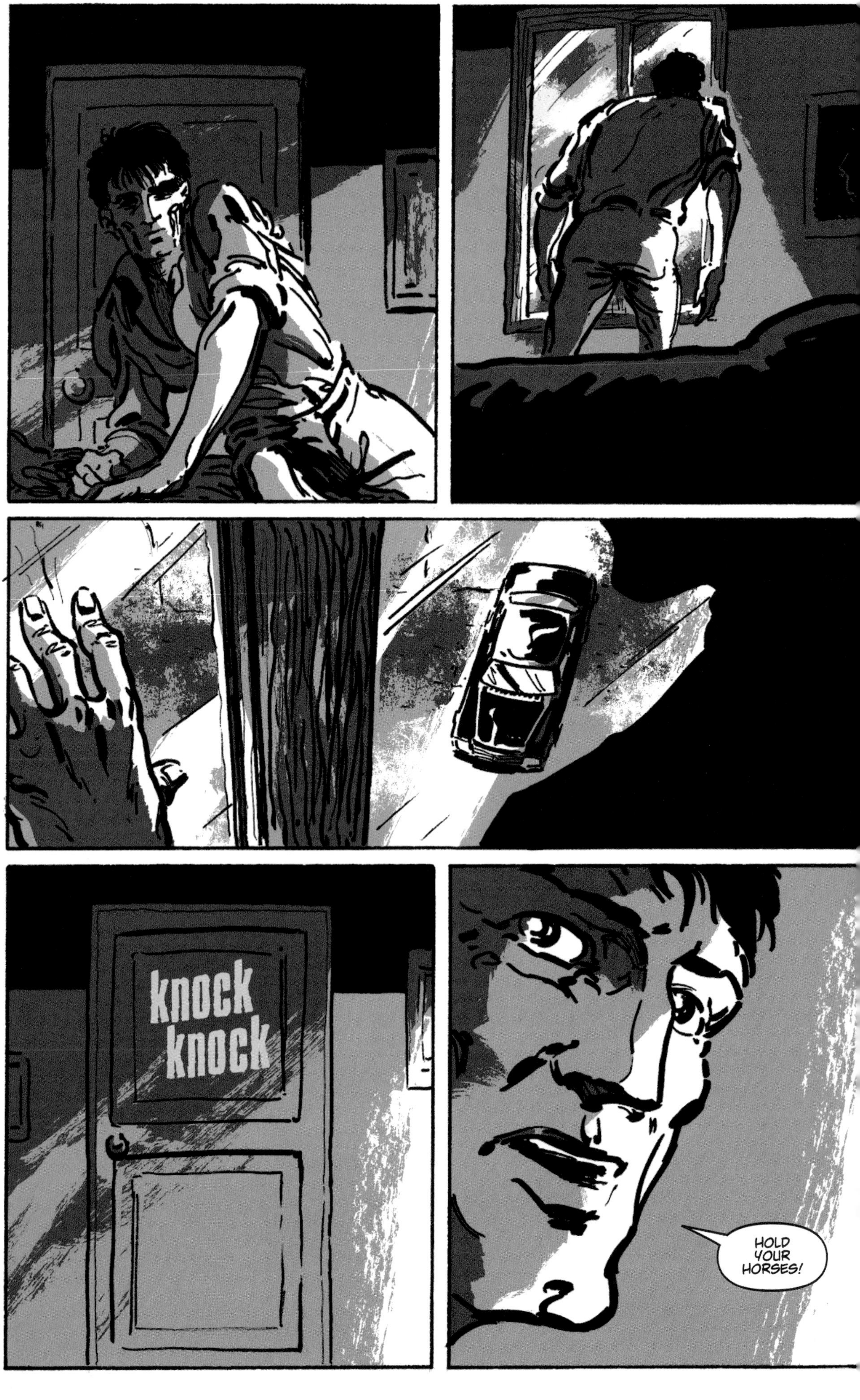
knock knock
HOLD YOUR HORSES!

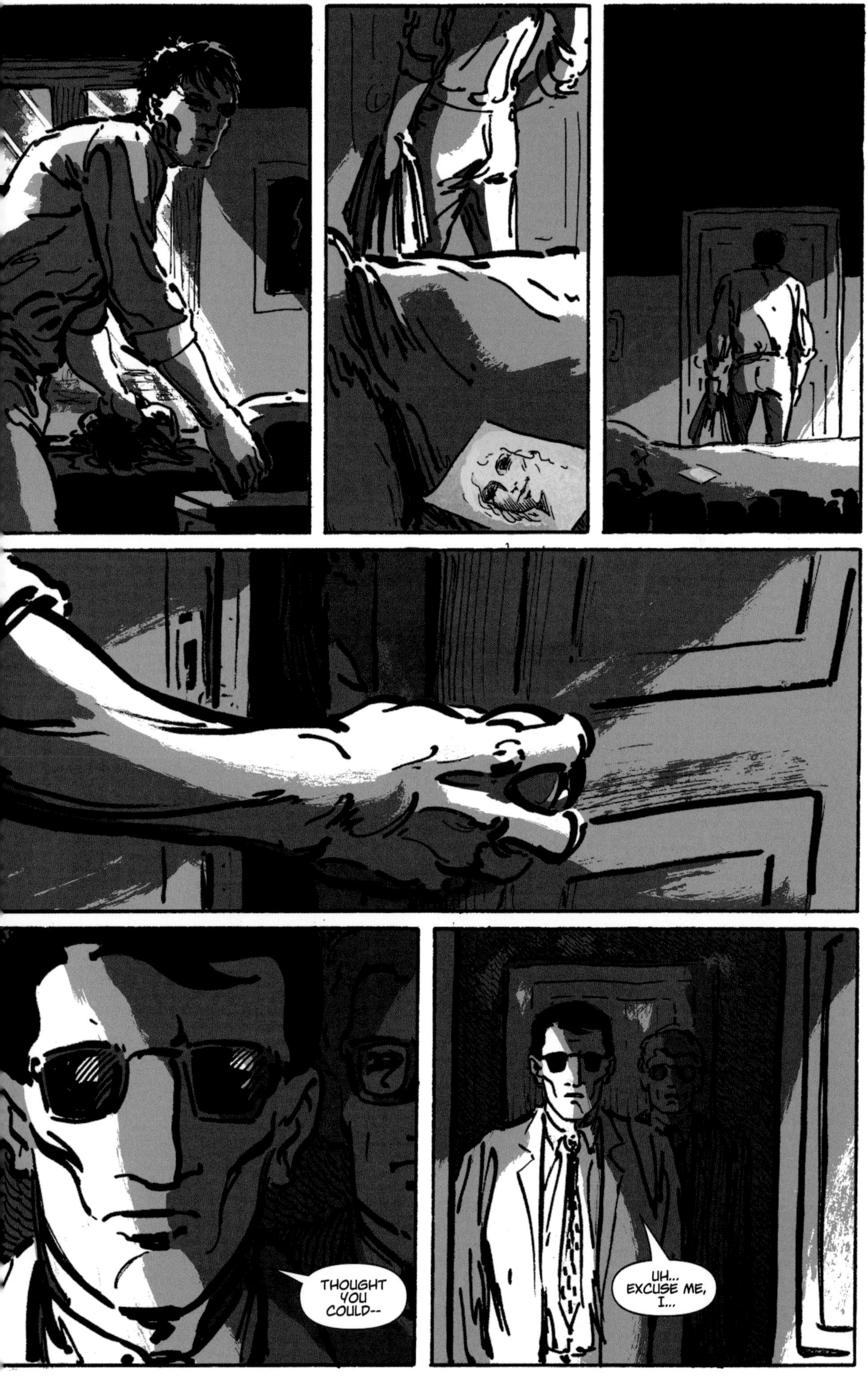
THOUGHT YOU COULD--
UH... EXCUSE ME, I...

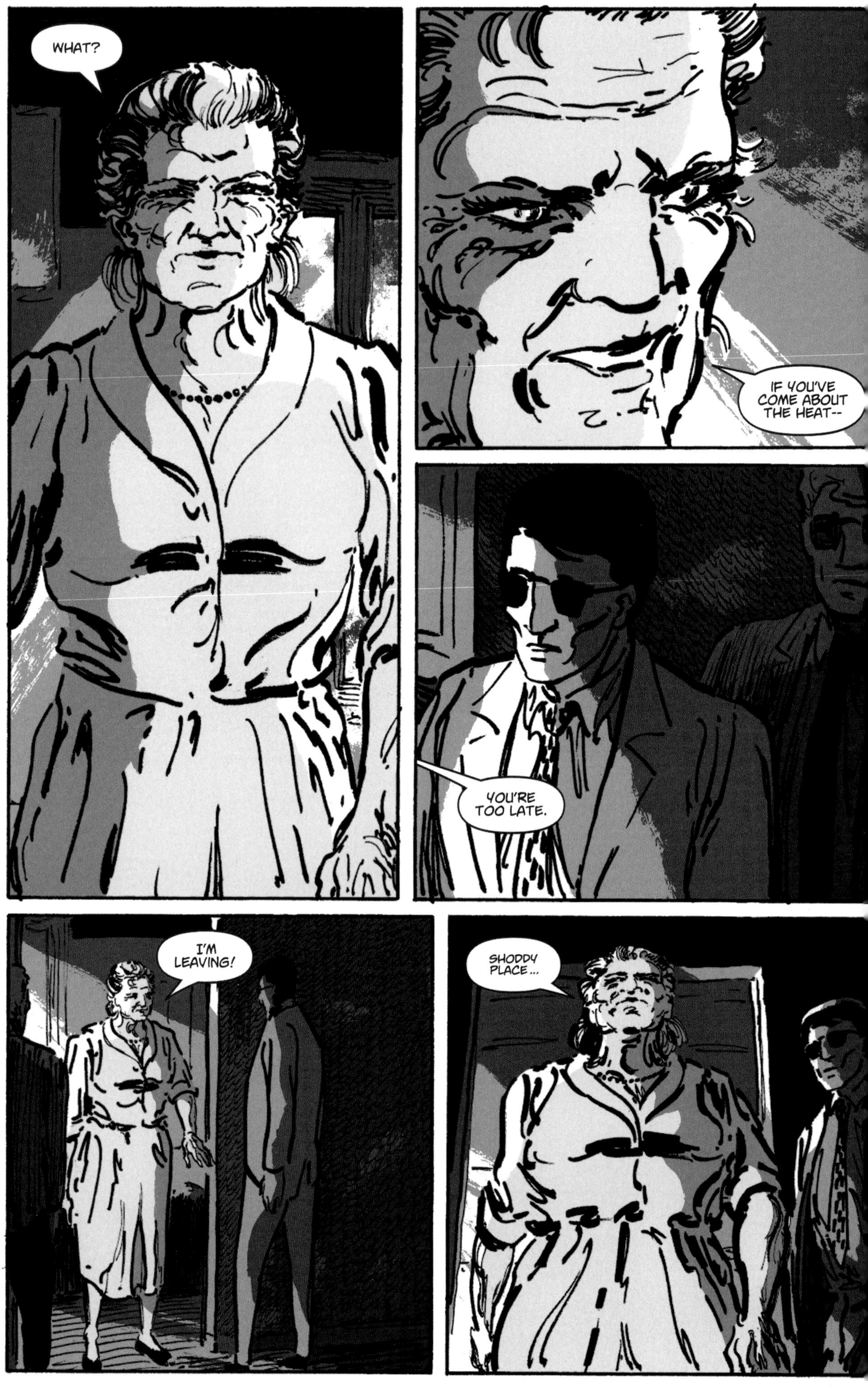
WHAT?
IF YOU'VE COME ABOUT THE HEAT--
YOU'RE TOO LATE.
I'M LEAVING!
SHODDY PLACE...

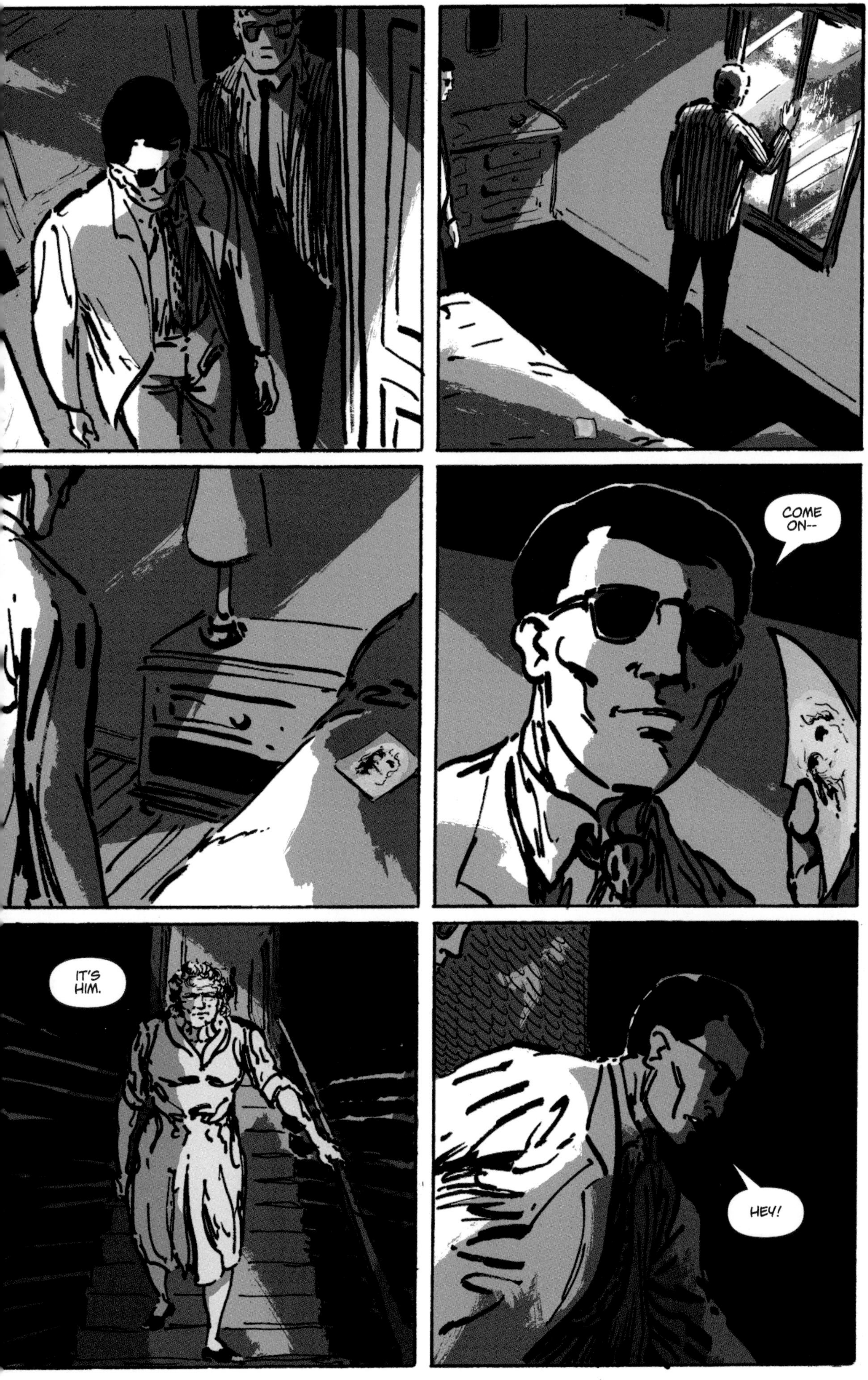
COME ON--
IT'S HIM.
HEY!

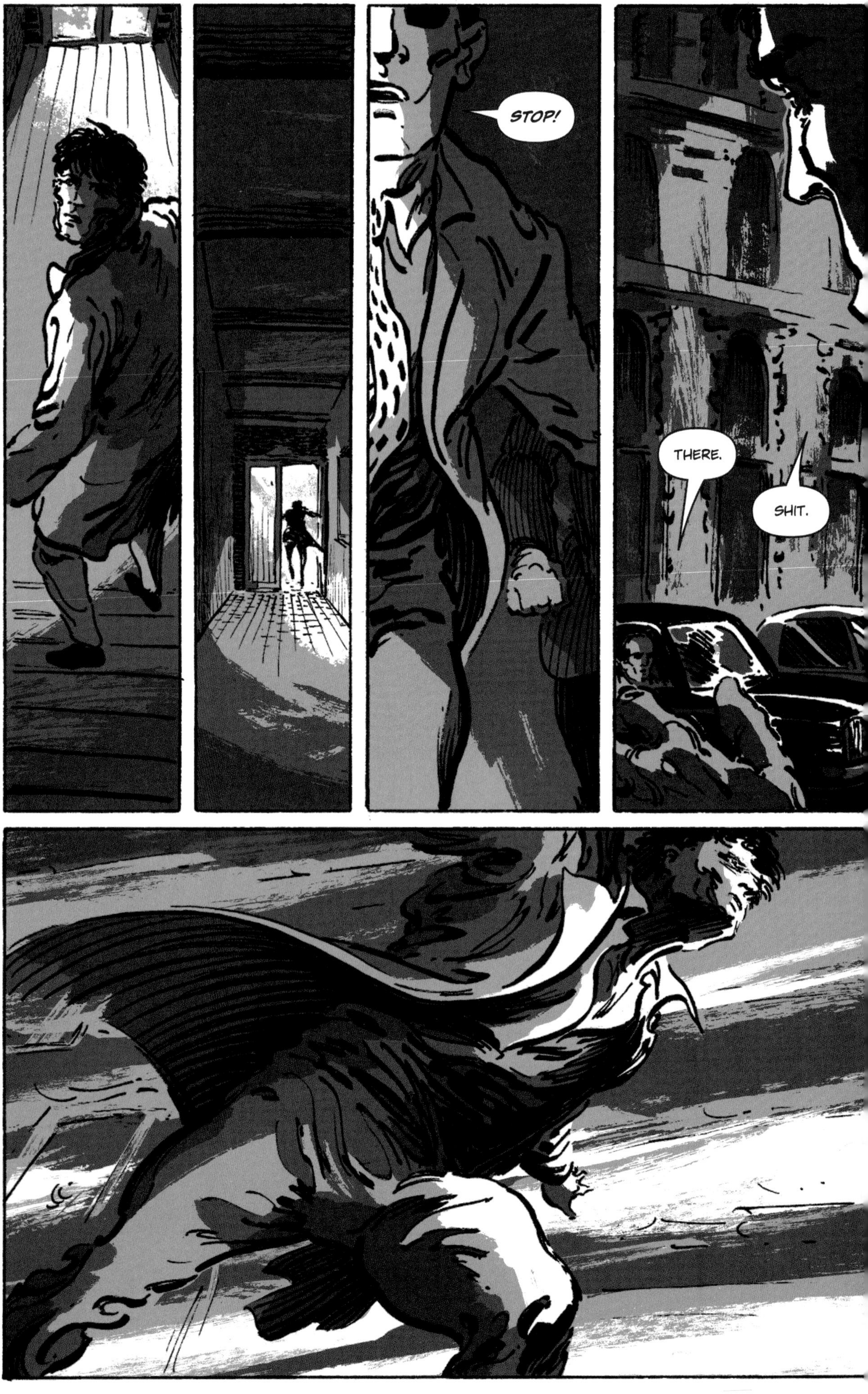
STOP!
THERE.
SHIT.

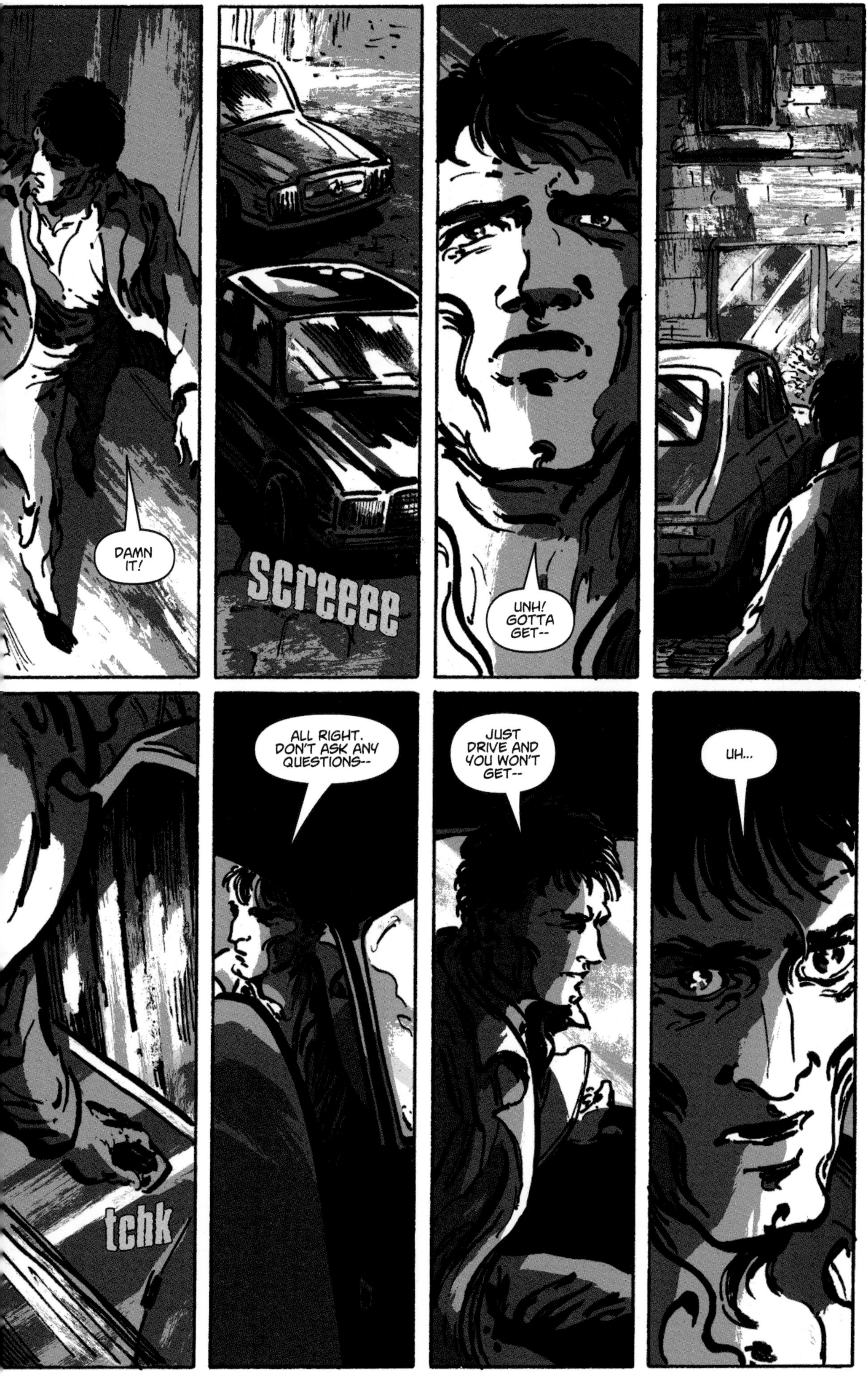
DAMN IT!
Screeee
UNH! GOTTA GET--
tchk
ALL RIGHT. DON'T ASK ANY QUESTIONS--
JUST DRIVE AND YOU WON'T GET--
UH...

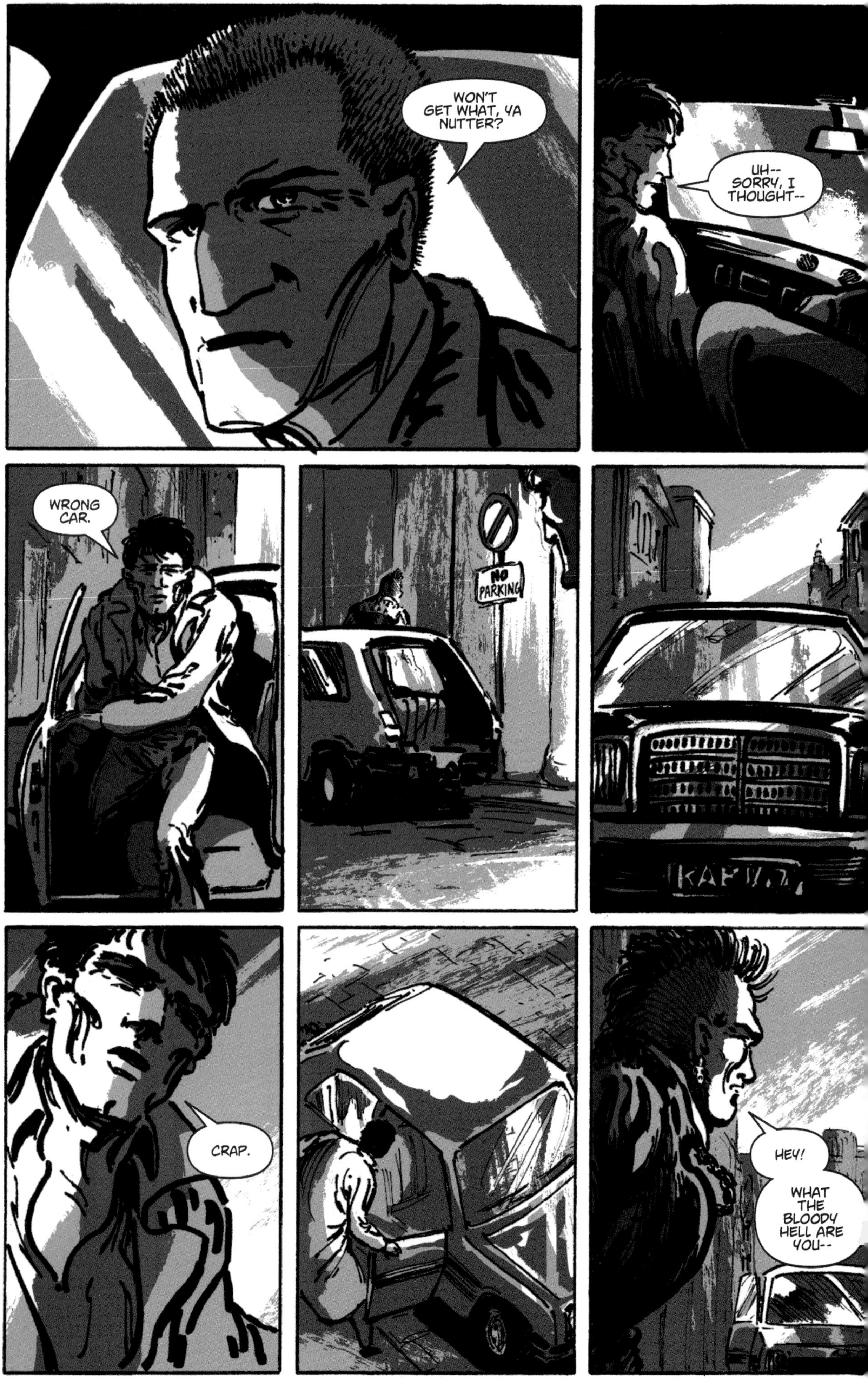
WON'T GET WHAT, YA NUTTER?
UH-- SORRY, I THOUGHT--
WRONG CAR.
NO PARKING
CRAP.
HEY!
WHAT THE BLOODY HELL ARE YOU--

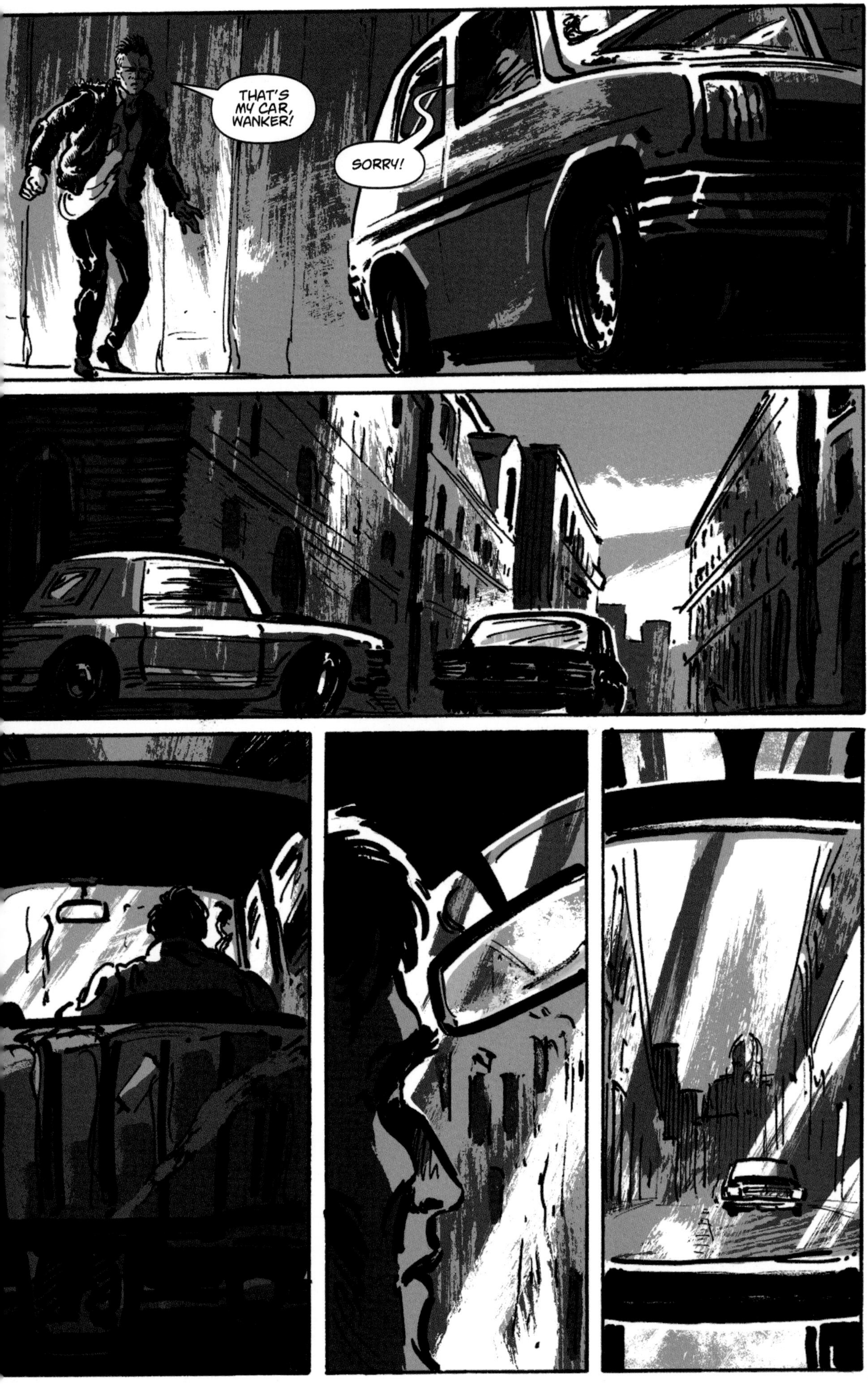
THAT'S MY CAR, WANKER!
SORRY!

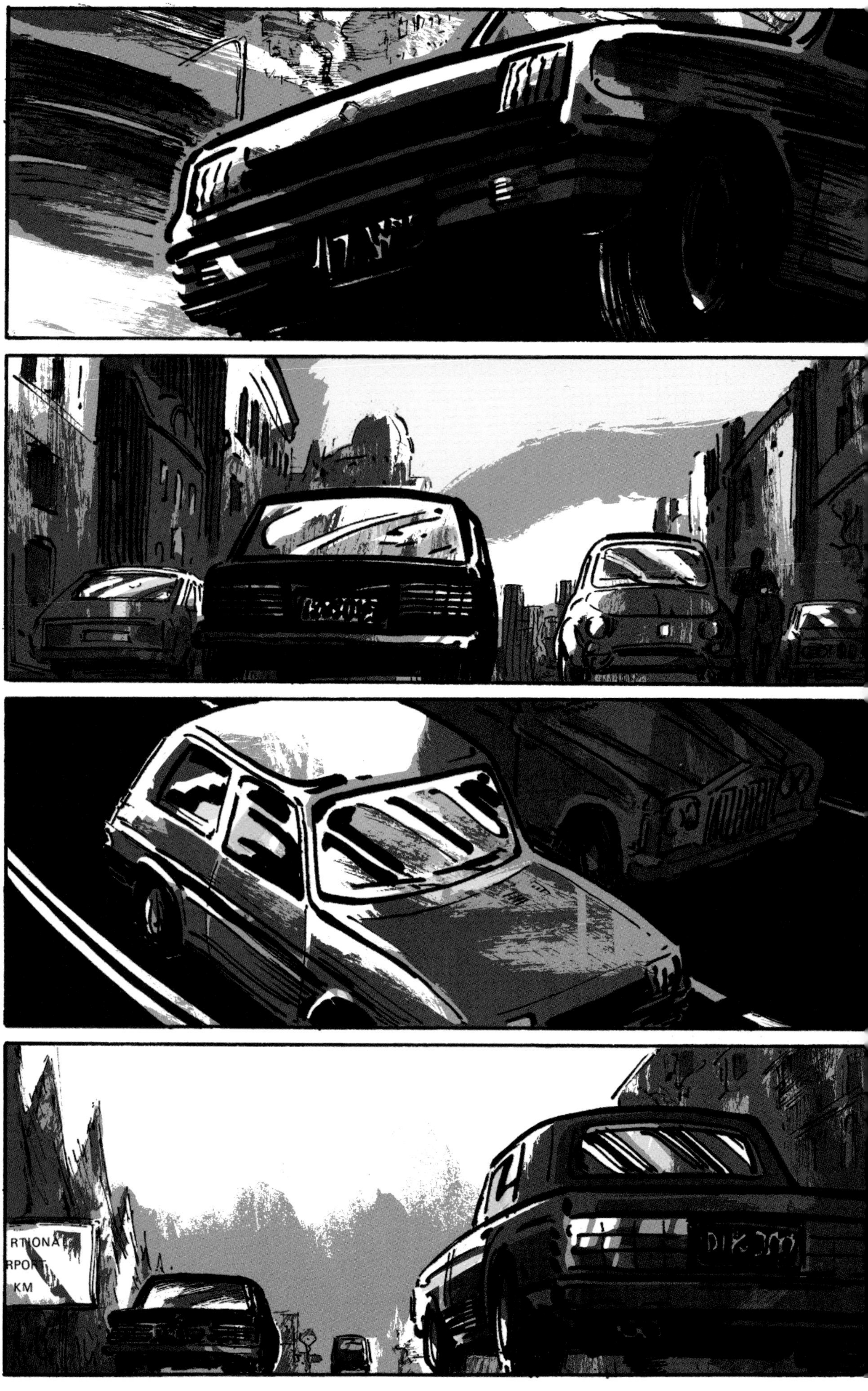
RTIONAL
RPORT
KM

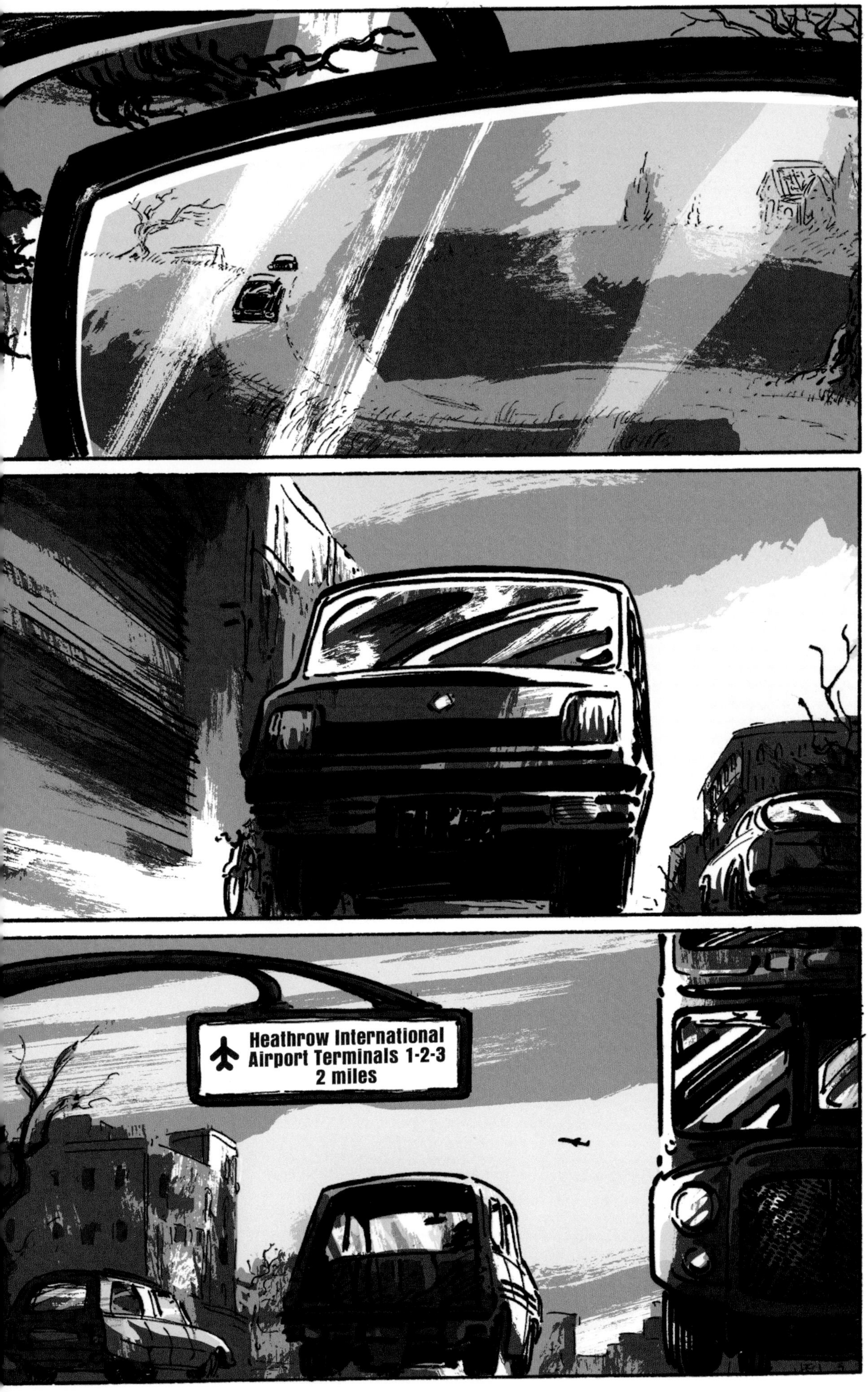
Heathrow International
Airport Terminals 1-2-3
2 miles

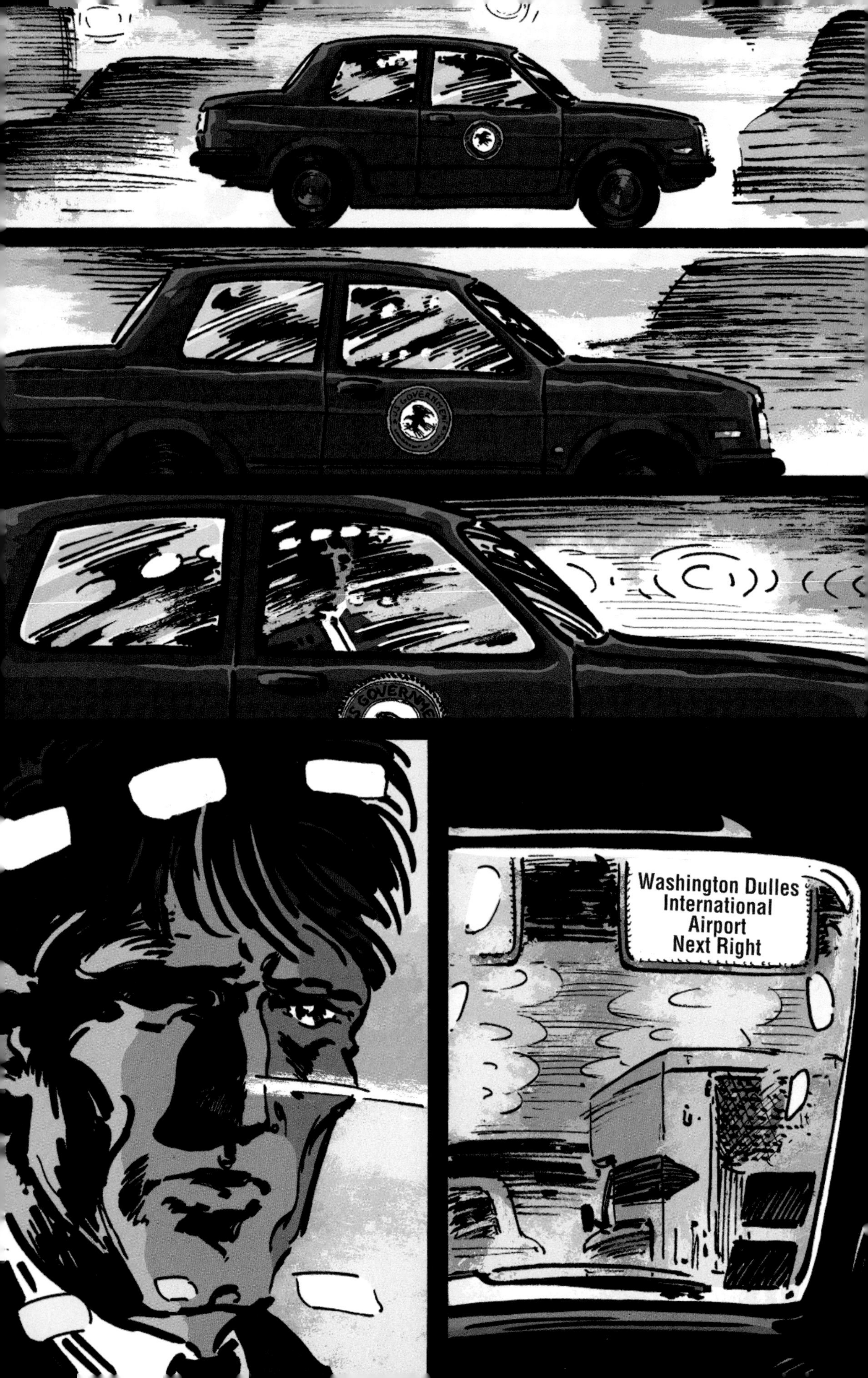
Washington Dulles
International
Airport
Next Right

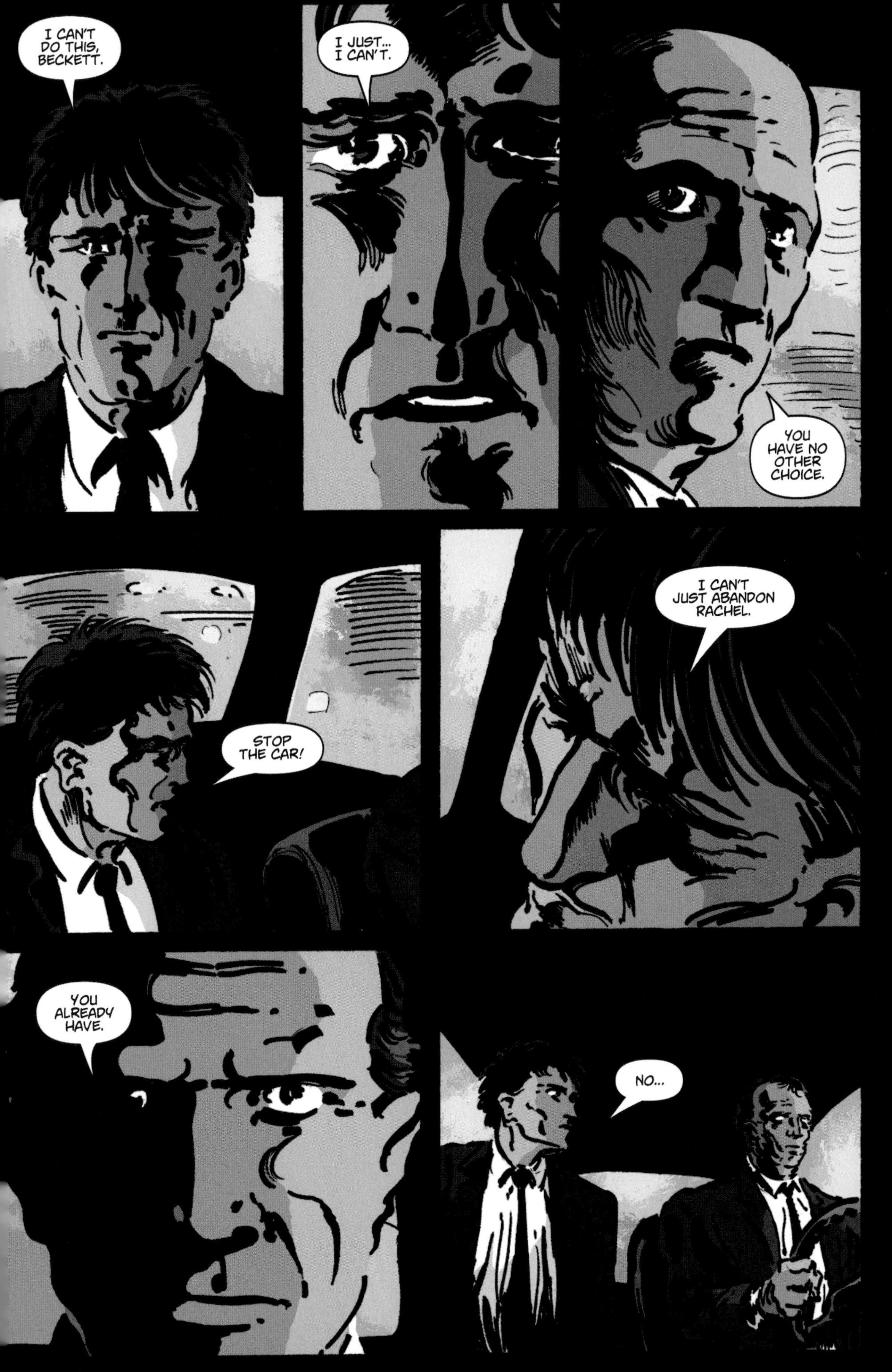

I CAN'T DO THIS, BECKETT.
I JUST... I CAN'T.
YOU HAVE NO OTHER CHOICE.
STOP THE CAR!
I CAN'T JUST ABANDON RACHEL.
YOU ALREADY HAVE.
NO...

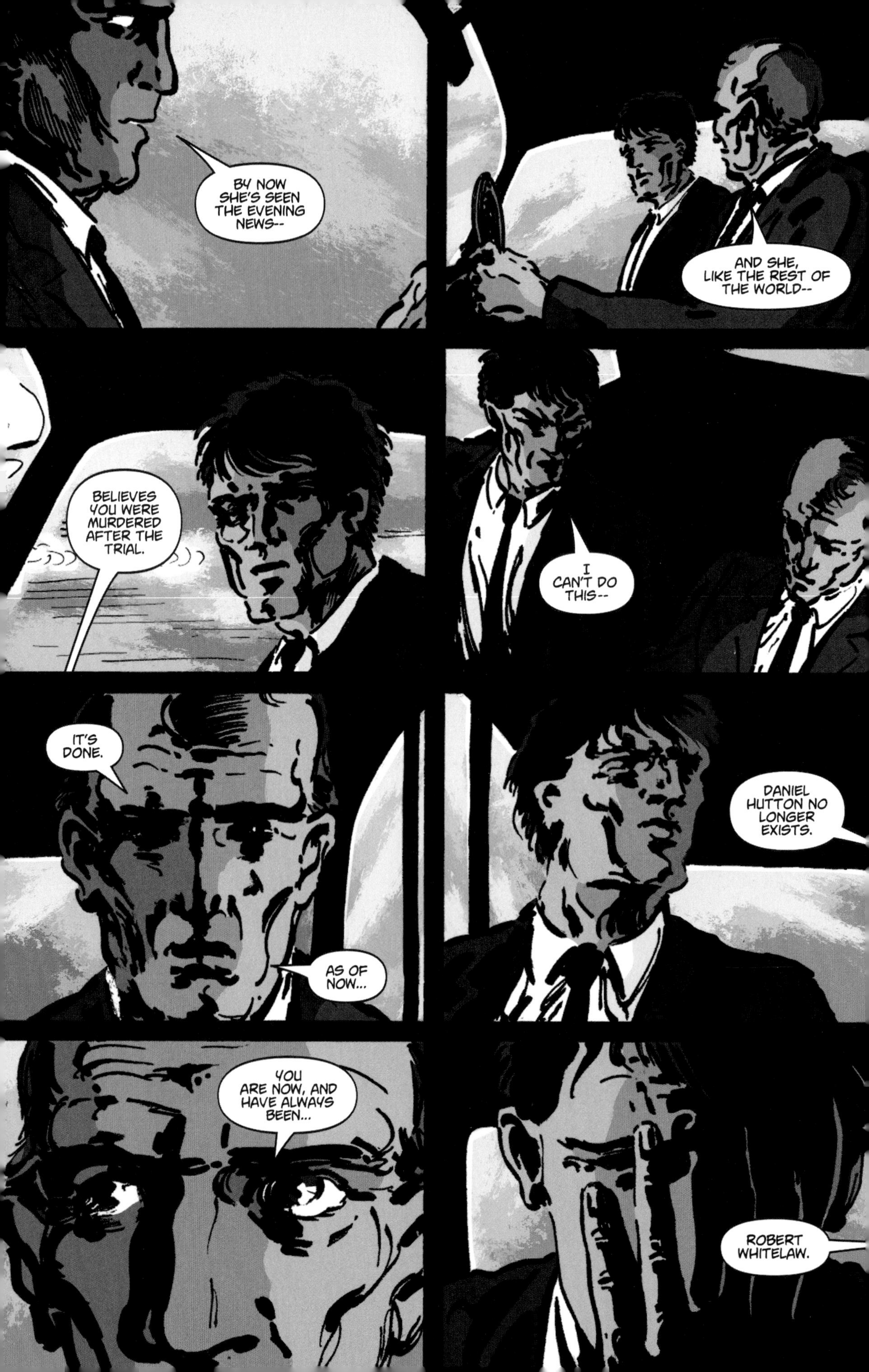
BY NOW SHE'S SEEN THE EVENING NEWS--
AND SHE, LIKE THE REST OF THE WORLD--
BELIEVES YOU WERE MURDERED AFTER THE TRIAL.
I CAN'T DO THIS--
IT'S DONE.
AS OF NOW...
DANIEL HUTTON NO LONGER EXISTS.
YOU ARE NOW, AND HAVE ALWAYS BEEN...
ROBERT WHITELAW.

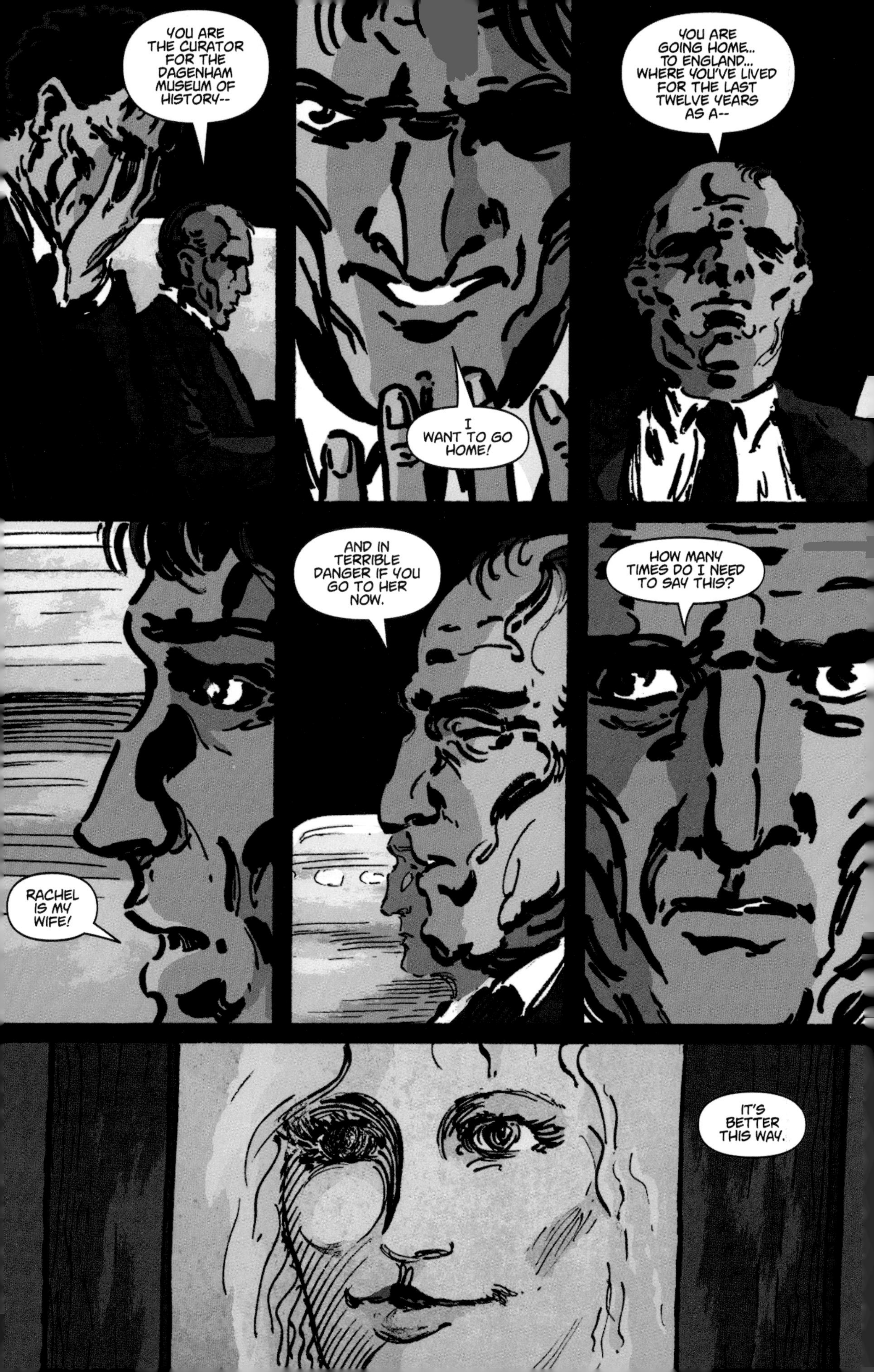
YOU ARE THE CURATOR FOR THE DAGENHAM MUSEUM OF HISTORY--
I WANT TO GO HOME!
YOU ARE GOING HOME... TO ENGLAND... WHERE YOU'VE LIVED FOR THE LAST TWELVE YEARS AS A--
RACHEL IS MY WIFE!
AND IN TERRIBLE DANGER IF YOU GO TO HER NOW.
HOW MANY TIMES DO I NEED TO SAY THIS?
IT'S BETTER THIS WAY.

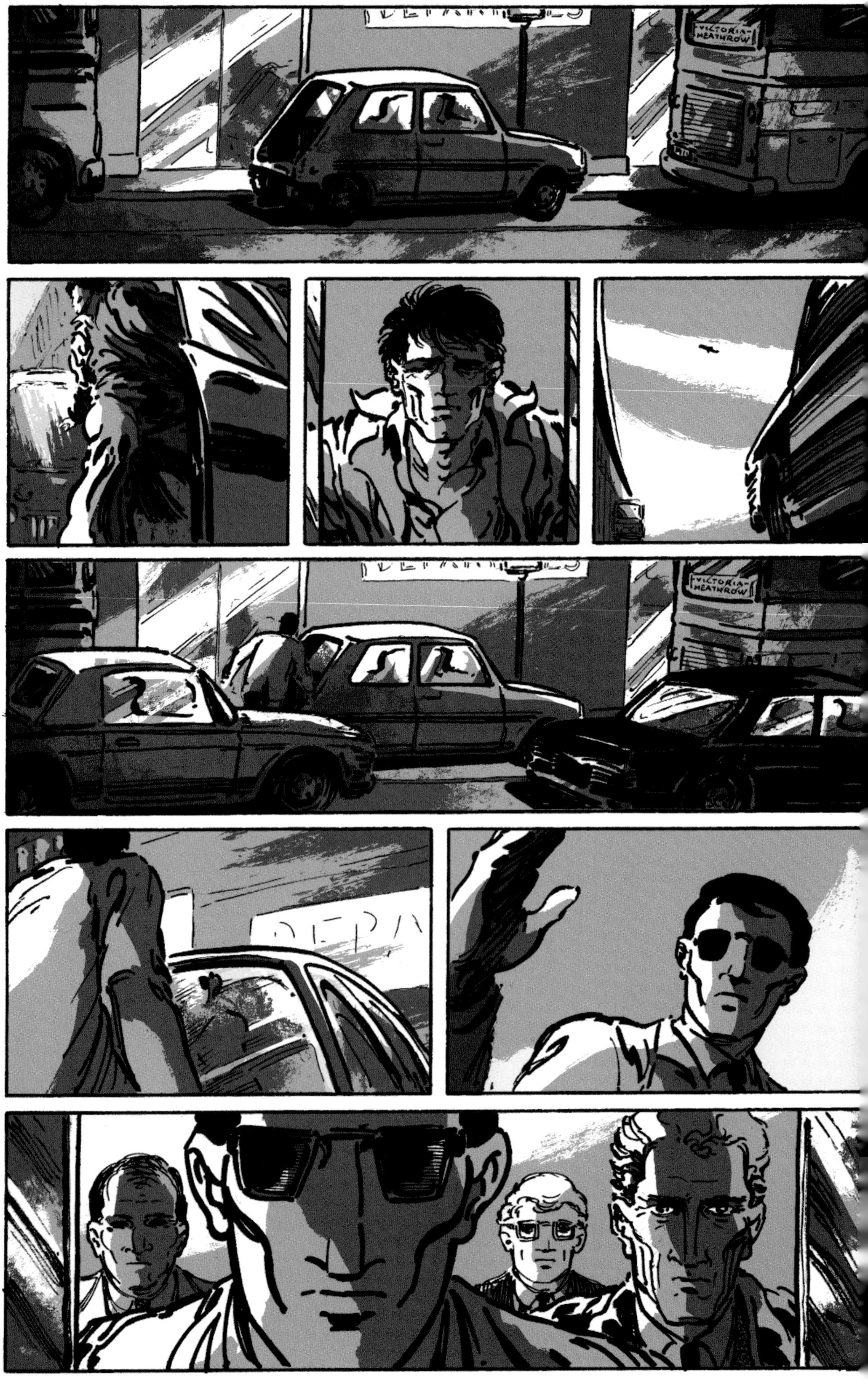
VICTORIA-HEATHROW
VICTORIA-HEATHROW

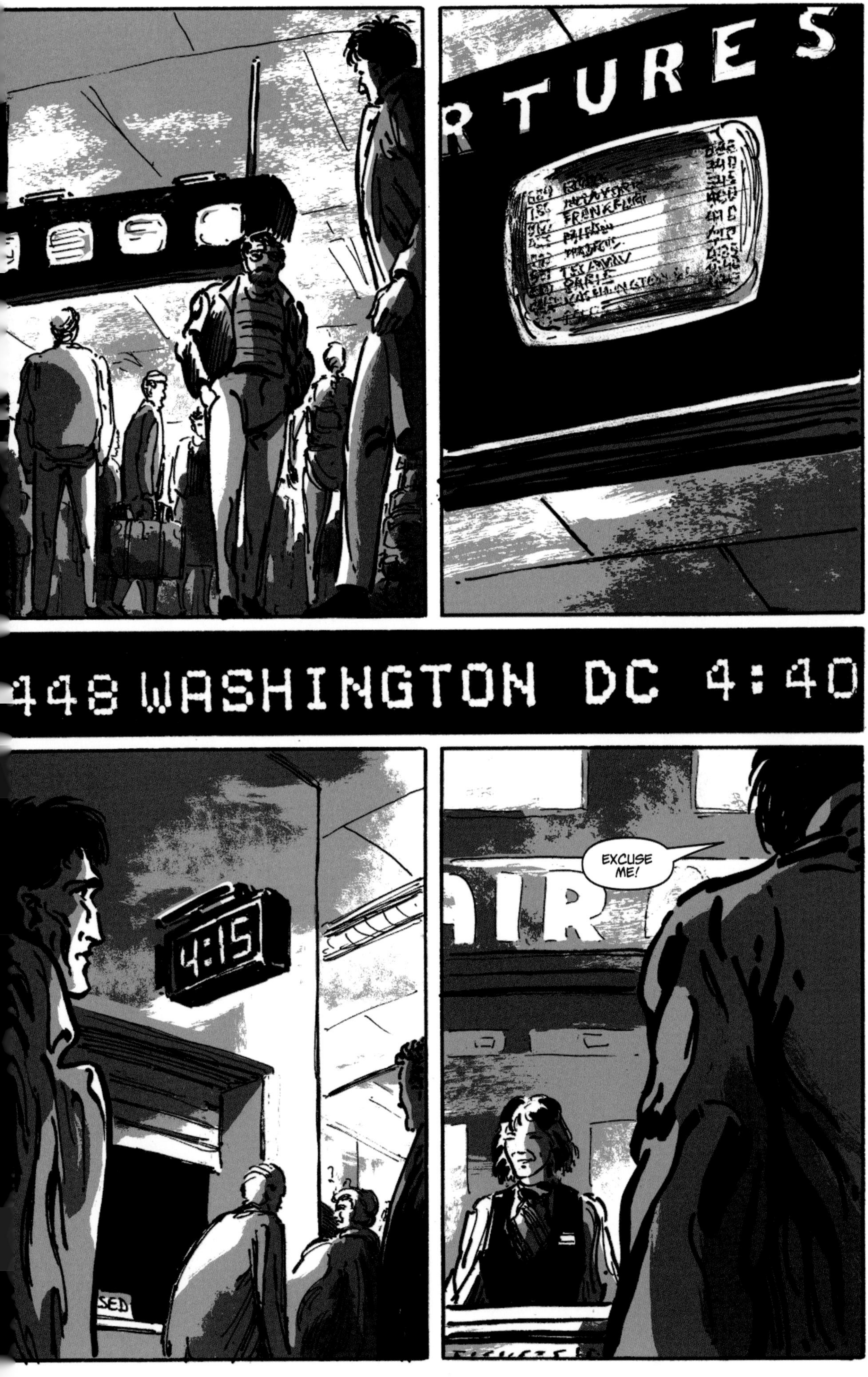
RTURES
448 WASHINGTON DC 4:40
4:15
SED
AIR
EXCUSE ME!

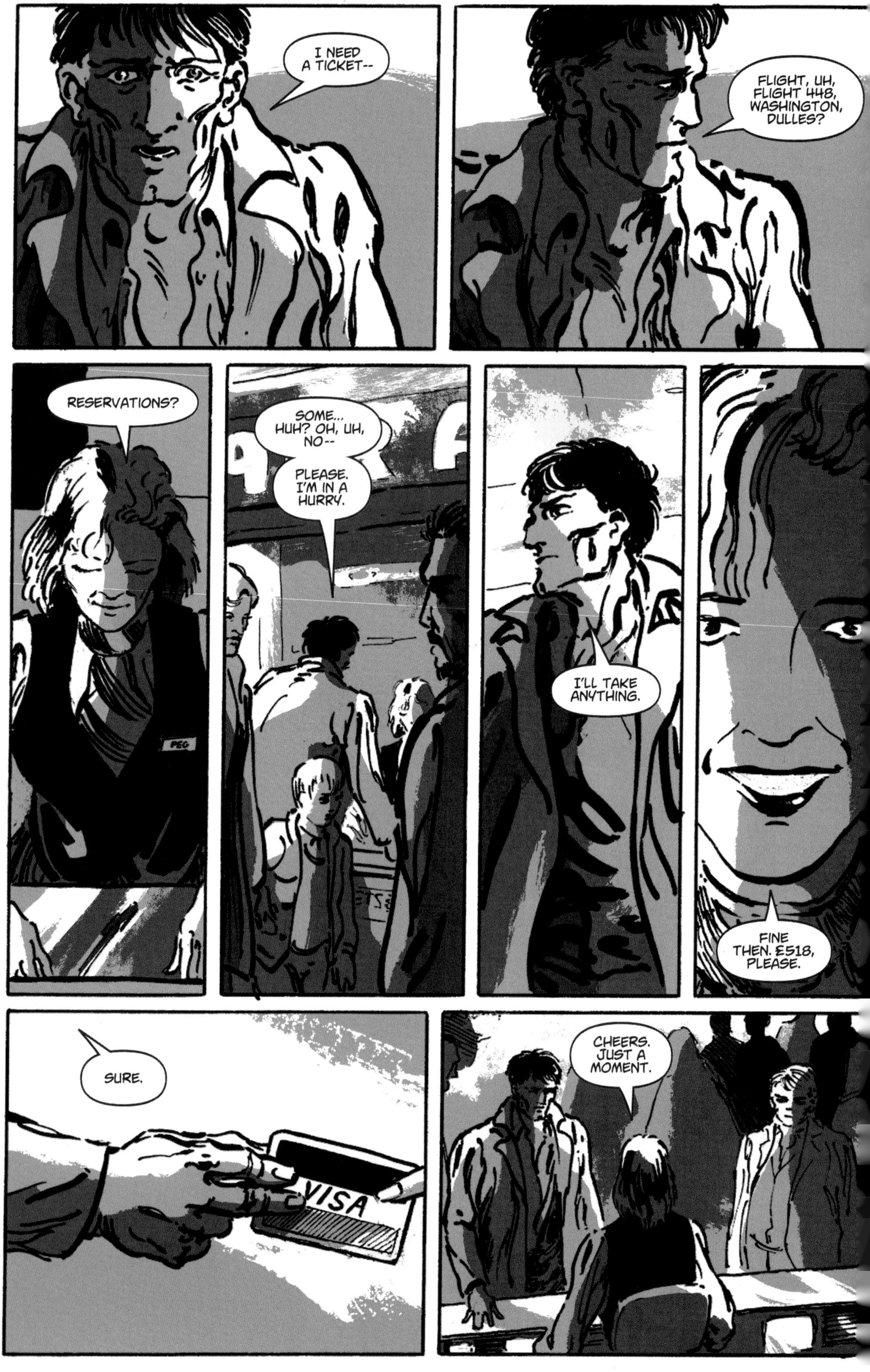

I NEED A TICKET--
FLIGHT, UH, FLIGHT 448, WASHINGTON, DULLES?
RESERVATIONS?
SOME... HUH? OH, UH, NO--
PLEASE. I'M IN A HURRY.
I'LL TAKE ANYTHING.
FINE THEN. £518, PLEASE.
SURE.
VISA
CHEERS. JUST A MOMENT.

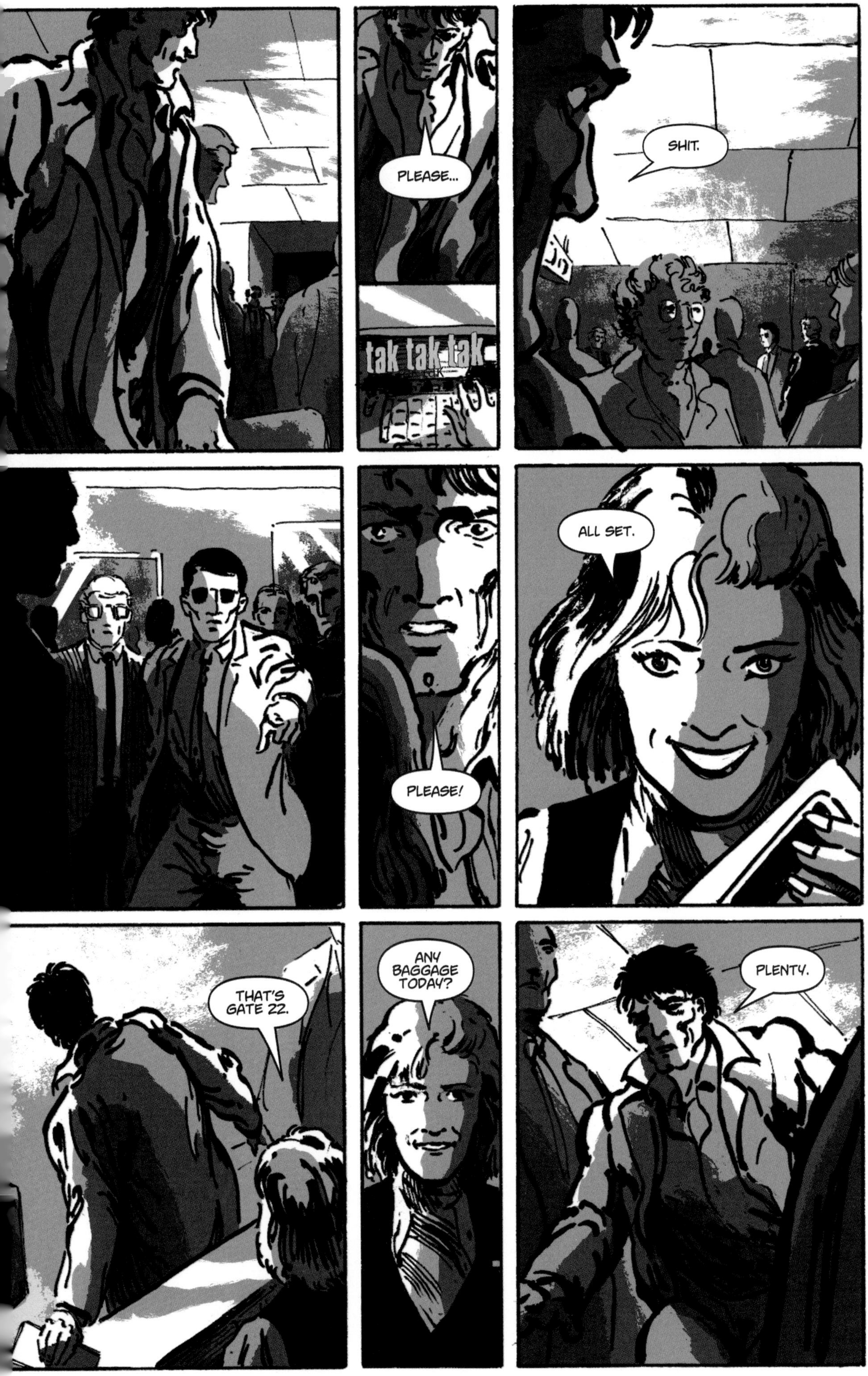
PLEASE...
tak tak tak
SHIT.
PLEASE!
ALL SET.
THAT'S GATE 22.
ANY BAGGAGE TODAY?
PLENTY.

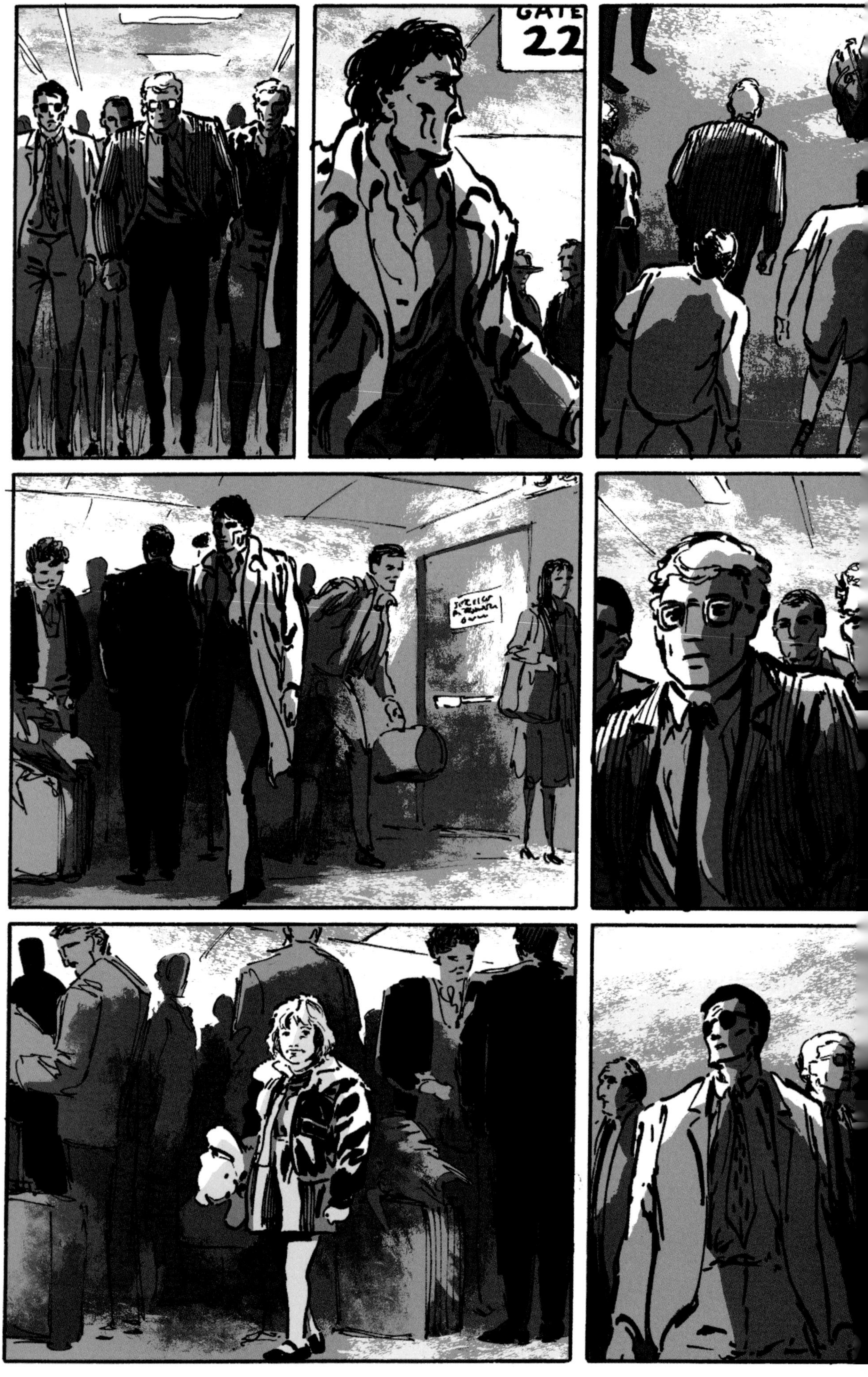
GATE
22

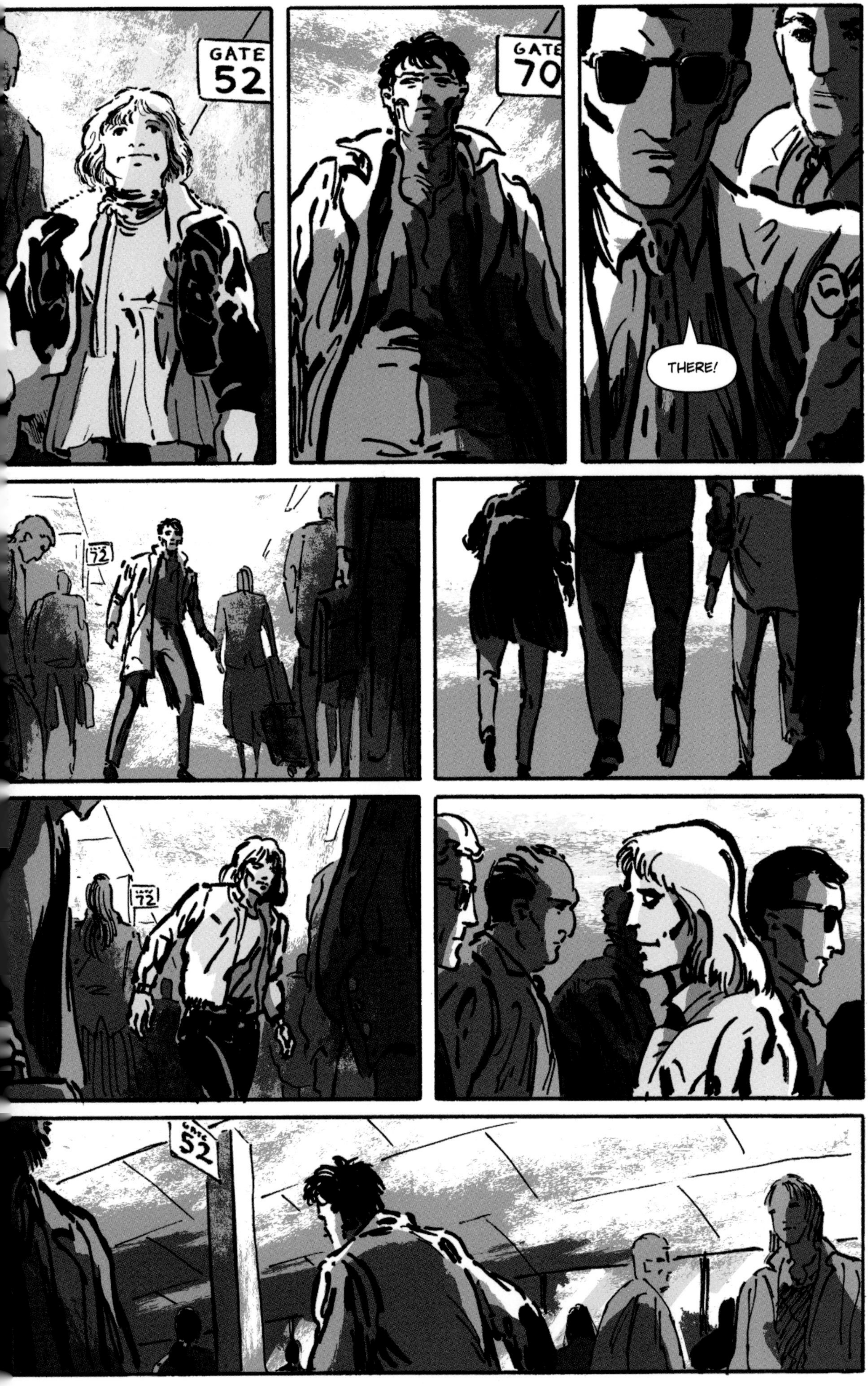
GATE
52
GATE
70
THERE!
72
72
GATE
52

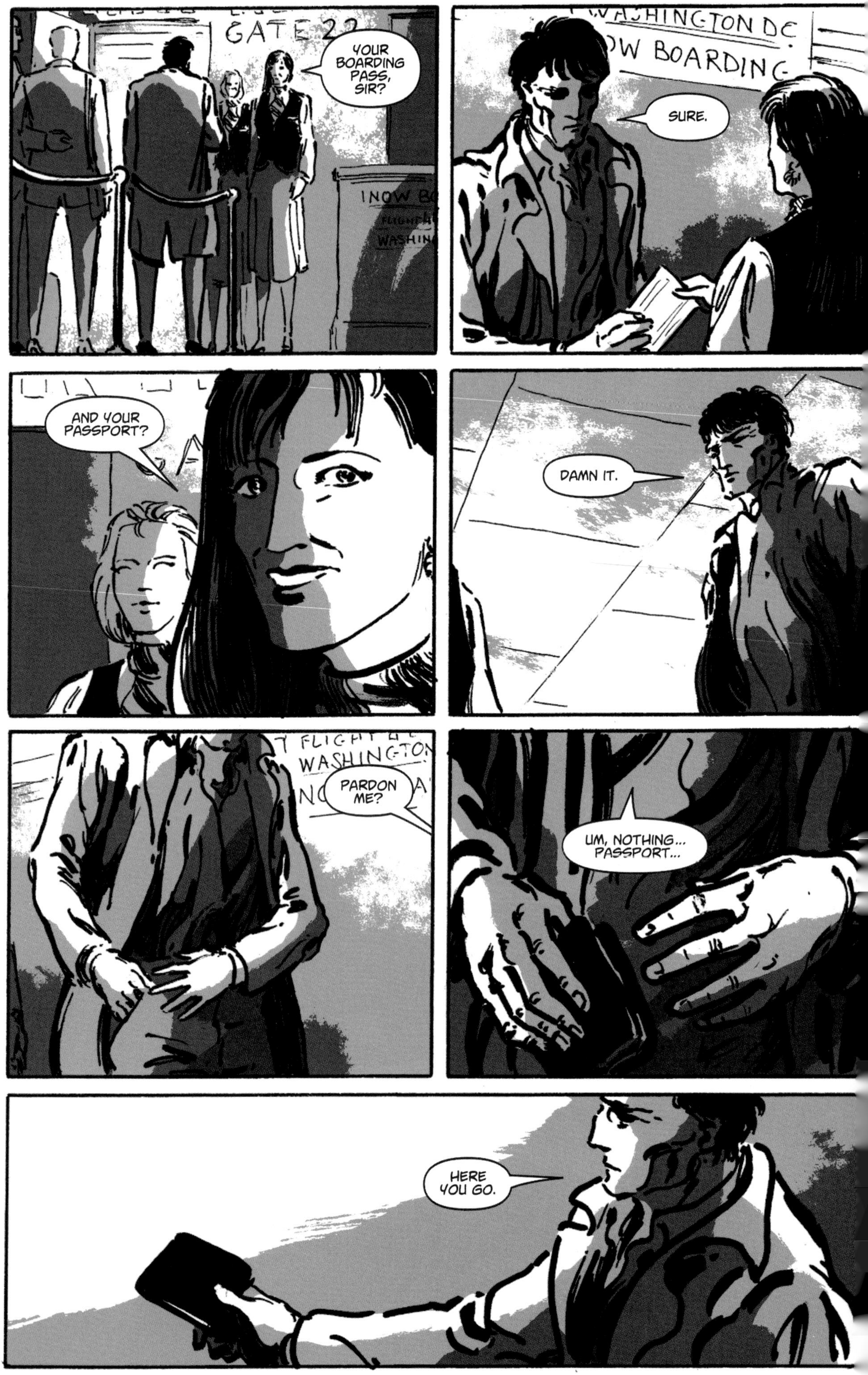
GATE 22
YOUR BOARDING PASS, SIR?
NOW BO
WASHIN
WASHINGTON DC
OW BOARDING
SURE.
AND YOUR PASSPORT?
DAMN IT.
WASHINGTON
PARDON ME?
UM, NOTHING... PASSPORT...
HERE YOU GO.

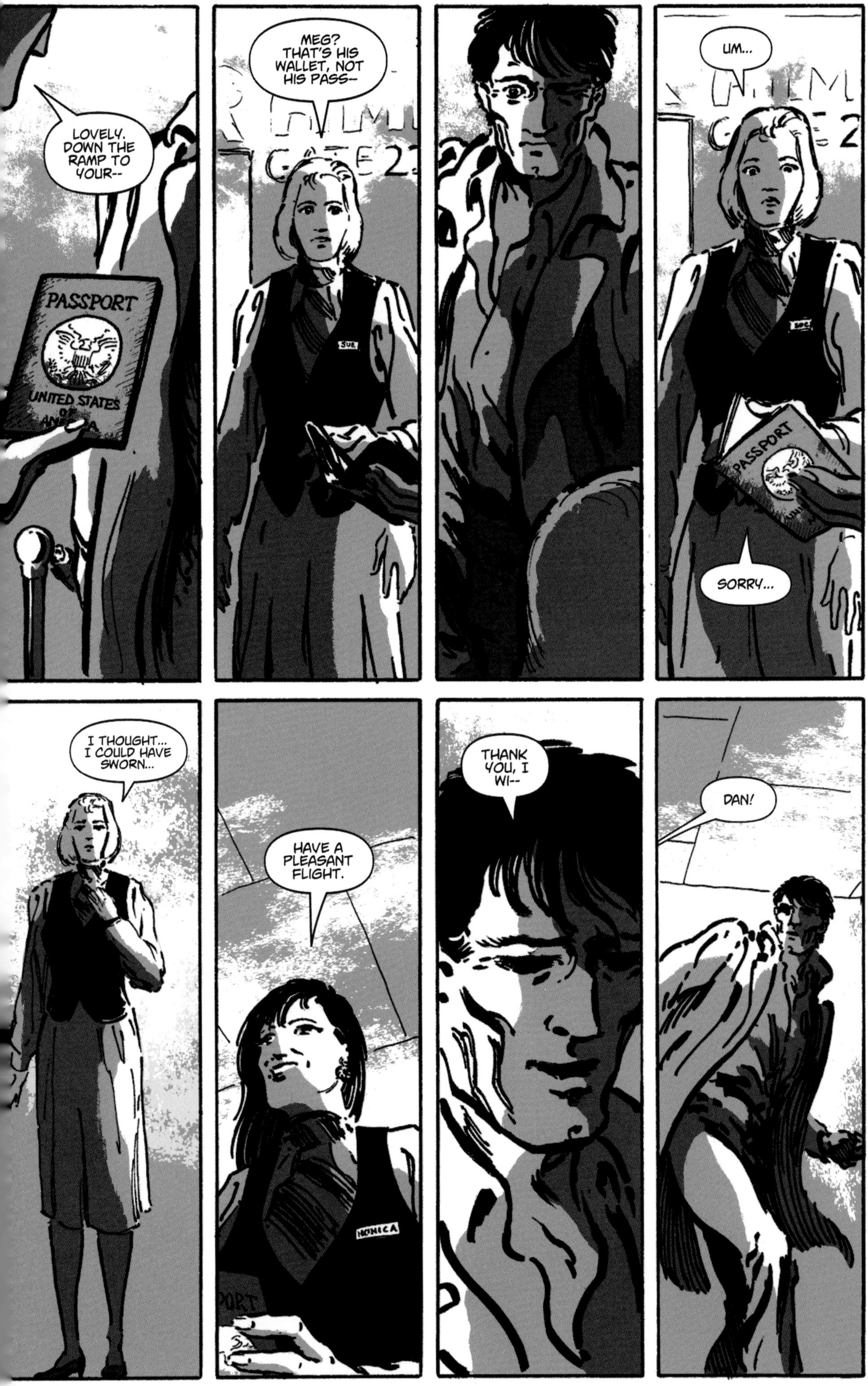
LOVELY. DOWN THE RAMP TO YOUR--
PASSPORT
UNITED STATES OF AMERICA
MEG? THAT'S HIS WALLET, NOT HIS PASS--
GATE 2
SUE
UM...
SUE
PASSPORT
SORRY...
I THOUGHT... I COULD HAVE SWORN...
HAVE A PLEASANT FLIGHT.
MONICA
THANK YOU, I WI--
DAN!

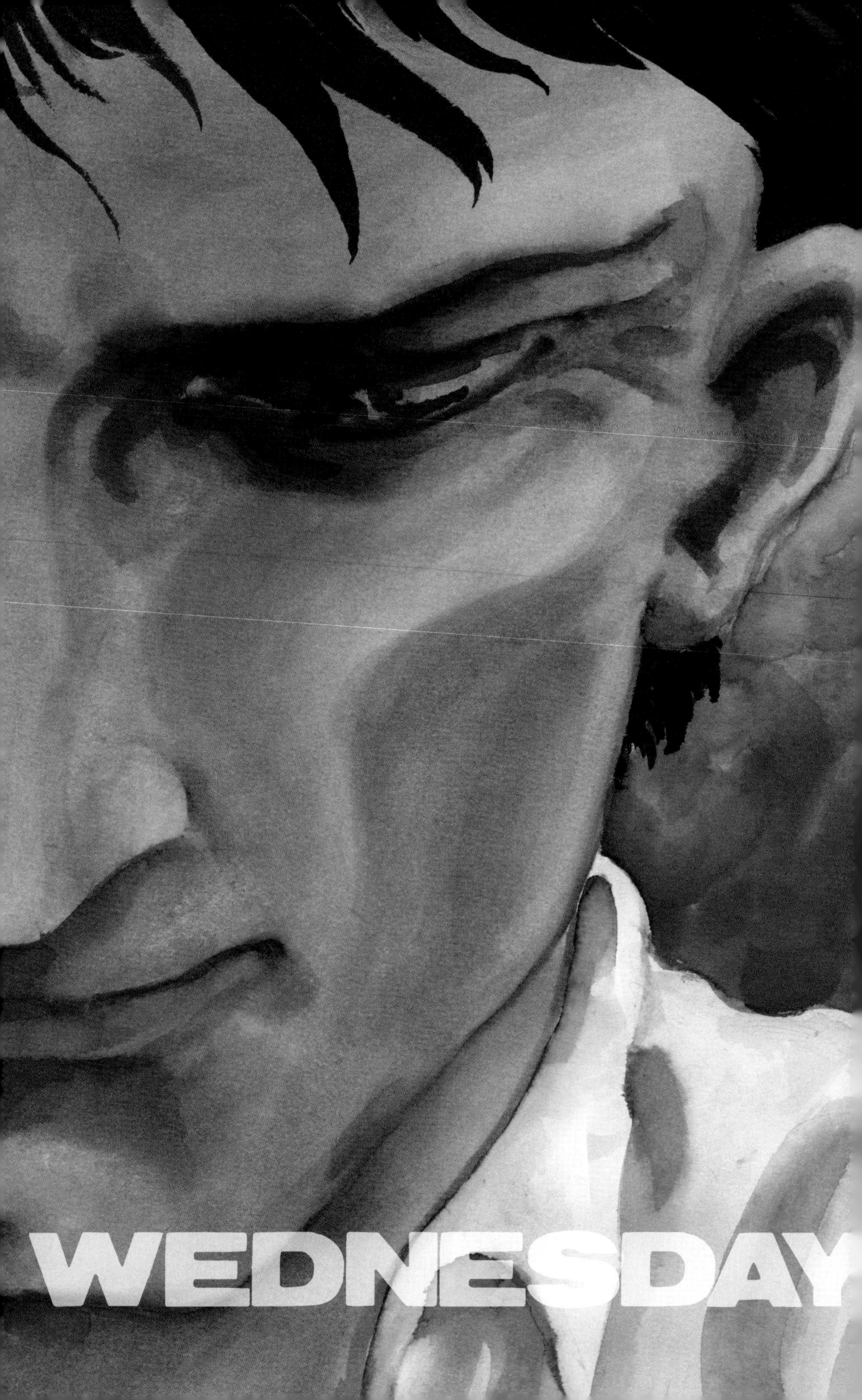
WEDNESDAY

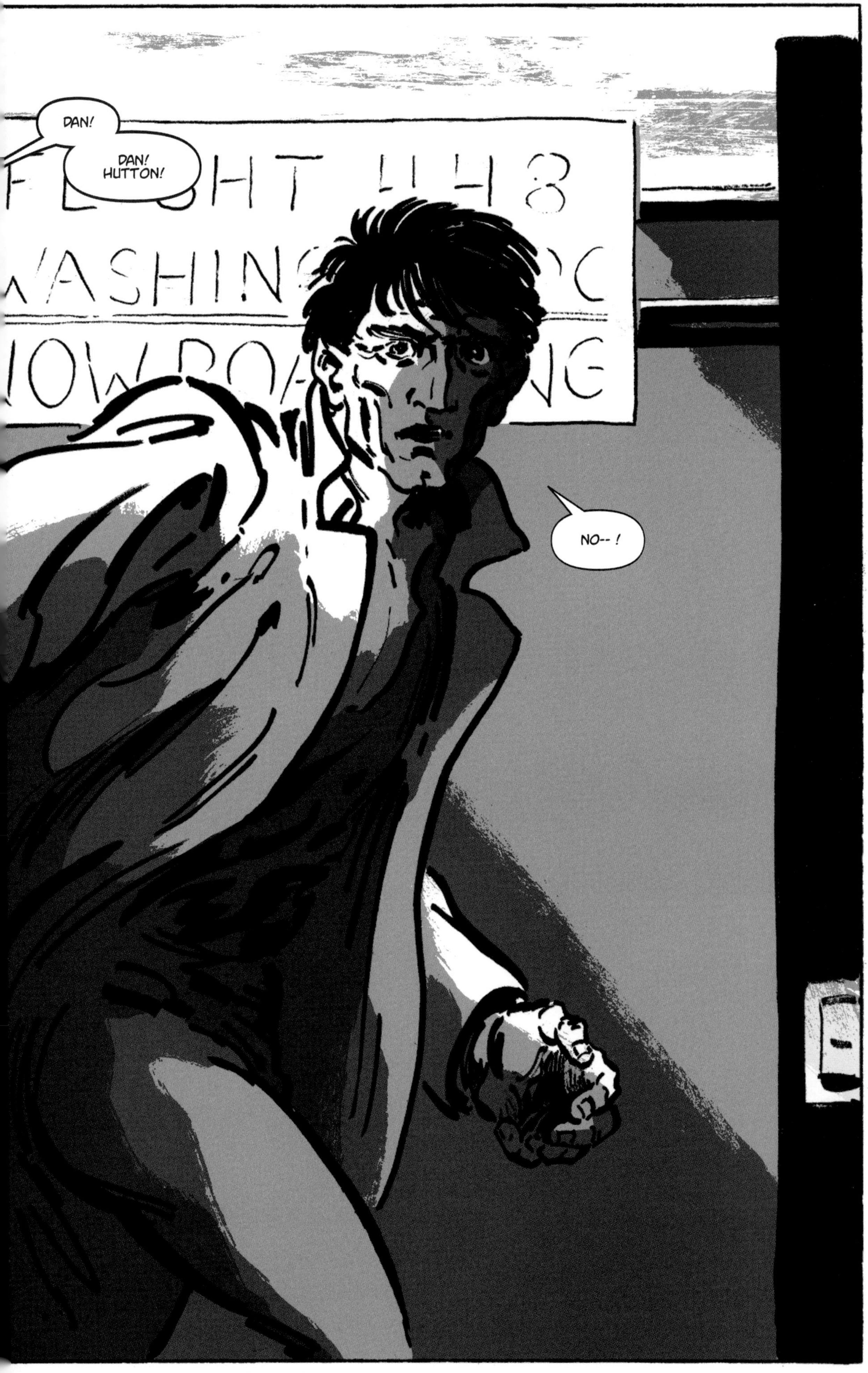
DAN!
DAN! HUTTON!
NO-- !

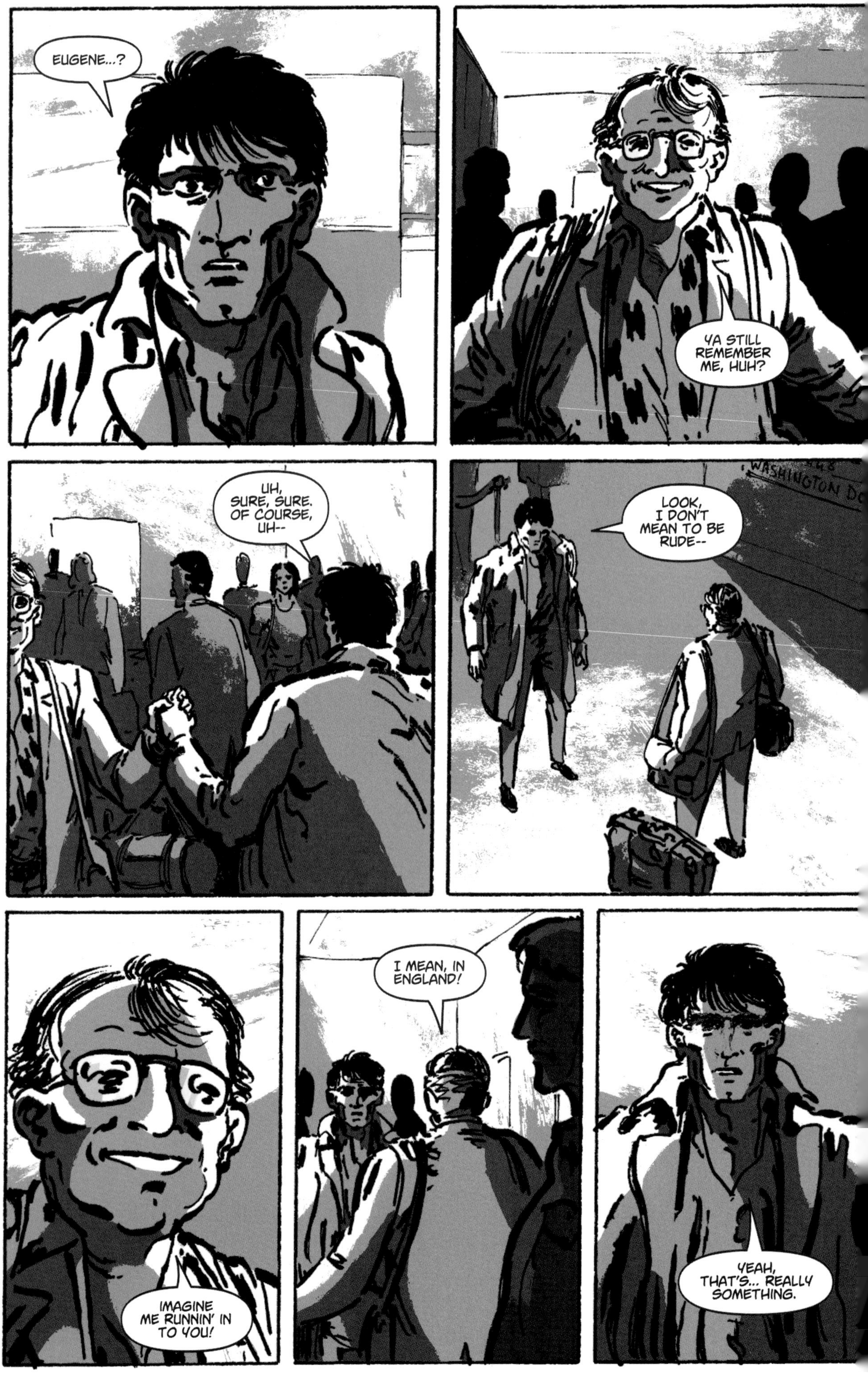
EUGENE...?
YA STILL REMEMBER ME, HUH?
UH, SURE, SURE. OF COURSE, UH--
LOOK, I DON'T MEAN TO BE RUDE--
WASHINGTON D
IMAGINE ME RUNNIN' IN TO YOU!
I MEAN, IN ENGLAND!
YEAH, THAT'S... REALLY SOMETHING.

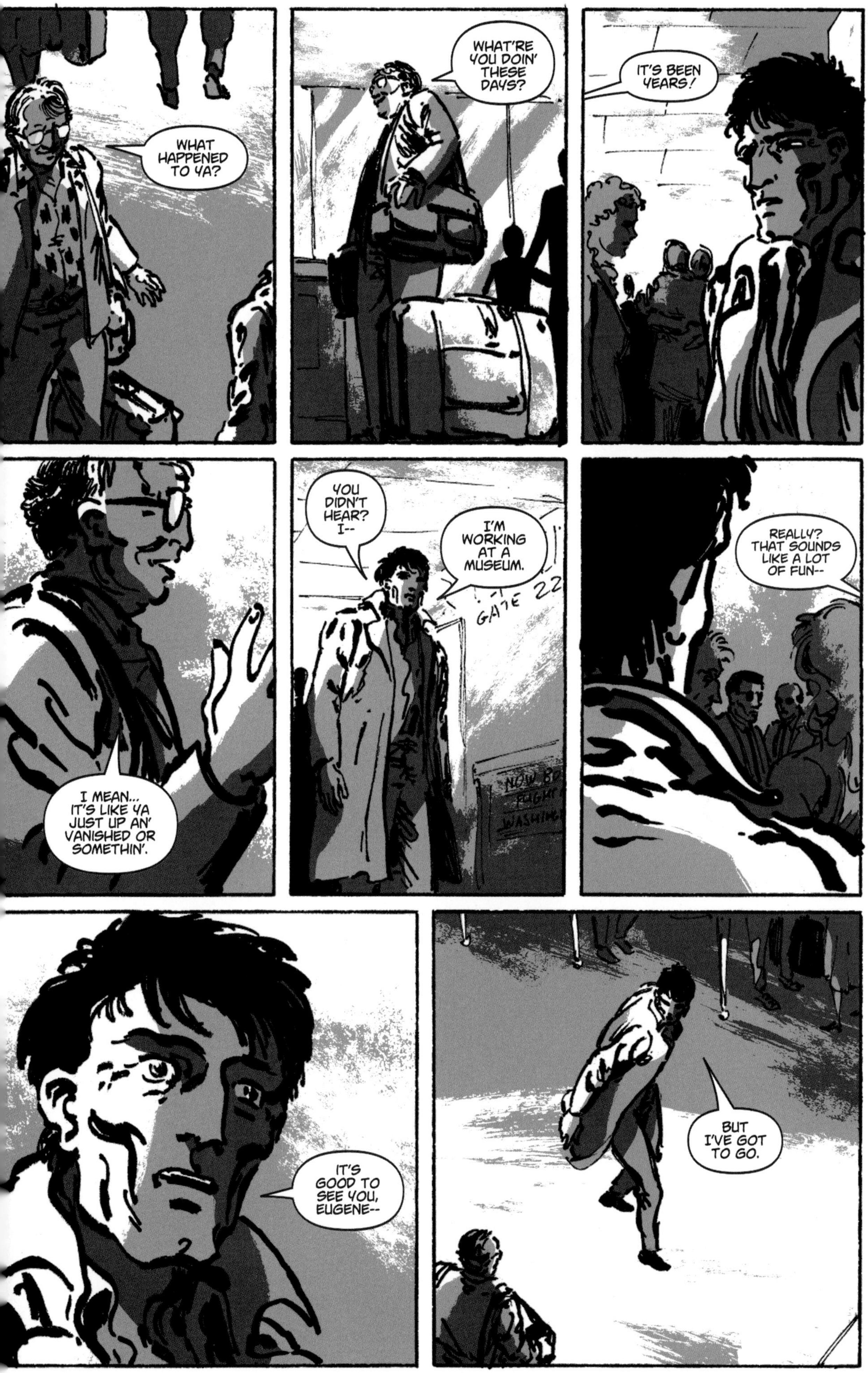
WHAT HAPPENED TO YA?
WHAT'RE YOU DOIN' THESE DAYS?
IT'S BEEN YEARS!
I MEAN... IT'S LIKE YA JUST UP AN' VANISHED OR SOMETHIN'.
YOU DIDN'T HEAR? I--
I'M WORKING AT A MUSEUM.
GATE 22
REALLY? THAT SOUNDS LIKE A LOT OF FUN--
IT'S GOOD TO SEE YOU, EUGENE--
BUT I'VE GOT TO GO.

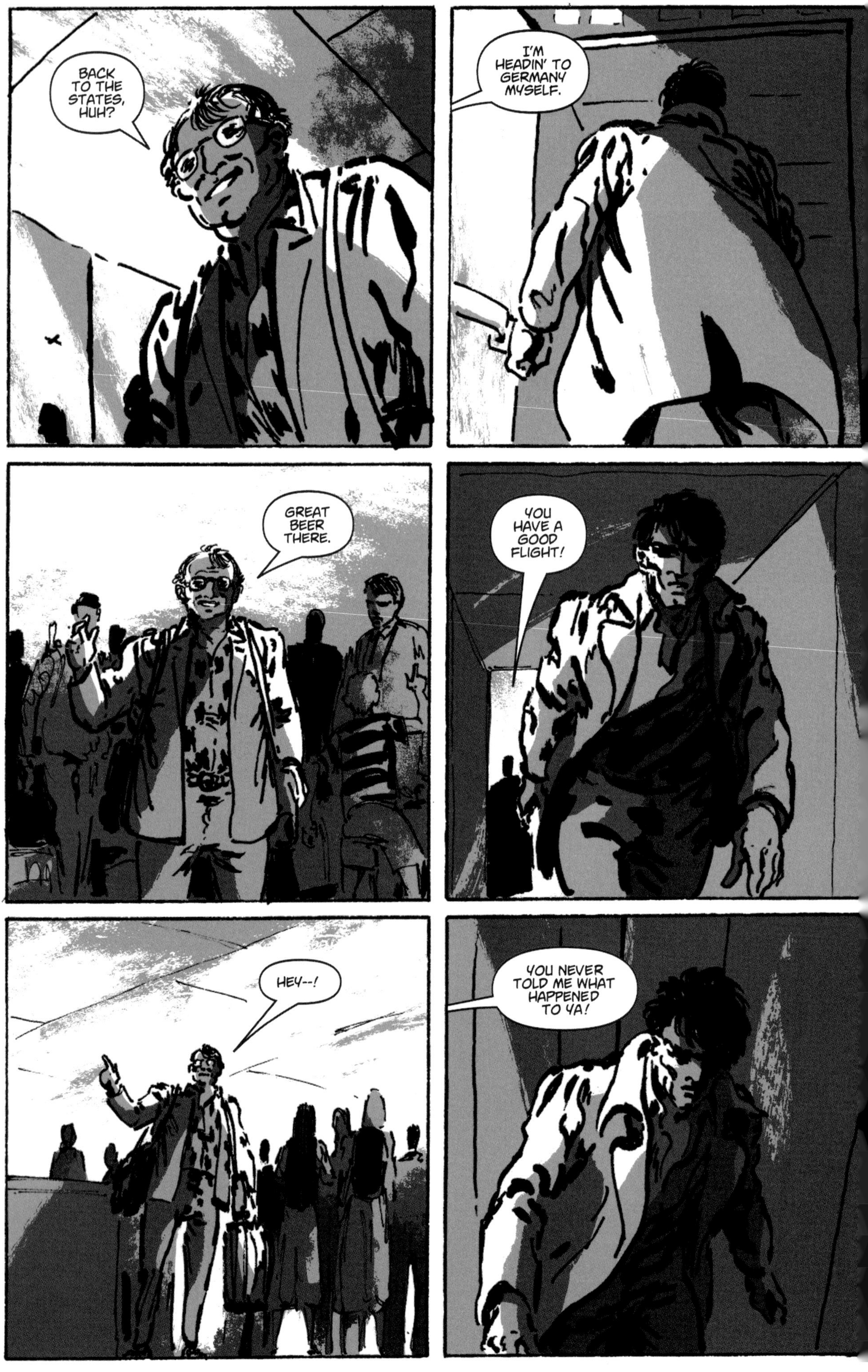
BACK TO THE STATES, HUH?
I'M HEADIN' TO GERMANY MYSELF.
GREAT BEER THERE.
YOU HAVE A GOOD FLIGHT!
HEY--!
YOU NEVER TOLD ME WHAT HAPPENED TO YA!

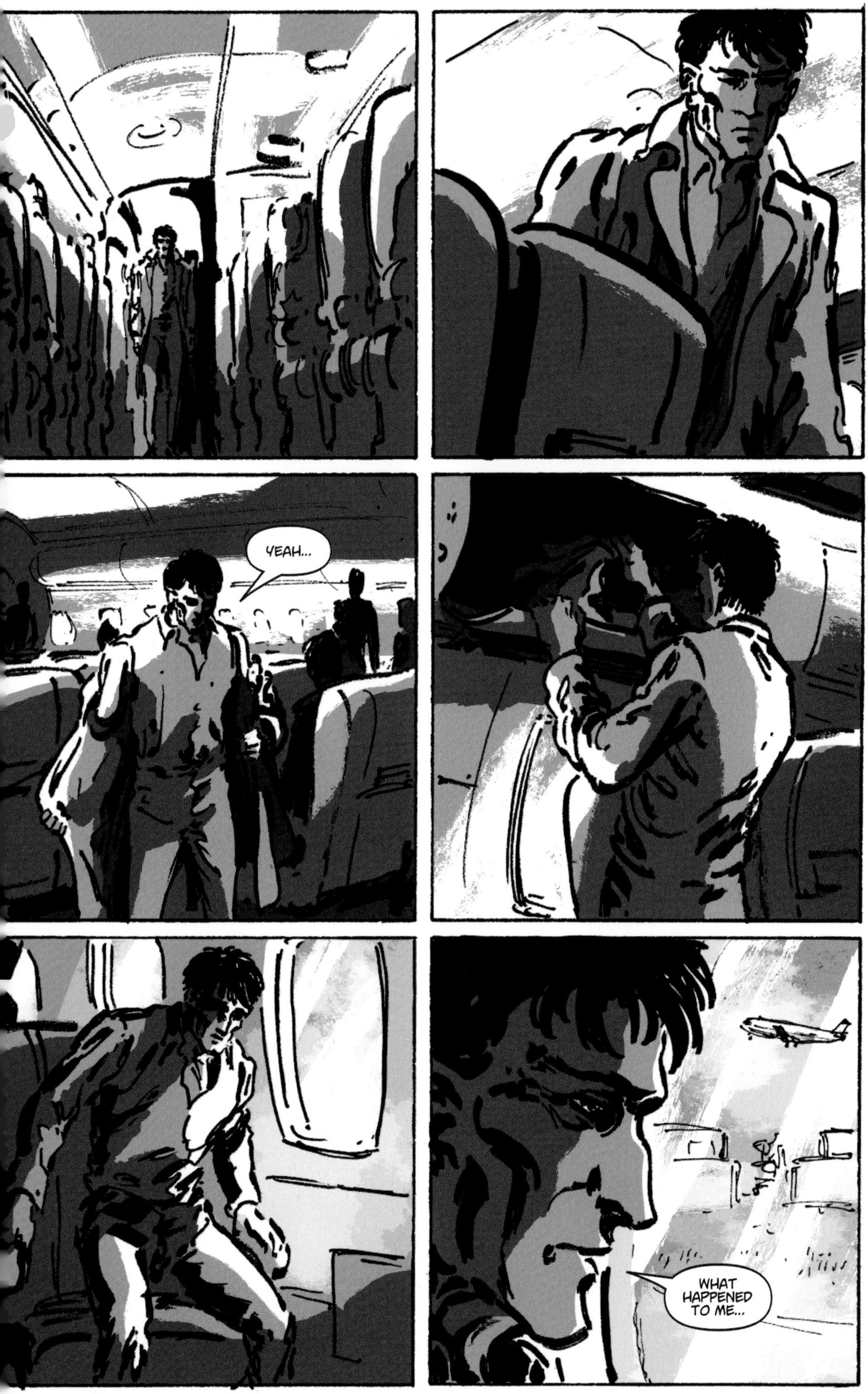
YEAH...
WHAT HAPPENED TO ME...

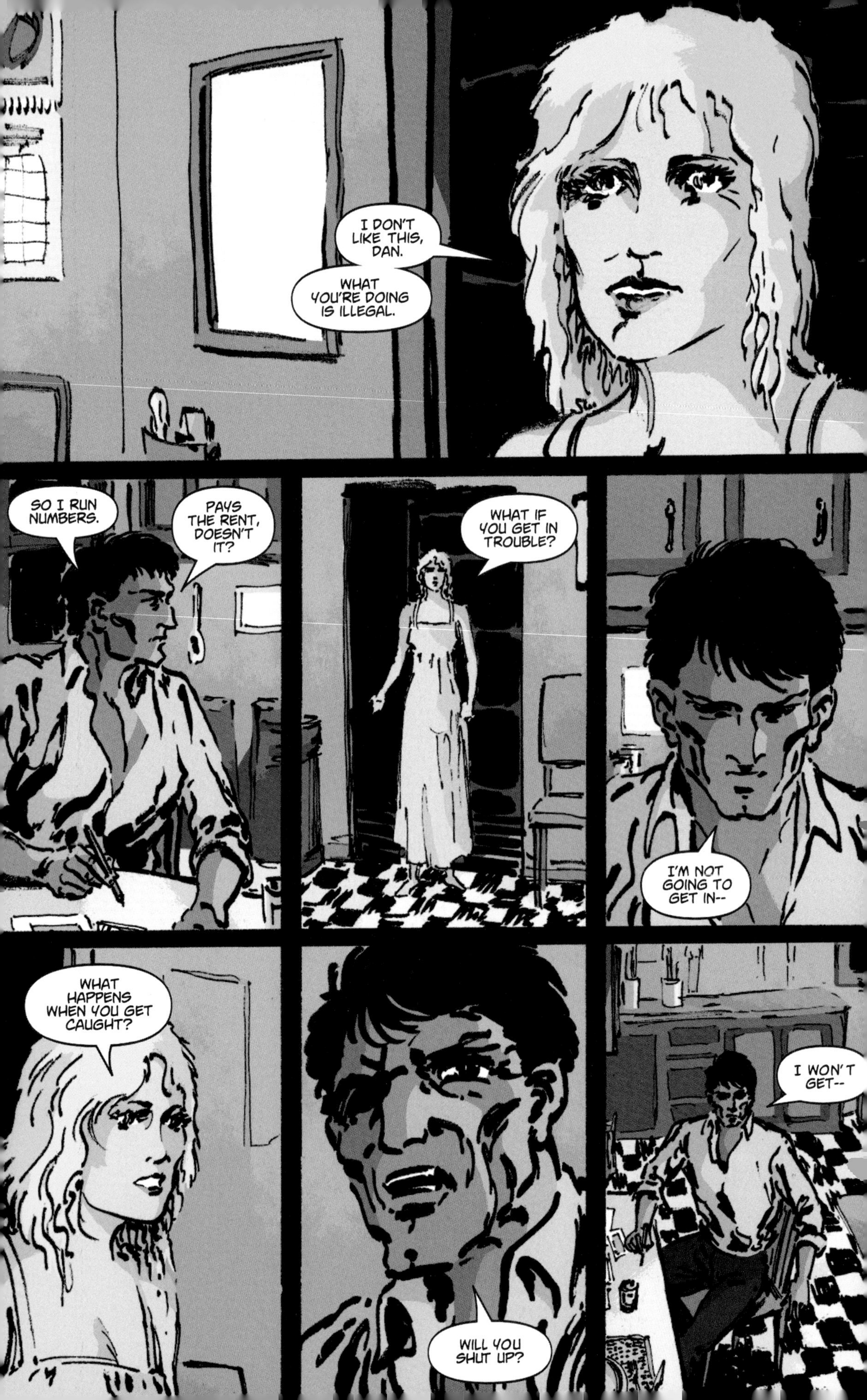
I DON'T LIKE THIS, DAN.
WHAT YOU'RE DOING IS ILLEGAL.
SO I RUN NUMBERS.
PAYS THE RENT, DOESN'T IT?
WHAT IF YOU GET IN TROUBLE?
I'M NOT GOING TO GET IN--
WHAT HAPPENS WHEN YOU GET CAUGHT?
WILL YOU SHUT UP?
I WON'T GET--

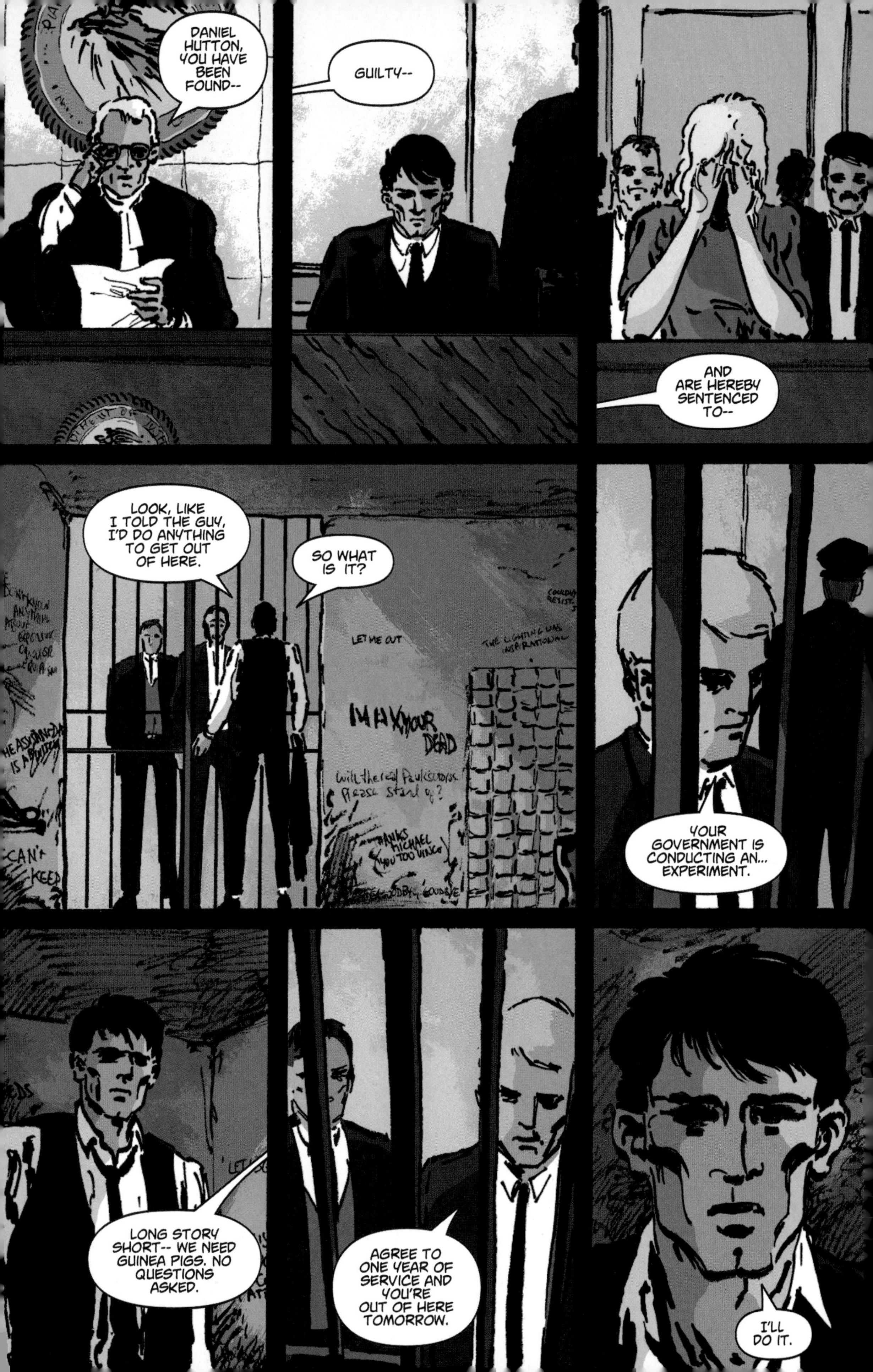
DANIEL HUTTON, YOU HAVE BEEN FOUND--
GUILTY--
AND ARE HEREBY SENTENCED TO--
LOOK, LIKE I TOLD THE GUY, I'D DO ANYTHING TO GET OUT OF HERE.
SO WHAT IS IT?
LET ME OUT
YOUR GOVERNMENT IS CONDUCTING AN... EXPERIMENT.
LONG STORY SHORT-- WE NEED GUINEA PIGS. NO QUESTIONS ASKED.
AGREE TO ONE YEAR OF SERVICE AND YOU'RE OUT OF HERE TOMORROW.
I'LL DO IT.

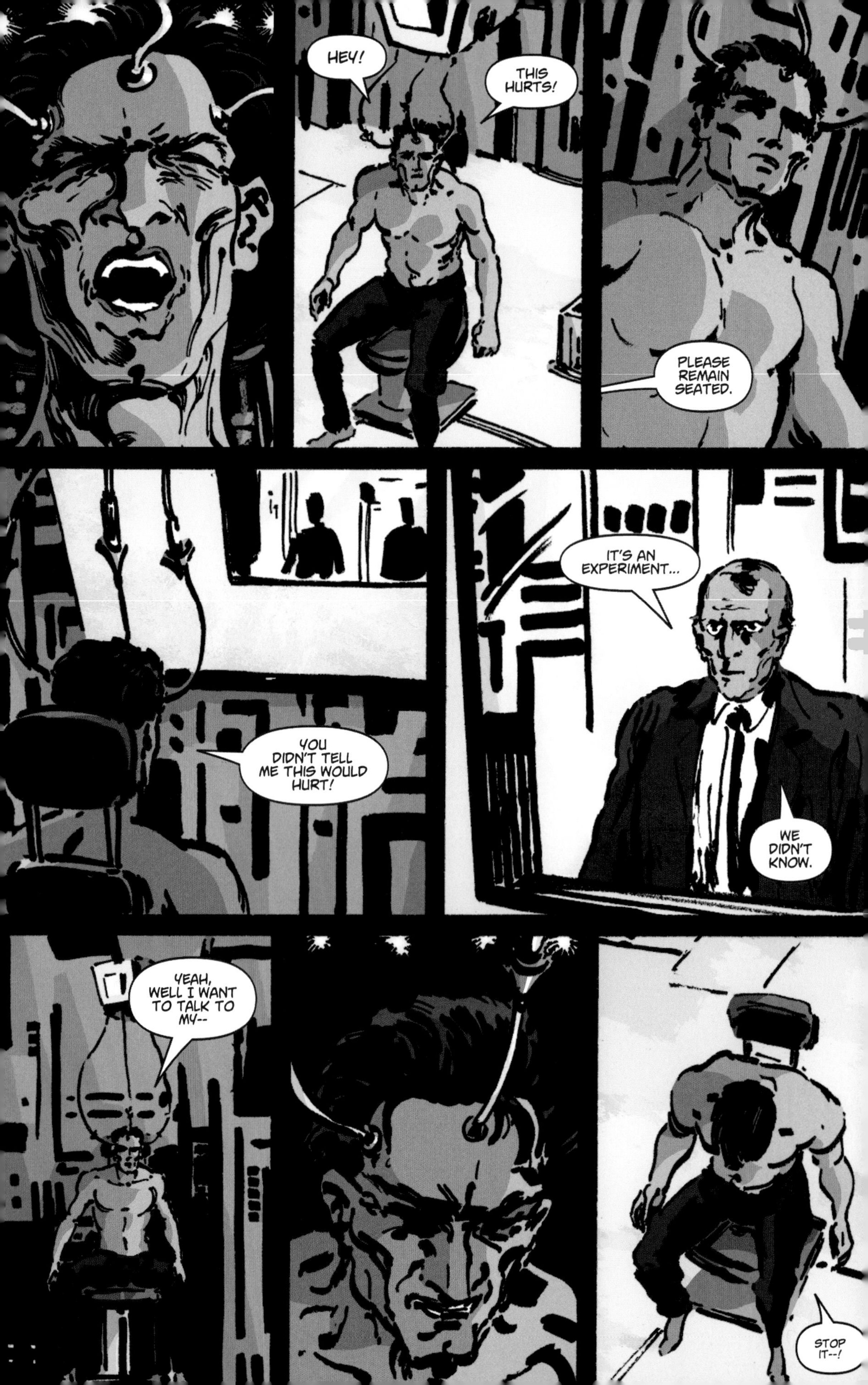
HEY!
THIS HURTS!
PLEASE REMAIN SEATED.
YOU DIDN'T TELL ME THIS WOULD HURT!
IT'S AN EXPERIMENT...
WE DIDN'T KNOW.
YEAH, WELL I WANT TO TALK TO MY--
STOP IT--!

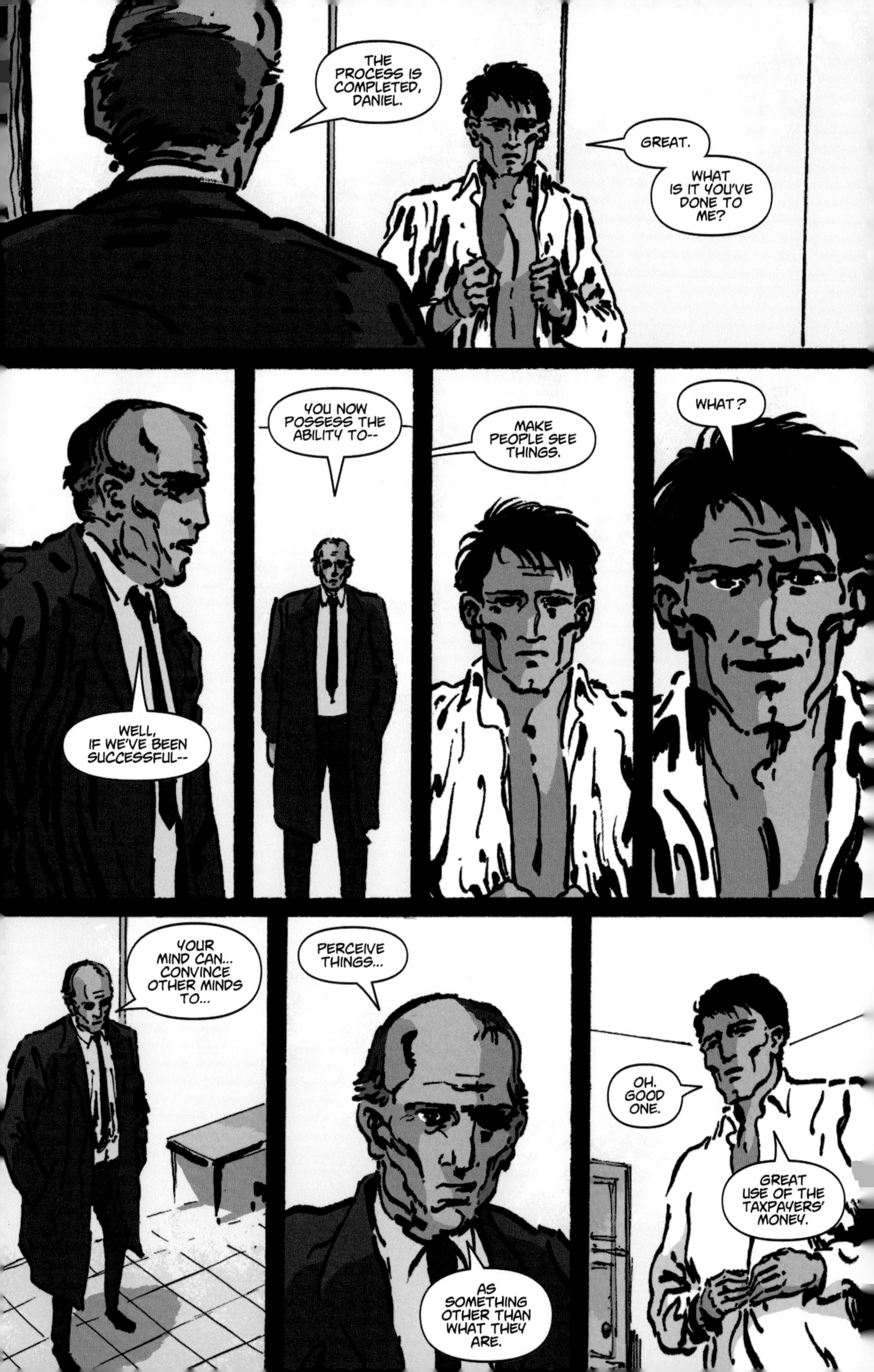
THE PROCESS IS COMPLETED, DANIEL.
GREAT.
WHAT IS IT YOU'VE DONE TO ME?
WELL, IF WE'VE BEEN SUCCESSFUL--
YOU NOW POSSESS THE ABILITY TO--
MAKE PEOPLE SEE THINGS.
WHAT?
YOUR MIND CAN... CONVINCE OTHER MINDS TO...
PERCEIVE THINGS...
AS SOMETHING OTHER THAN WHAT THEY ARE.
OH. GOOD ONE.
GREAT USE OF THE TAXPAYERS' MONEY.

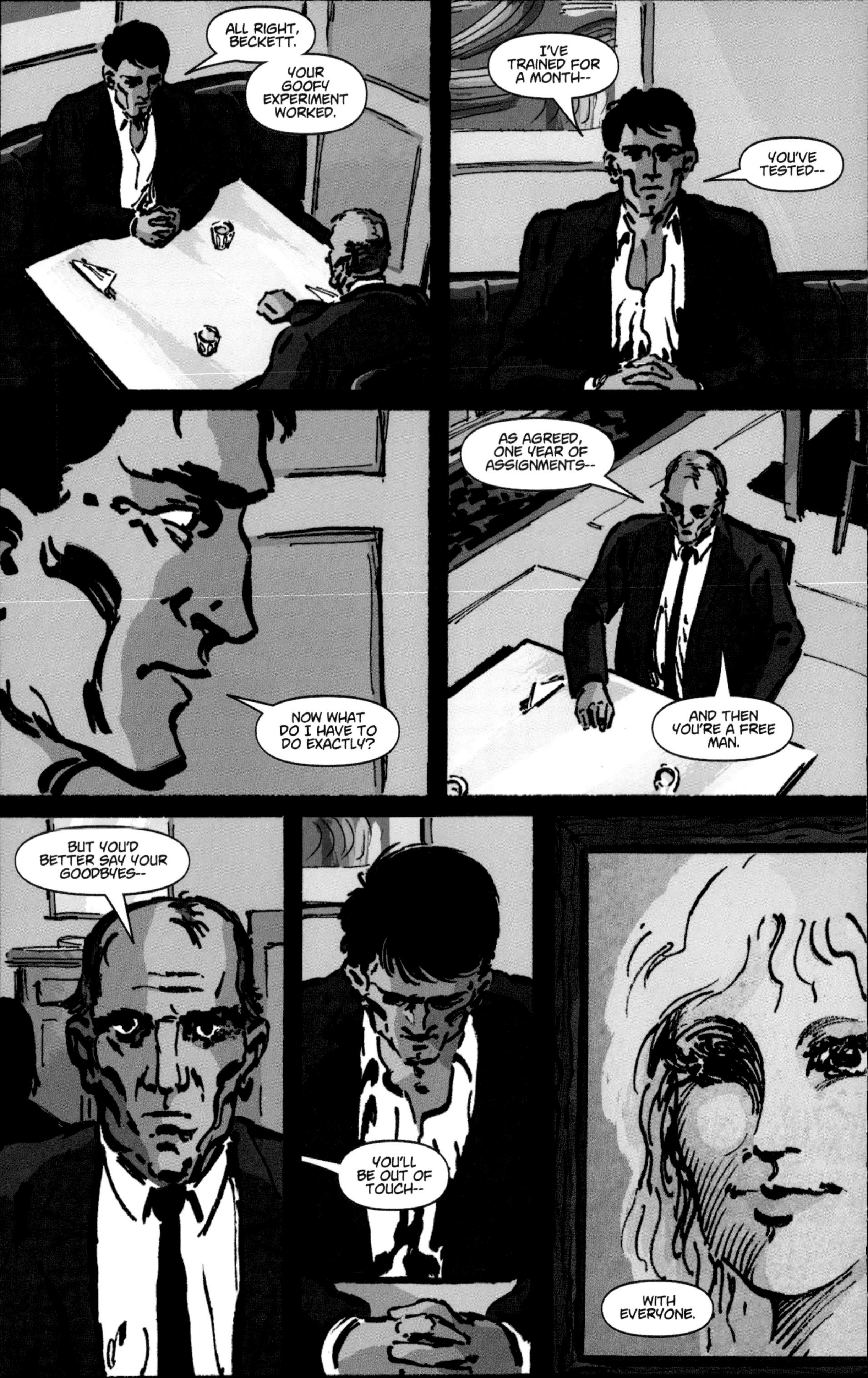
ALL RIGHT, BECKETT.
YOUR GOOFY EXPERIMENT WORKED.
I'VE TRAINED FOR A MONTH--
YOU'VE TESTED--
NOW WHAT DO I HAVE TO DO EXACTLY?
AS AGREED, ONE YEAR OF ASSIGNMENTS--
AND THEN YOU'RE A FREE MAN.
BUT YOU'D BETTER SAY YOUR GOODBYES--
YOU'LL BE OUT OF TOUCH--
WITH EVERYONE.

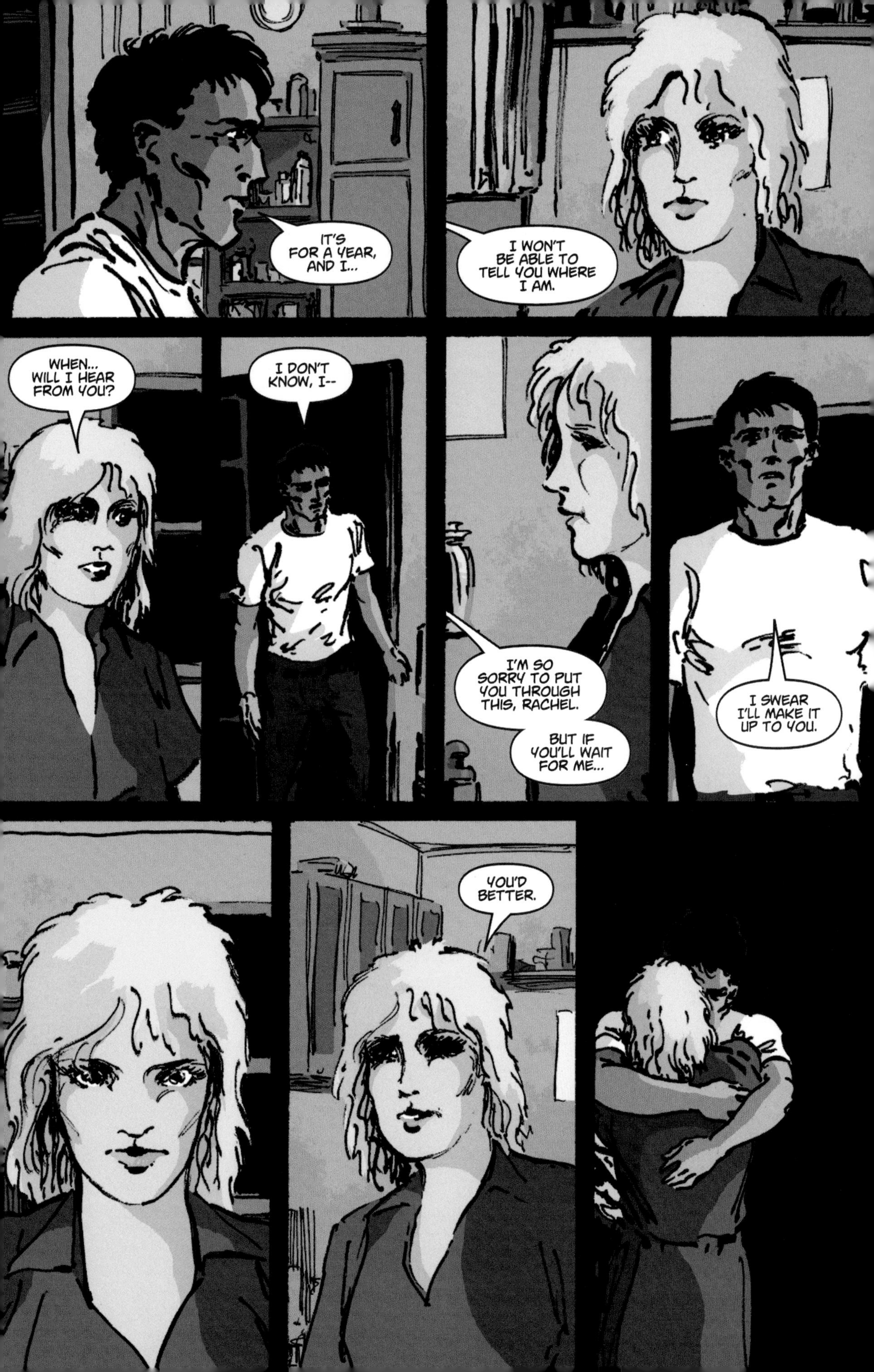
IT'S FOR A YEAR, AND I...
I WON'T BE ABLE TO TELL YOU WHERE I AM.
WHEN... WILL I HEAR FROM YOU?
I DON'T KNOW, I--
I'M SO SORRY TO PUT YOU THROUGH THIS, RACHEL.
BUT IF YOU'LL WAIT FOR ME...
I SWEAR I'LL MAKE IT UP TO YOU.
YOU'D BETTER.

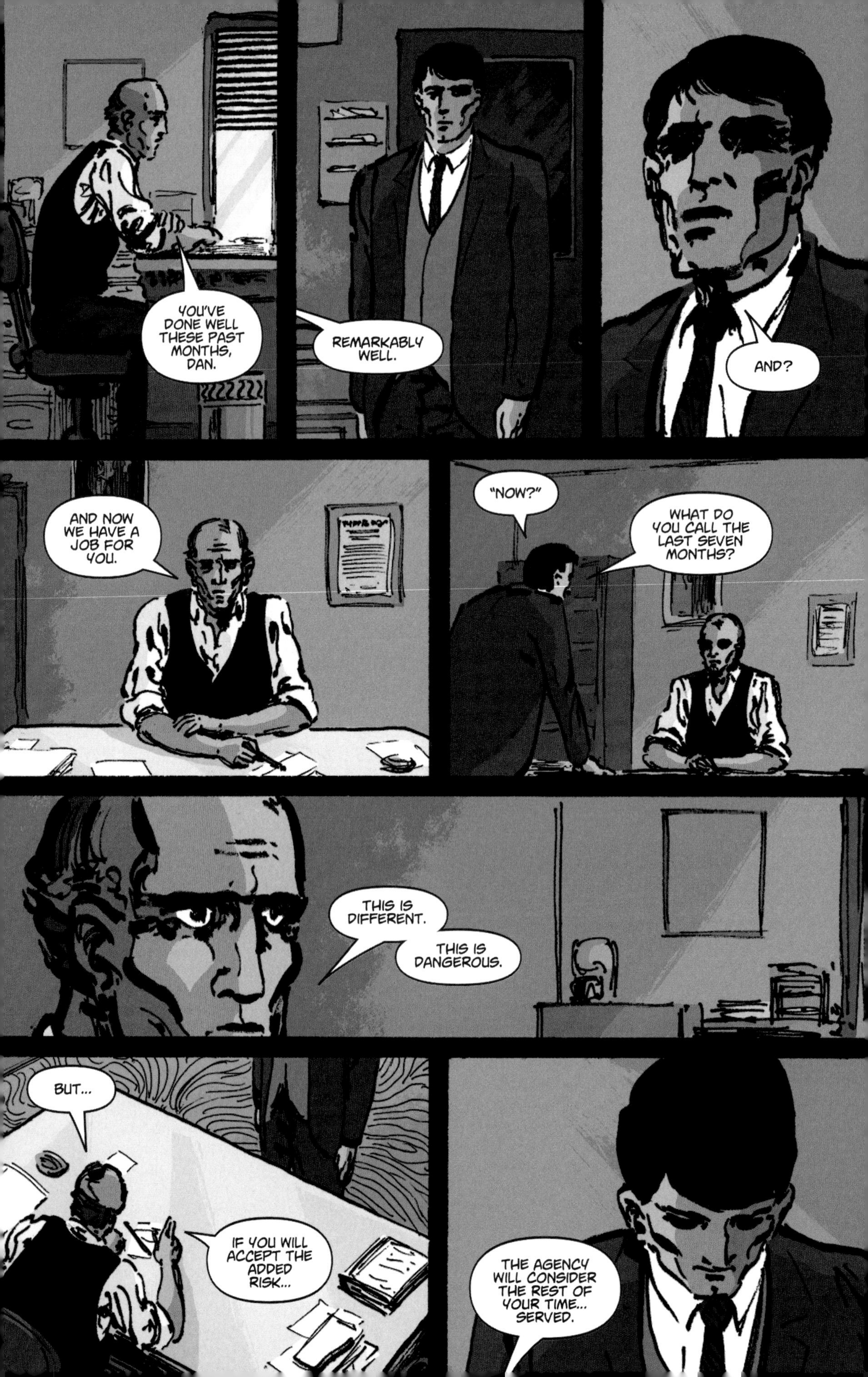
YOU'VE DONE WELL THESE PAST MONTHS, DAN.
REMARKABLY WELL.
AND?
AND NOW WE HAVE A JOB FOR YOU.
"NOW?"
WHAT DO YOU CALL THE LAST SEVEN MONTHS?
THIS IS DIFFERENT.
THIS IS DANGEROUS.
BUT...
IF YOU WILL ACCEPT THE ADDED RISK...
THE AGENCY WILL CONSIDER THE REST OF YOUR TIME... SERVED.

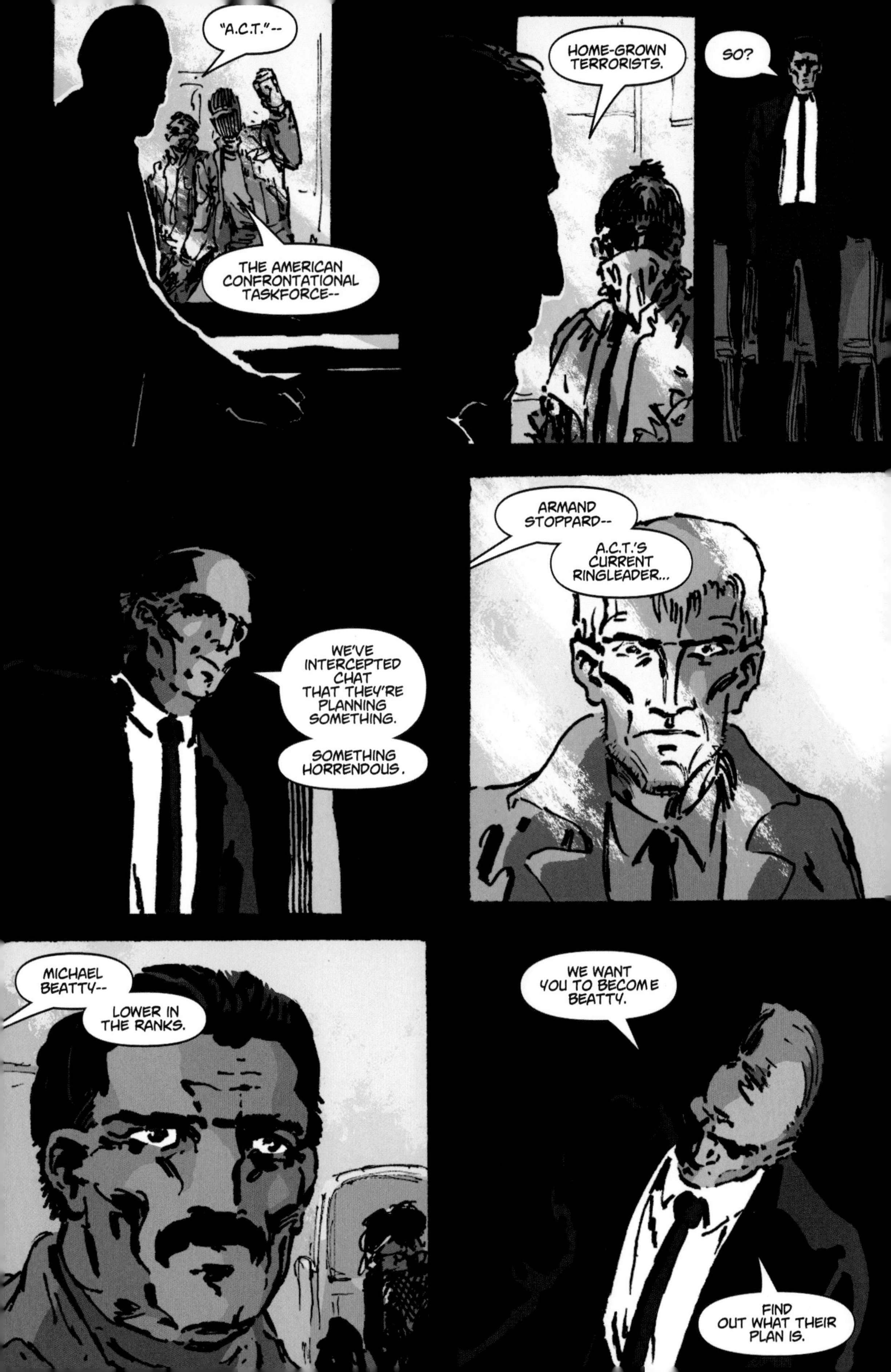
"A.C.T."--
THE AMERICAN CONFRONTATIONAL TASKFORCE--
HOME-GROWN TERRORISTS.
SO?
WE'VE INTERCEPTED CHAT THAT THEY'RE PLANNING SOMETHING.
SOMETHING HORRENDOUS.
ARMAND STOPPARD--
A.C.T.'S CURRENT RINGLEADER...
MICHAEL BEATTY--
LOWER IN THE RANKS.
WE WANT YOU TO BECOME BEATTY.
FIND OUT WHAT THEIR PLAN IS.

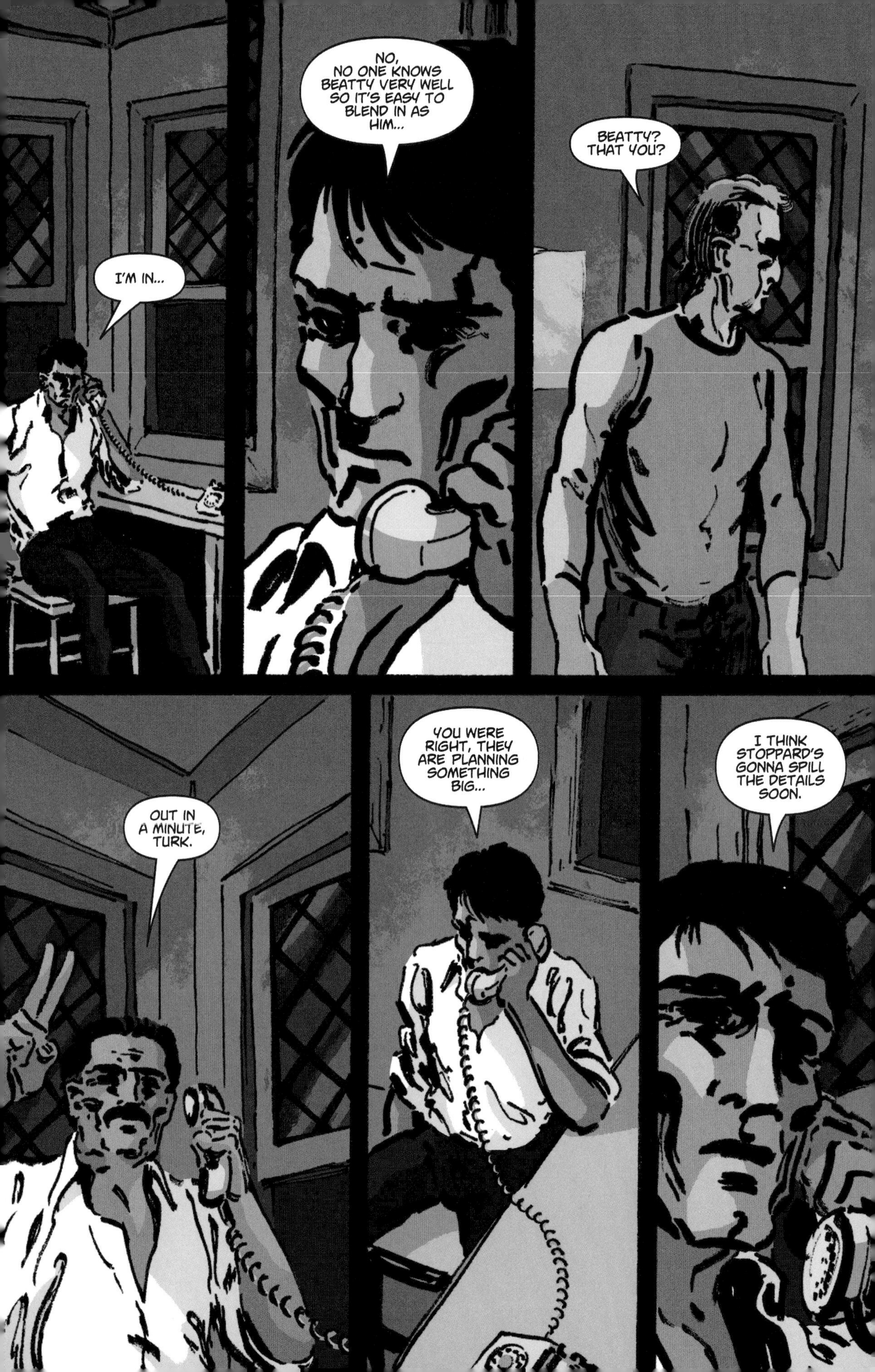
I'M IN...
NO, NO ONE KNOWS BEATTY VERY WELL SO IT'S EASY TO BLEND IN AS HIM...
BEATTY? THAT YOU?
OUT IN A MINUTE, TURK.
YOU WERE RIGHT, THEY ARE PLANNING SOMETHING BIG...
I THINK STOPPARD'S GONNA SPILL THE DETAILS SOON.

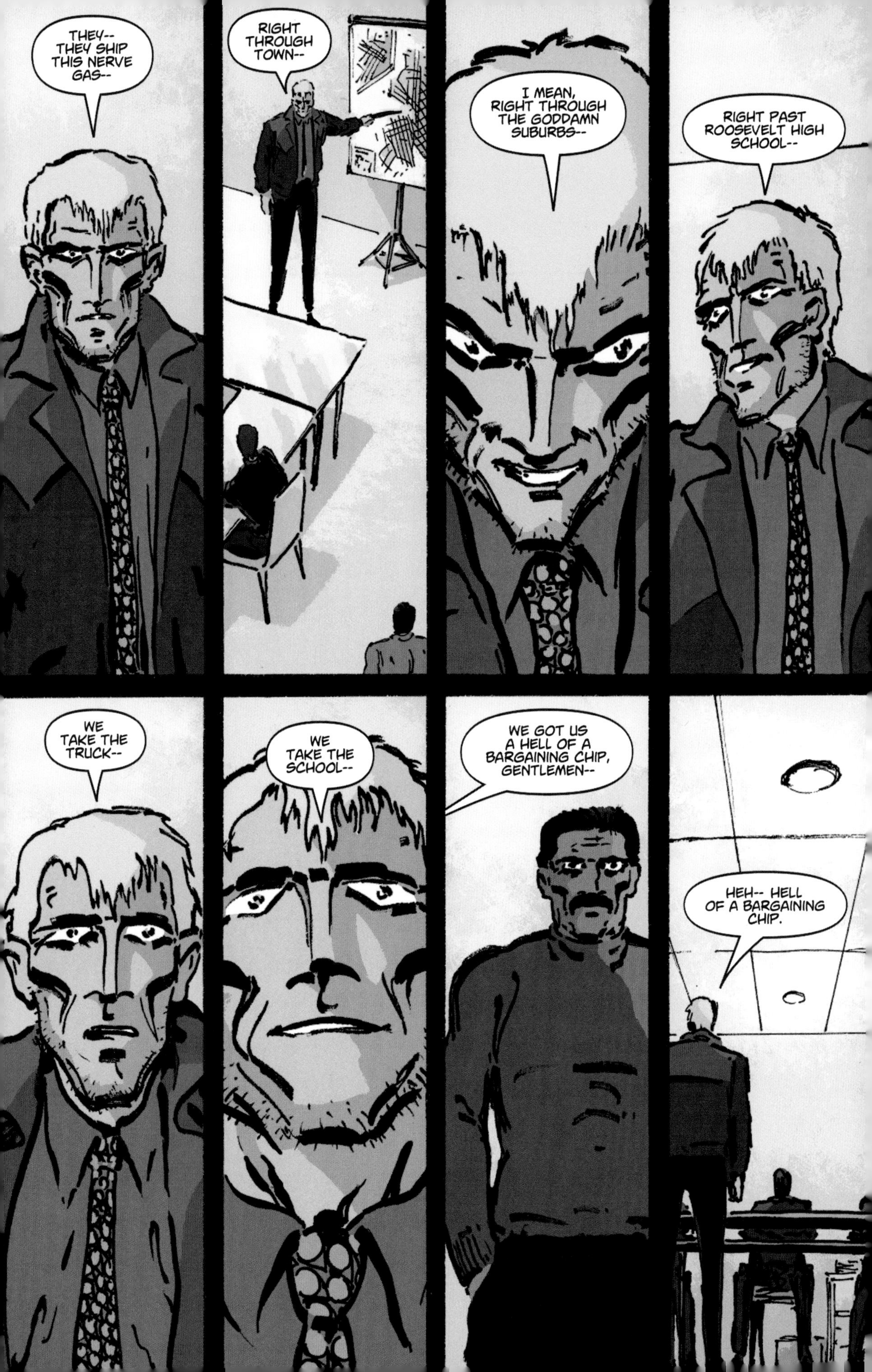
THEY-- THEY SHIP THIS NERVE GAS--
RIGHT THROUGH TOWN--
I MEAN, RIGHT THROUGH THE GODDAMN SUBURBS--
RIGHT PAST ROOSEVELT HIGH SCHOOL--
WE TAKE THE TRUCK--
WE TAKE THE SCHOOL--
WE GOT US A HELL OF A BARGAINING CHIP, GENTLEMEN--
HEH-- HELL OF A BARGAINING CHIP.

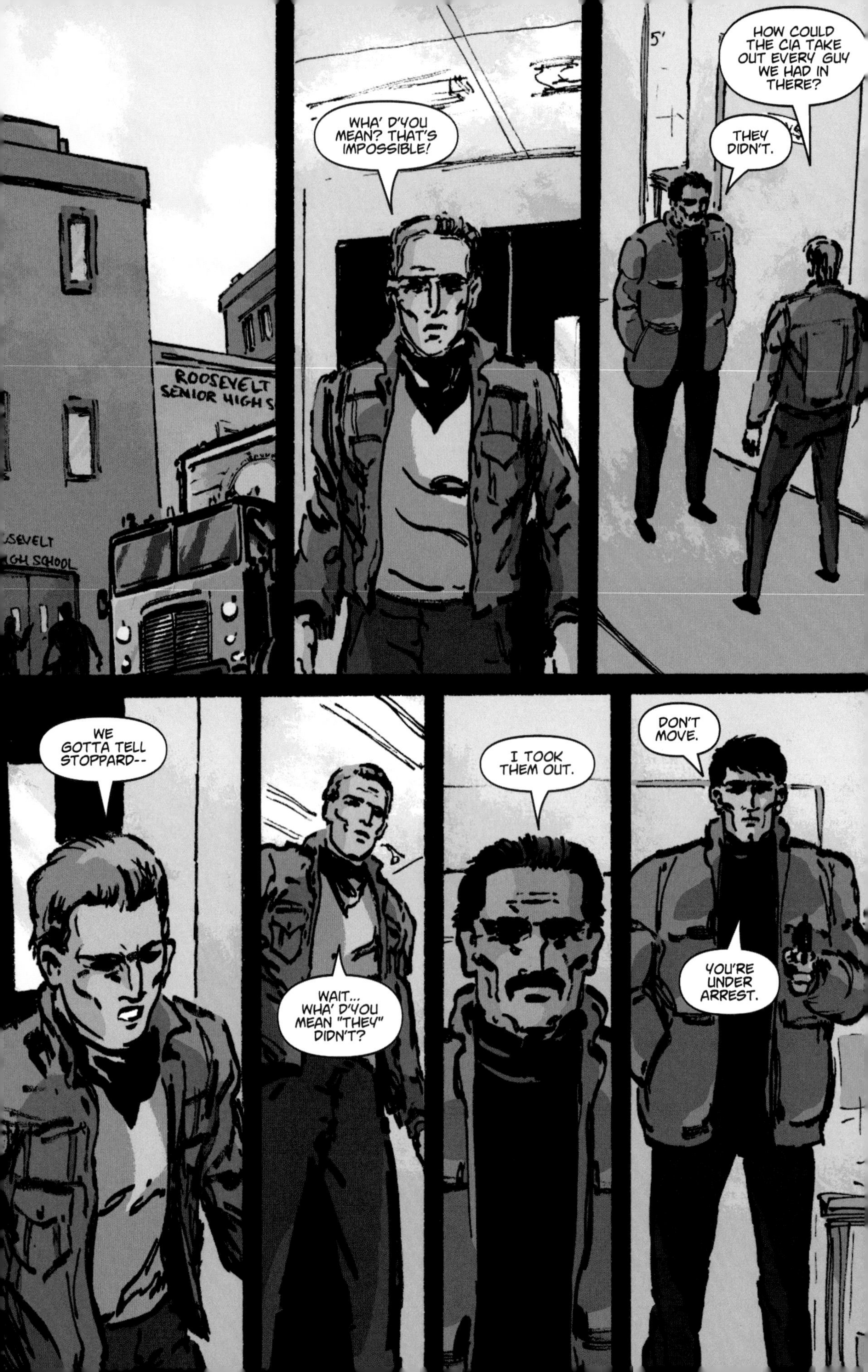
ROOSEVELT SENIOR HIGH S
SEVELT
GH SCHOOL
WHA' D'YOU MEAN? THAT'S IMPOSSIBLE!
HOW COULD THE CIA TAKE OUT EVERY GUY WE HAD IN THERE?
THEY DIDN'T.
WE GOTTA TELL STOPPARD--
WAIT... WHA' D'YOU MEAN "THEY" DIDN'T?
I TOOK THEM OUT.
DON'T MOVE.
YOU'RE UNDER ARREST.

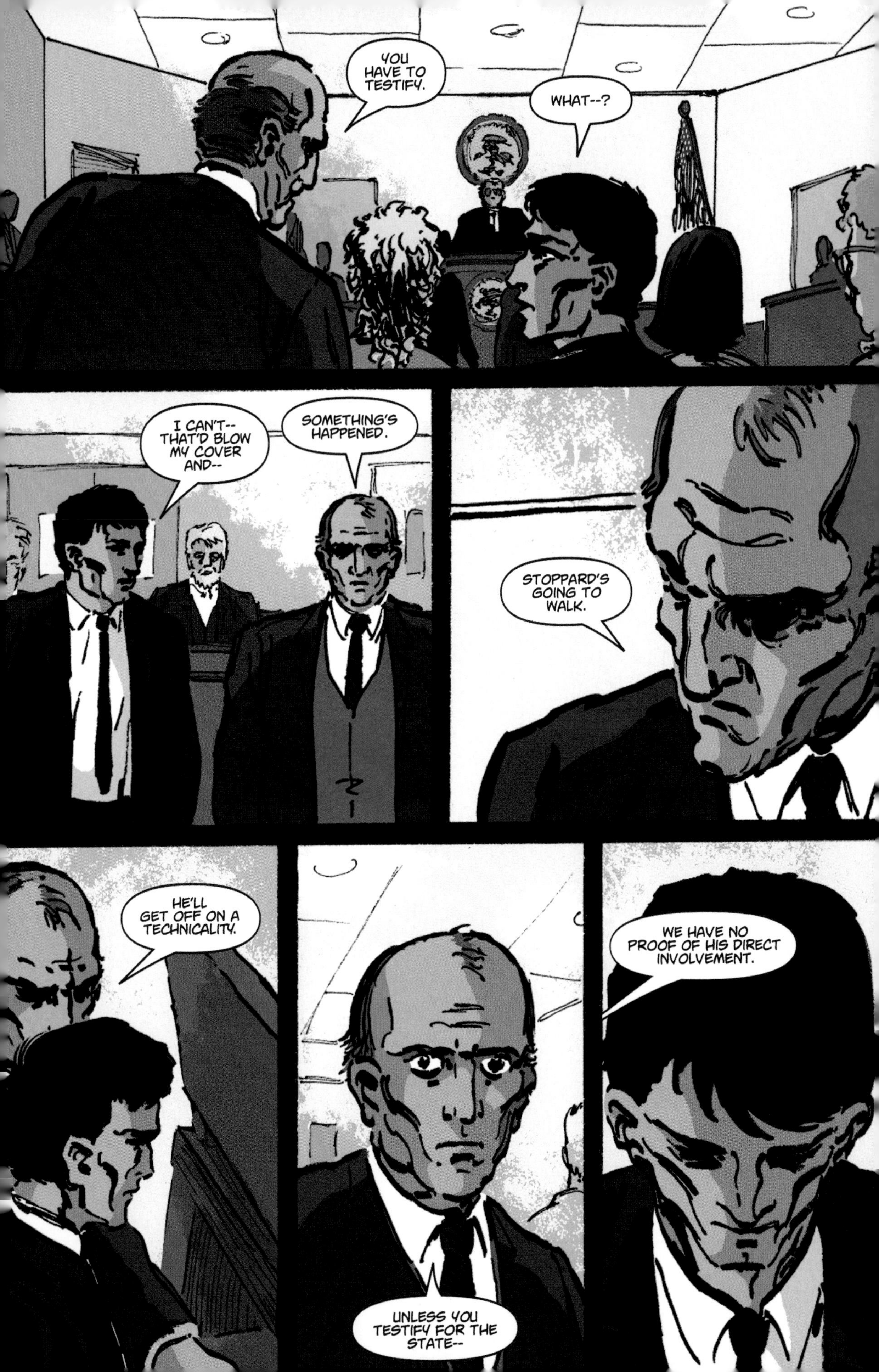
YOU HAVE TO TESTIFY.
WHAT--?
I CAN'T--THAT'D BLOW MY COVER AND--
SOMETHING'S HAPPENED.
STOPPARD'S GOING TO WALK.
HE'LL GET OFF ON A TECHNICALITY.
UNLESS YOU TESTIFY FOR THE STATE--
WE HAVE NO PROOF OF HIS DIRECT INVOLVEMENT.

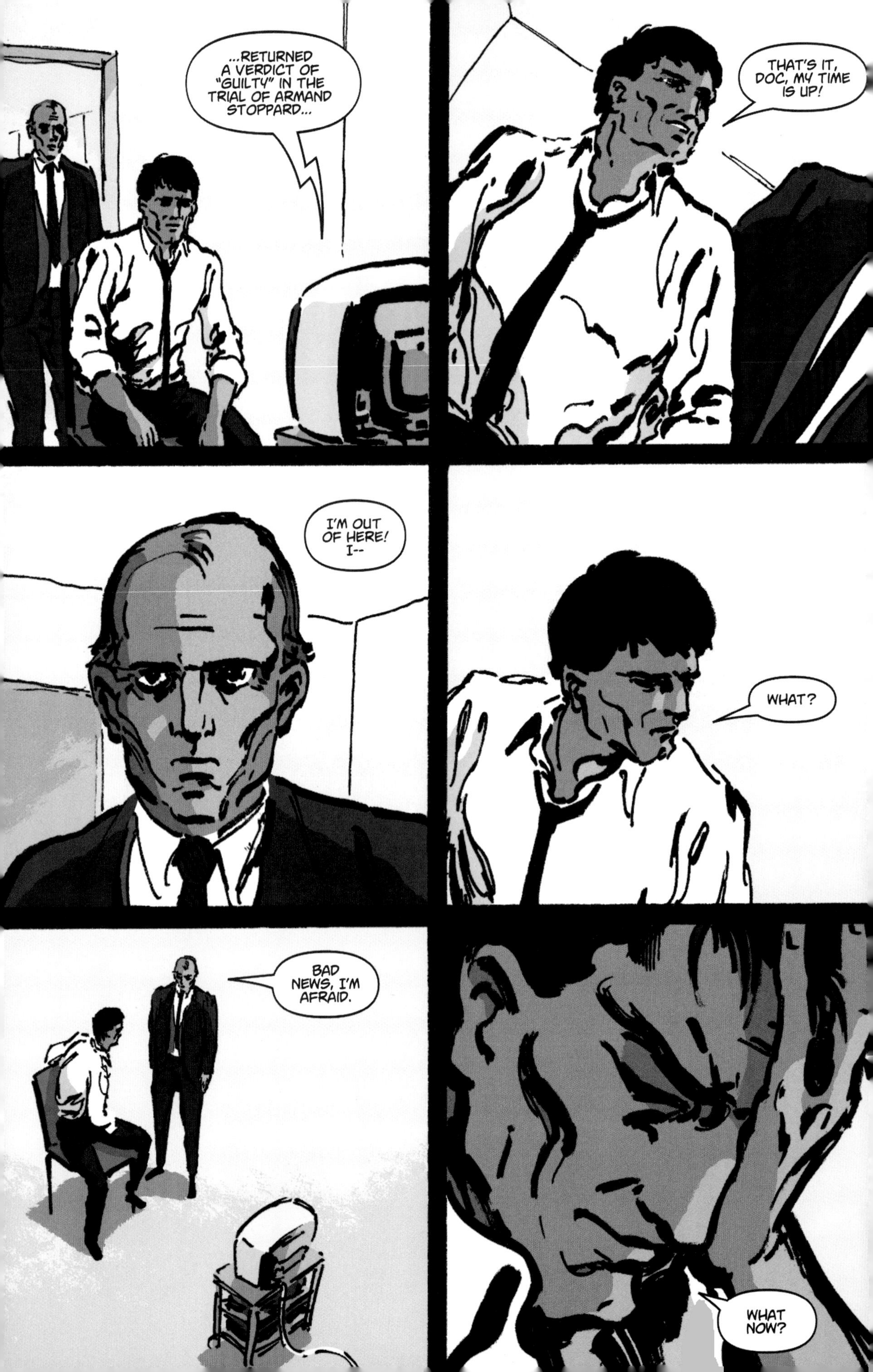
...RETURNED A VERDICT OF "GUILTY" IN THE TRIAL OF ARMAND STOPPARD...
THAT'S IT, DOC, MY TIME IS UP!
I'M OUT OF HERE! I--
WHAT?
BAD NEWS, I'M AFRAID.
WHAT NOW?

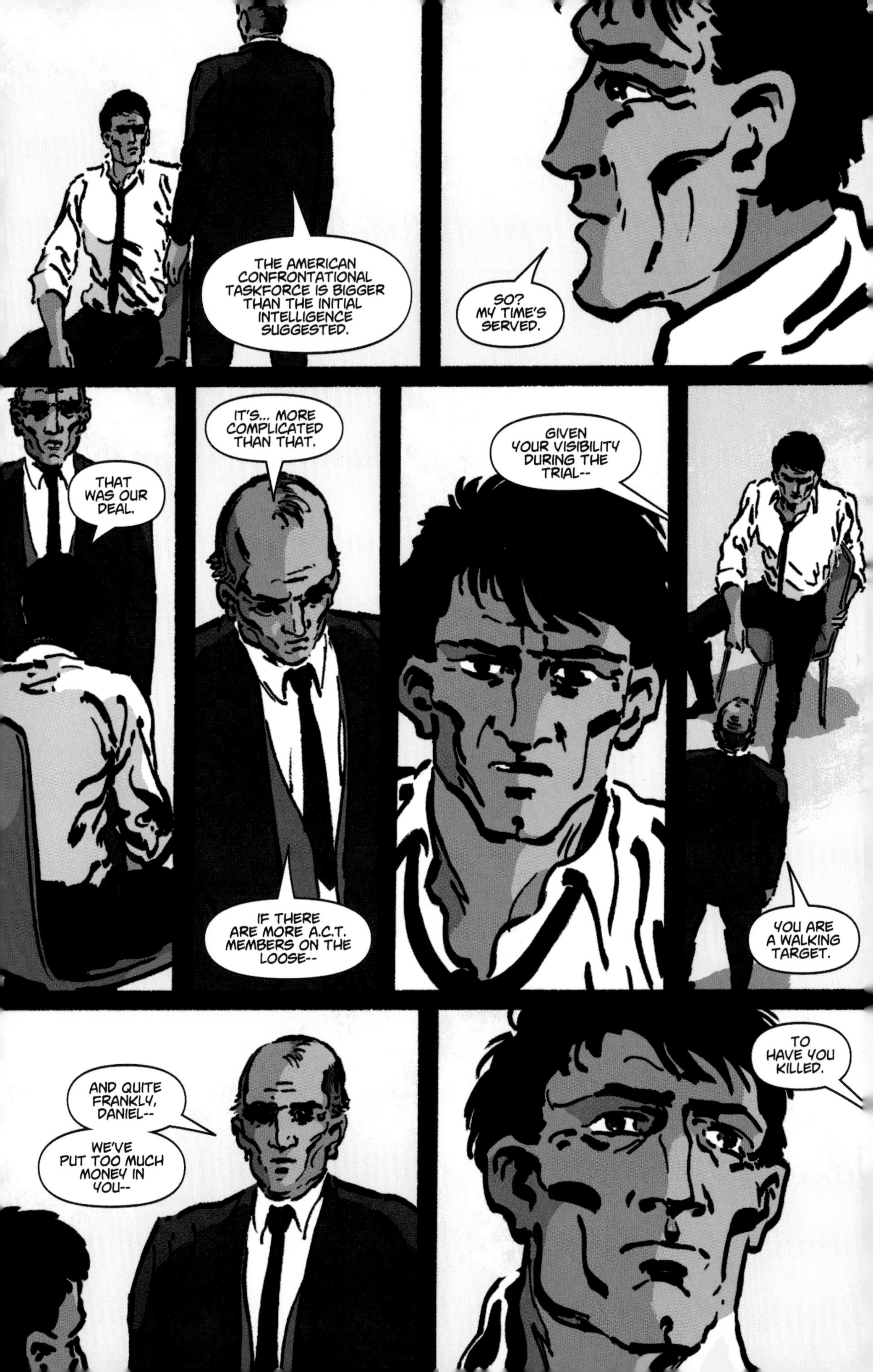
THE AMERICAN CONFRONTATIONAL TASKFORCE IS BIGGER THAN THE INITIAL INTELLIGENCE SUGGESTED.
SO? MY TIME'S SERVED.
THAT WAS OUR DEAL.
IT'S... MORE COMPLICATED THAN THAT.
IF THERE ARE MORE A.C.T. MEMBERS ON THE LOOSE--
GIVEN YOUR VISIBILITY DURING THE TRIAL--
YOU ARE A WALKING TARGET.
AND QUITE FRANKLY, DANIEL--
WE'VE PUT TOO MUCH MONEY IN YOU--
TO HAVE YOU KILLED.

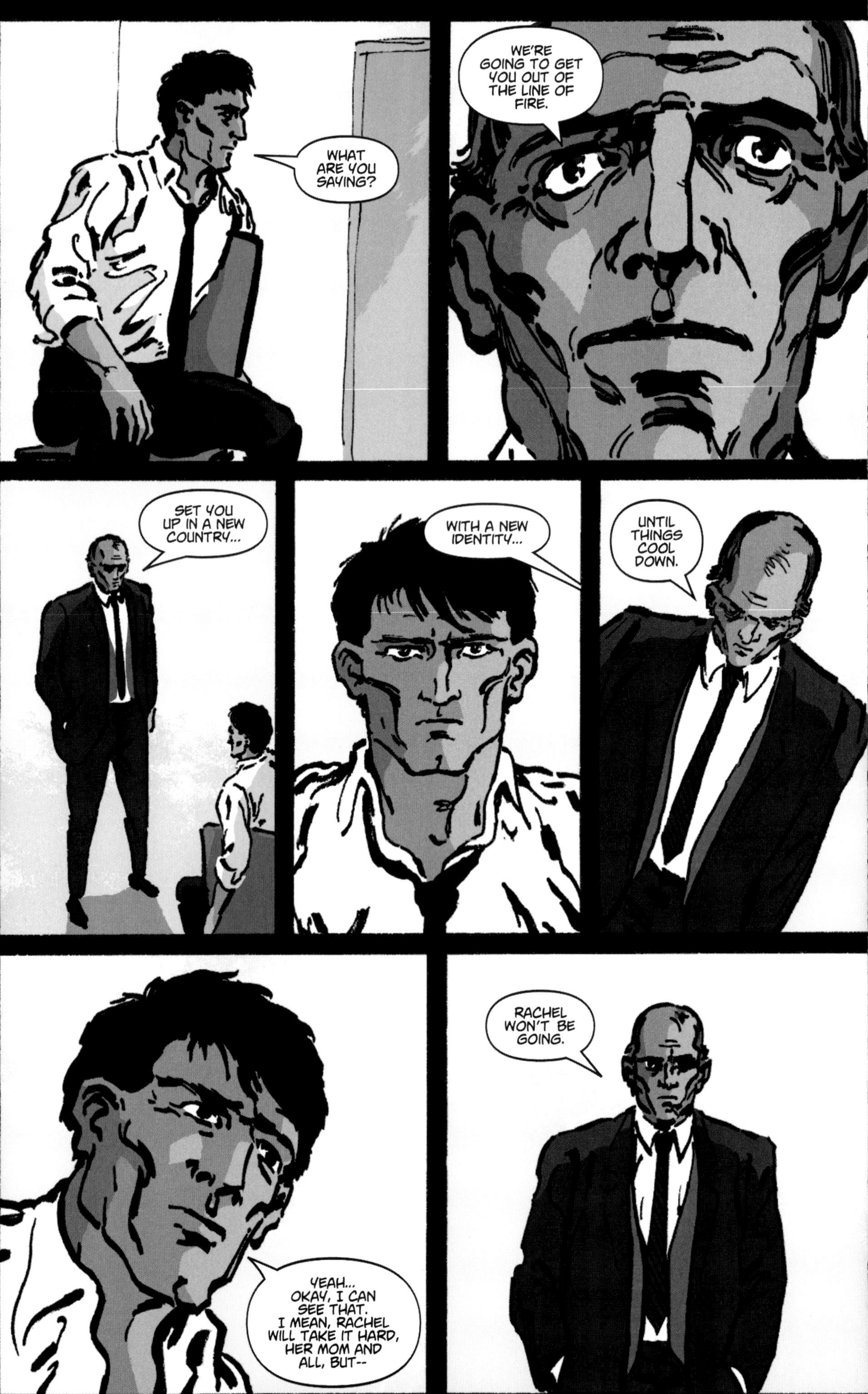
WHAT ARE YOU SAYING?
WE'RE GOING TO GET YOU OUT OF THE LINE OF FIRE.
SET YOU UP IN A NEW COUNTRY...
WITH A NEW IDENTITY...
UNTIL THINGS COOL DOWN.
YEAH... OKAY, I CAN SEE THAT. I MEAN, RACHEL WILL TAKE IT HARD, HER MOM AND ALL, BUT--
RACHEL WON'T BE GOING.

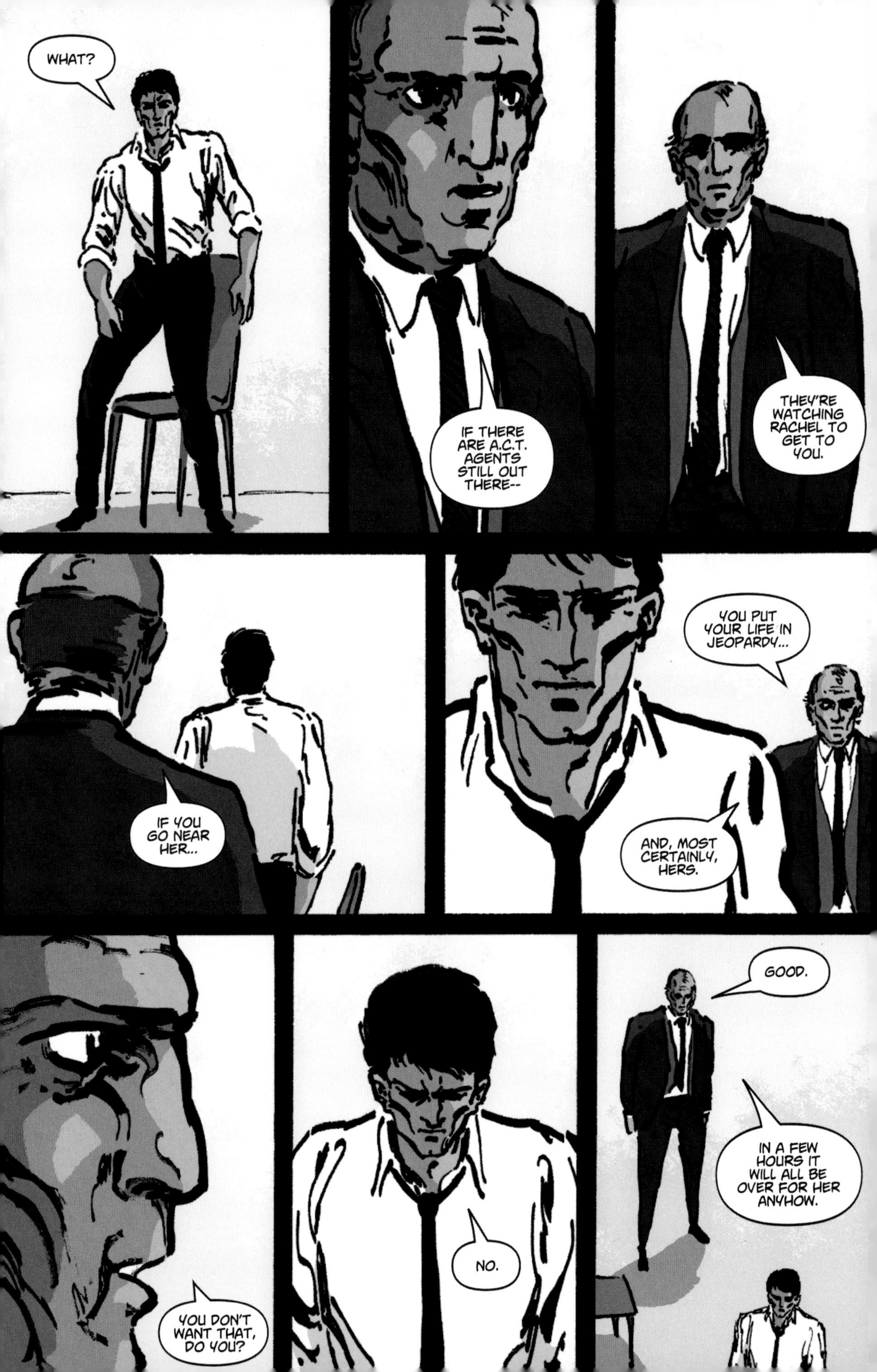
WHAT?
IF THERE ARE A.C.T. AGENTS STILL OUT THERE--
THEY'RE WATCHING RACHEL TO GET TO YOU.
IF YOU GO NEAR HER...
YOU PUT YOUR LIFE IN JEOPARDY...
AND, MOST CERTAINLY, HERS.
YOU DON'T WANT THAT, DO YOU?
NO.
GOOD.
IN A FEW HOURS IT WILL ALL BE OVER FOR HER ANYHOW.

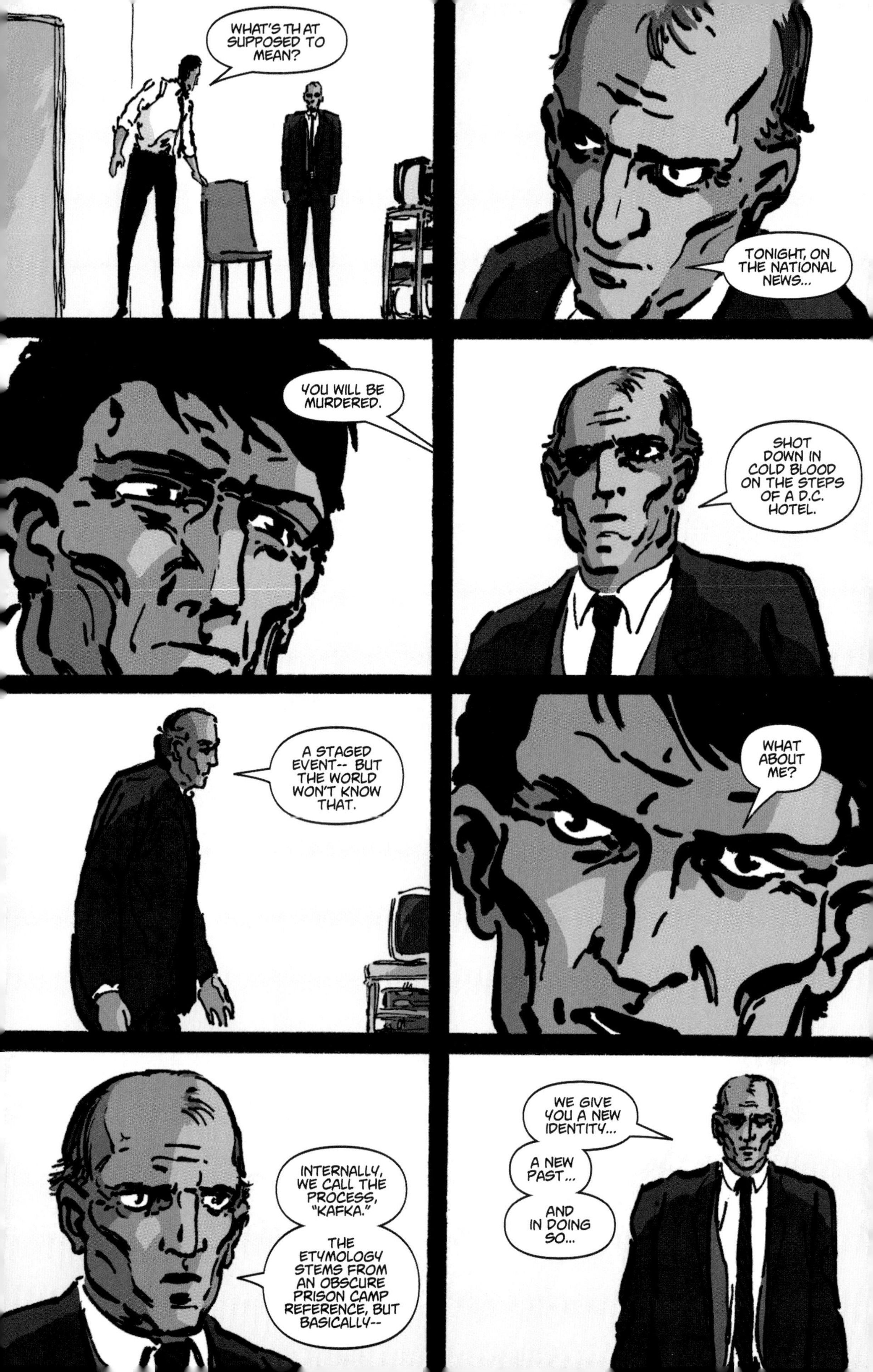
WHAT'S THAT SUPPOSED TO MEAN?
TONIGHT, ON THE NATIONAL NEWS...
YOU WILL BE MURDERED.
SHOT DOWN IN COLD BLOOD ON THE STEPS OF A D.C. HOTEL.
A STAGED EVENT-- BUT THE WORLD WON'T KNOW THAT.
WHAT ABOUT ME?
INTERNALLY, WE CALL THE PROCESS, "KAFKA."
THE ETYMOLOGY STEMS FROM AN OBSCURE PRISON CAMP REFERENCE, BUT BASICALLY--
WE GIVE YOU A NEW IDENTITY...
A NEW PAST...
AND IN DOING SO...

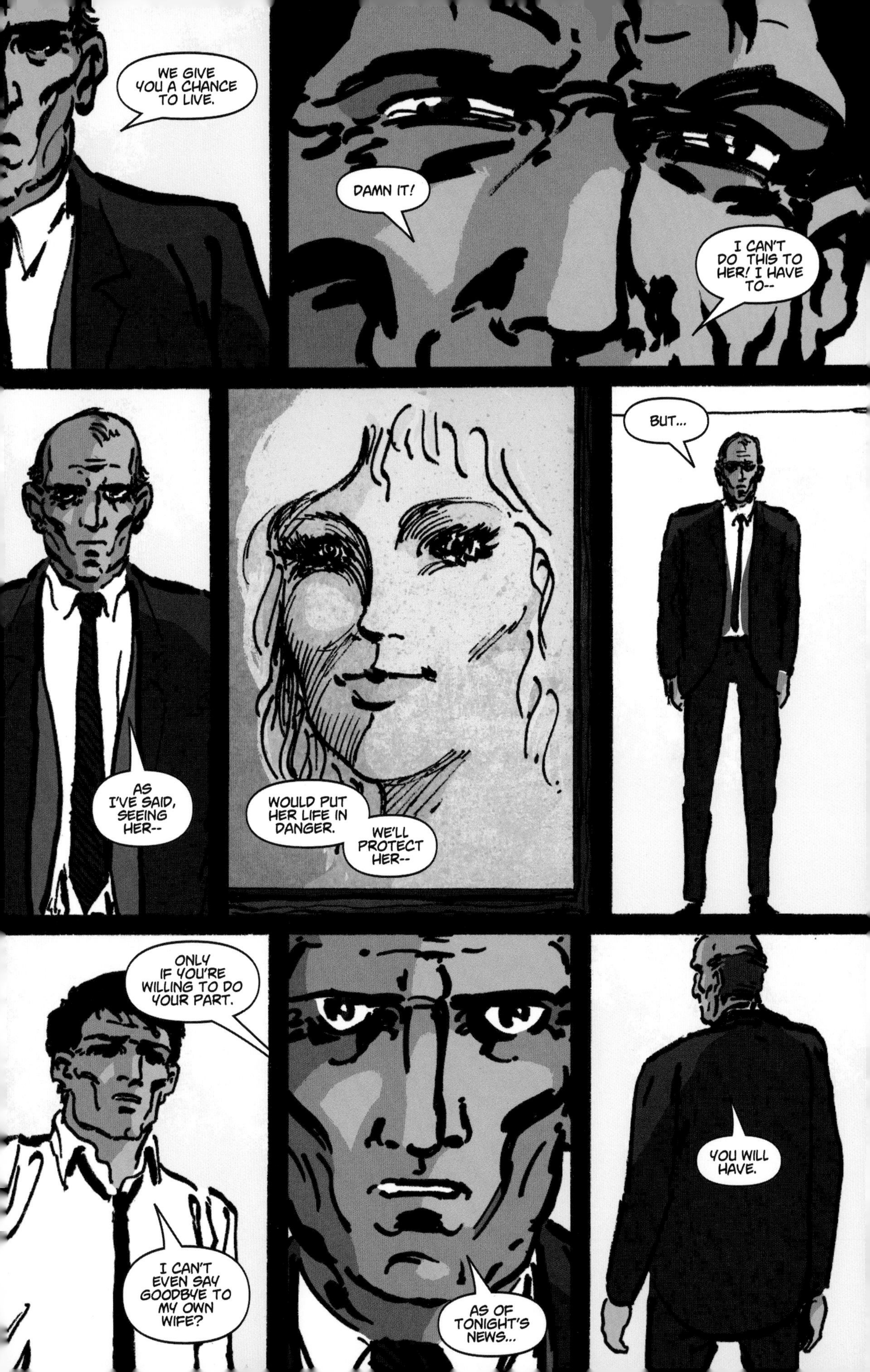
WE GIVE YOU A CHANCE TO LIVE.
DAMN IT!
I CAN'T DO THIS TO HER! I HAVE TO--
AS I'VE SAID, SEEING HER--
WOULD PUT HER LIFE IN DANGER.
WE'LL PROTECT HER--
BUT...
ONLY IF YOU'RE WILLING TO DO YOUR PART.
I CAN'T EVEN SAY GOODBYE TO MY OWN WIFE?
AS OF TONIGHT'S NEWS...
YOU WILL HAVE.

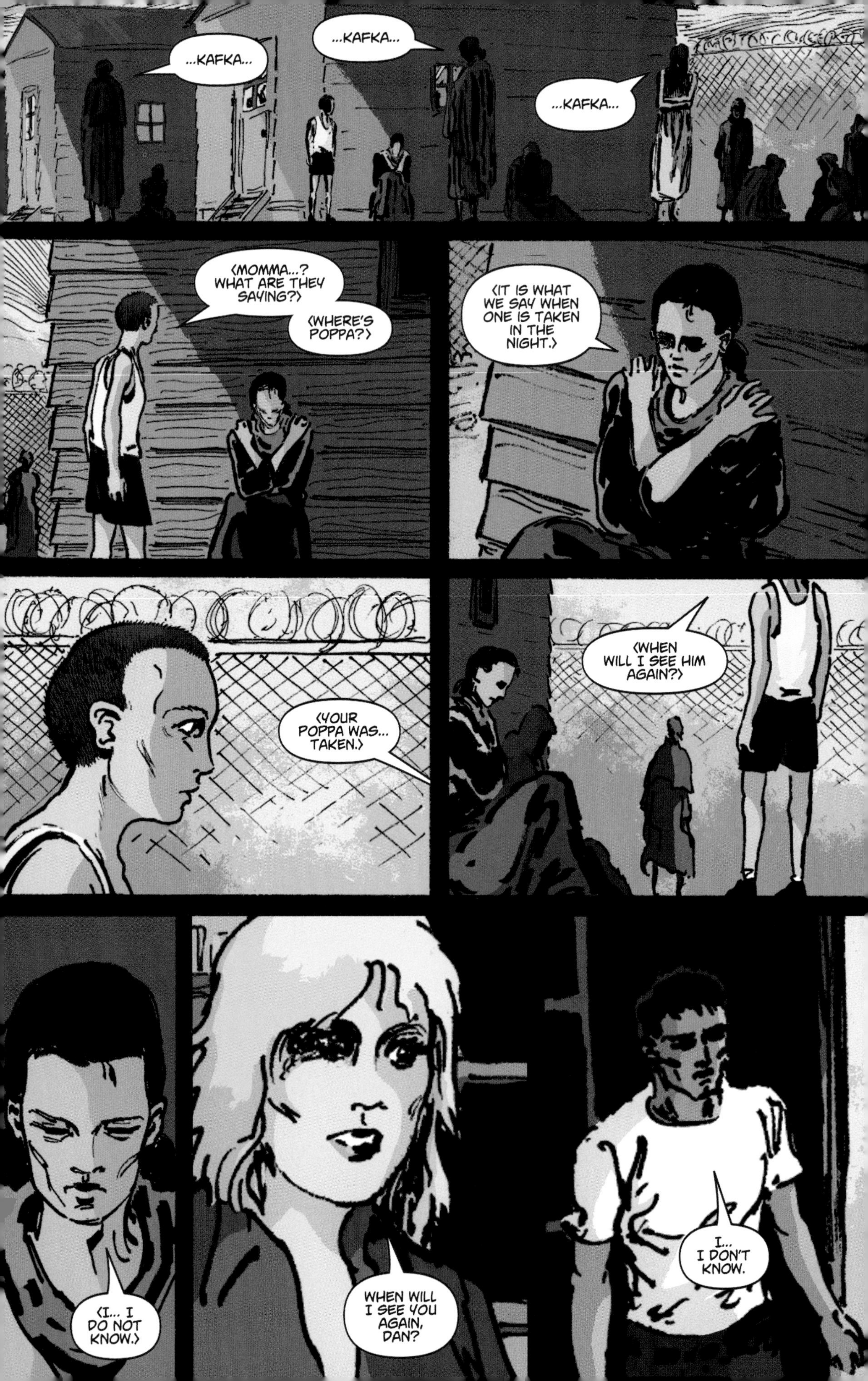

...KAFKA...
...KAFKA...
...KAFKA...
‹MOMMA...? WHAT ARE THEY SAYING?›
‹WHERE'S POPPA?›
‹IT IS WHAT WE SAY WHEN ONE IS TAKEN IN THE NIGHT.›
‹YOUR POPPA WAS... TAKEN.›
‹WHEN WILL I SEE HIM AGAIN?›
‹I... I DO NOT KNOW.›
WHEN WILL I SEE YOU AGAIN, DAN?
I... I DON'T KNOW.

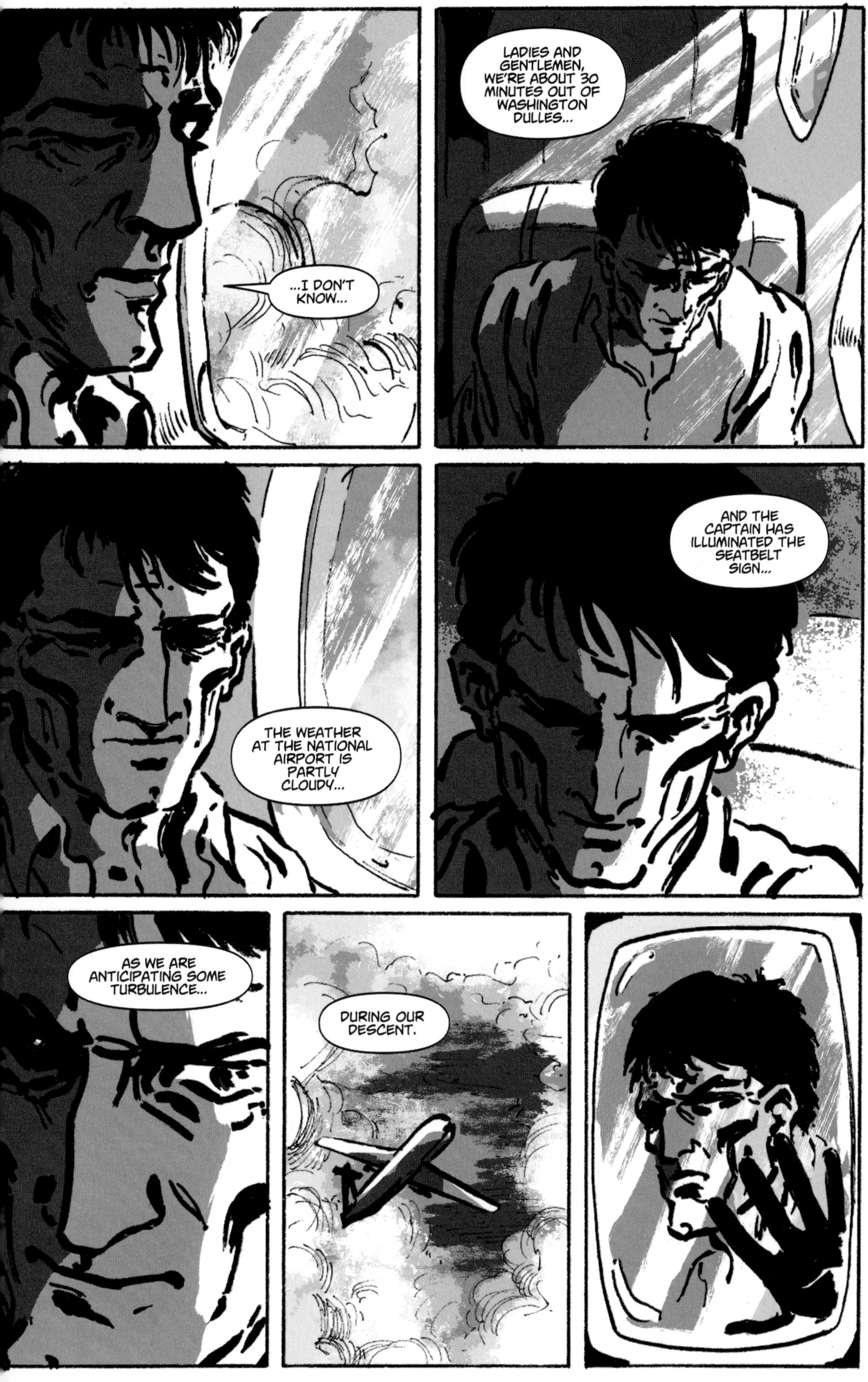

...I DON'T KNOW...
LADIES AND GENTLEMEN, WE'RE ABOUT 30 MINUTES OUT OF WASHINGTON DULLES...
THE WEATHER AT THE NATIONAL AIRPORT IS PARTLY CLOUDY...
AND THE CAPTAIN HAS ILLUMINATED THE SEATBELT SIGN...
AS WE ARE ANTICIPATING SOME TURBULENCE...
DURING OUR DESCENT.

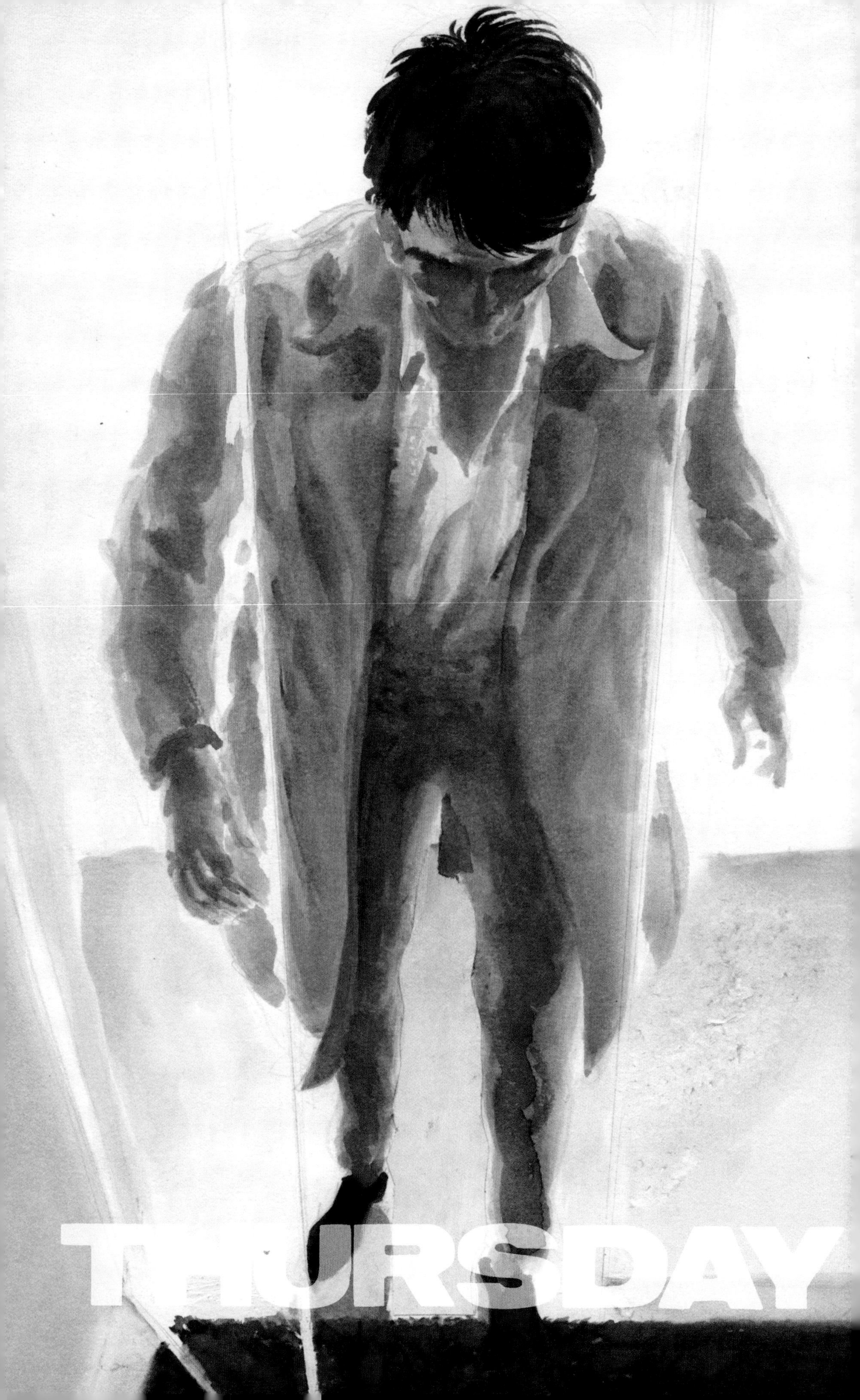
THURSDAY

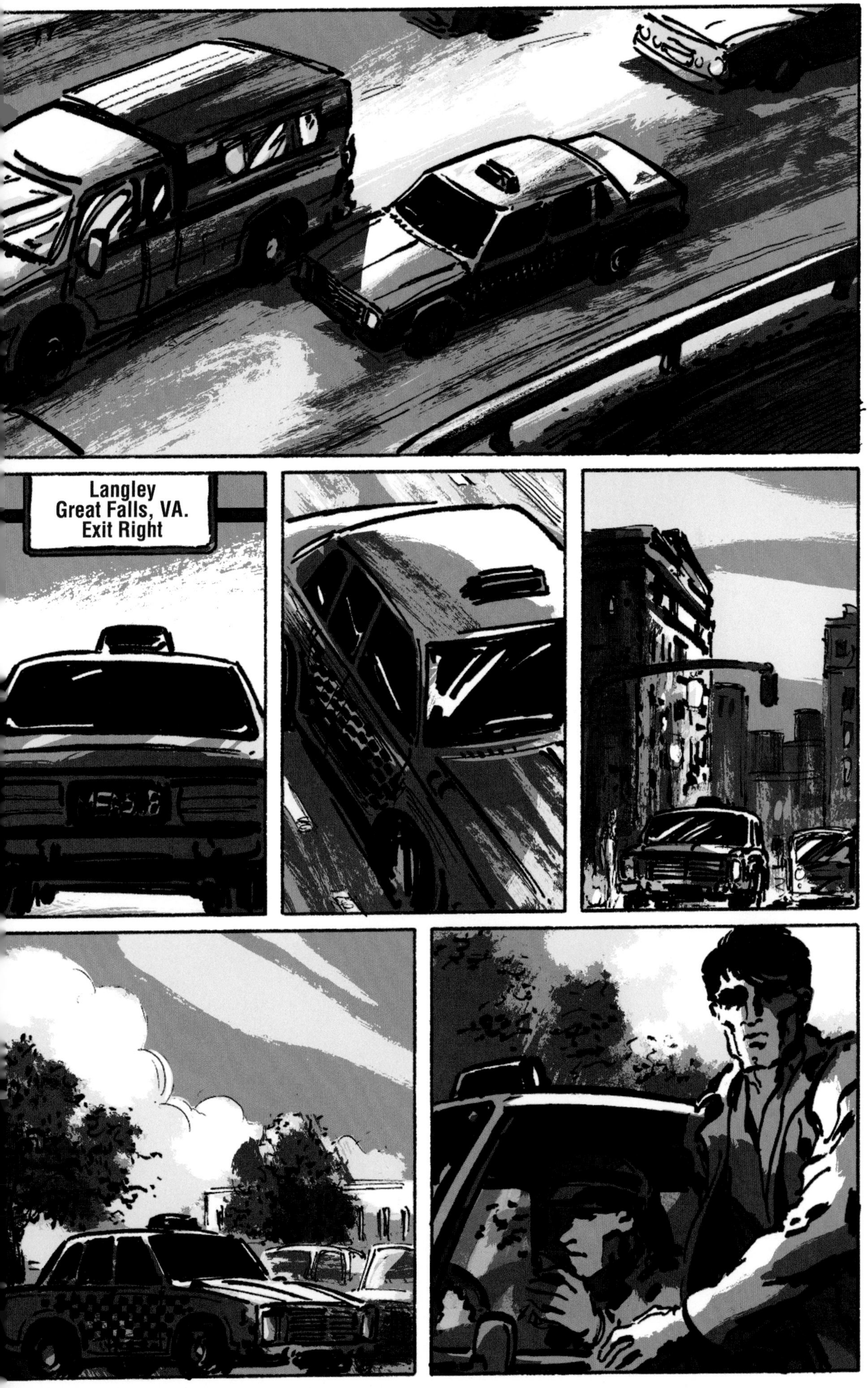
Langley
Great Falls, VA.
Exit Right

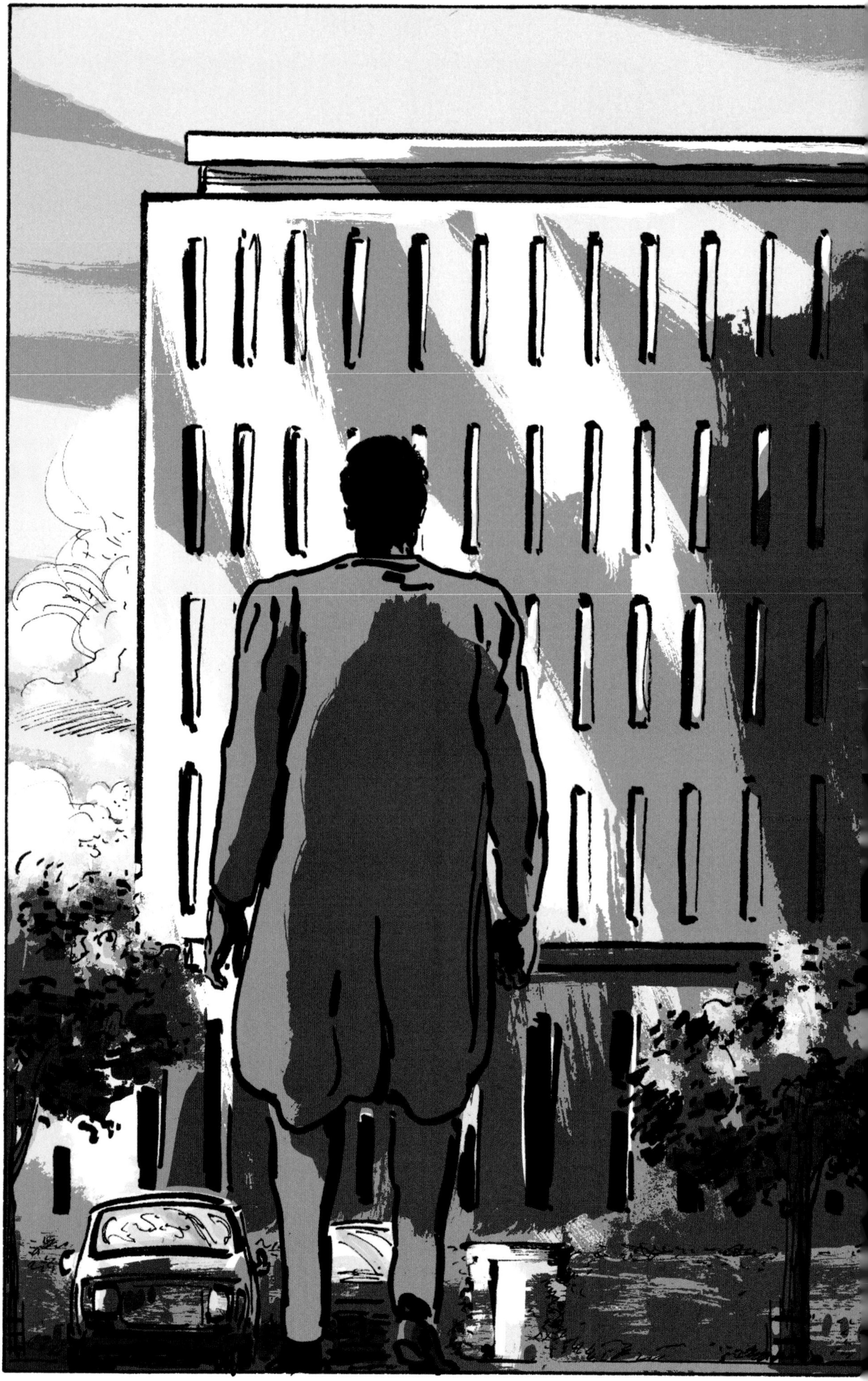

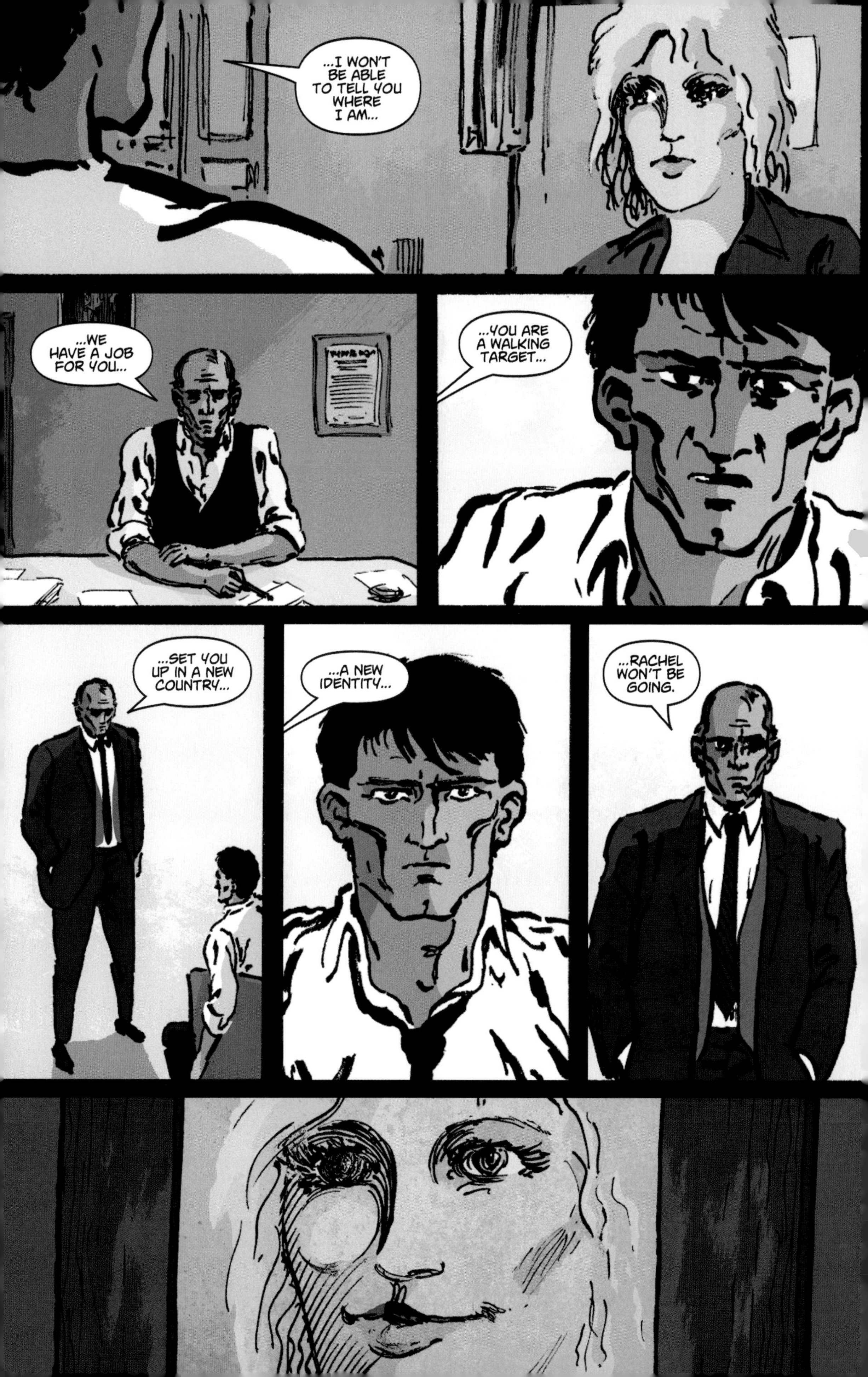
...I WON'T BE ABLE TO TELL YOU WHERE I AM...
...WE HAVE A JOB FOR YOU...
...YOU ARE A WALKING TARGET...
...SET YOU UP IN A NEW COUNTRY...
...A NEW IDENTITY...
...RACHEL WON'T BE GOING.

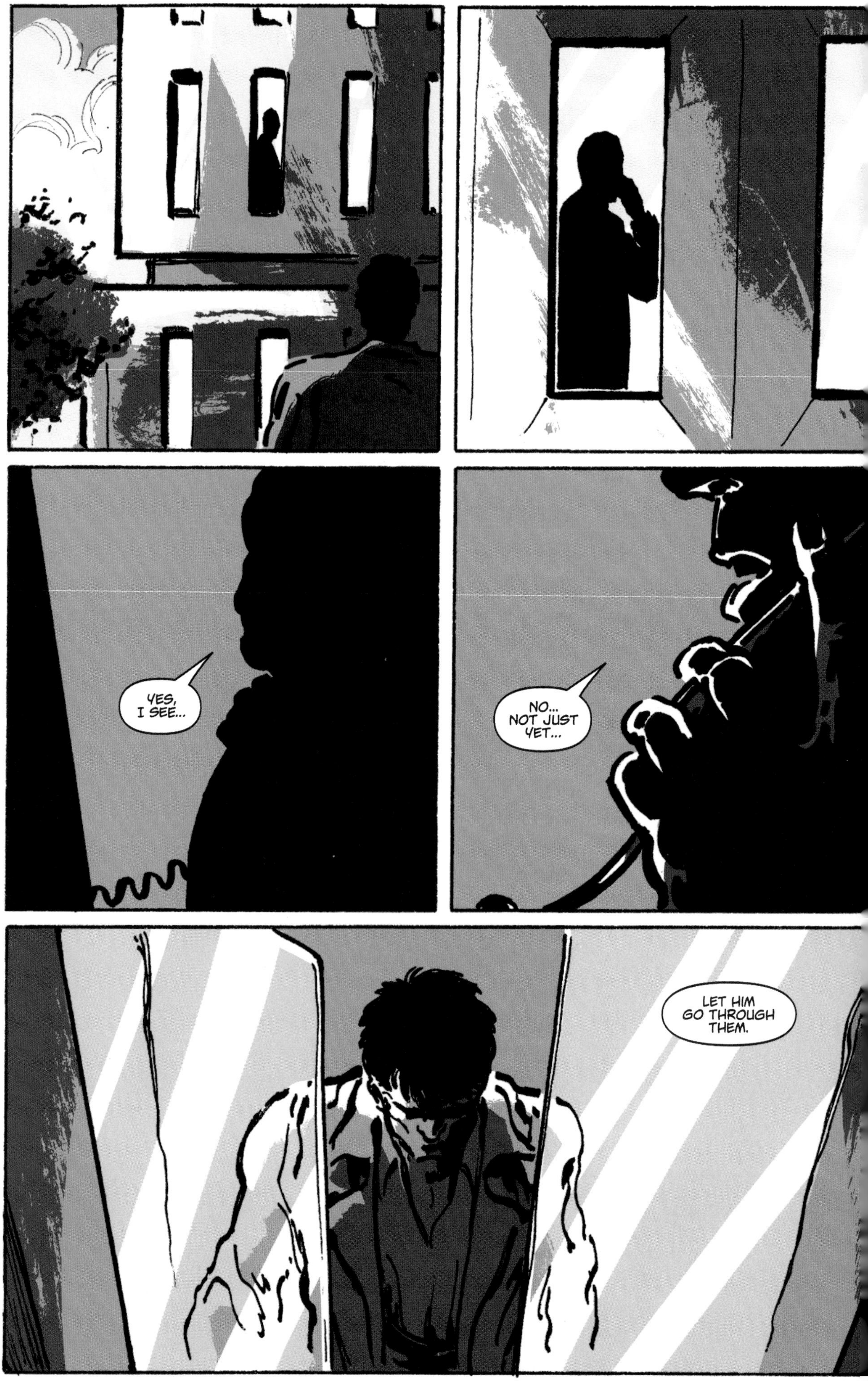
YES, I SEE...
NO... NOT JUST YET...
LET HIM GO THROUGH THEM.

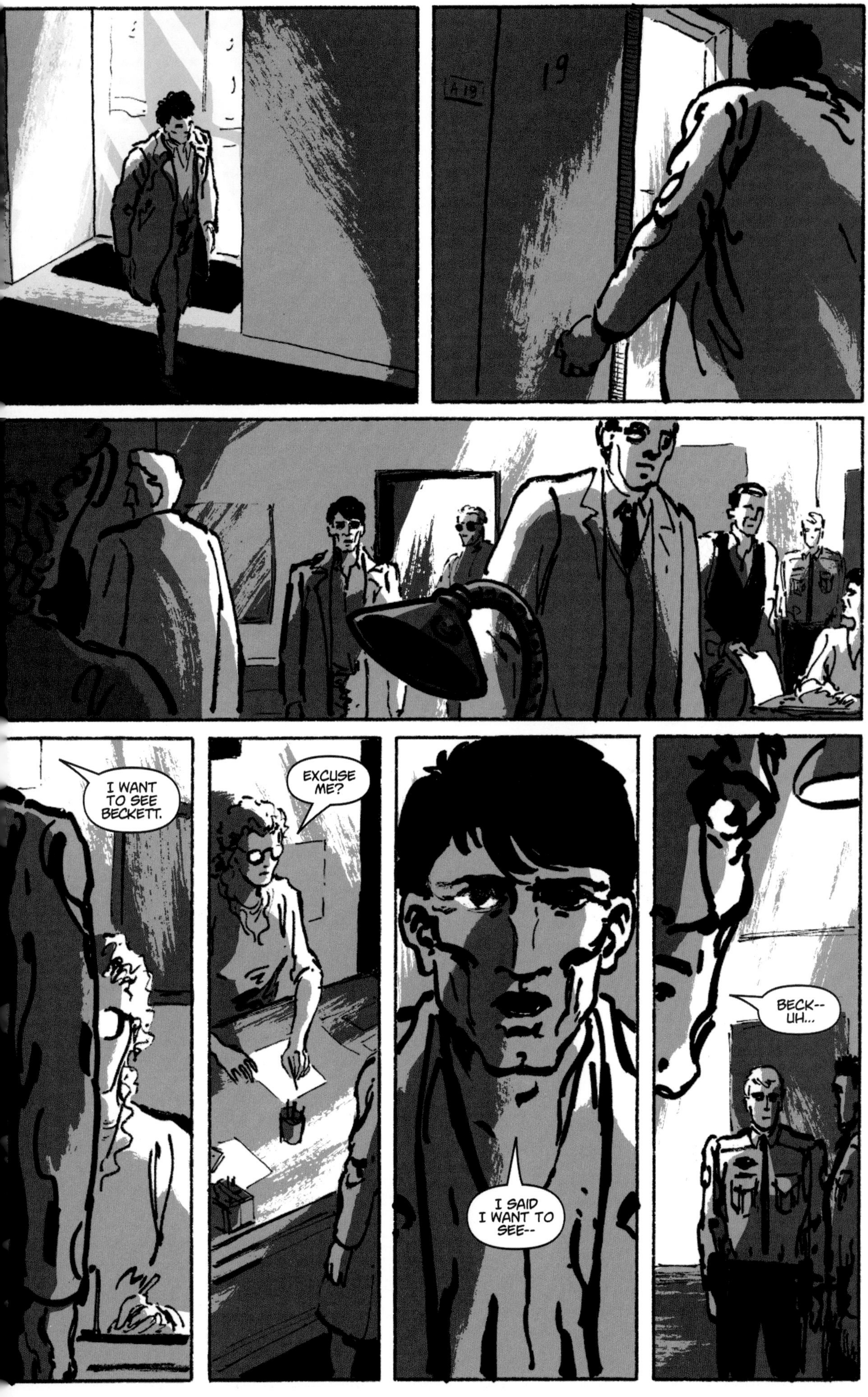
I WANT TO SEE BECKETT.
EXCUSE ME?
I SAID I WANT TO SEE--
BECK-- UH...

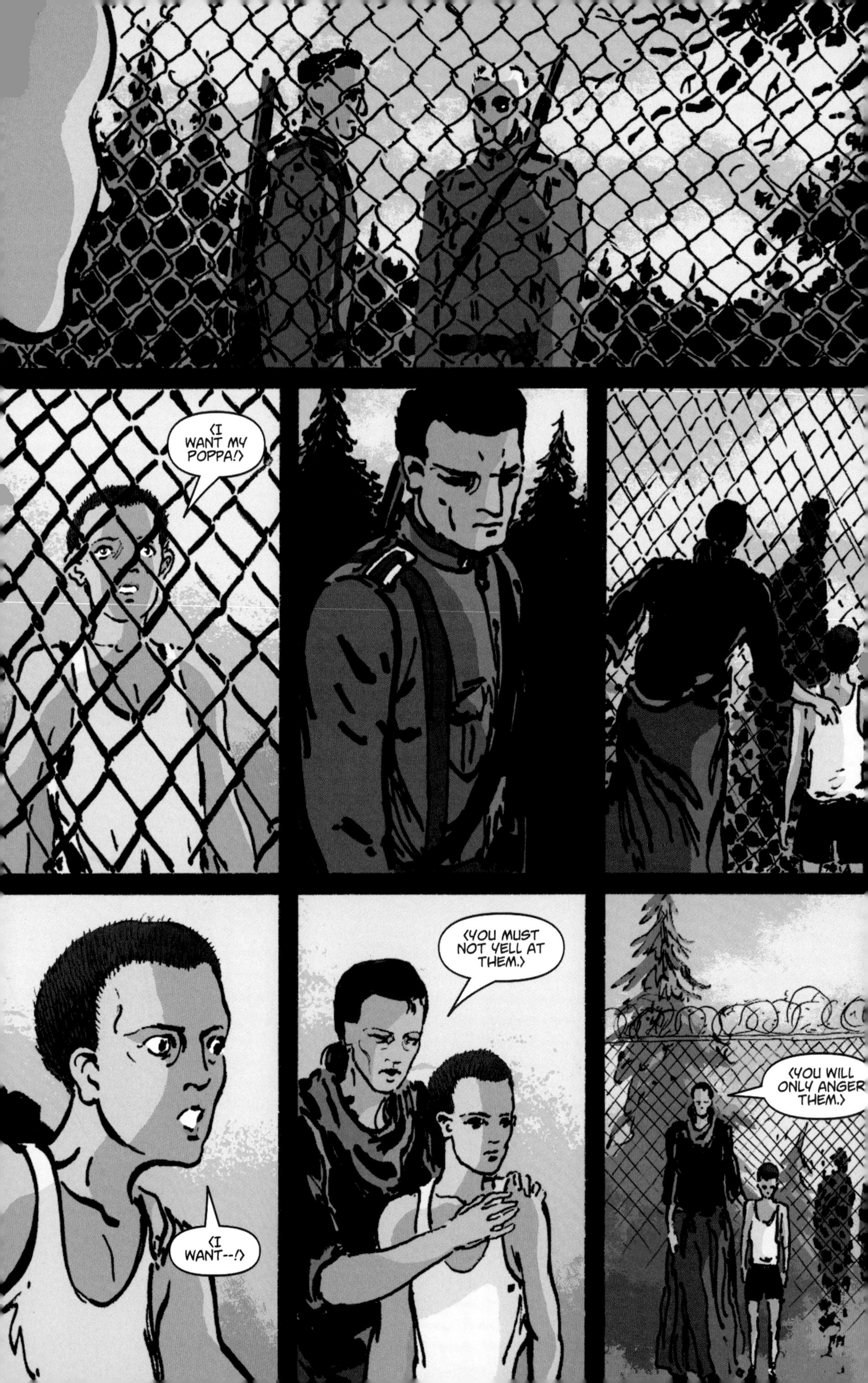
⟨I WANT MY POPPA!⟩
⟨I WANT--!⟩
⟨YOU MUST NOT YELL AT THEM.⟩
⟨YOU WILL ONLY ANGER THEM.⟩

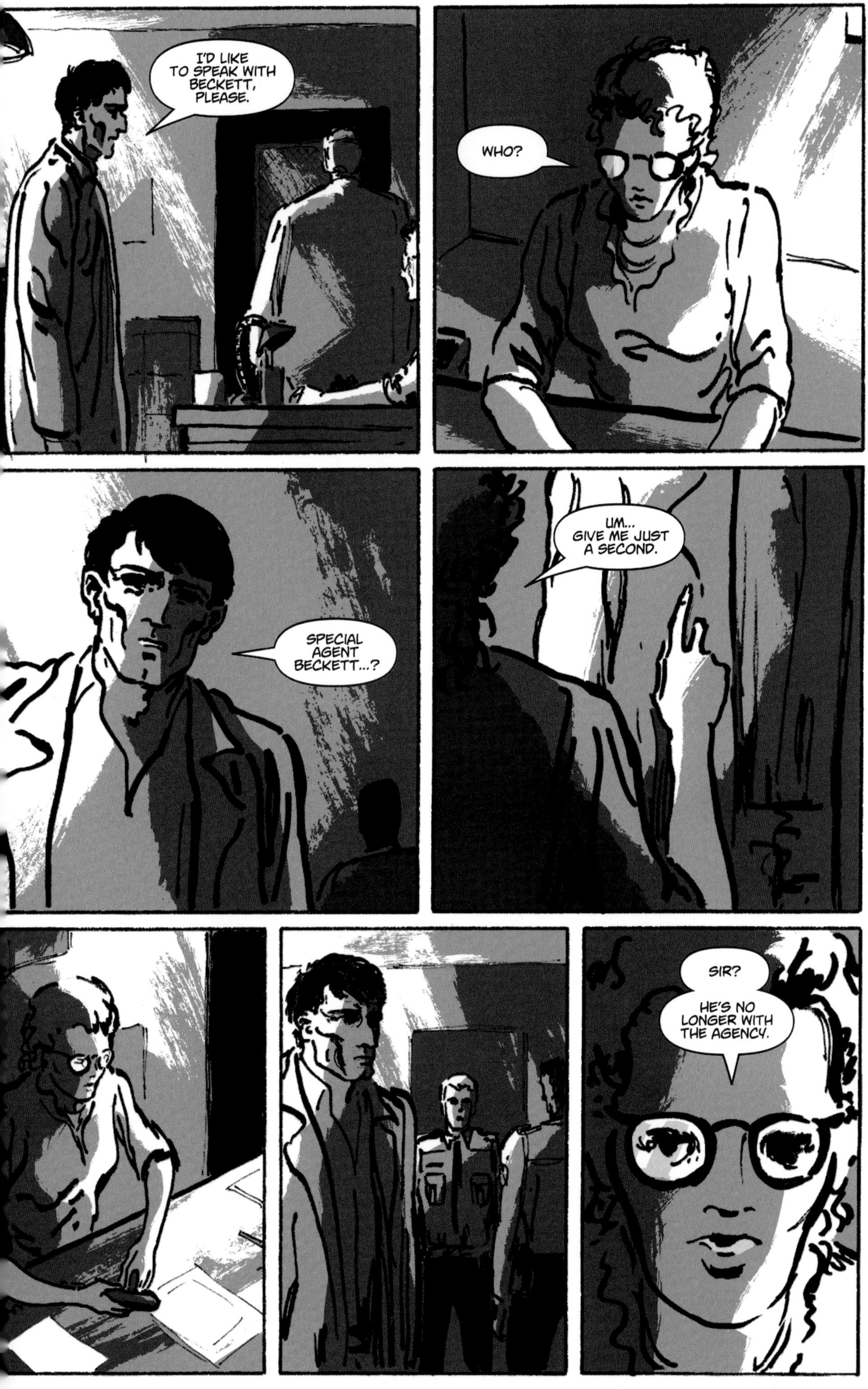
I'D LIKE TO SPEAK WITH BECKETT, PLEASE.
WHO?
SPECIAL AGENT BECKETT...?
UM... GIVE ME JUST A SECOND.
SIR?
HE'S NO LONGER WITH THE AGENCY.

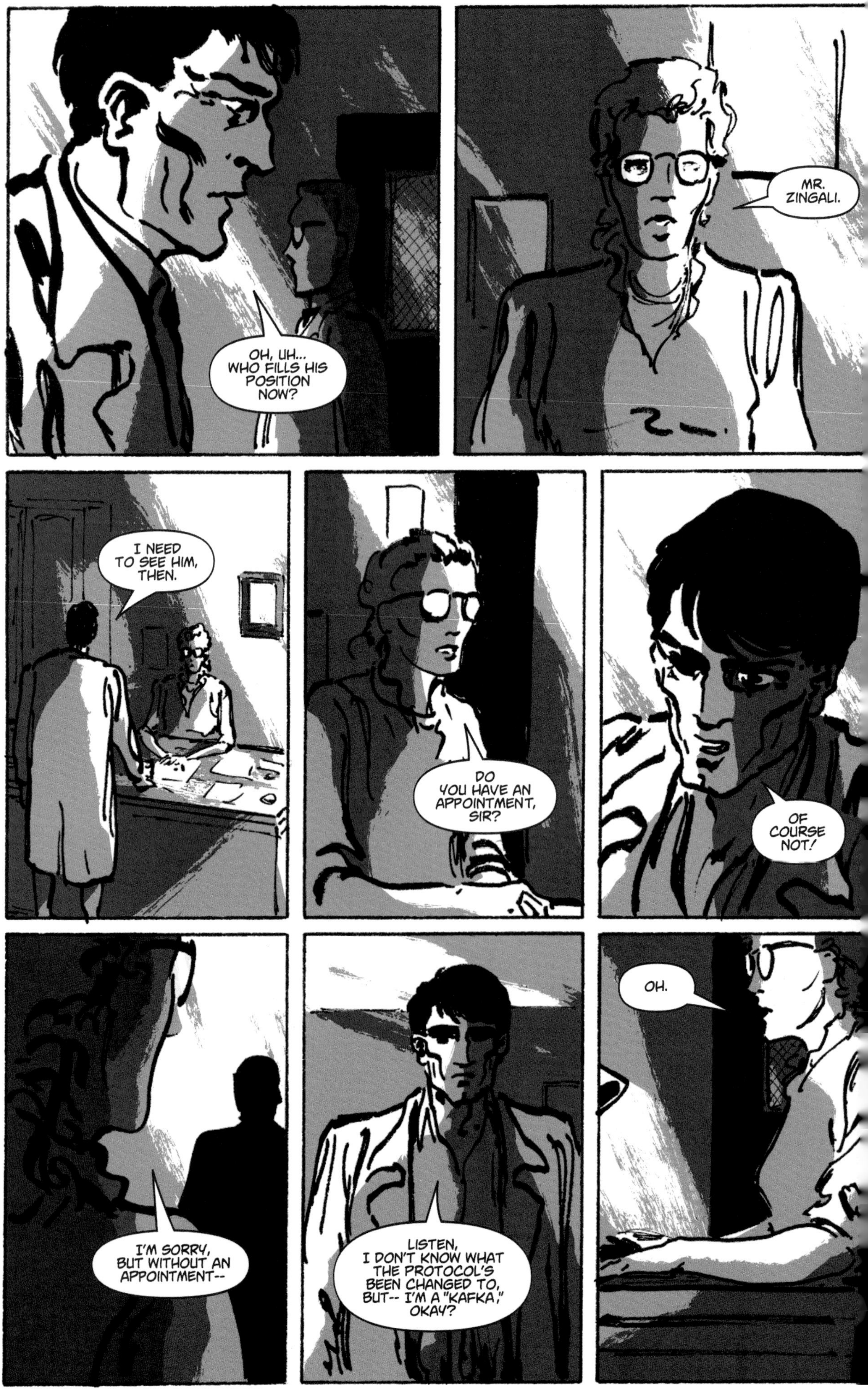
OH, UH... WHO FILLS HIS POSITION NOW?
MR. ZINGALI.
I NEED TO SEE HIM, THEN.
DO YOU HAVE AN APPOINTMENT, SIR?
OF COURSE NOT!
I'M SORRY, BUT WITHOUT AN APPOINTMENT--
LISTEN, I DON'T KNOW WHAT THE PROTOCOL'S BEEN CHANGED TO, BUT-- I'M A "KAFKA," OKAY?
OH.

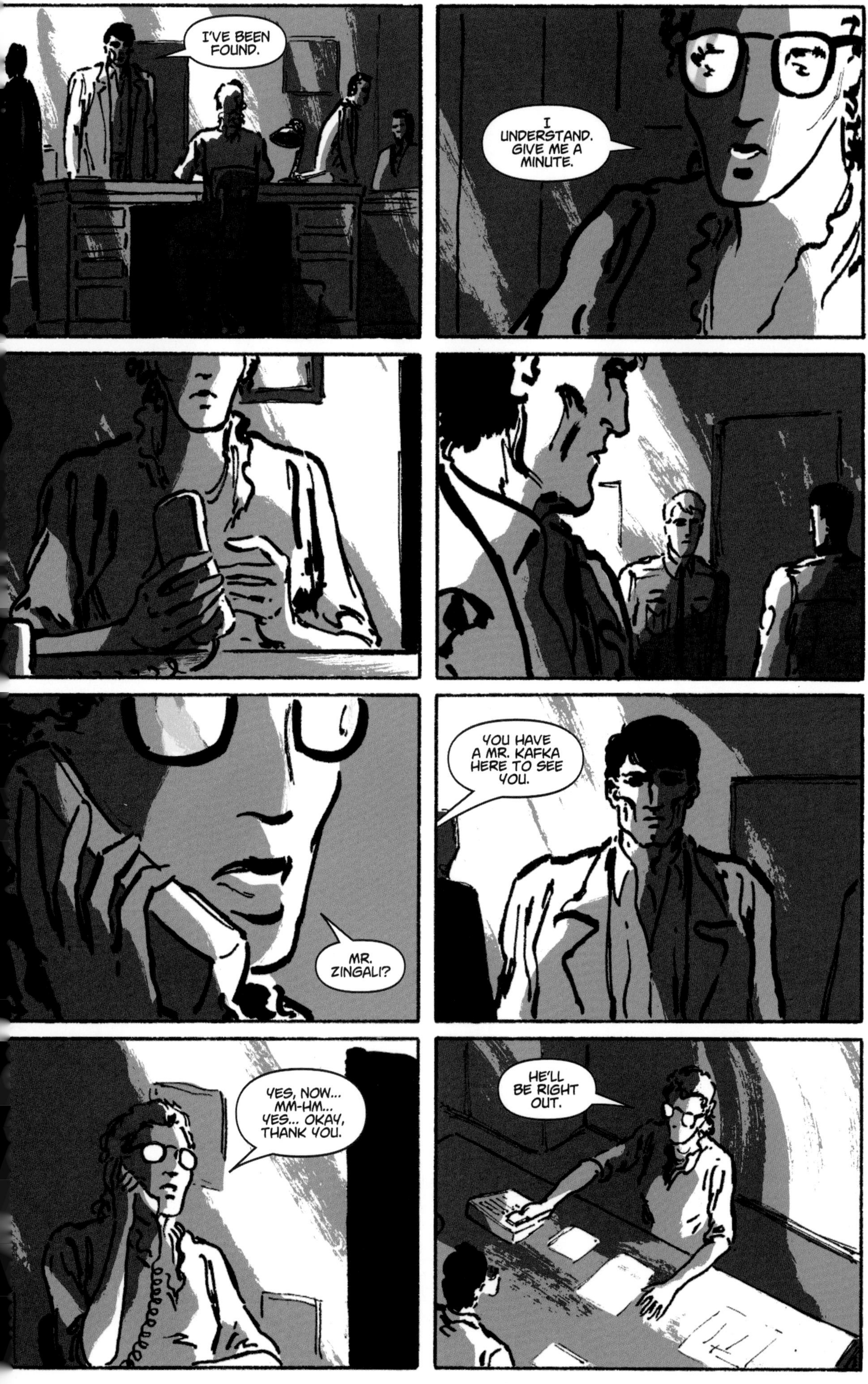

I'VE BEEN FOUND.
I UNDERSTAND. GIVE ME A MINUTE.
MR. ZINGALI?
YOU HAVE A MR. KAFKA HERE TO SEE YOU.
YES, NOW... MM-HM... YES... OKAY, THANK YOU.
HE'LL BE RIGHT OUT.

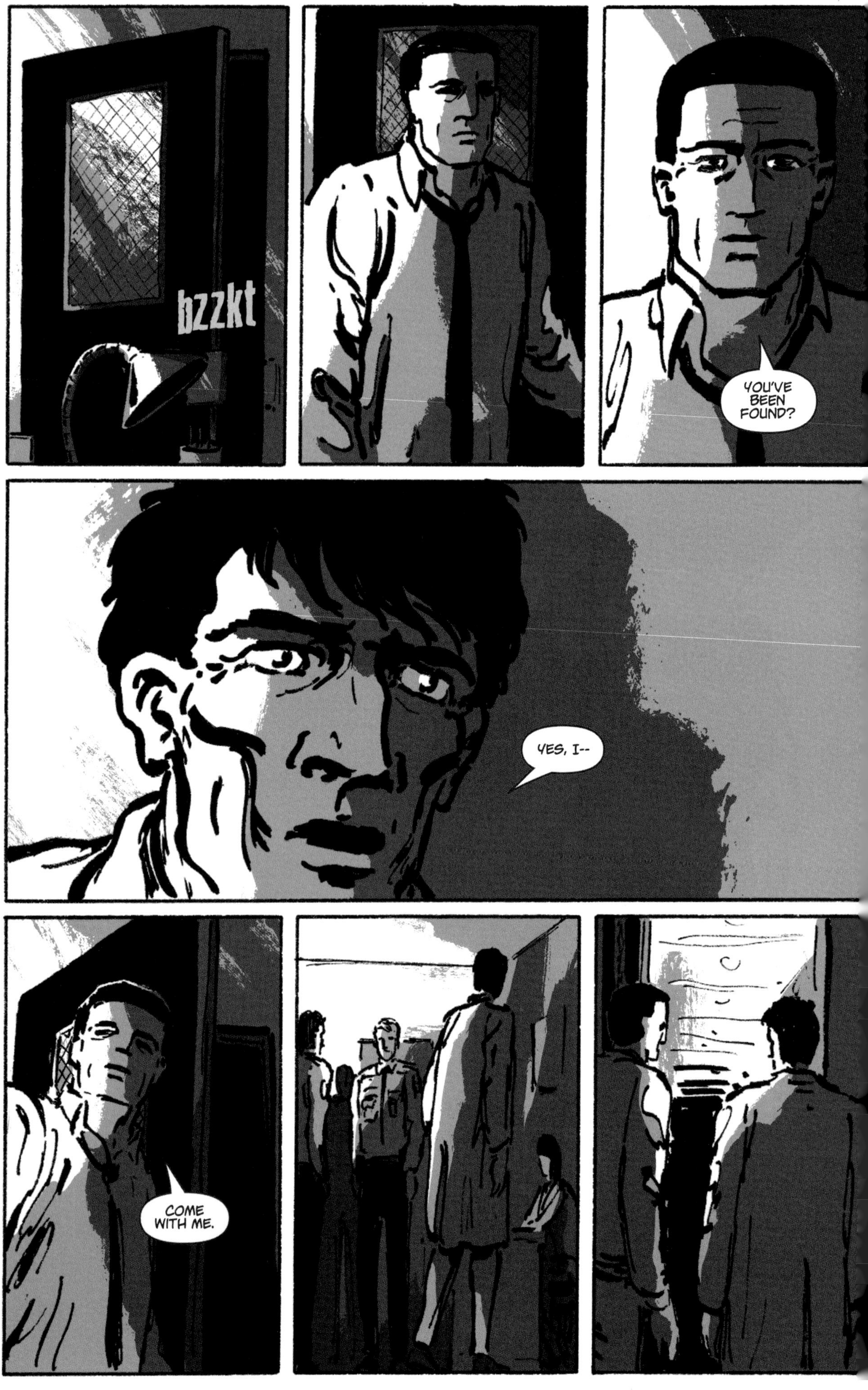
bzzkt
YOU'VE BEEN FOUND?
YES, I--
COME WITH ME.

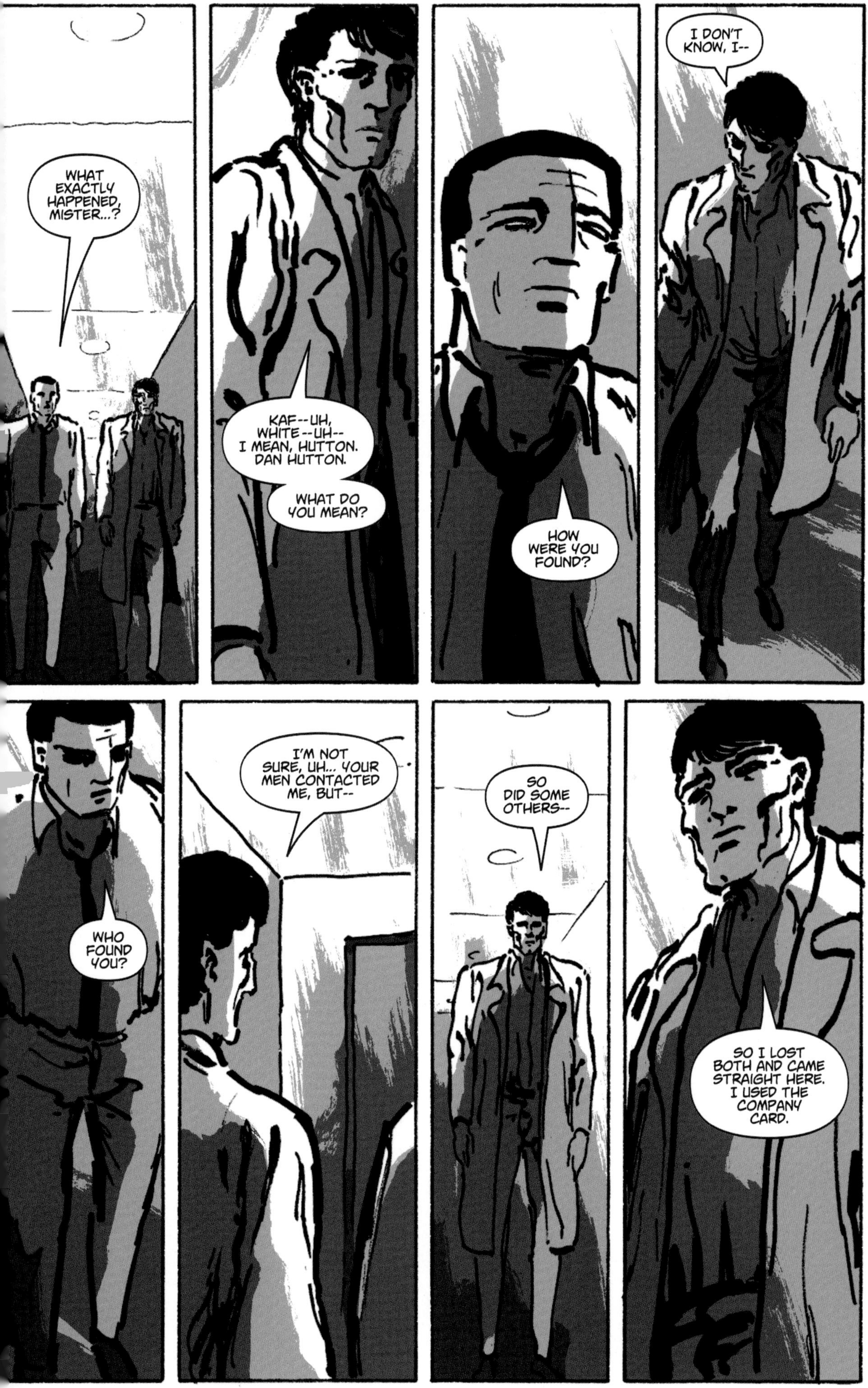
WHAT EXACTLY HAPPENED, MISTER...?
KAF--UH, WHITE--UH-- I MEAN, HUTTON. DAN HUTTON.
WHAT DO YOU MEAN?
HOW WERE YOU FOUND?
I DON'T KNOW, I--
WHO FOUND YOU?
I'M NOT SURE, UH... YOUR MEN CONTACTED ME, BUT--
SO DID SOME OTHERS--
SO I LOST BOTH AND CAME STRAIGHT HERE. I USED THE COMPANY CARD.

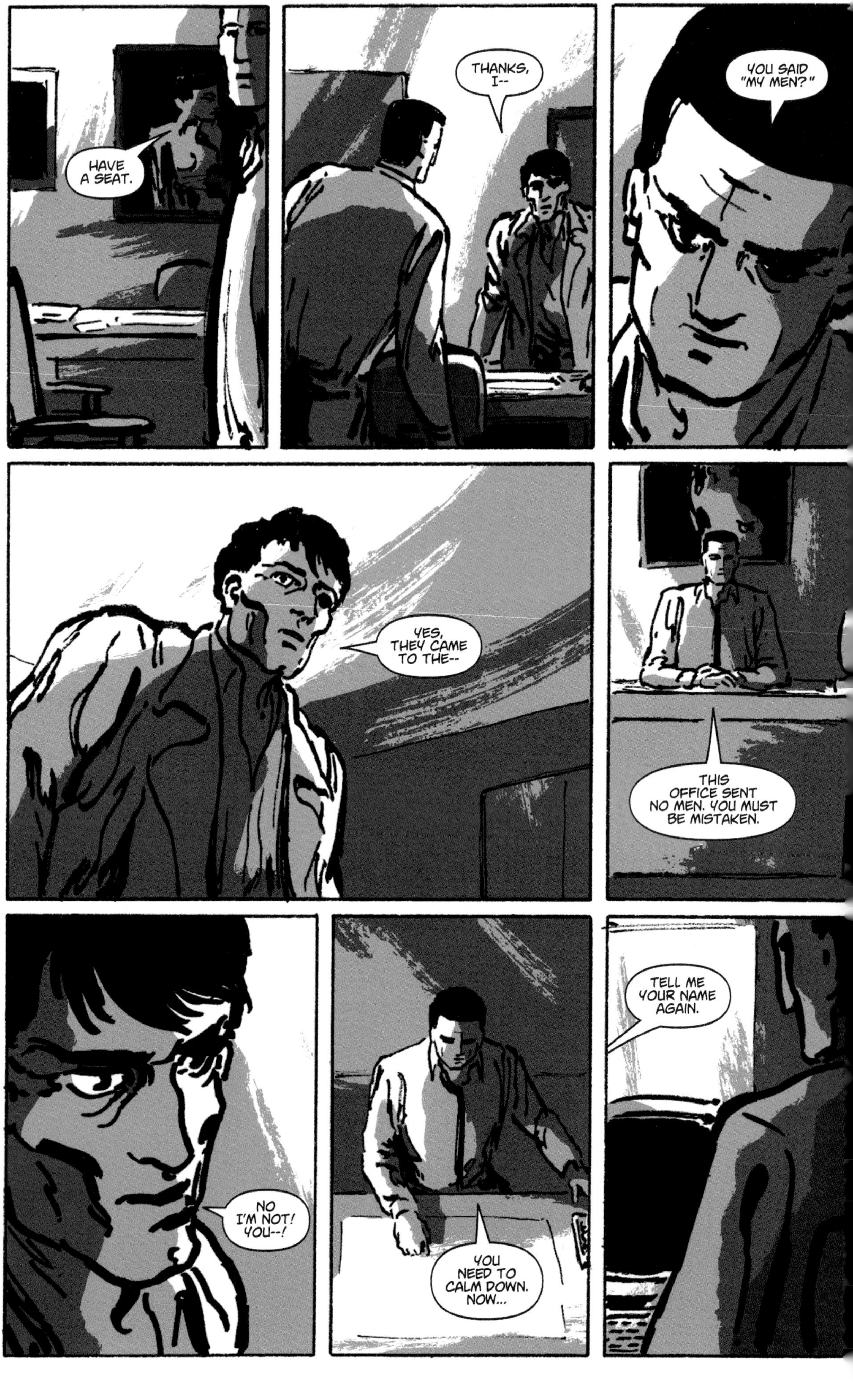

HAVE A SEAT.
THANKS, I--
YOU SAID "MY MEN?"
YES, THEY CAME TO THE--
THIS OFFICE SENT NO MEN. YOU MUST BE MISTAKEN.
NO I'M NOT! YOU--!
YOU NEED TO CALM DOWN. NOW...
TELL ME YOUR NAME AGAIN.

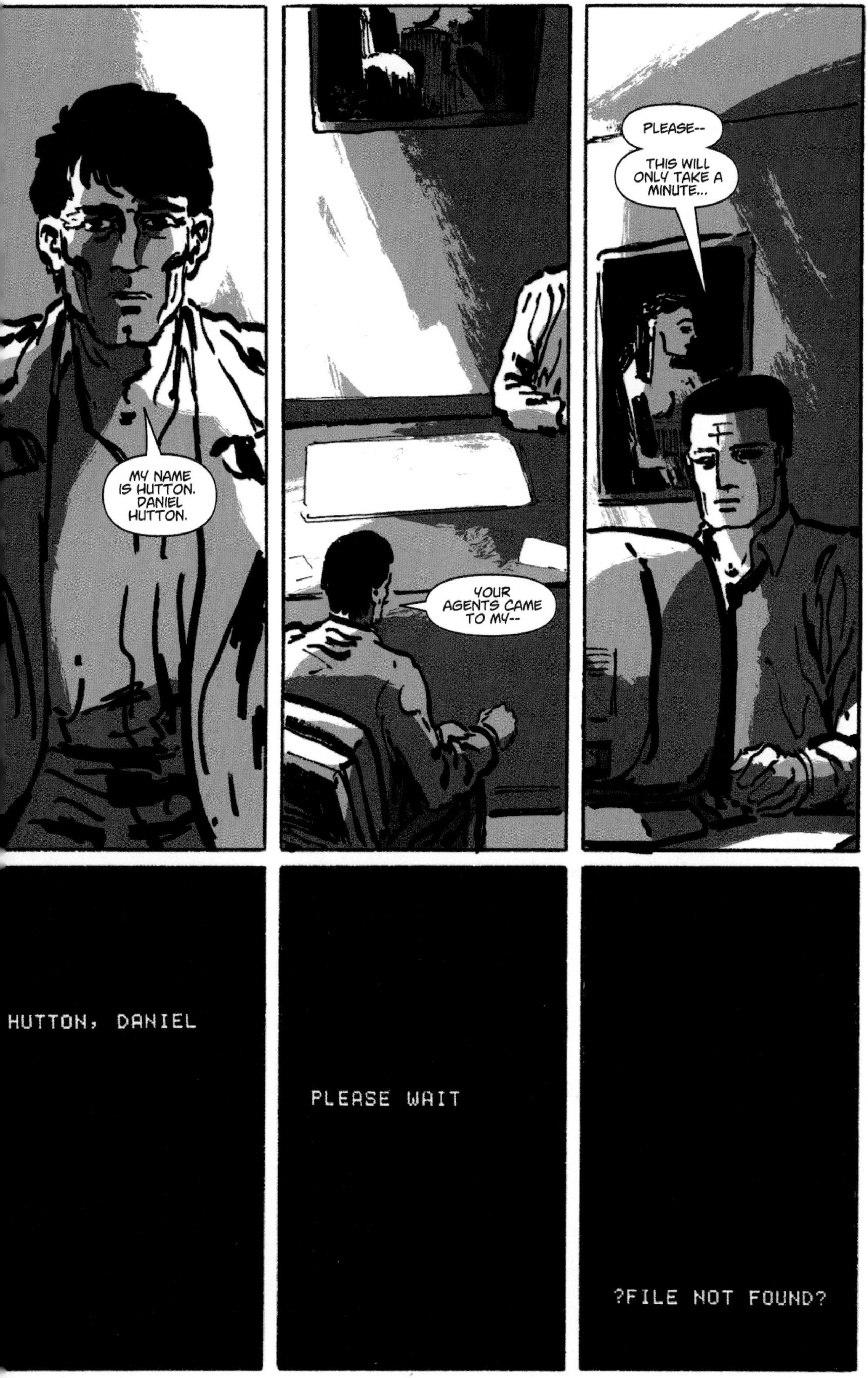
MY NAME IS HUTTON. DANIEL HUTTON.
YOUR AGENTS CAME TO MY--
PLEASE--
THIS WILL ONLY TAKE A MINUTE...
HUTTON, DANIEL
PLEASE WAIT
?FILE NOT FOUND?

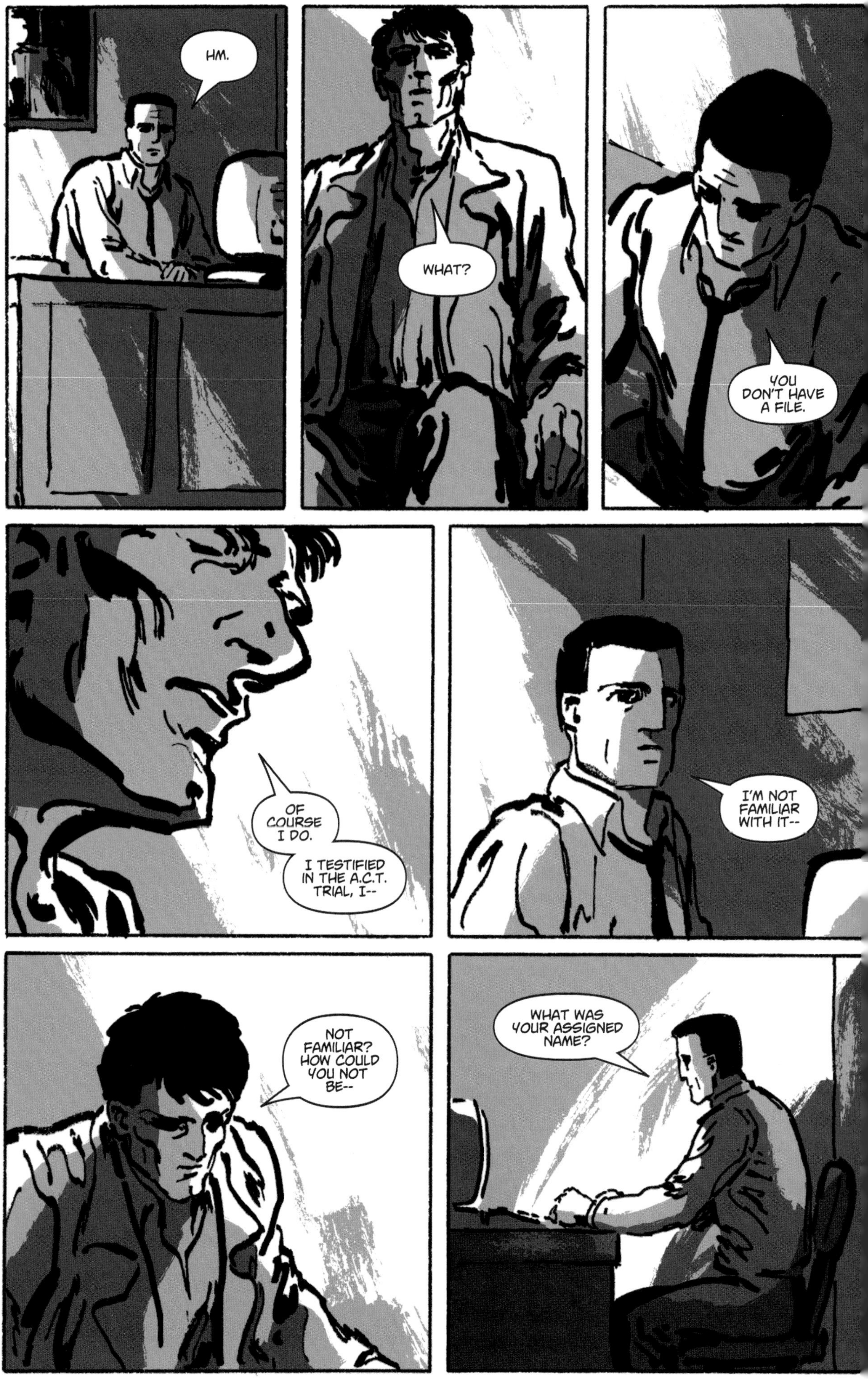
HM.
WHAT?
YOU DON'T HAVE A FILE.
OF COURSE I DO.
I TESTIFIED IN THE A.C.T. TRIAL, I--
I'M NOT FAMILIAR WITH IT--
NOT FAMILIAR? HOW COULD YOU NOT BE--
WHAT WAS YOUR ASSIGNED NAME?

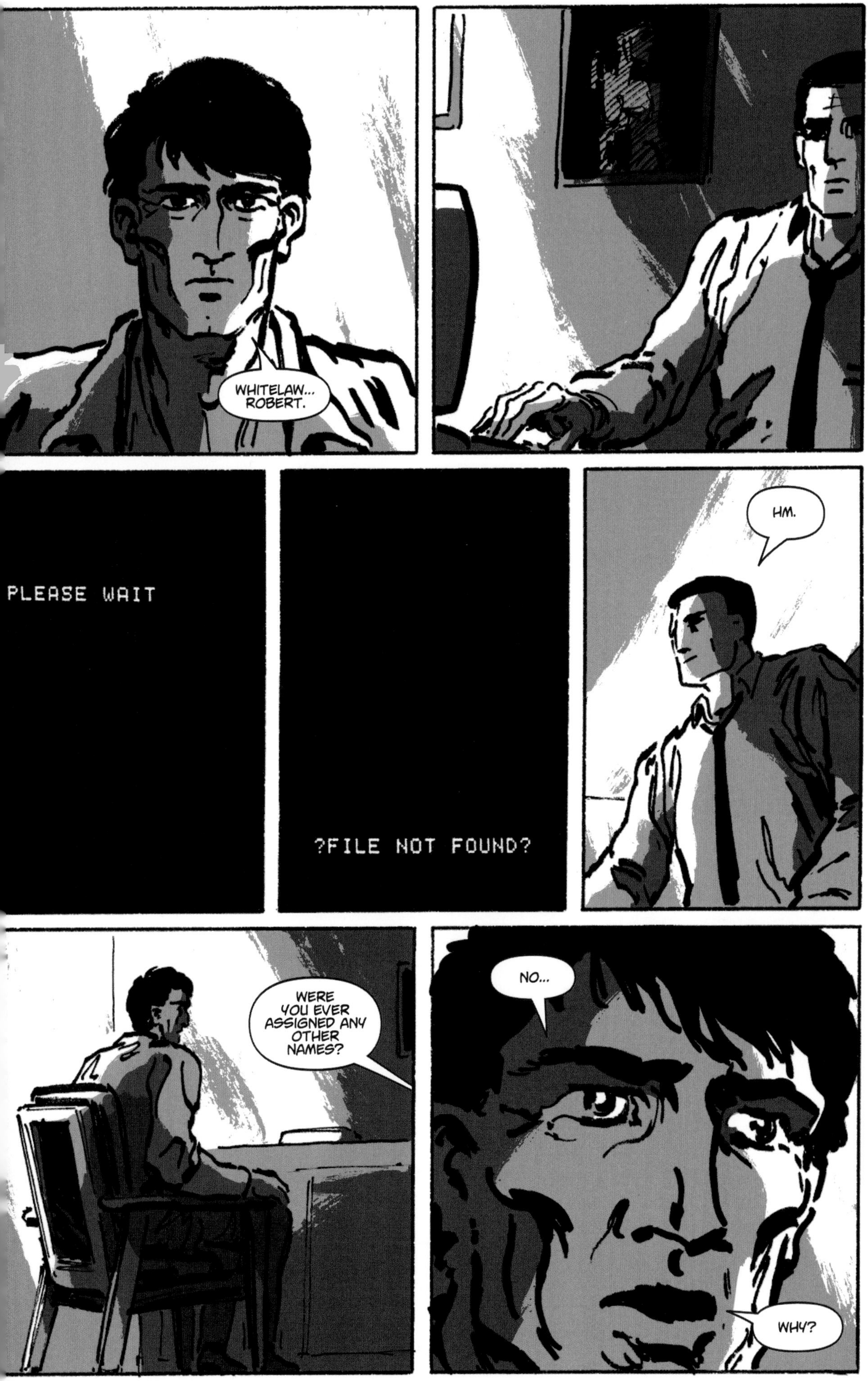
WHITELAW... ROBERT.
PLEASE WAIT
?FILE NOT FOUND?
HM.
WERE YOU EVER ASSIGNED ANY OTHER NAMES?
NO...
WHY?

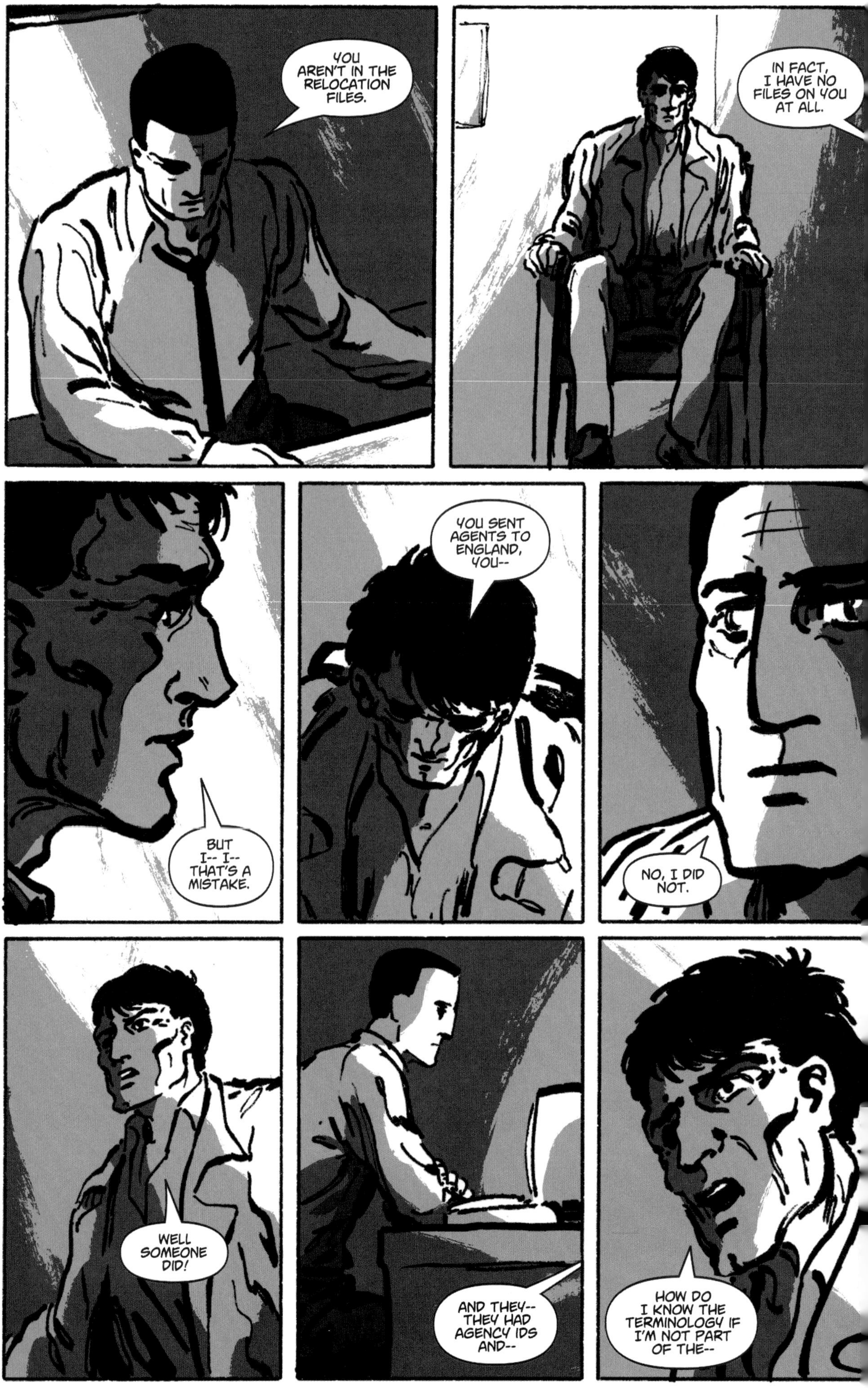
YOU AREN'T IN THE RELOCATION FILES.
IN FACT, I HAVE NO FILES ON YOU AT ALL.
BUT I-- I-- THAT'S A MISTAKE.
YOU SENT AGENTS TO ENGLAND, YOU--
NO, I DID NOT.
WELL SOMEONE DID!
AND THEY-- THEY HAD AGENCY IDS AND--
HOW DO I KNOW THE TERMINOLOGY IF I'M NOT PART OF THE--

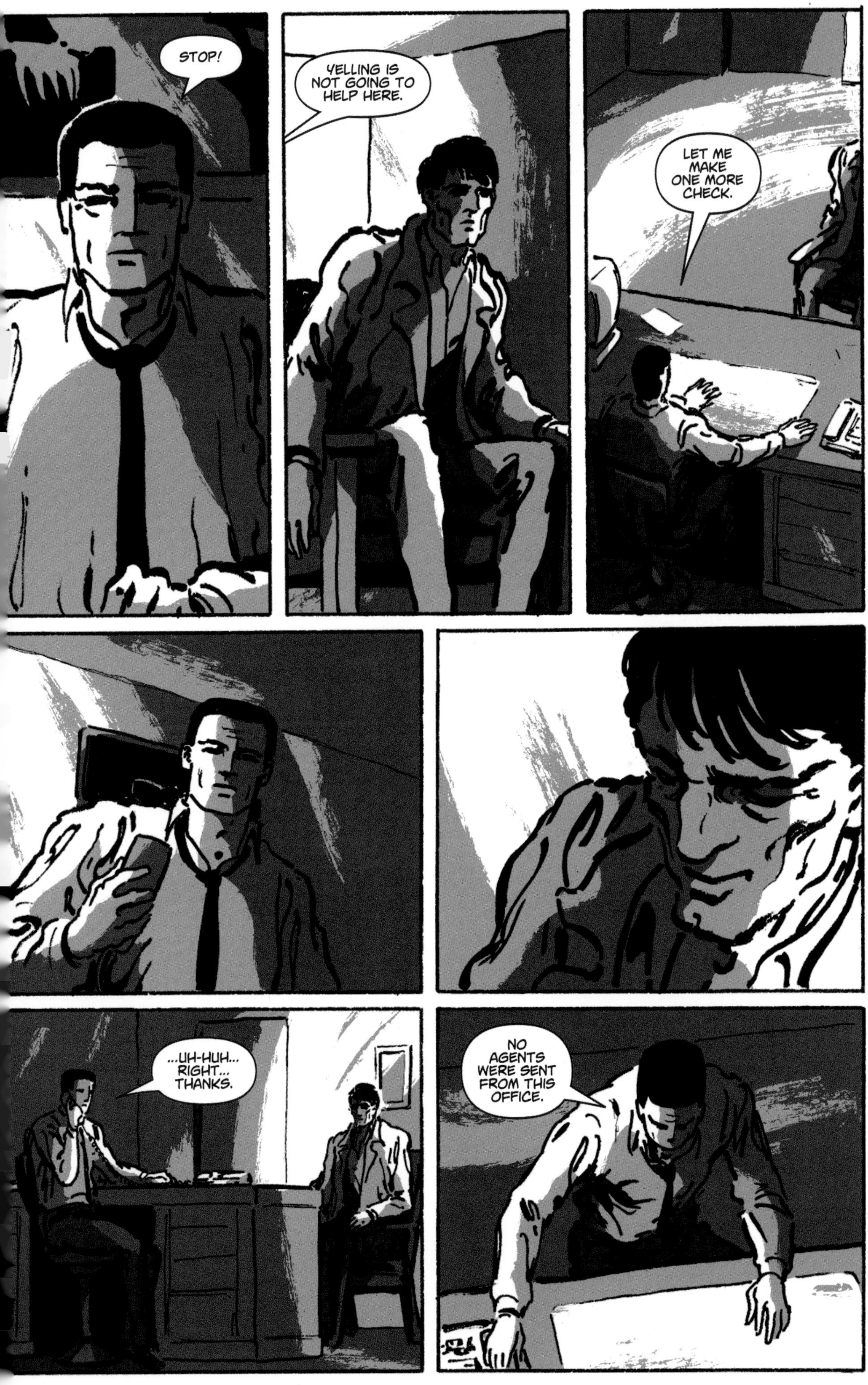
STOP!
YELLING IS NOT GOING TO HELP HERE.
LET ME MAKE ONE MORE CHECK.
...UH-HUH... RIGHT... THANKS.
NO AGENTS WERE SENT FROM THIS OFFICE.

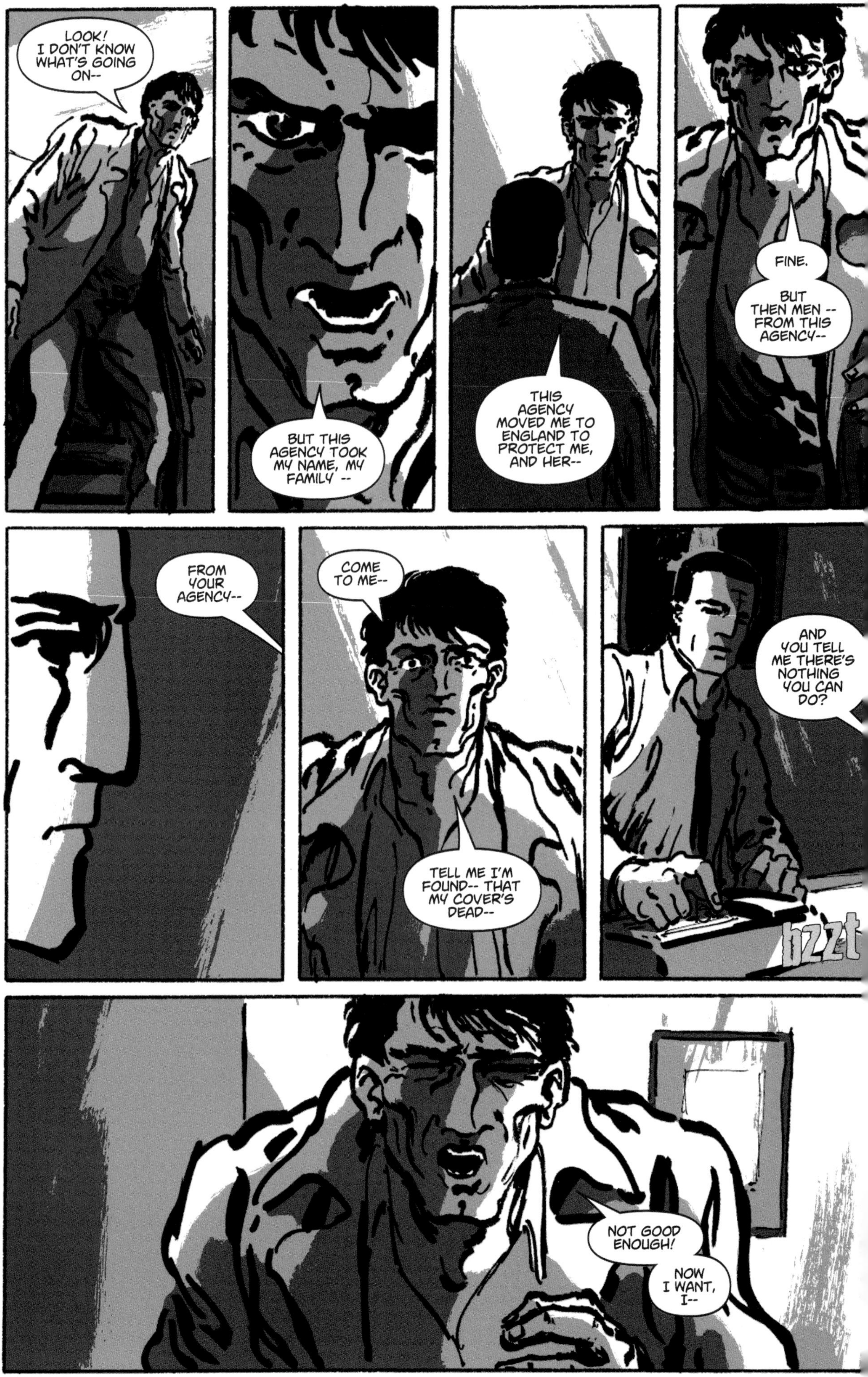
LOOK! I DON'T KNOW WHAT'S GOING ON--
BUT THIS AGENCY TOOK MY NAME, MY FAMILY --
THIS AGENCY MOVED ME TO ENGLAND TO PROTECT ME, AND HER--
FINE.
BUT THEN MEN -- FROM THIS AGENCY--
FROM YOUR AGENCY--
COME TO ME--
TELL ME I'M FOUND-- THAT MY COVER'S DEAD--
AND YOU TELL ME THERE'S NOTHING YOU CAN DO?
bzzt
NOT GOOD ENOUGH!
NOW I WANT, I--

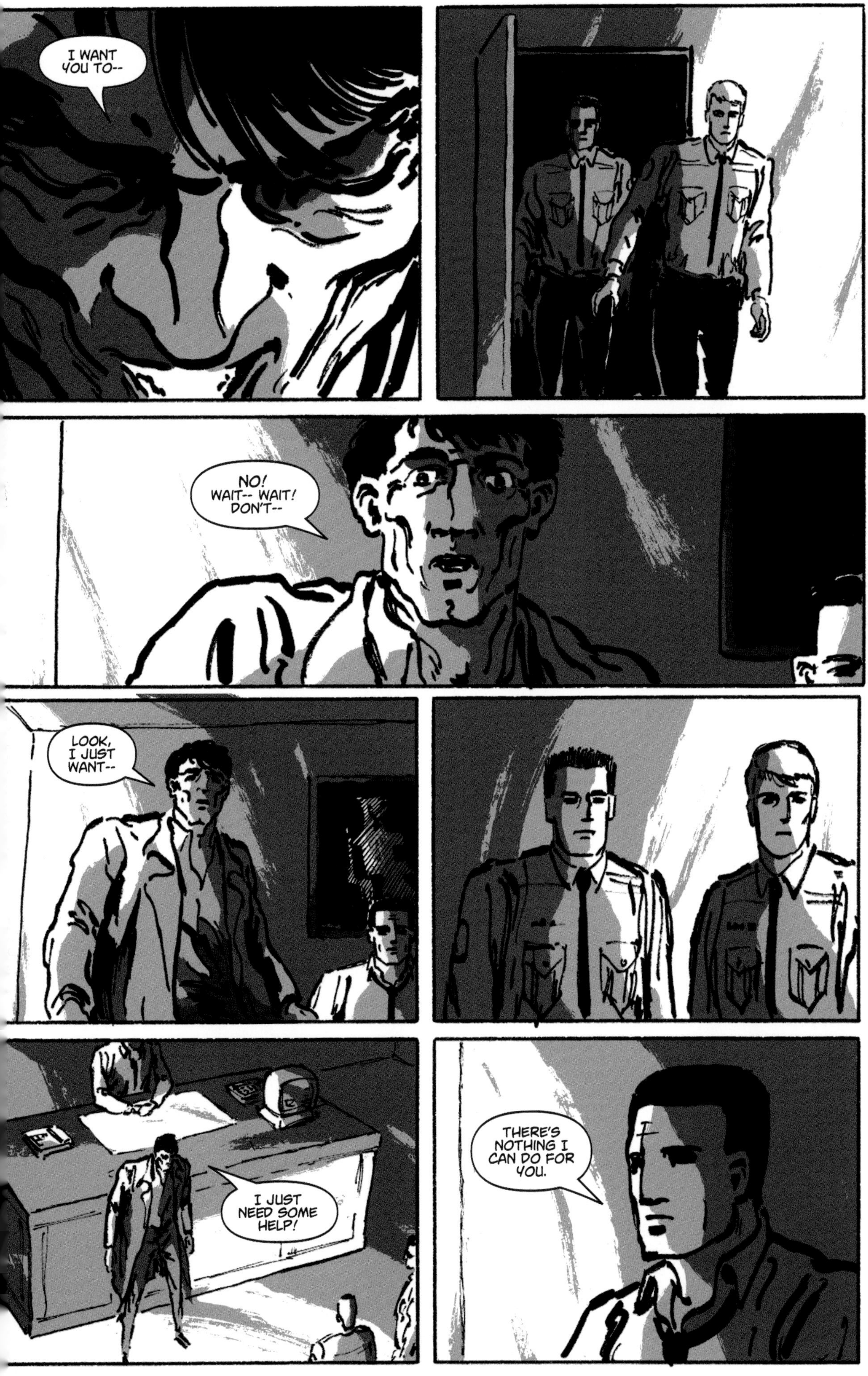
I WANT YOU TO--
NO! WAIT-- WAIT! DON'T--
LOOK, I JUST WANT--
I JUST NEED SOME HELP!
THERE'S NOTHING I CAN DO FOR YOU.

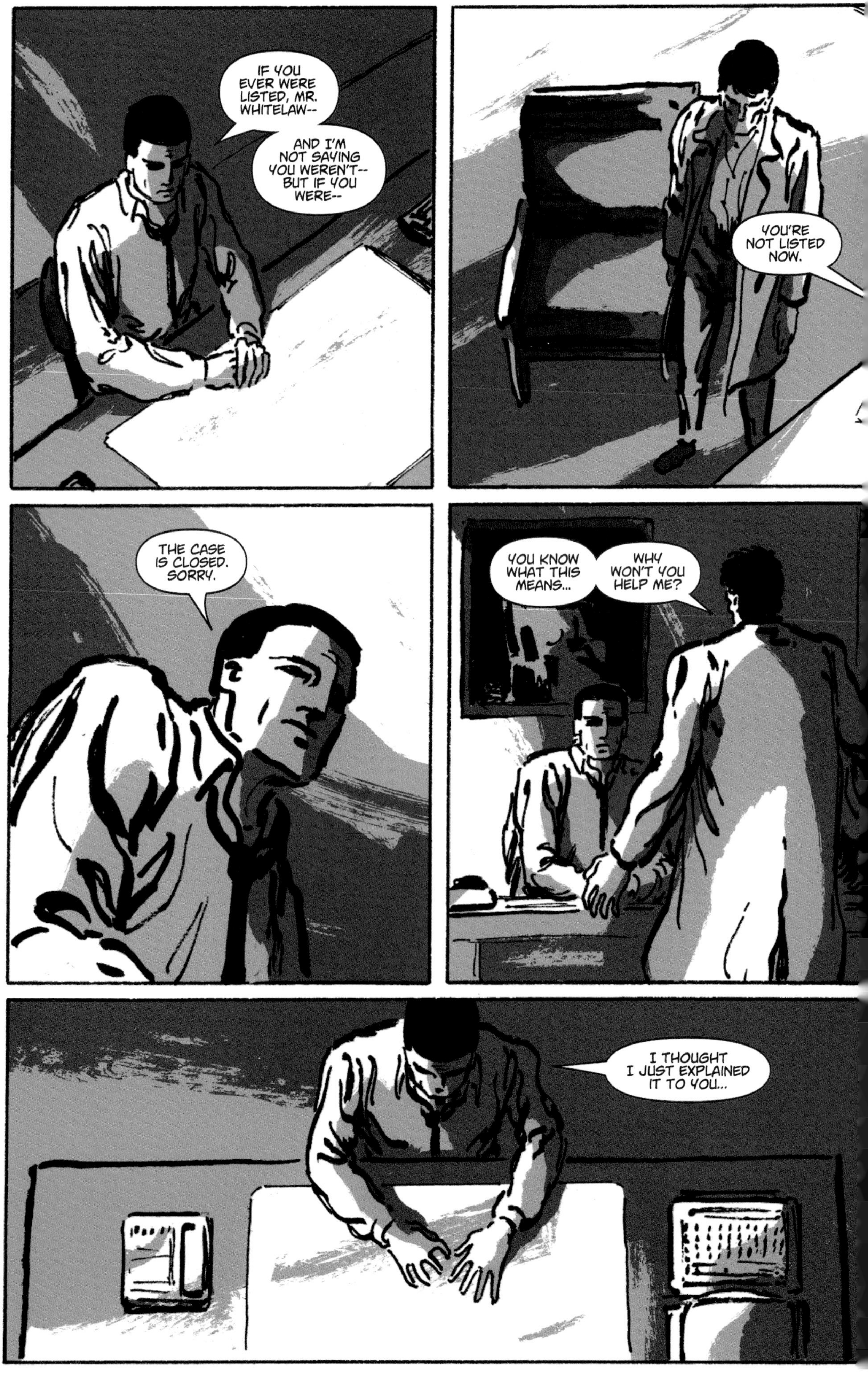
IF YOU EVER WERE LISTED, MR. WHITELAW--
AND I'M NOT SAYING YOU WEREN'T-- BUT IF YOU WERE--
YOU'RE NOT LISTED NOW.
THE CASE IS CLOSED. SORRY.
YOU KNOW WHAT THIS MEANS...
WHY WON'T YOU HELP ME?
I THOUGHT I JUST EXPLAINED IT TO YOU...

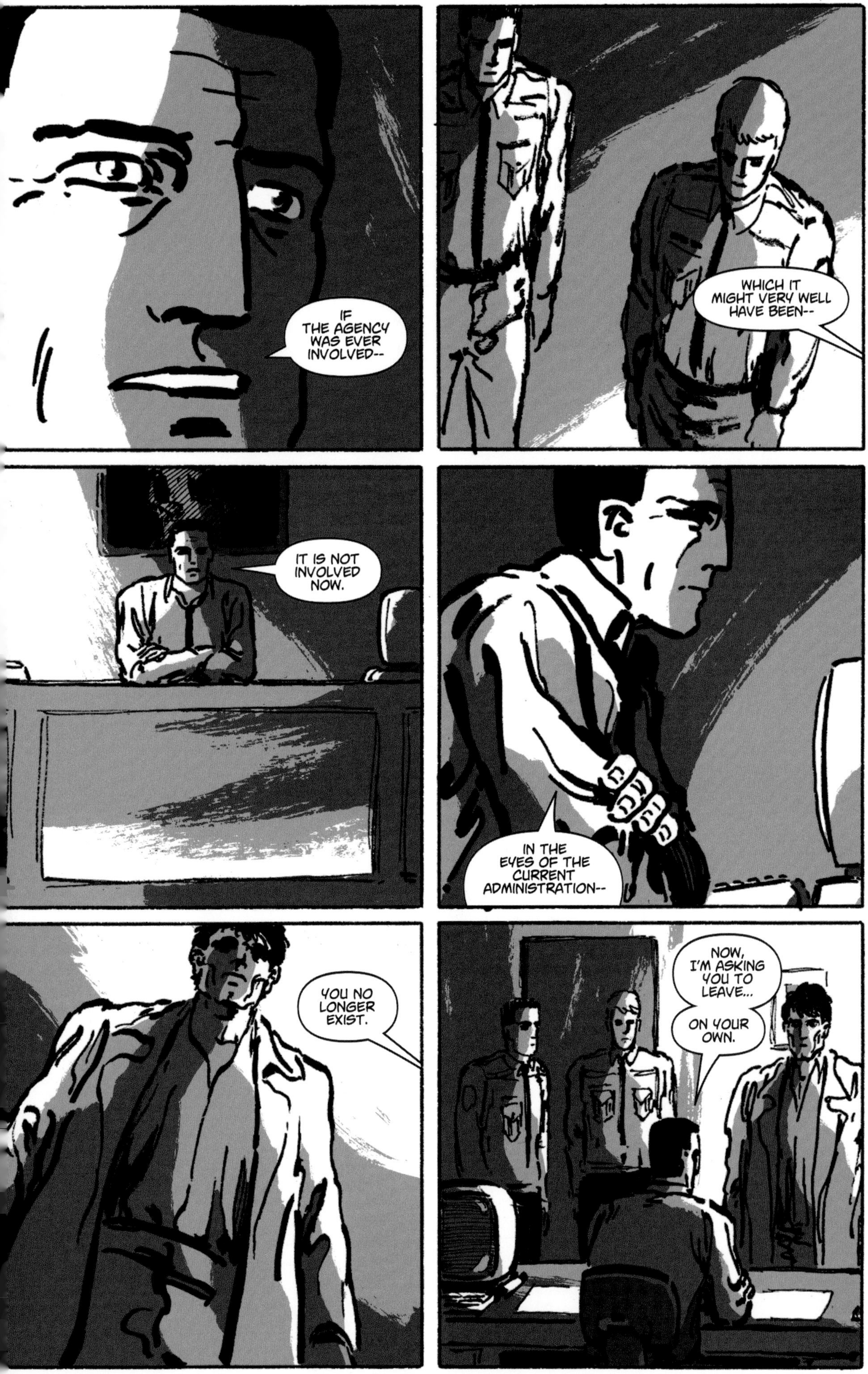
IF THE AGENCY WAS EVER INVOLVED--
WHICH IT MIGHT VERY WELL HAVE BEEN--
IT IS NOT INVOLVED NOW.
IN THE EYES OF THE CURRENT ADMINISTRATION--
YOU NO LONGER EXIST.
NOW, I'M ASKING YOU TO LEAVE...
ON YOUR OWN.

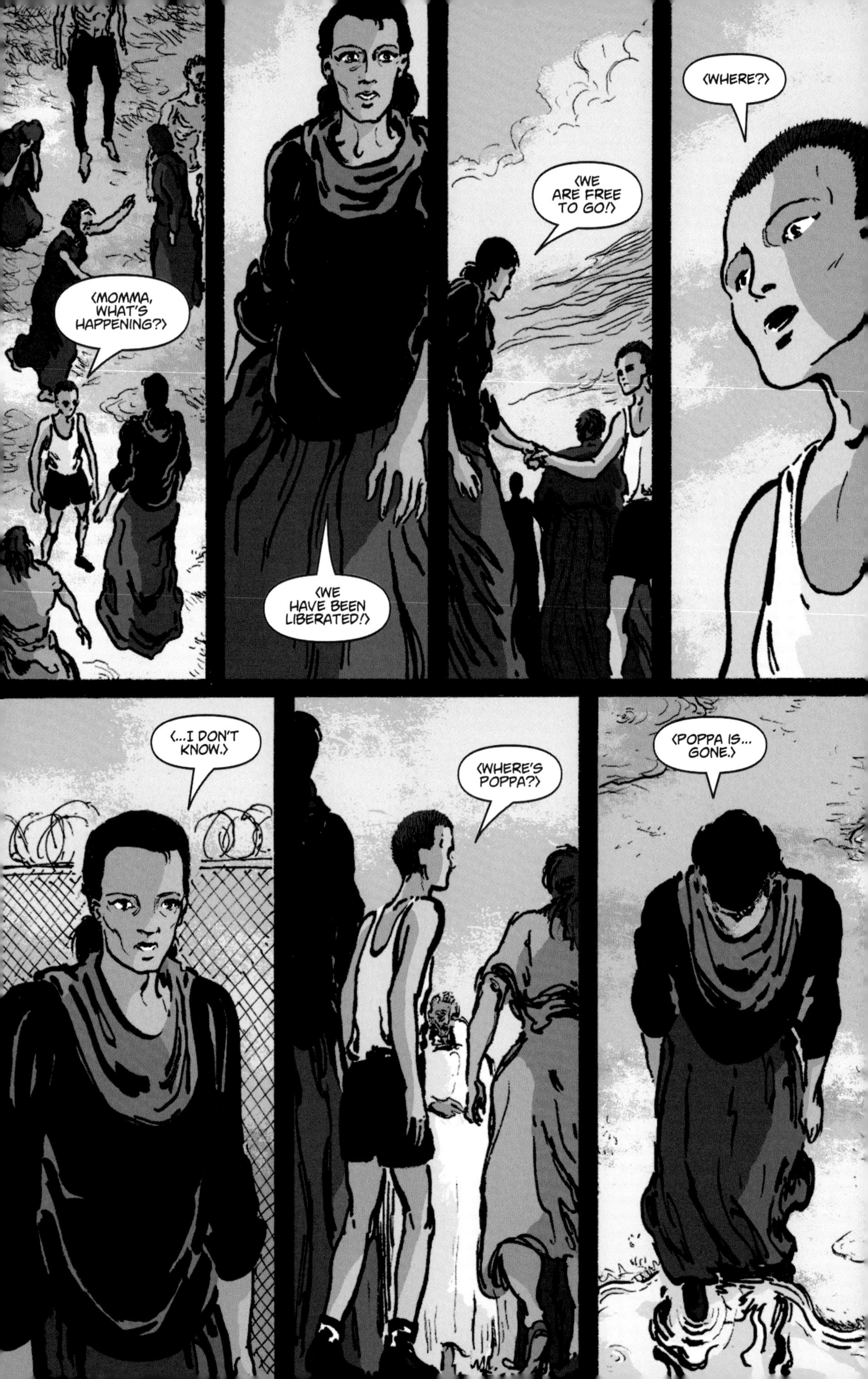
〈MOMMA, WHAT'S HAPPENING?〉
〈WE HAVE BEEN LIBERATED!〉
〈WE ARE FREE TO GO!〉
〈WHERE?〉
〈...I DON'T KNOW.〉
〈WHERE'S POPPA?〉
〈POPPA IS... GONE.〉

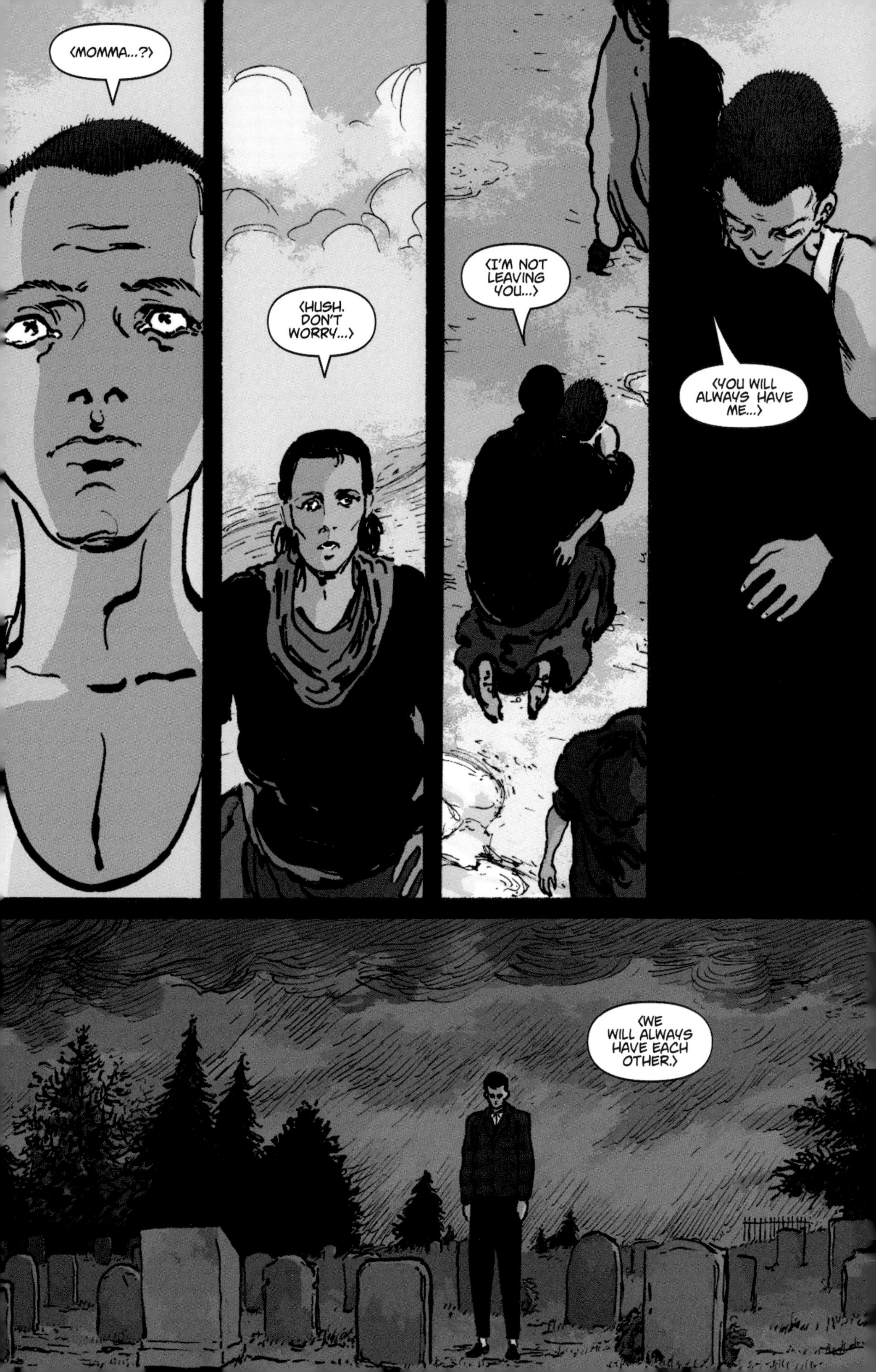

⟨MOMMA...?⟩
⟨HUSH. DON'T WORRY...⟩
⟨I'M NOT LEAVING YOU...⟩
⟨YOU WILL ALWAYS HAVE ME...⟩
⟨WE WILL ALWAYS HAVE EACH OTHER.⟩

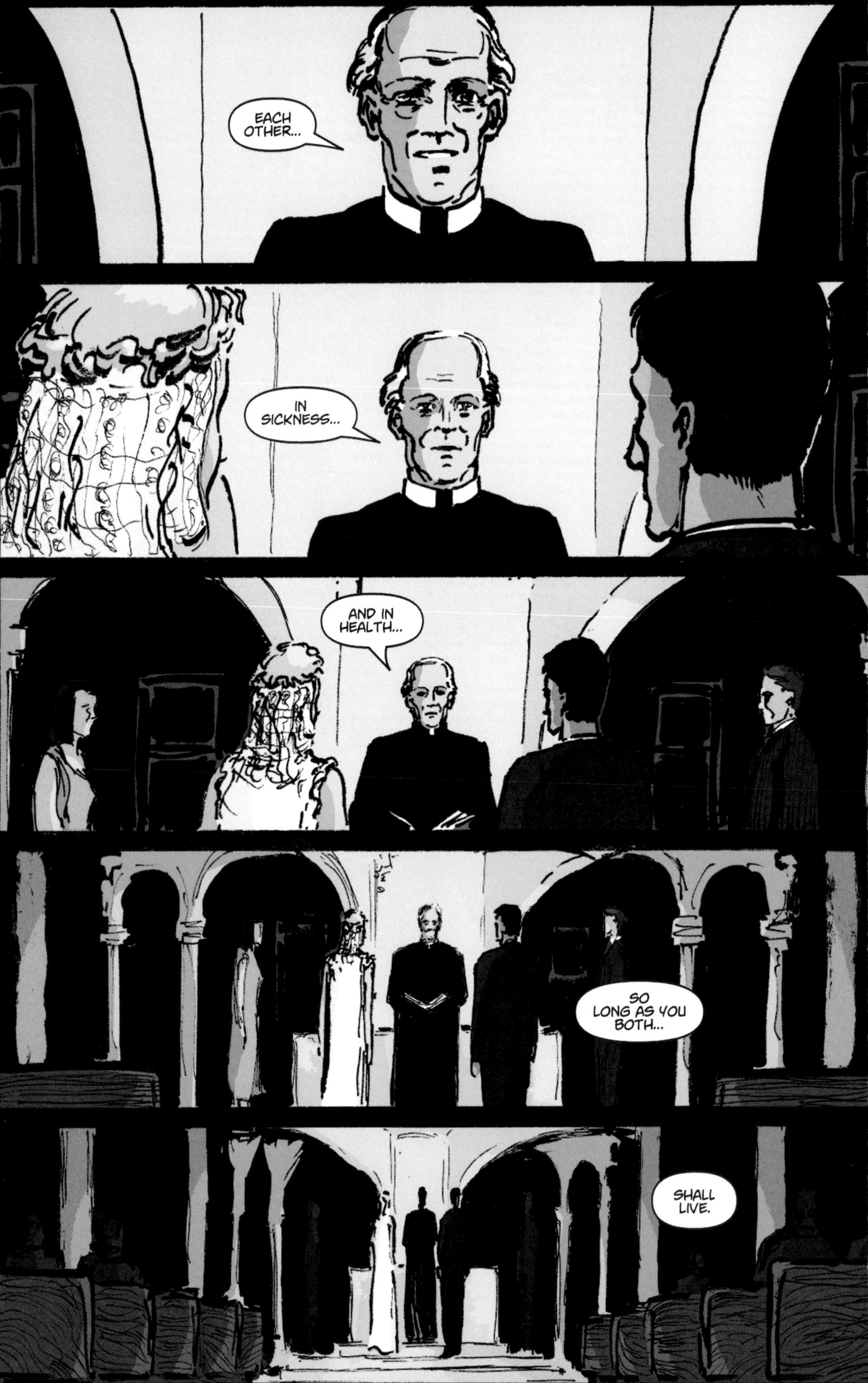
EACH OTHER...
IN SICKNESS...
AND IN HEALTH...
SO LONG AS YOU BOTH...
SHALL LIVE.

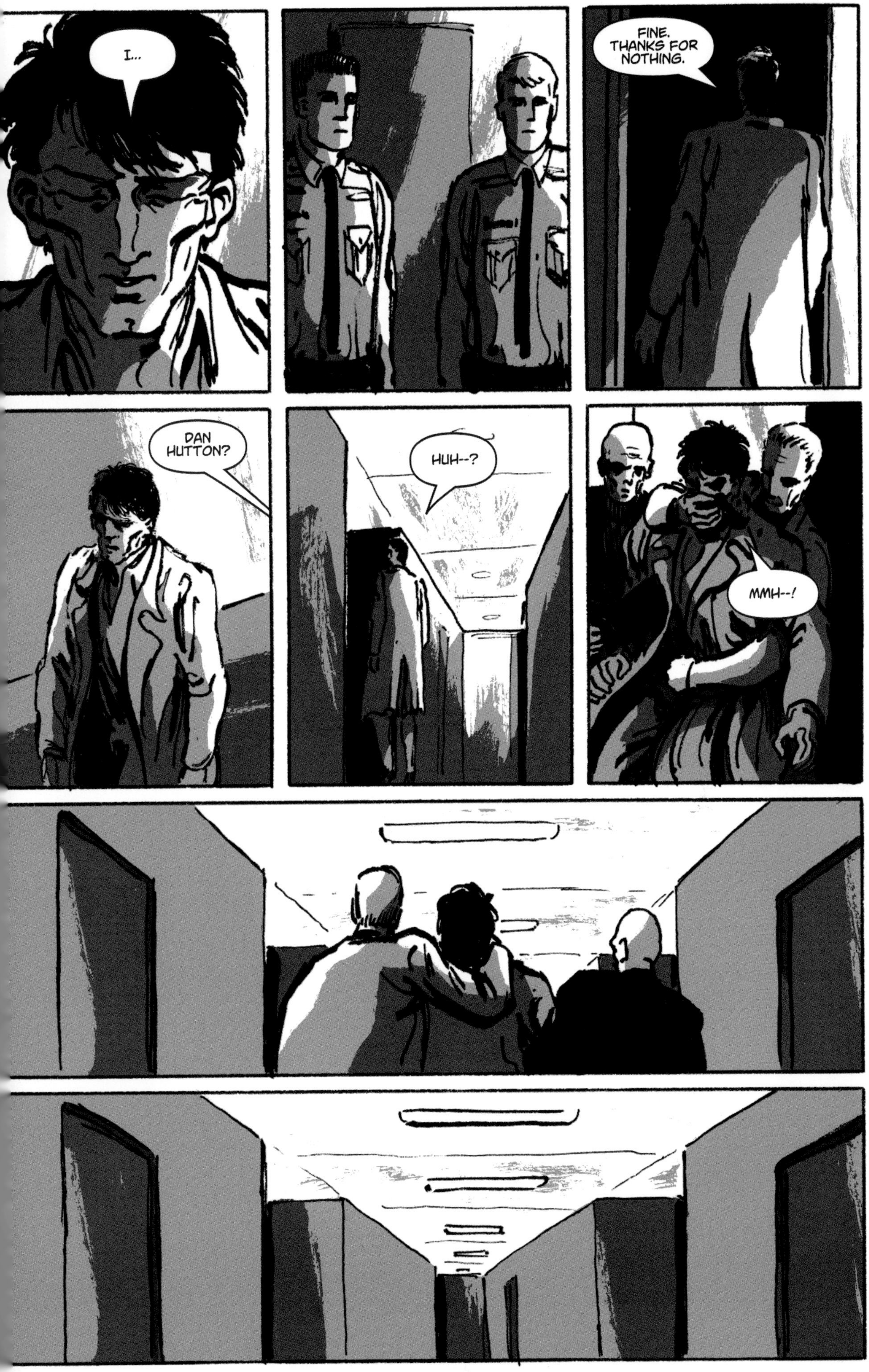
I...
FINE. THANKS FOR NOTHING.
DAN HUTTON?
HUH--?
MMH--!

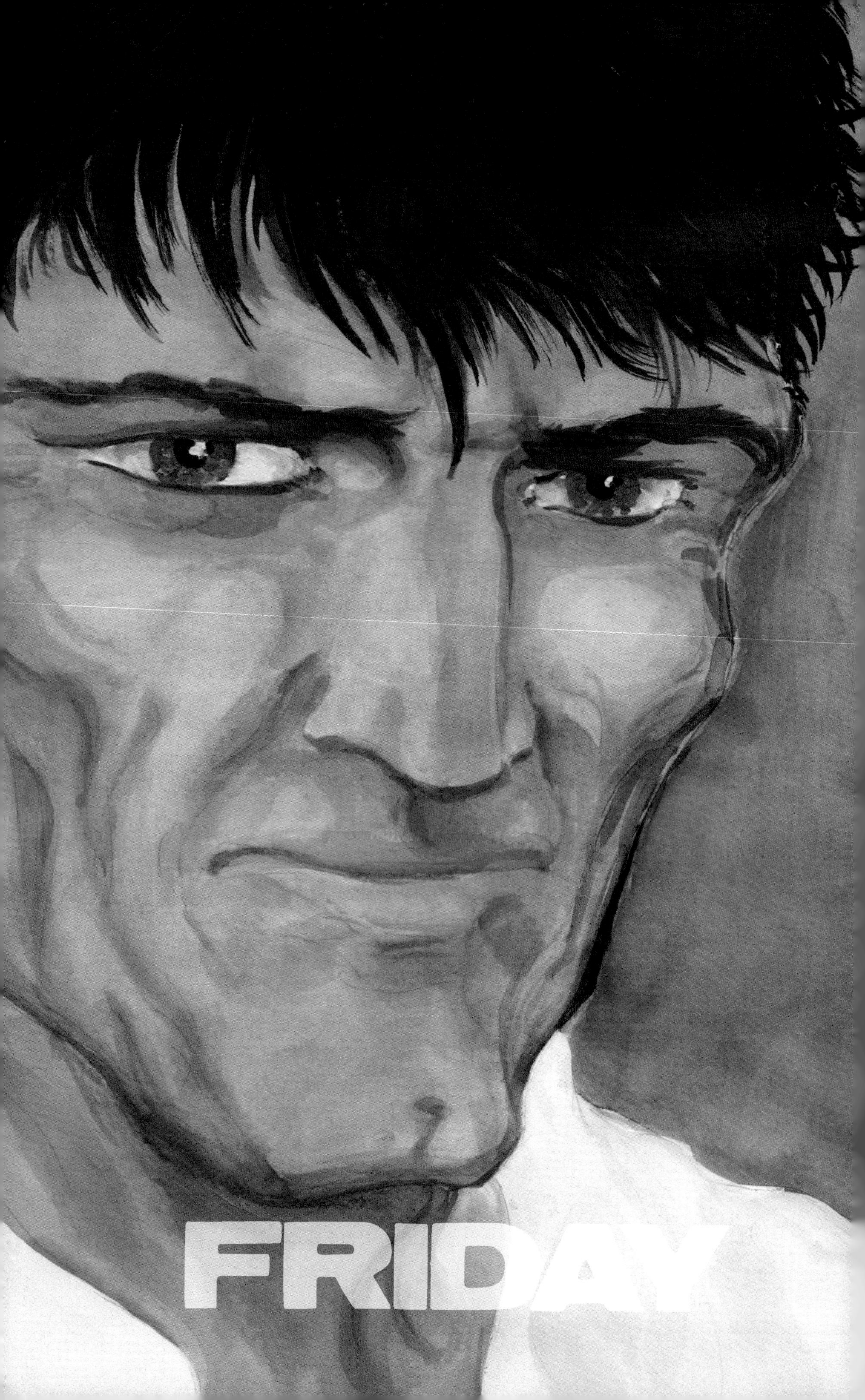
FRIDAY

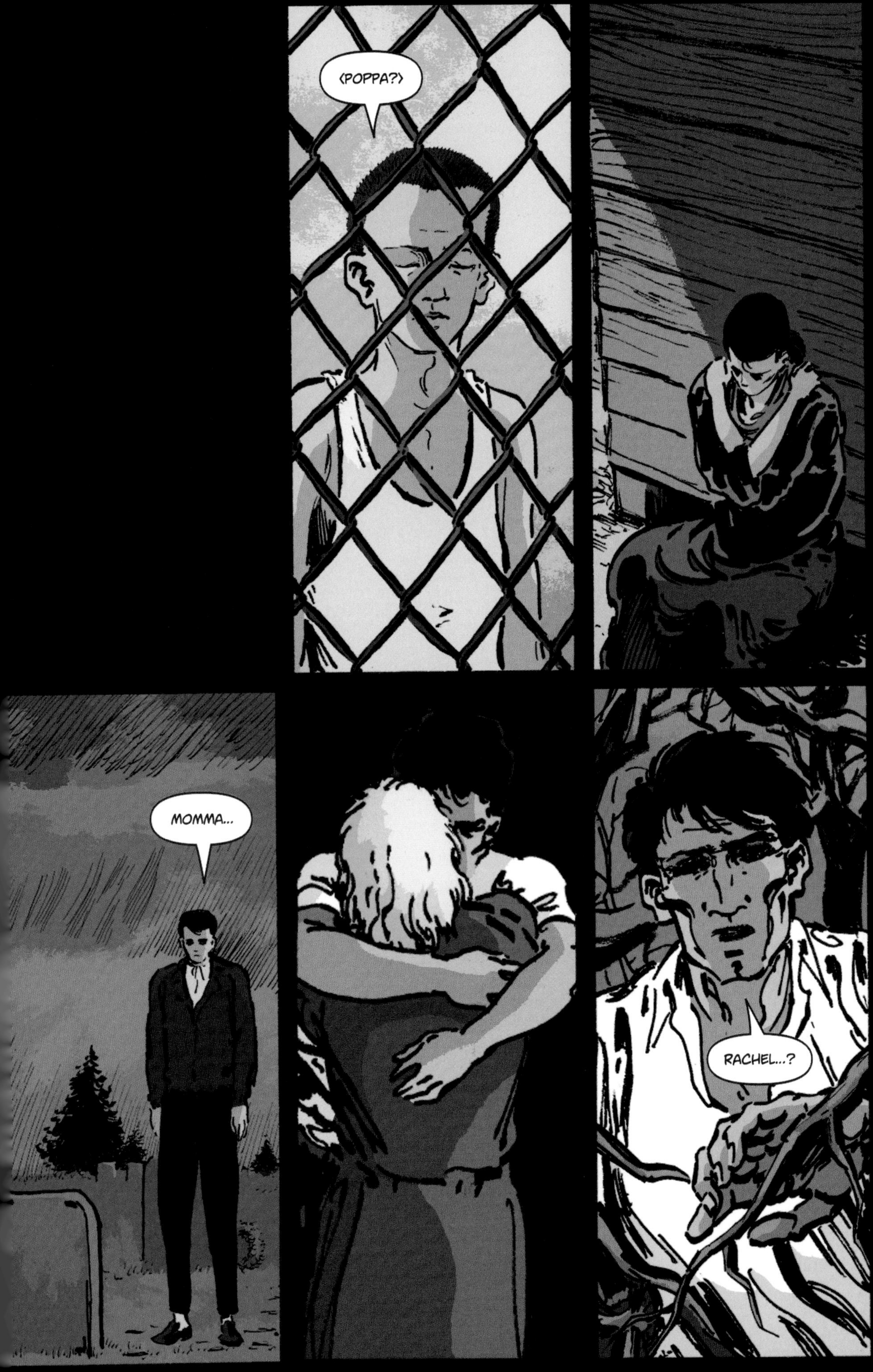
‹POPPA?›
MOMMA...
RACHEL...?

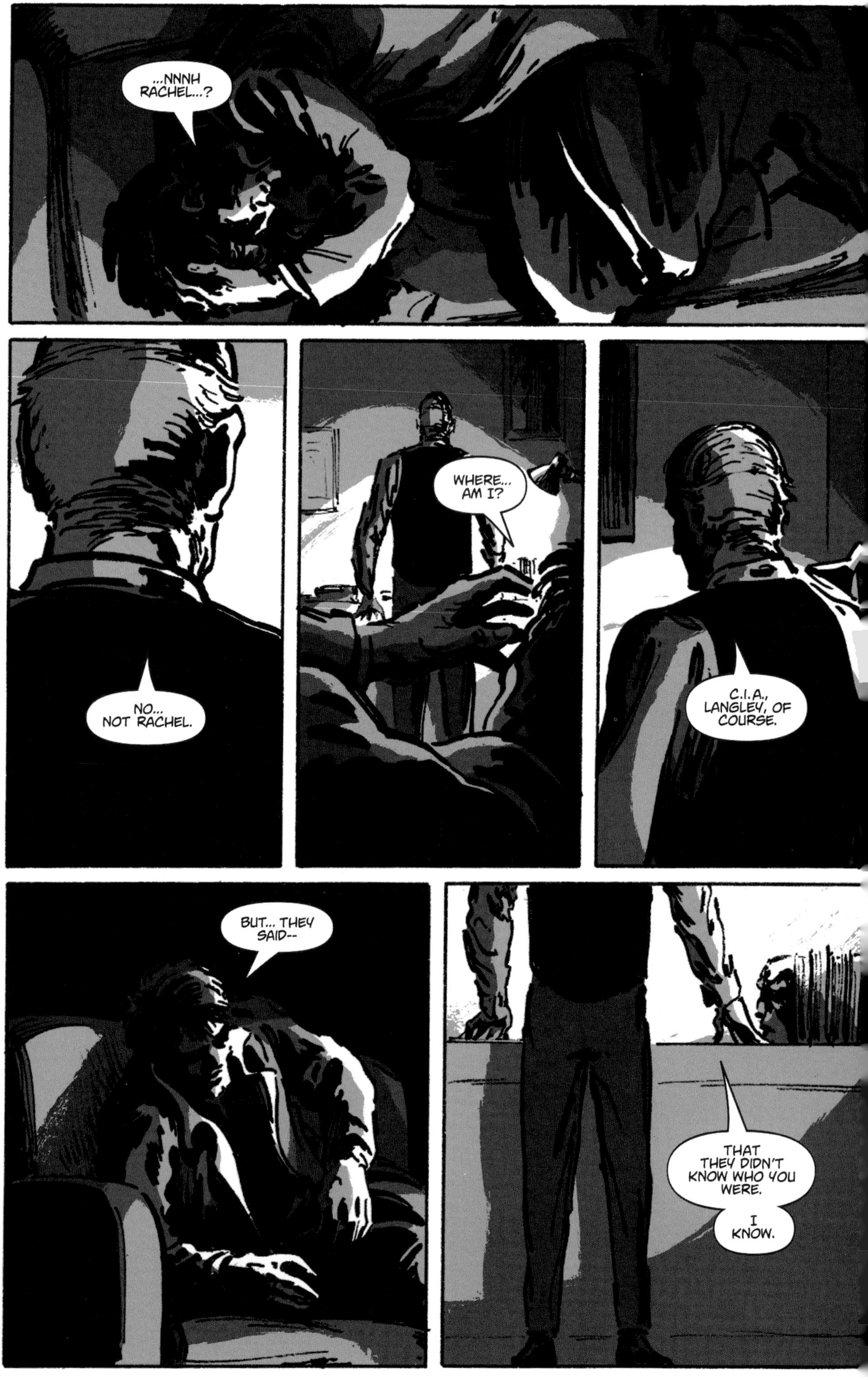
...NNNH RACHEL...?
NO... NOT RACHEL.
WHERE... AM I?
C.I.A., LANGLEY, OF COURSE.
BUT... THEY SAID--
THAT THEY DIDN'T KNOW WHO YOU WERE.
I KNOW.

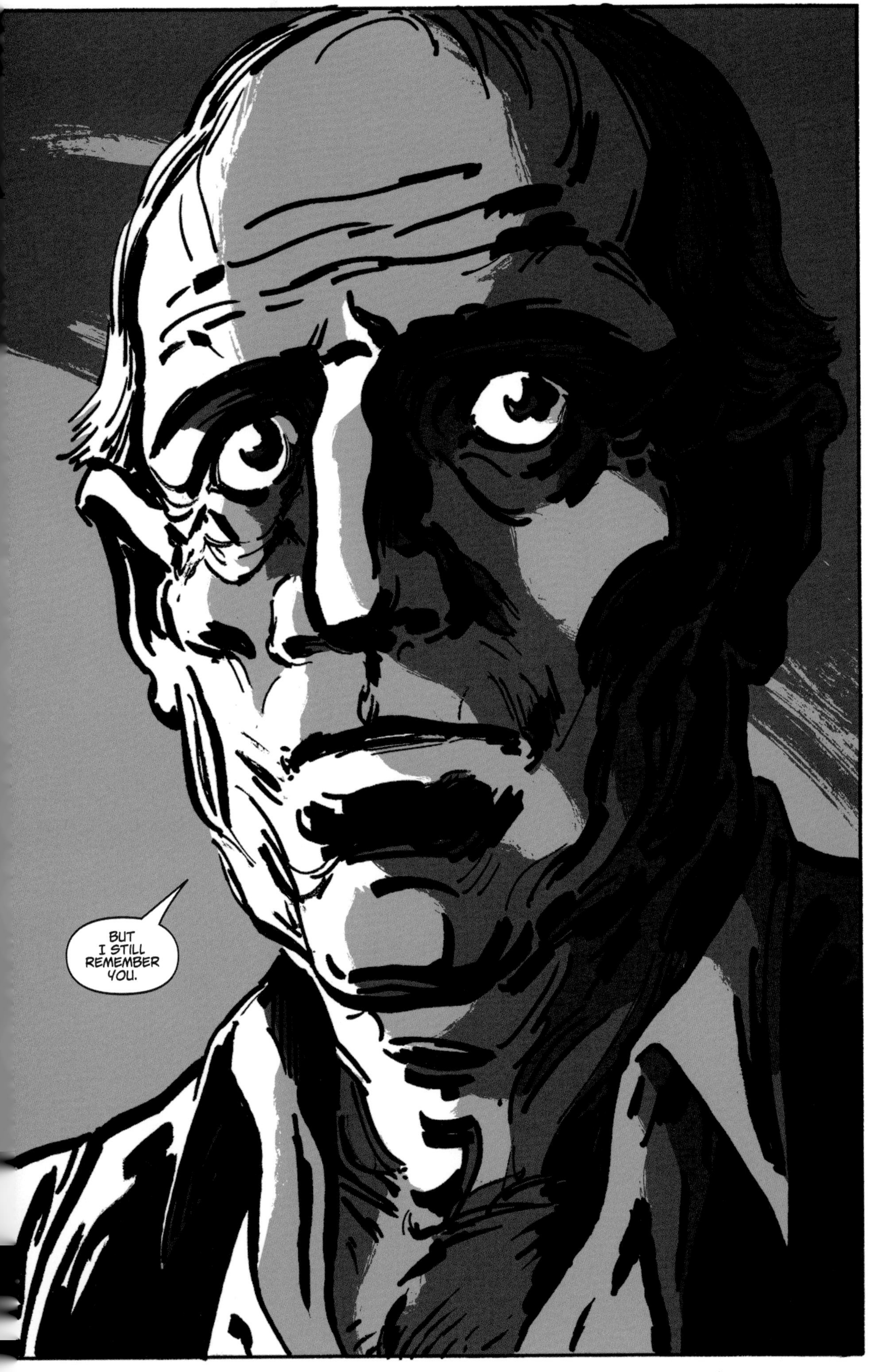
BUT I STILL REMEMBER YOU.

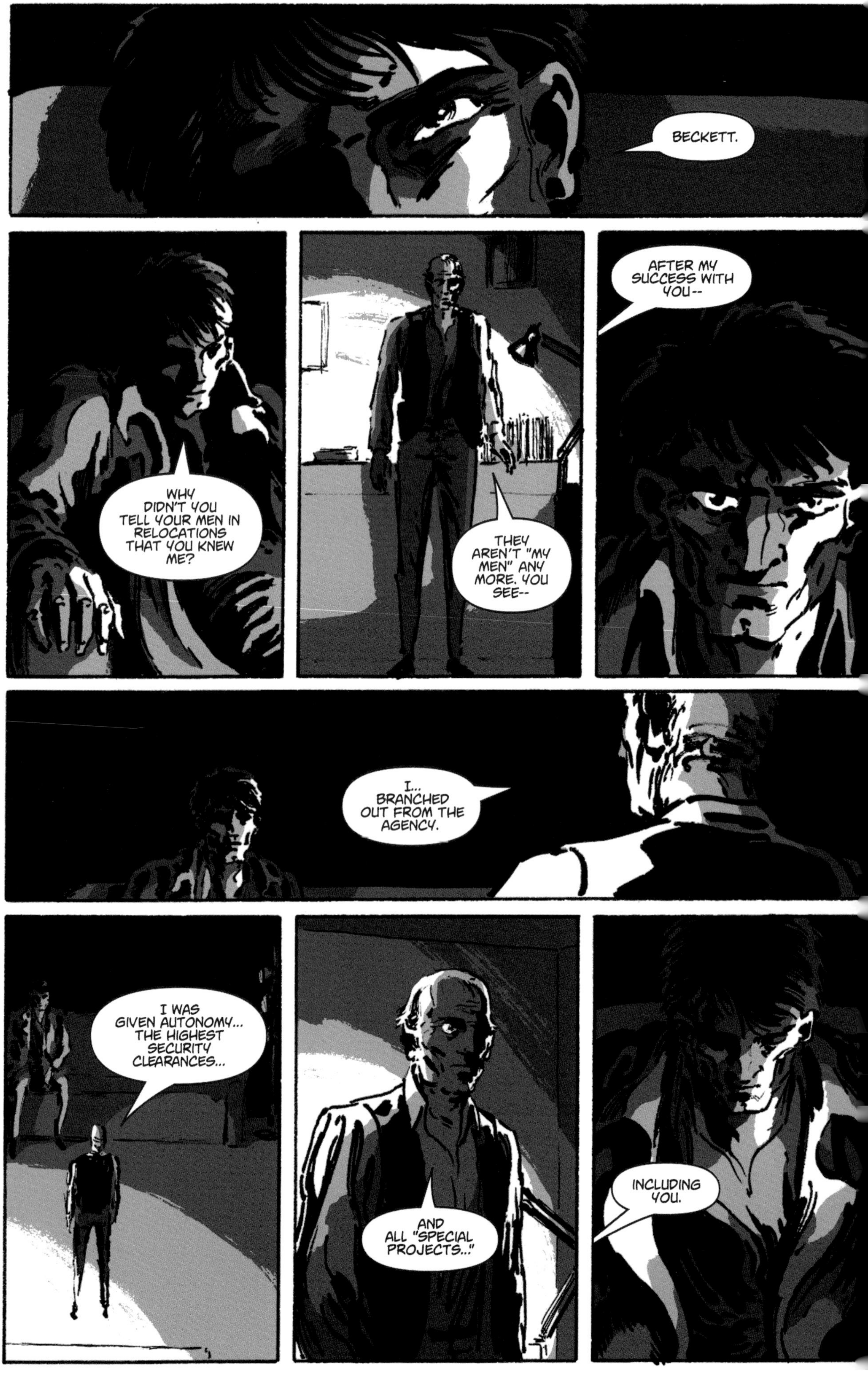
BECKETT.
WHY DIDN'T YOU TELL YOUR MEN IN RELOCATIONS THAT YOU KNEW ME?
THEY AREN'T "MY MEN" ANY MORE. YOU SEE--
AFTER MY SUCCESS WITH YOU--
I... BRANCHED OUT FROM THE AGENCY.
I WAS GIVEN AUTONOMY... THE HIGHEST SECURITY CLEARANCES...
AND ALL "SPECIAL PROJECTS..."
INCLUDING YOU.

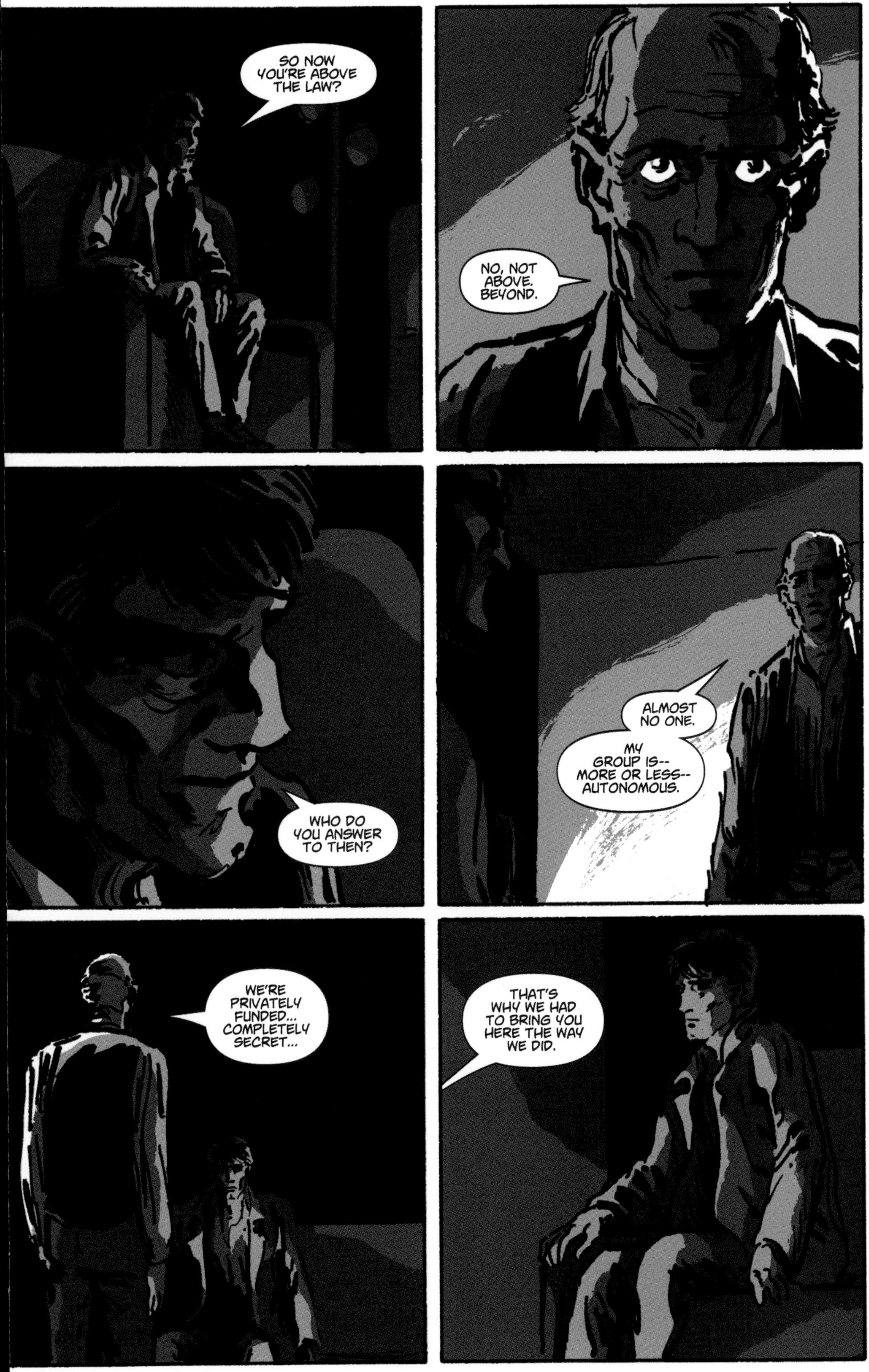
SO NOW YOU'RE ABOVE THE LAW?
NO, NOT ABOVE. BEYOND.
WHO DO YOU ANSWER TO THEN?
ALMOST NO ONE.
MY GROUP IS-- MORE OR LESS-- AUTONOMOUS.
WE'RE PRIVATELY FUNDED... COMPLETELY SECRET...
THAT'S WHY WE HAD TO BRING YOU HERE THE WAY WE DID.

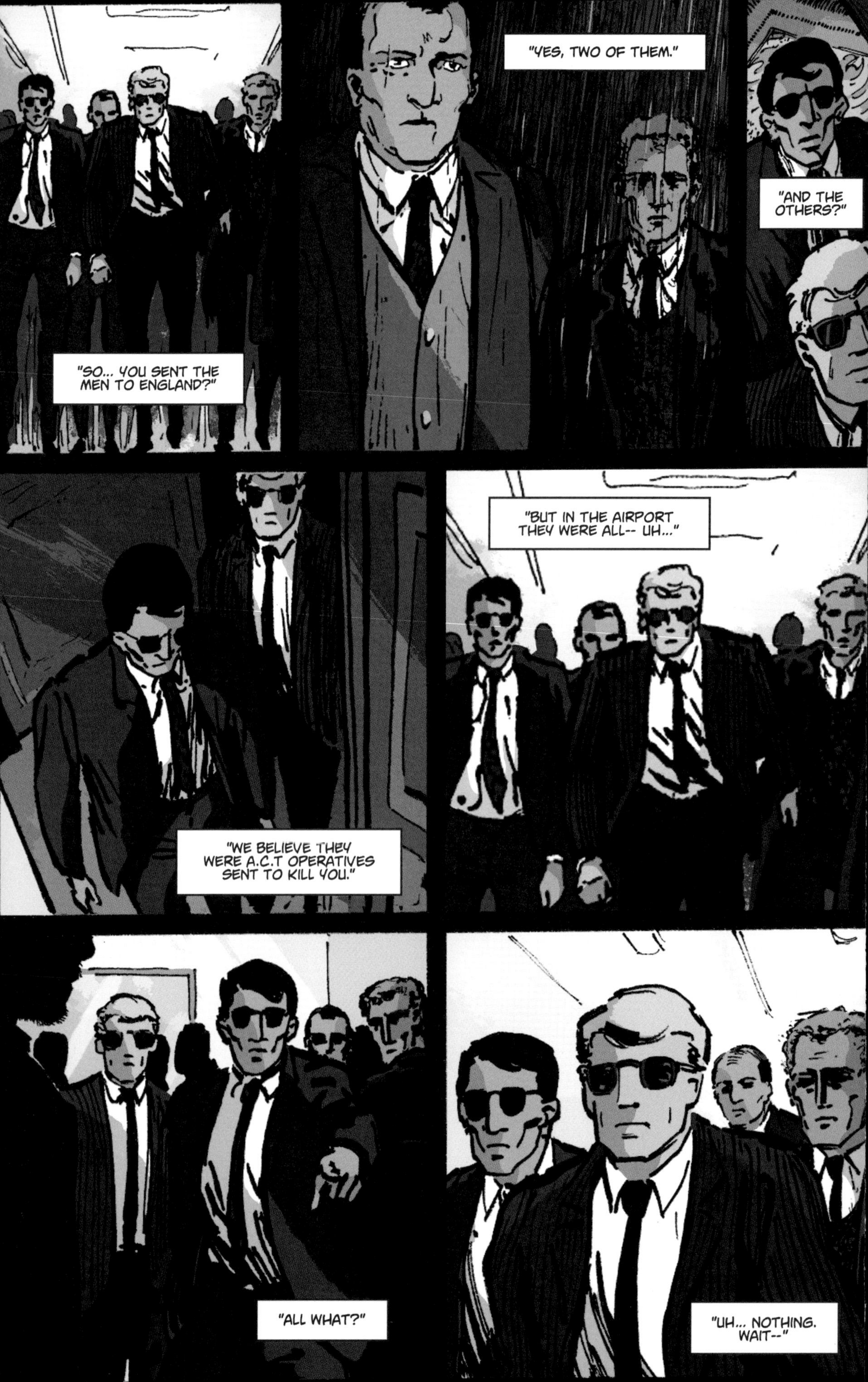
"SO... YOU SENT THE MEN TO ENGLAND?"
"YES, TWO OF THEM."
"AND THE OTHERS?"
"WE BELIEVE THEY WERE A.C.T OPERATIVES SENT TO KILL YOU."
"BUT IN THE AIRPORT THEY WERE ALL-- UH..."
"ALL WHAT?"
"UH... NOTHING. WAIT--"

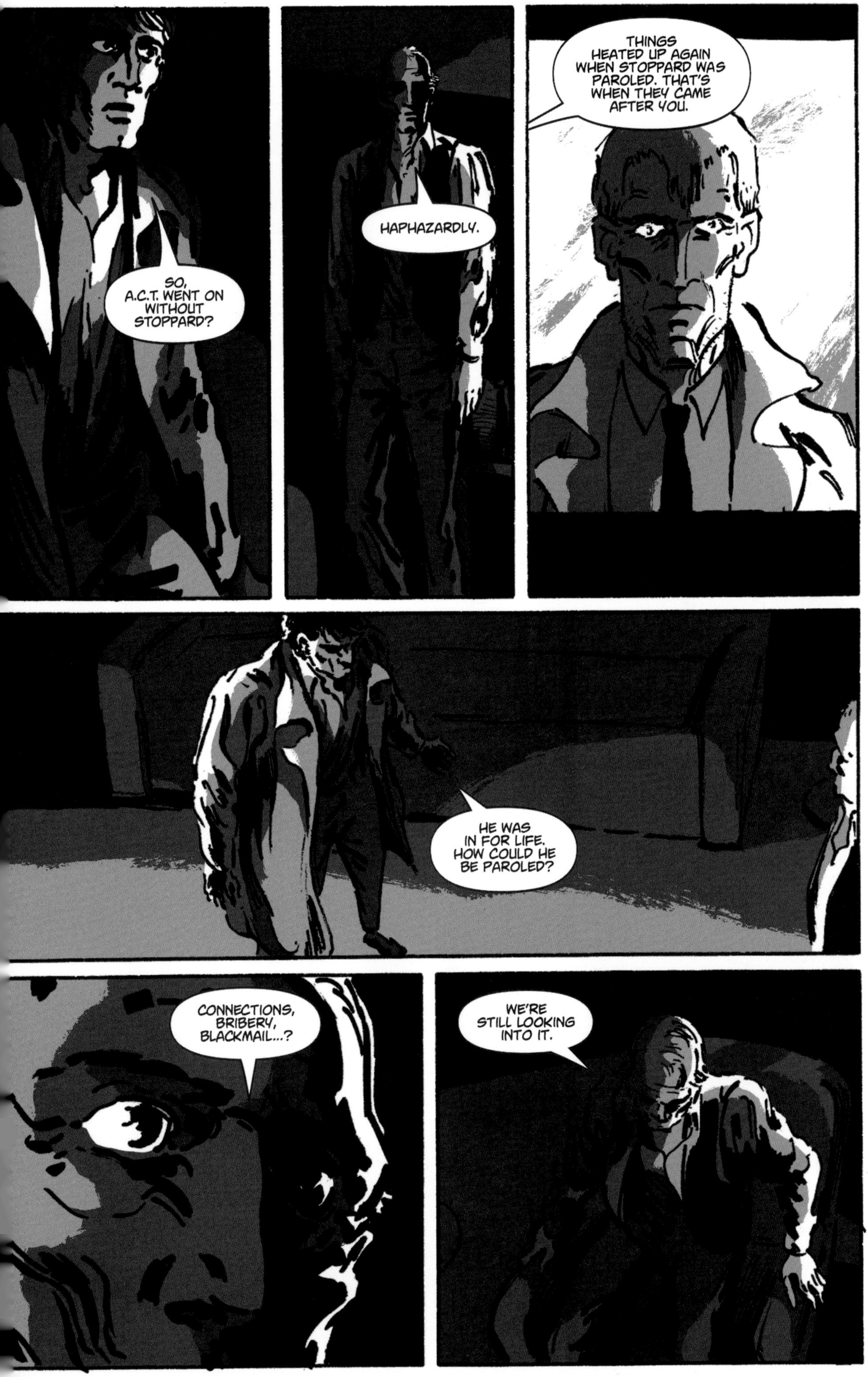
SO, A.C.T. WENT ON WITHOUT STOPPARD?
HAPHAZARDLY.
THINGS HEATED UP AGAIN WHEN STOPPARD WAS PAROLED. THAT'S WHEN THEY CAME AFTER YOU.
HE WAS IN FOR LIFE. HOW COULD HE BE PAROLED?
CONNECTIONS, BRIBERY, BLACKMAIL...?
WE'RE STILL LOOKING INTO IT.

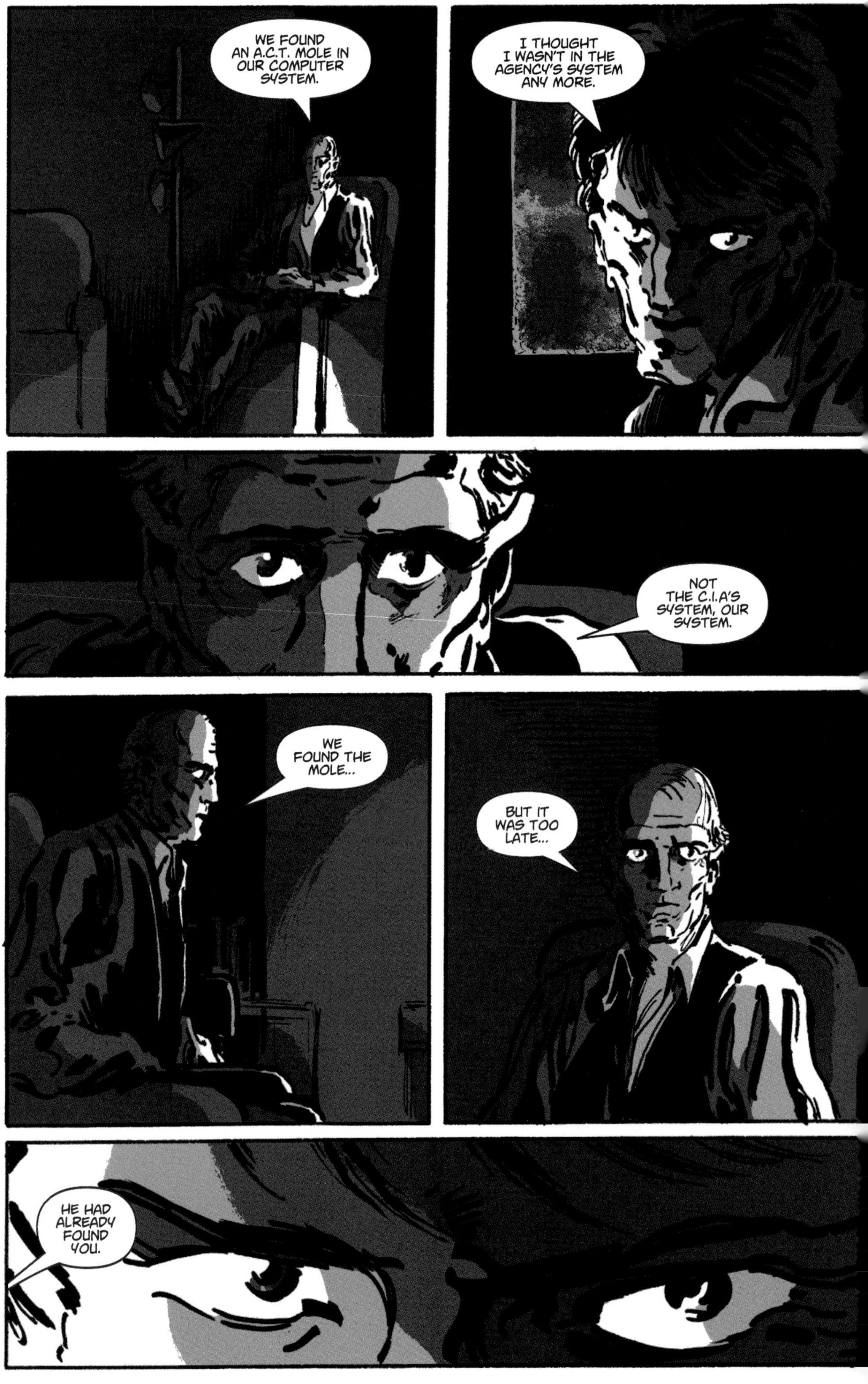
WE FOUND AN A.C.T. MOLE IN OUR COMPUTER SYSTEM.
I THOUGHT I WASN'T IN THE AGENCY'S SYSTEM ANY MORE.
NOT THE C.I.A'S SYSTEM, OUR SYSTEM.
WE FOUND THE MOLE...
BUT IT WAS TOO LATE...
HE HAD ALREADY FOUND YOU.

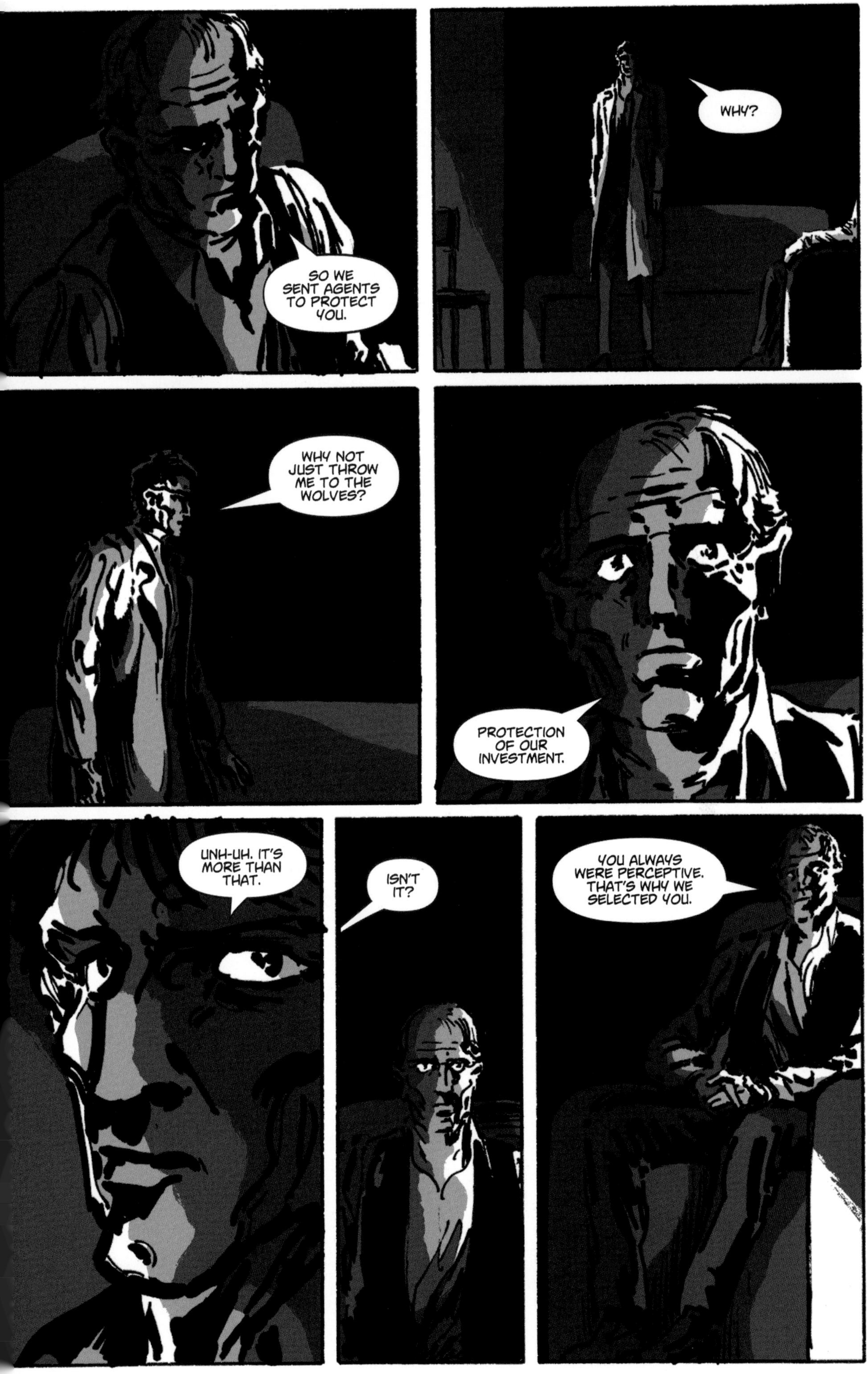
SO WE SENT AGENTS TO PROTECT YOU.
WHY?
WHY NOT JUST THROW ME TO THE WOLVES?
PROTECTION OF OUR INVESTMENT.
UNH-UH. IT'S MORE THAN THAT.
ISN'T IT?
YOU ALWAYS WERE PERCEPTIVE. THAT'S WHY WE SELECTED YOU.

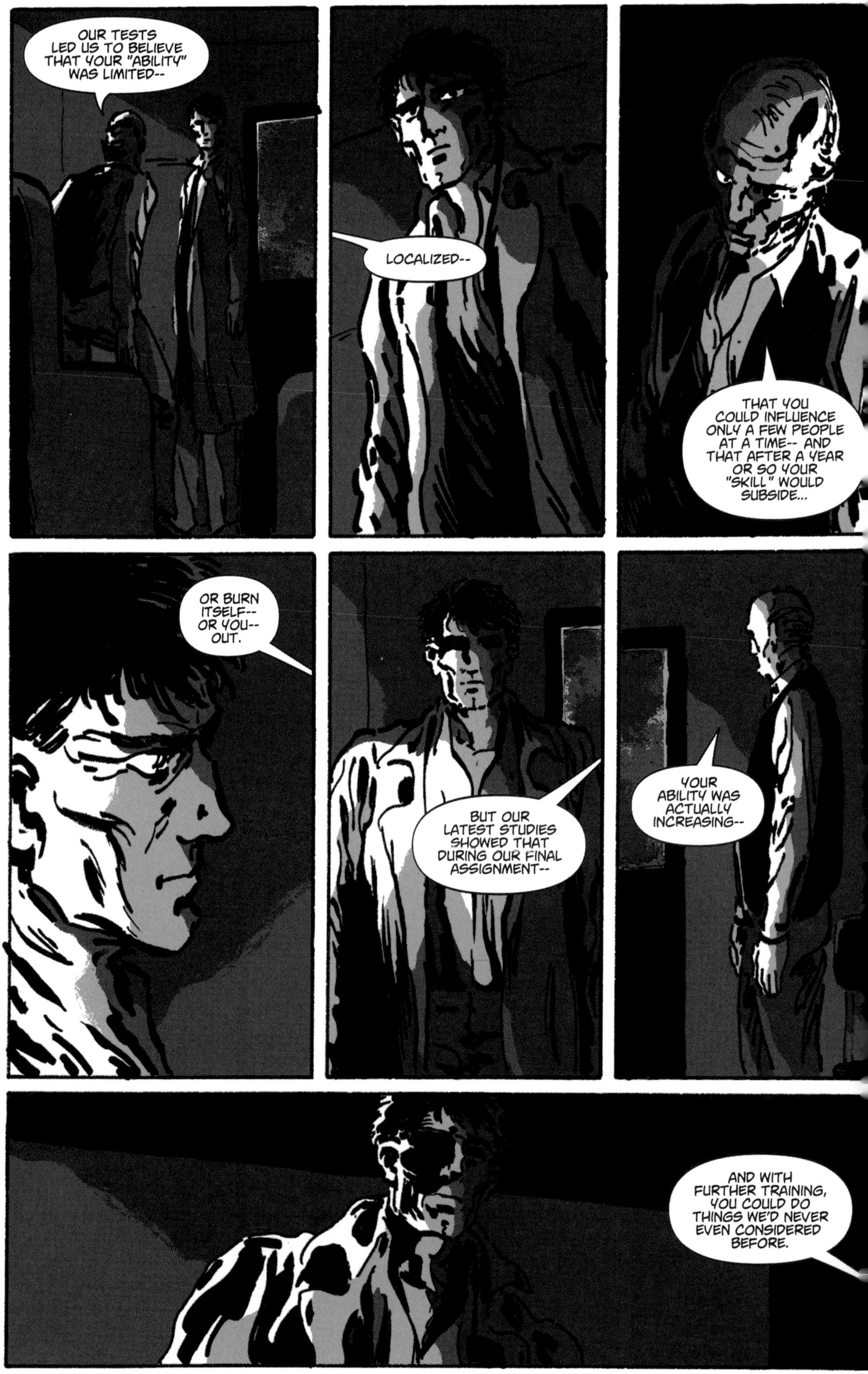
OUR TESTS LED US TO BELIEVE THAT YOUR "ABILITY" WAS LIMITED--
LOCALIZED--
THAT YOU COULD INFLUENCE ONLY A FEW PEOPLE AT A TIME-- AND THAT AFTER A YEAR OR SO YOUR "SKILL" WOULD SUBSIDE...
OR BURN ITSELF-- OR YOU-- OUT.
BUT OUR LATEST STUDIES SHOWED THAT DURING OUR FINAL ASSIGNMENT--
YOUR ABILITY WAS ACTUALLY INCREASING--
AND WITH FURTHER TRAINING, YOU COULD DO THINGS WE'D NEVER EVEN CONSIDERED BEFORE.

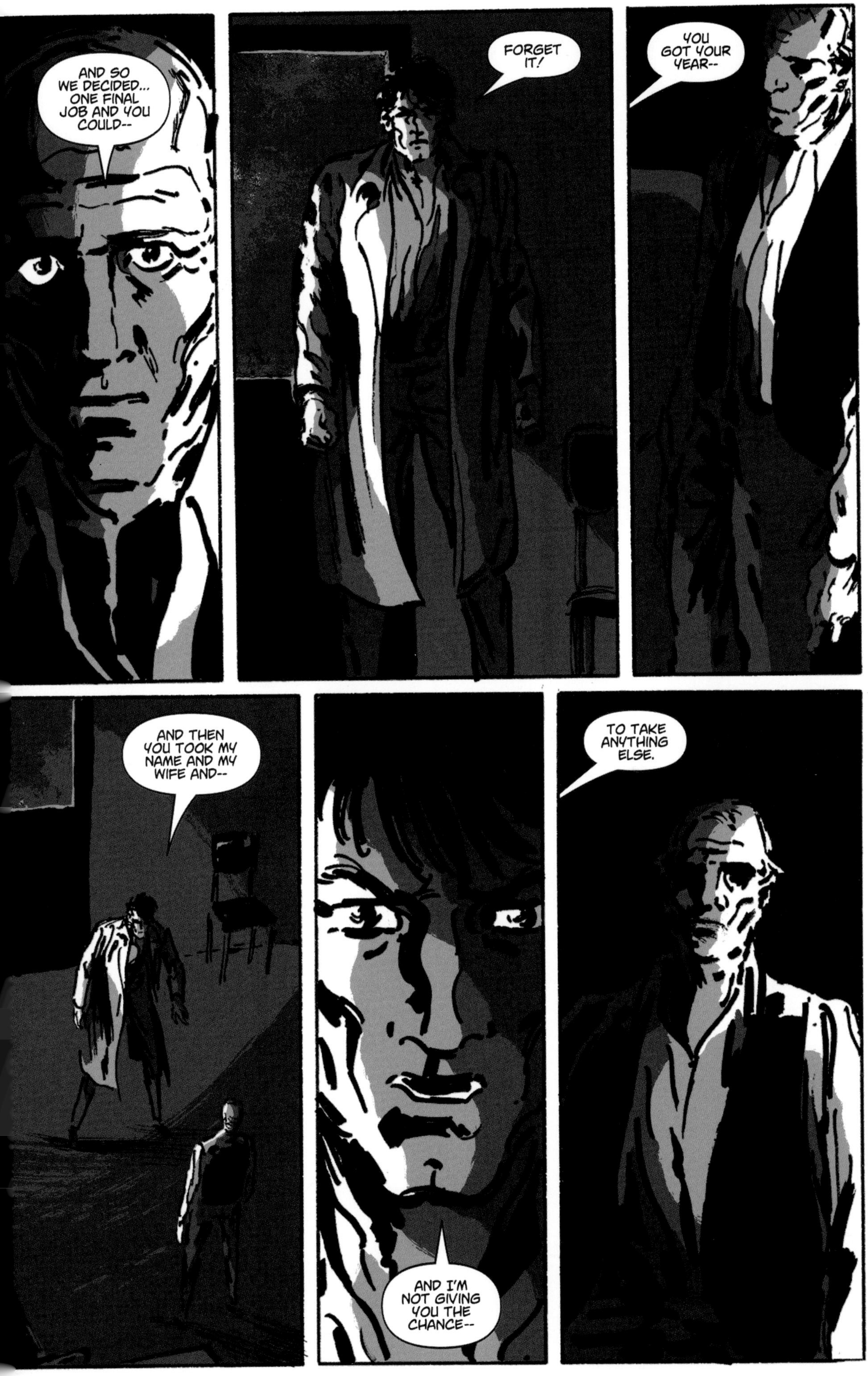
AND SO WE DECIDED... ONE FINAL JOB AND YOU COULD--
FORGET IT!
YOU GOT YOUR YEAR--
AND THEN YOU TOOK MY NAME AND MY WIFE AND--
AND I'M NOT GIVING YOU THE CHANCE--
TO TAKE ANYTHING ELSE.

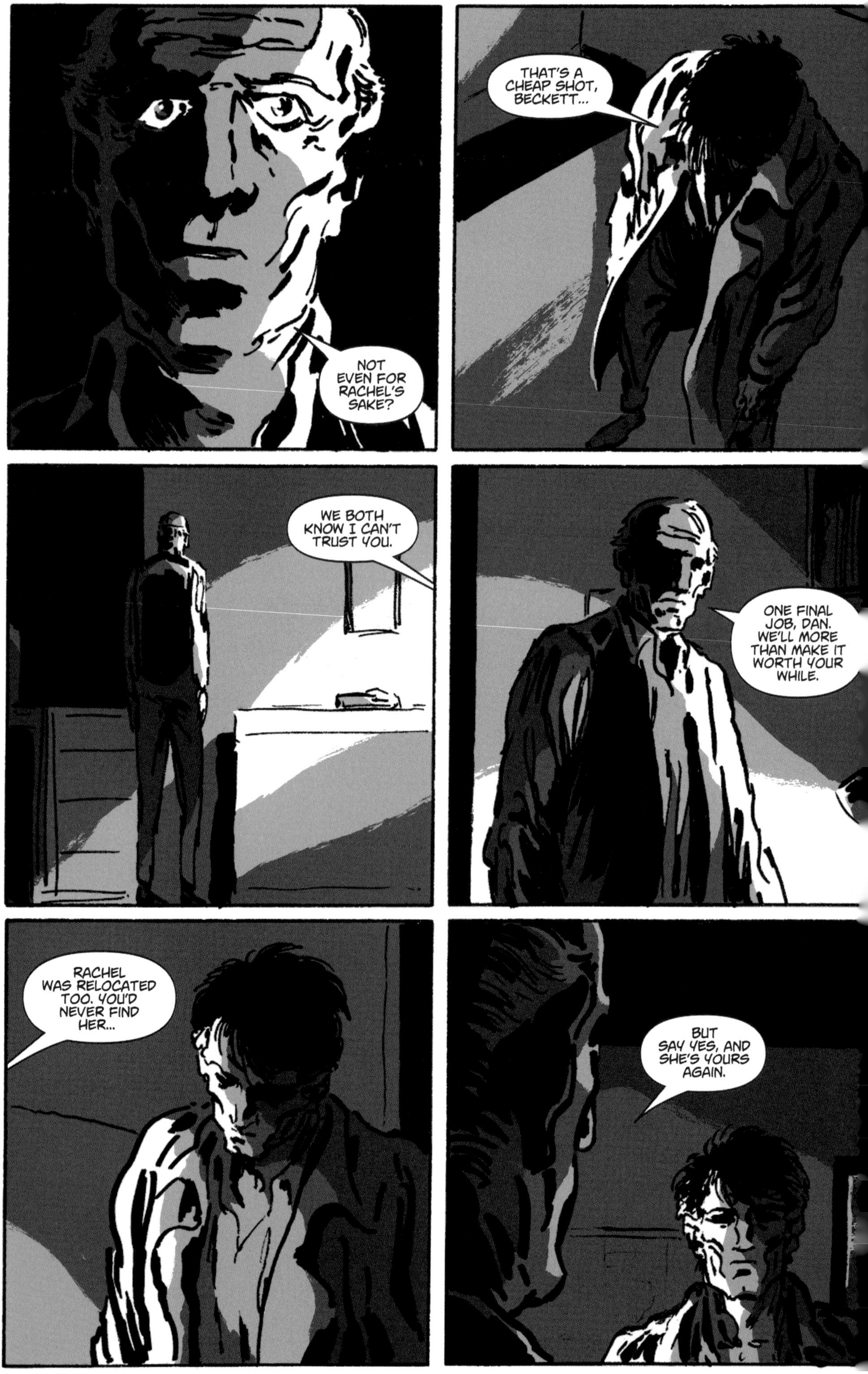
NOT EVEN FOR RACHEL'S SAKE?
THAT'S A CHEAP SHOT, BECKETT...
WE BOTH KNOW I CAN'T TRUST YOU.
ONE FINAL JOB, DAN. WE'LL MORE THAN MAKE IT WORTH YOUR WHILE.
RACHEL WAS RELOCATED TOO. YOU'D NEVER FIND HER...
BUT SAY YES, AND SHE'S YOURS AGAIN.

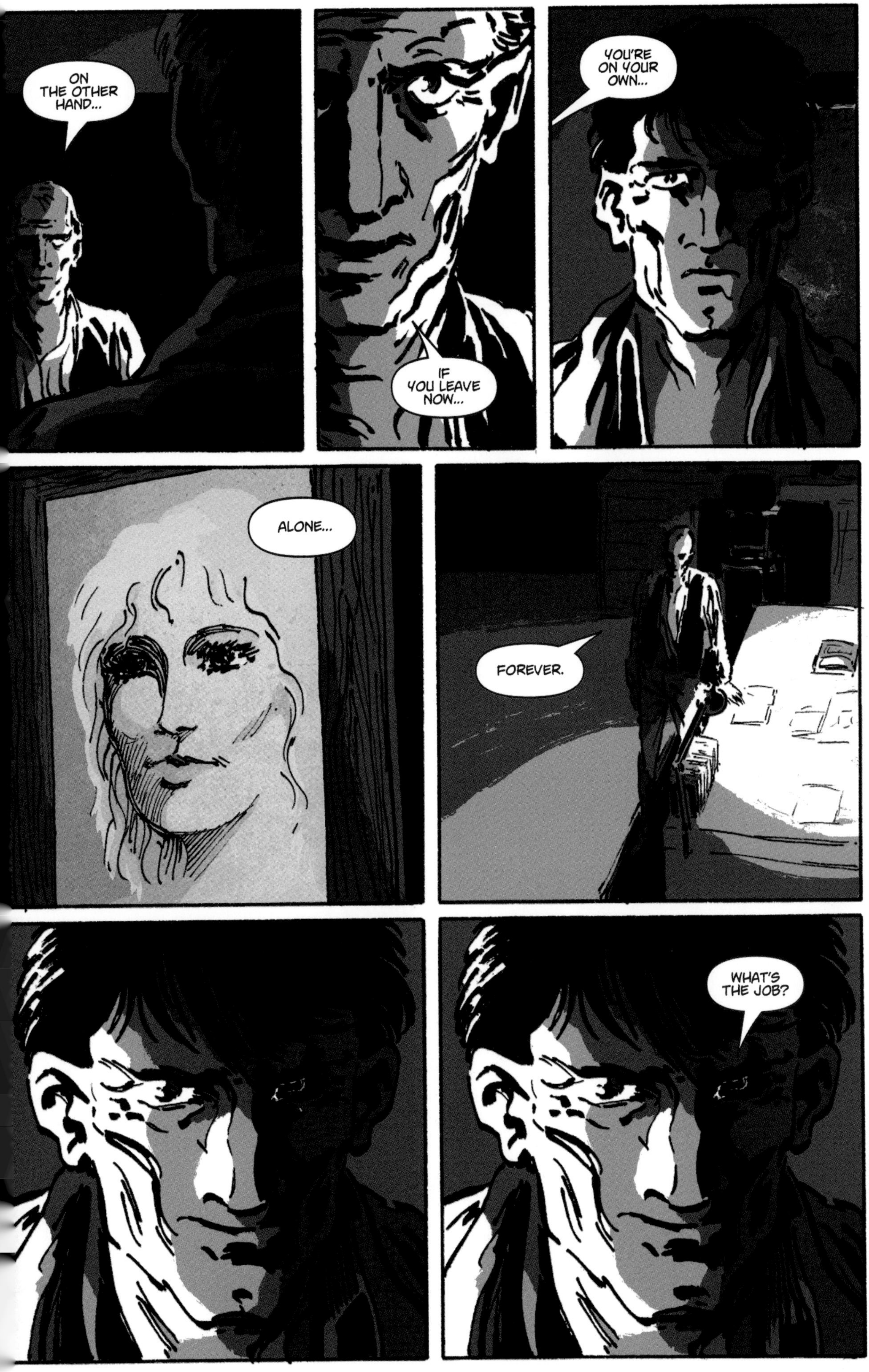
ON
THE OTHER
HAND...
IF
YOU LEAVE
NOW...
YOU'RE
ON YOUR
OWN...
ALONE...
FOREVER.
WHAT'S
THE JOB?

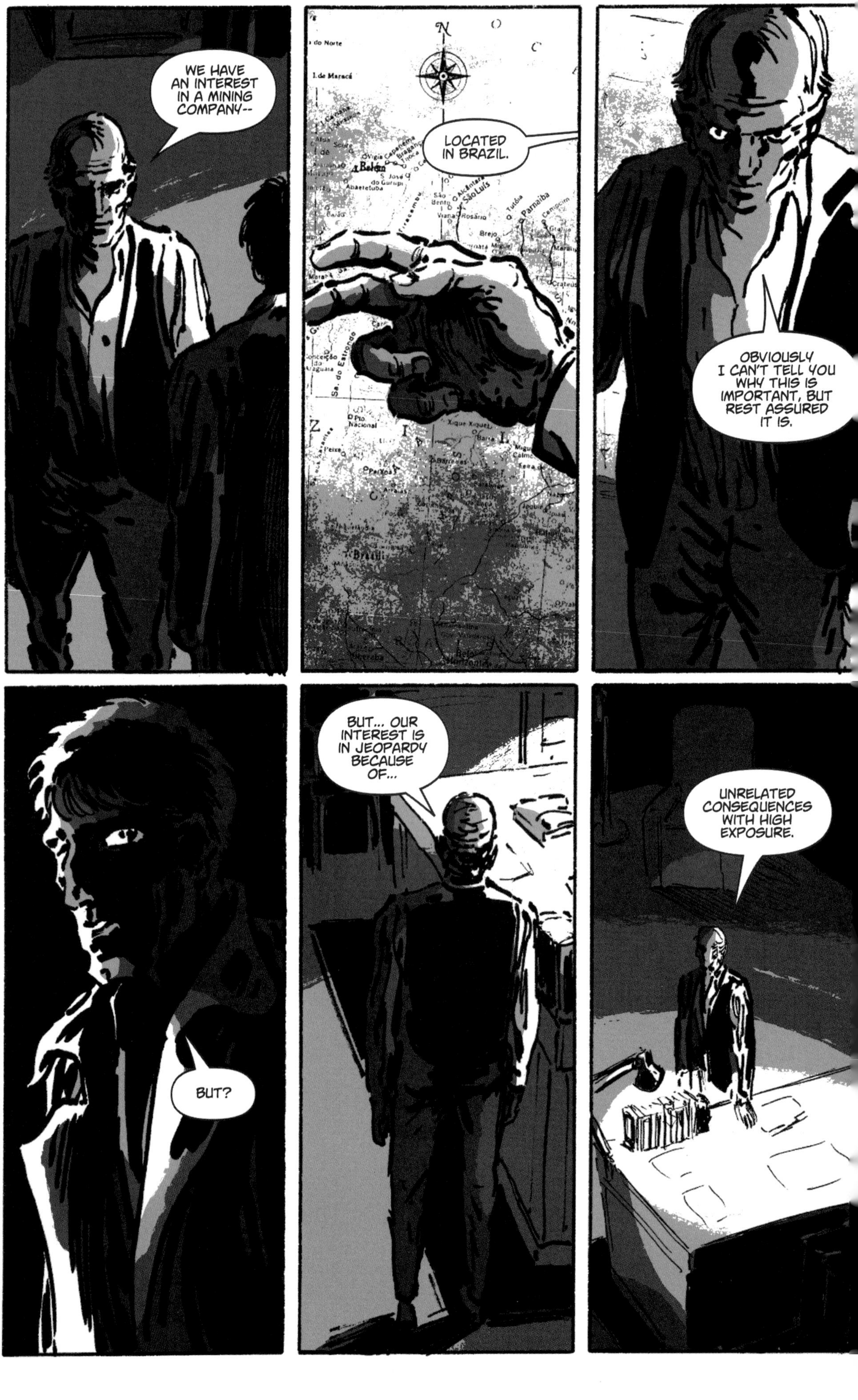
WE HAVE AN INTEREST IN A MINING COMPANY--
LOCATED IN BRAZIL.
OBVIOUSLY I CAN'T TELL YOU WHY THIS IS IMPORTANT, BUT REST ASSURED IT IS.
BUT?
BUT... OUR INTEREST IS IN JEOPARDY BECAUSE OF...
UNRELATED CONSEQUENCES WITH HIGH EXPOSURE.

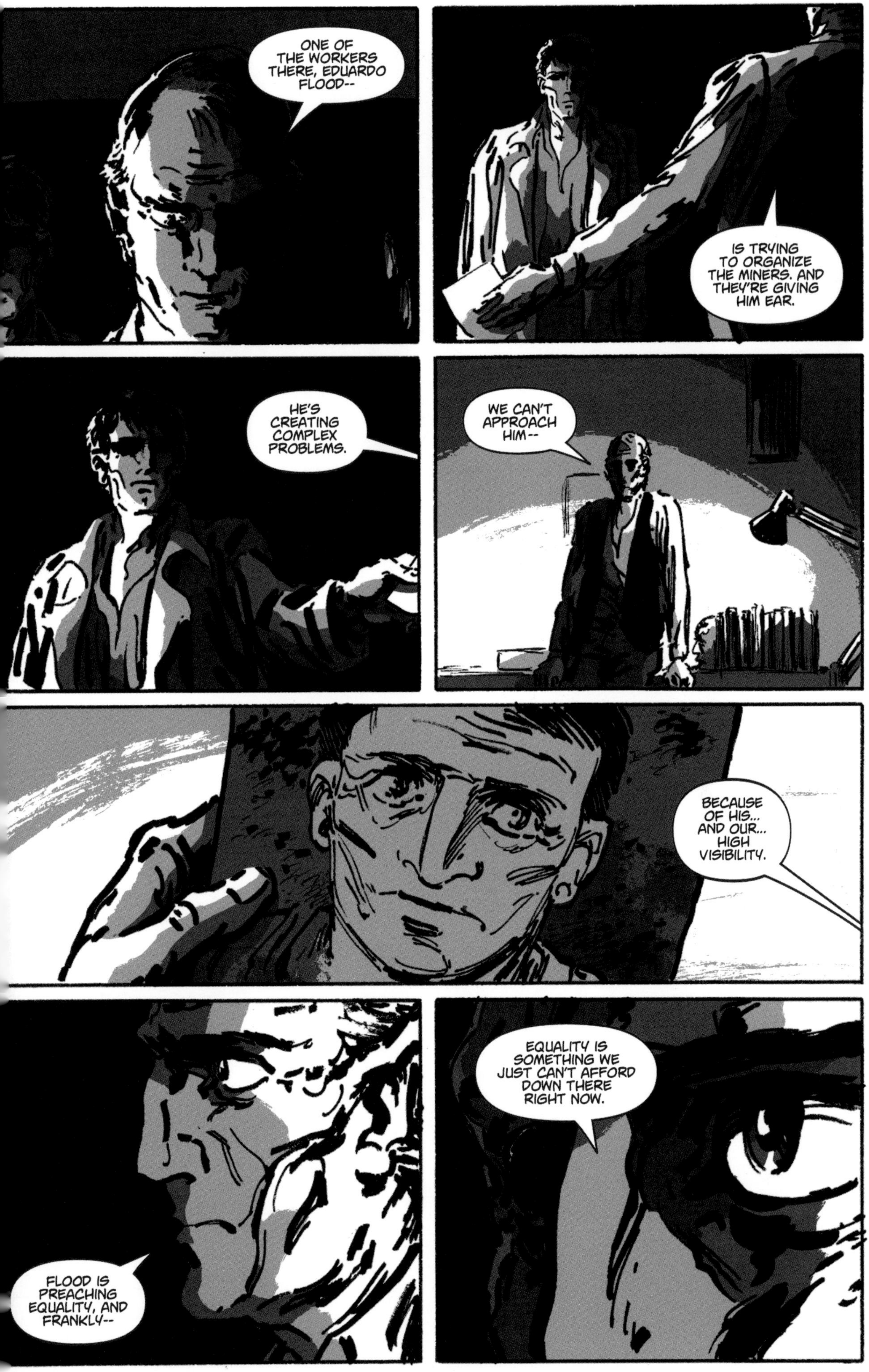
ONE OF THE WORKERS THERE, EDUARDO FLOOD--
IS TRYING TO ORGANIZE THE MINERS. AND THEY'RE GIVING HIM EAR.
HE'S CREATING COMPLEX PROBLEMS.
WE CAN'T APPROACH HIM--
BECAUSE OF HIS... AND OUR... HIGH VISIBILITY.
FLOOD IS PREACHING EQUALITY, AND FRANKLY--
EQUALITY IS SOMETHING WE JUST CAN'T AFFORD DOWN THERE RIGHT NOW.

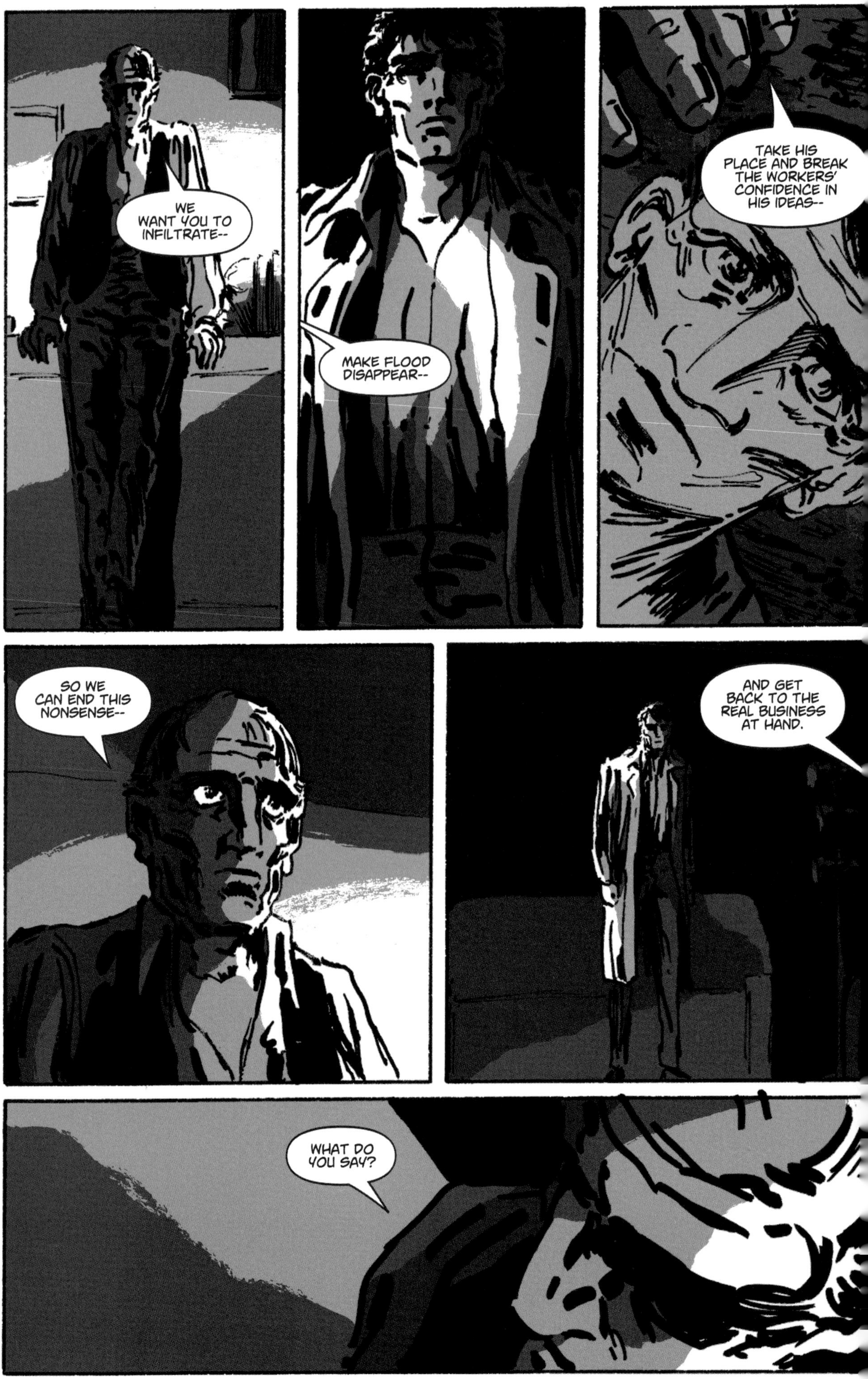
WE WANT YOU TO INFILTRATE--
MAKE FLOOD DISAPPEAR--
TAKE HIS PLACE AND BREAK THE WORKERS' CONFIDENCE IN HIS IDEAS--
SO WE CAN END THIS NONSENSE--
AND GET BACK TO THE REAL BUSINESS AT HAND.
WHAT DO YOU SAY?

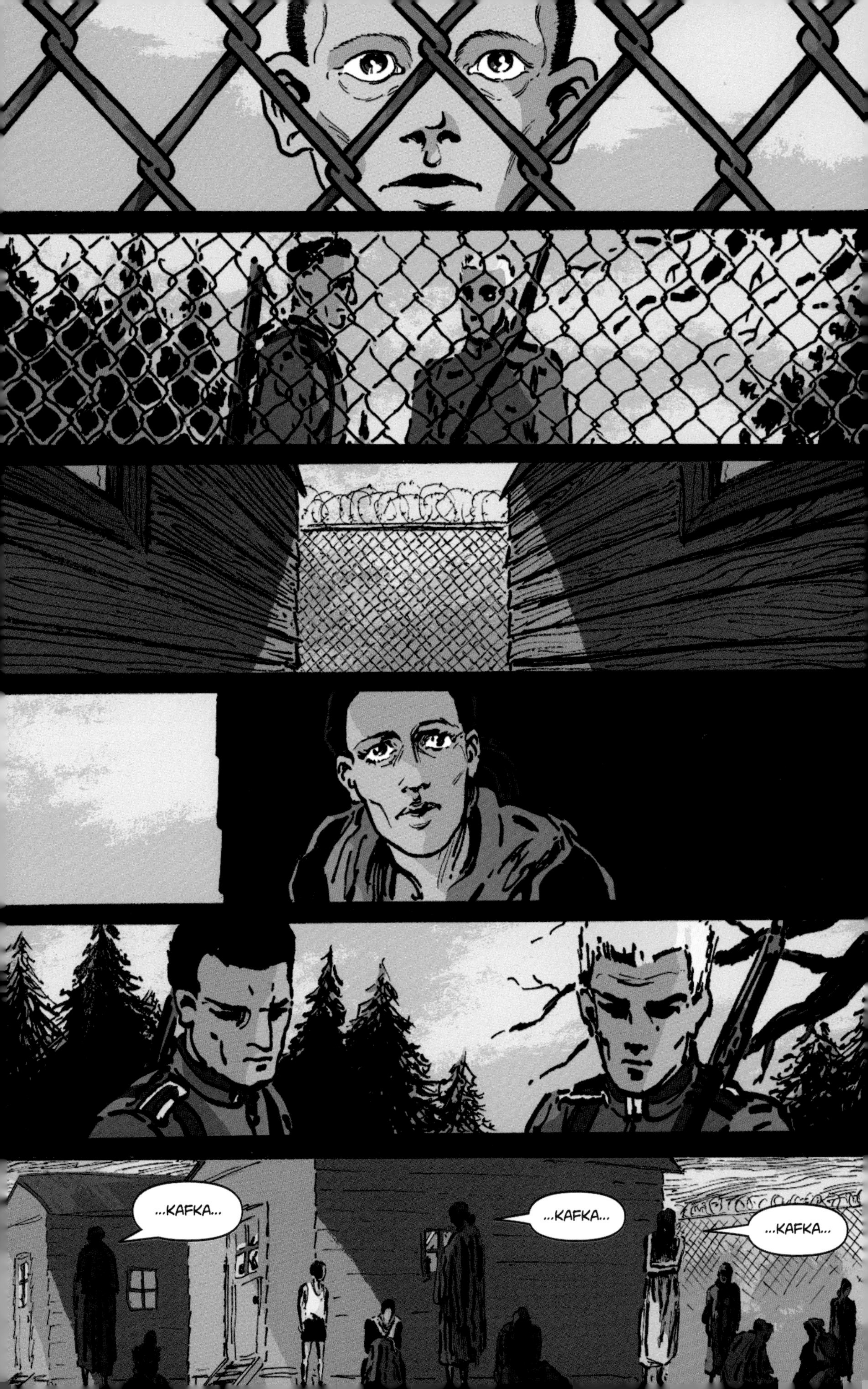
...KAFKA...
...KAFKA...
...KAFKA...

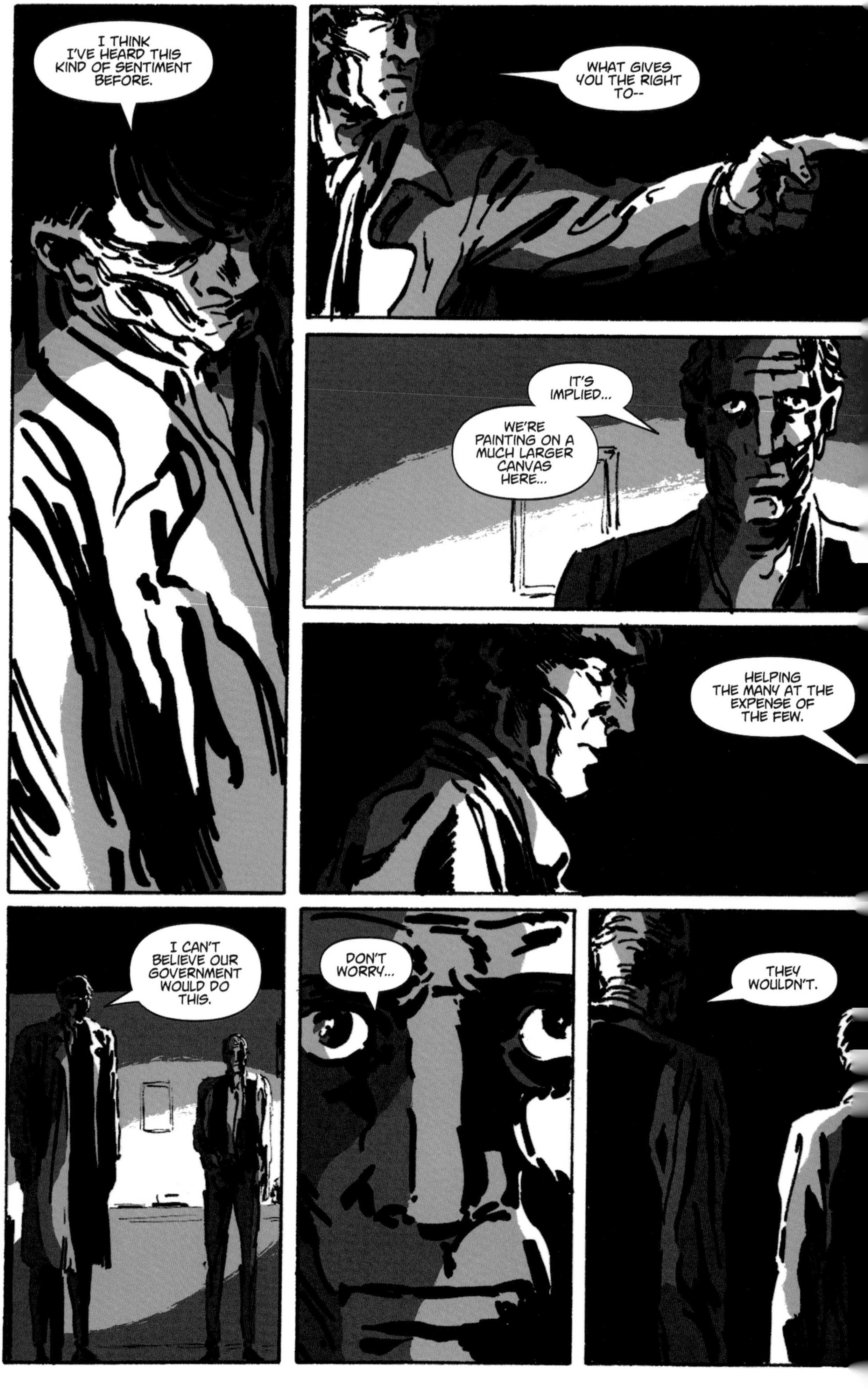
I THINK I'VE HEARD THIS KIND OF SENTIMENT BEFORE.
WHAT GIVES YOU THE RIGHT TO--
IT'S IMPLIED...
WE'RE PAINTING ON A MUCH LARGER CANVAS HERE...
HELPING THE MANY AT THE EXPENSE OF THE FEW.
I CAN'T BELIEVE OUR GOVERNMENT WOULD DO THIS.
DON'T WORRY...
THEY WOULDN'T.

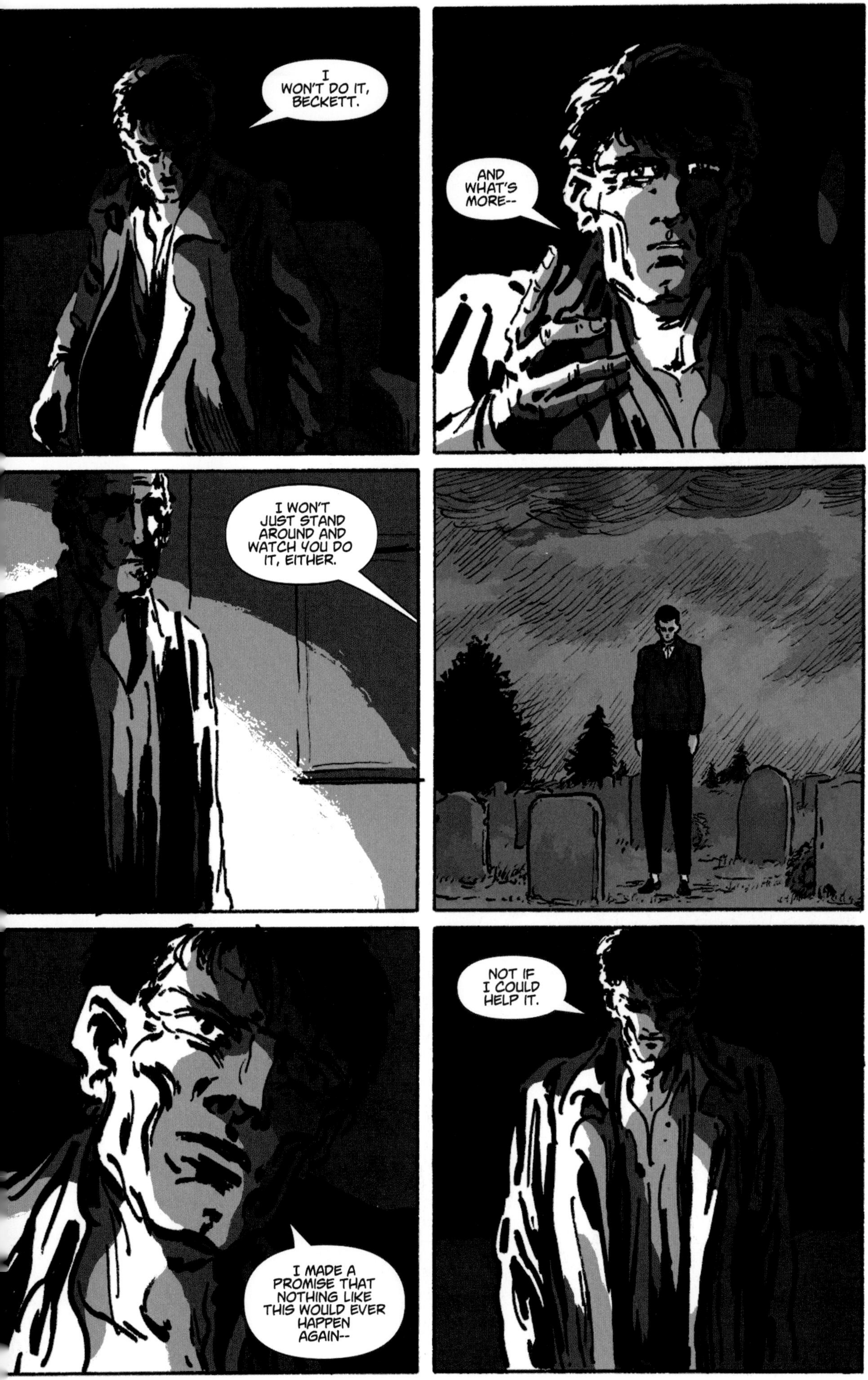
I WON'T DO IT, BECKETT.
AND WHAT'S MORE--
I WON'T JUST STAND AROUND AND WATCH YOU DO IT, EITHER.
I MADE A PROMISE THAT NOTHING LIKE THIS WOULD EVER HAPPEN AGAIN--
NOT IF I COULD HELP IT.

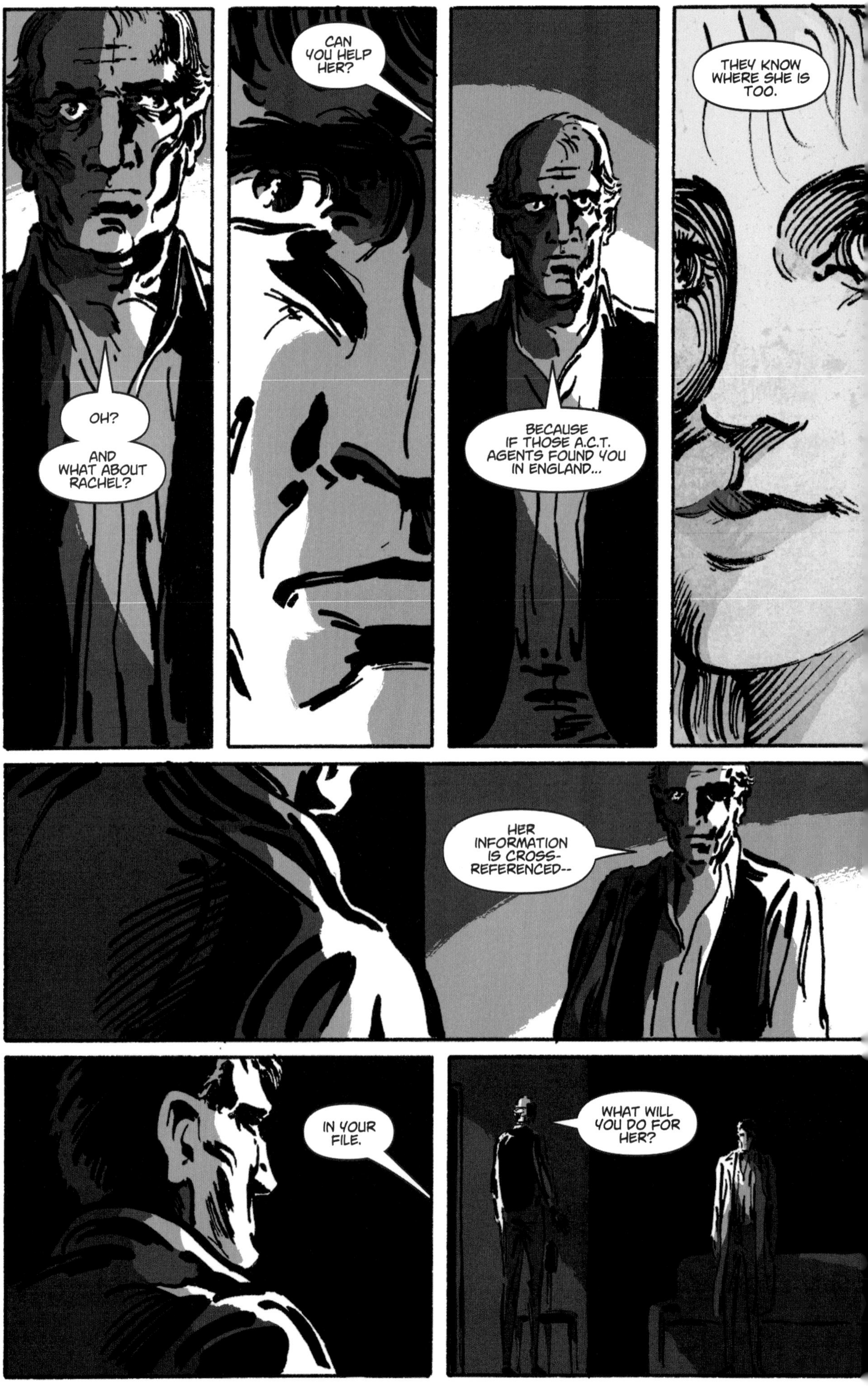
OH?
AND WHAT ABOUT RACHEL?
CAN YOU HELP HER?
BECAUSE IF THOSE A.C.T. AGENTS FOUND YOU IN ENGLAND...
THEY KNOW WHERE SHE IS TOO.
HER INFORMATION IS CROSS-REFERENCED--
IN YOUR FILE.
WHAT WILL YOU DO FOR HER?

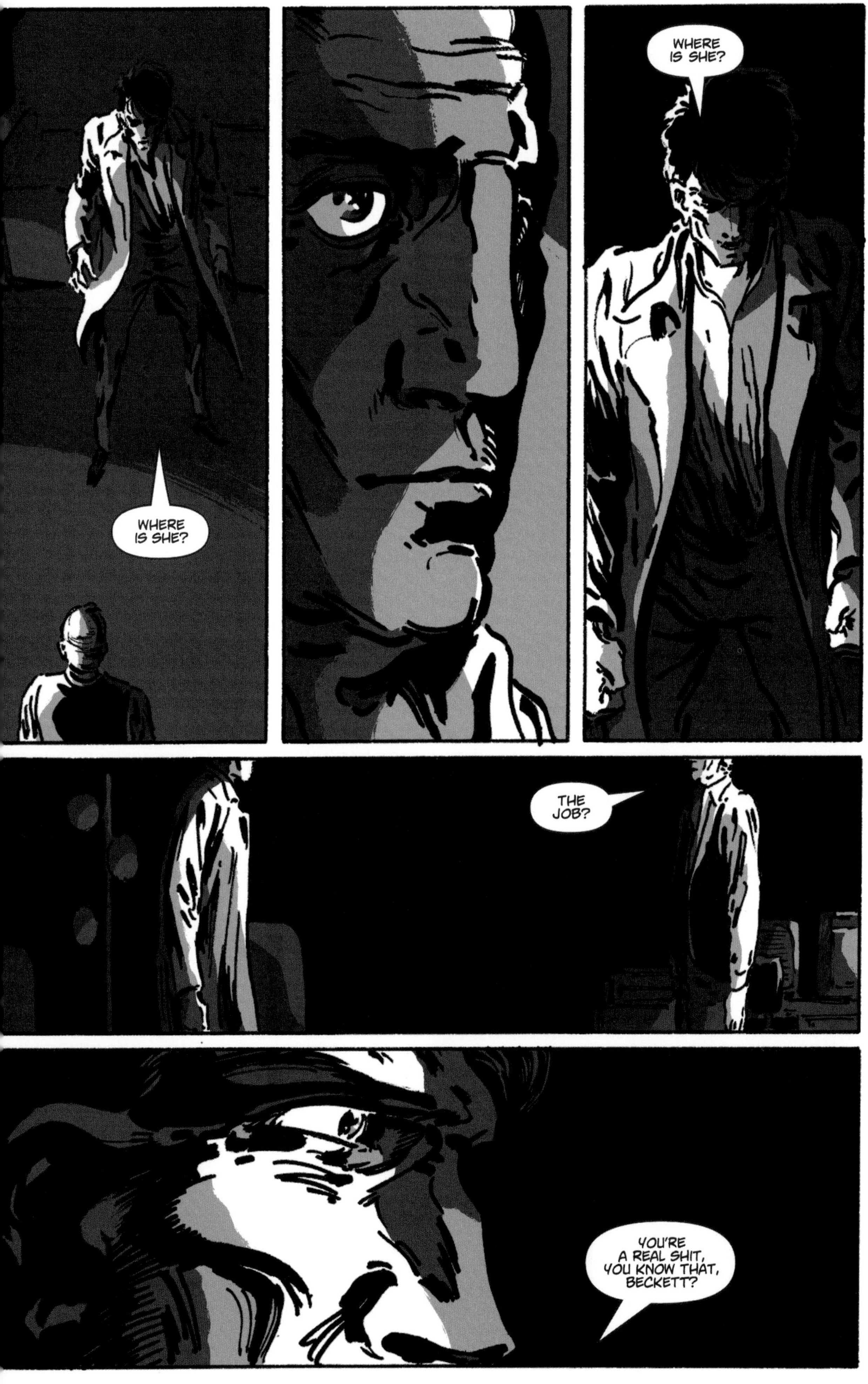
WHERE IS SHE?
WHERE IS SHE?
THE JOB?
YOU'RE A REAL SHIT, YOU KNOW THAT, BECKETT?

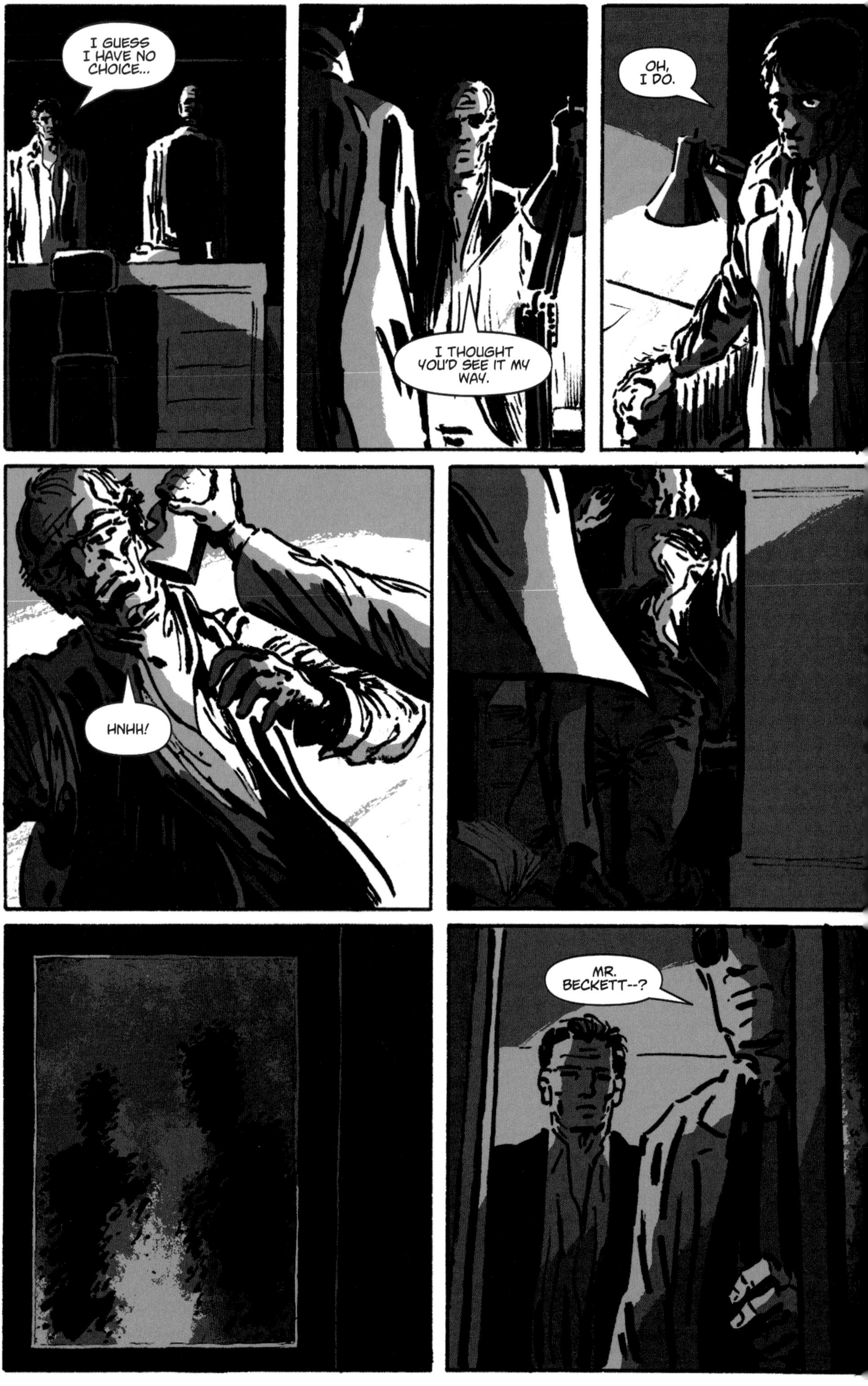
I GUESS I HAVE NO CHOICE...
I THOUGHT YOU'D SEE IT MY WAY.
OH, I DO.
HNHH!
MR. BECKETT--?

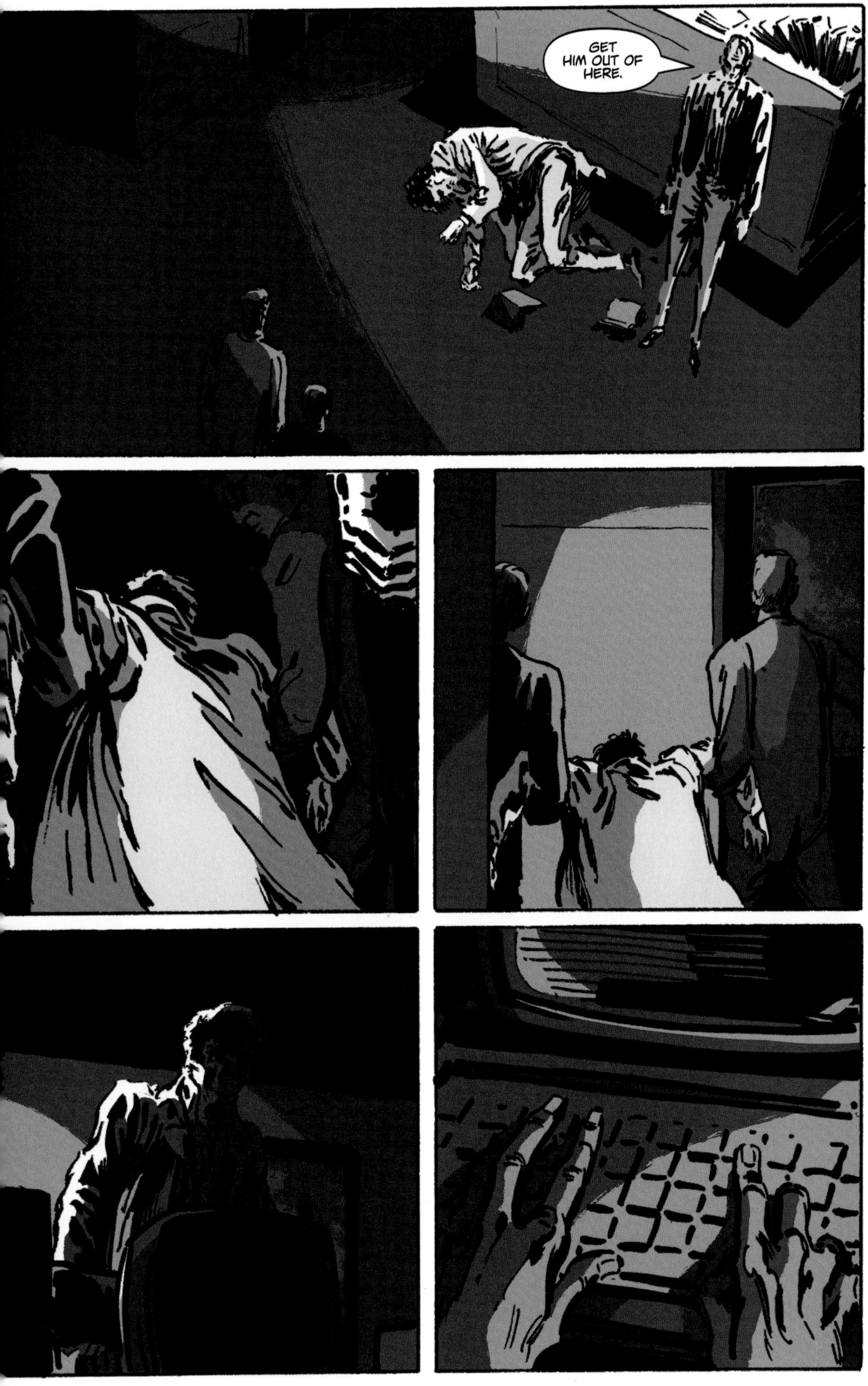
GET HIM OUT OF HERE.

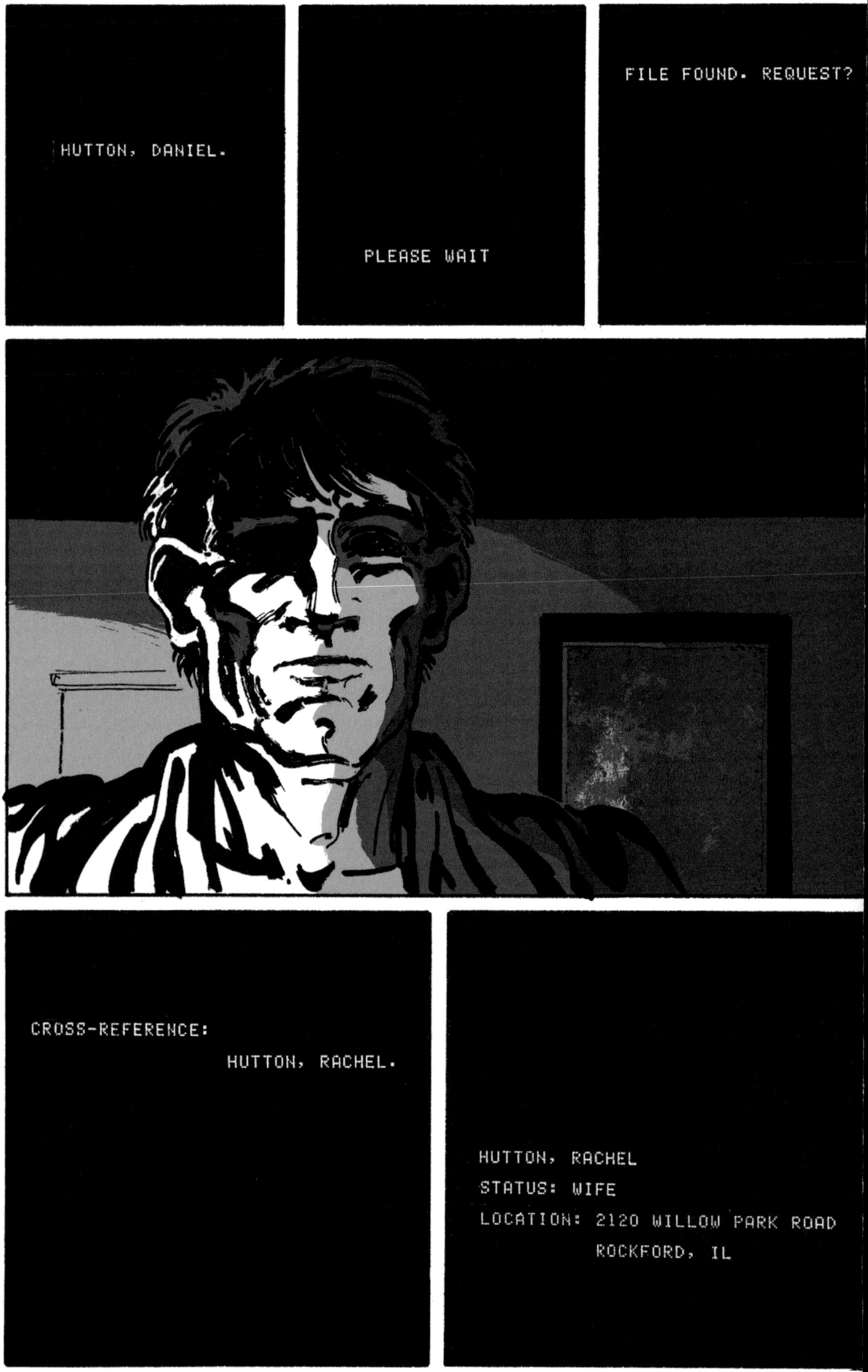
HUTTON, DANIEL.
PLEASE WAIT
FILE FOUND. REQUEST?
CROSS-REFERENCE:
HUTTON, RACHEL.
HUTTON, RACHEL
STATUS: WIFE
LOCATION: 2120 WILLOW PARK ROAD
ROCKFORD, IL

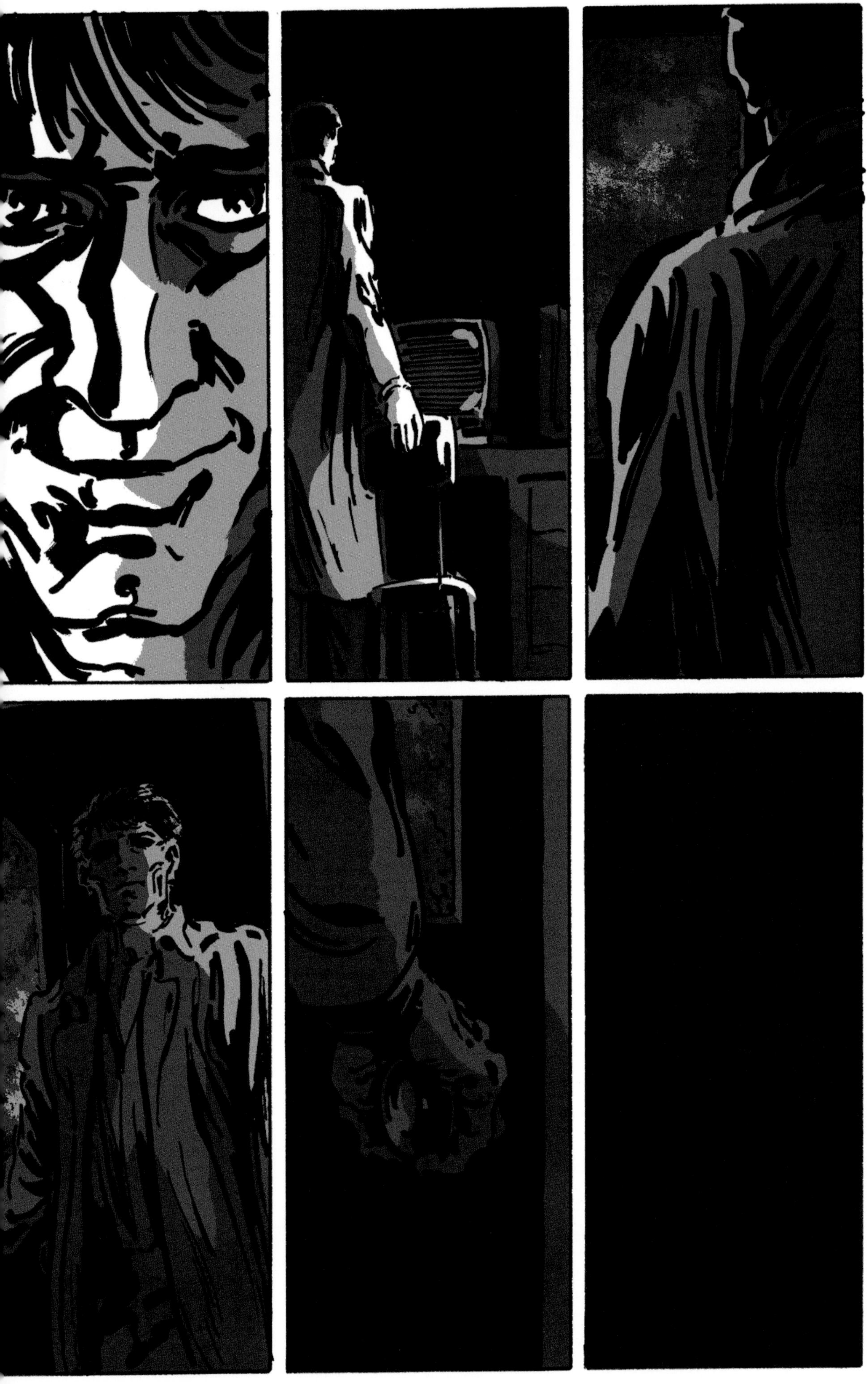

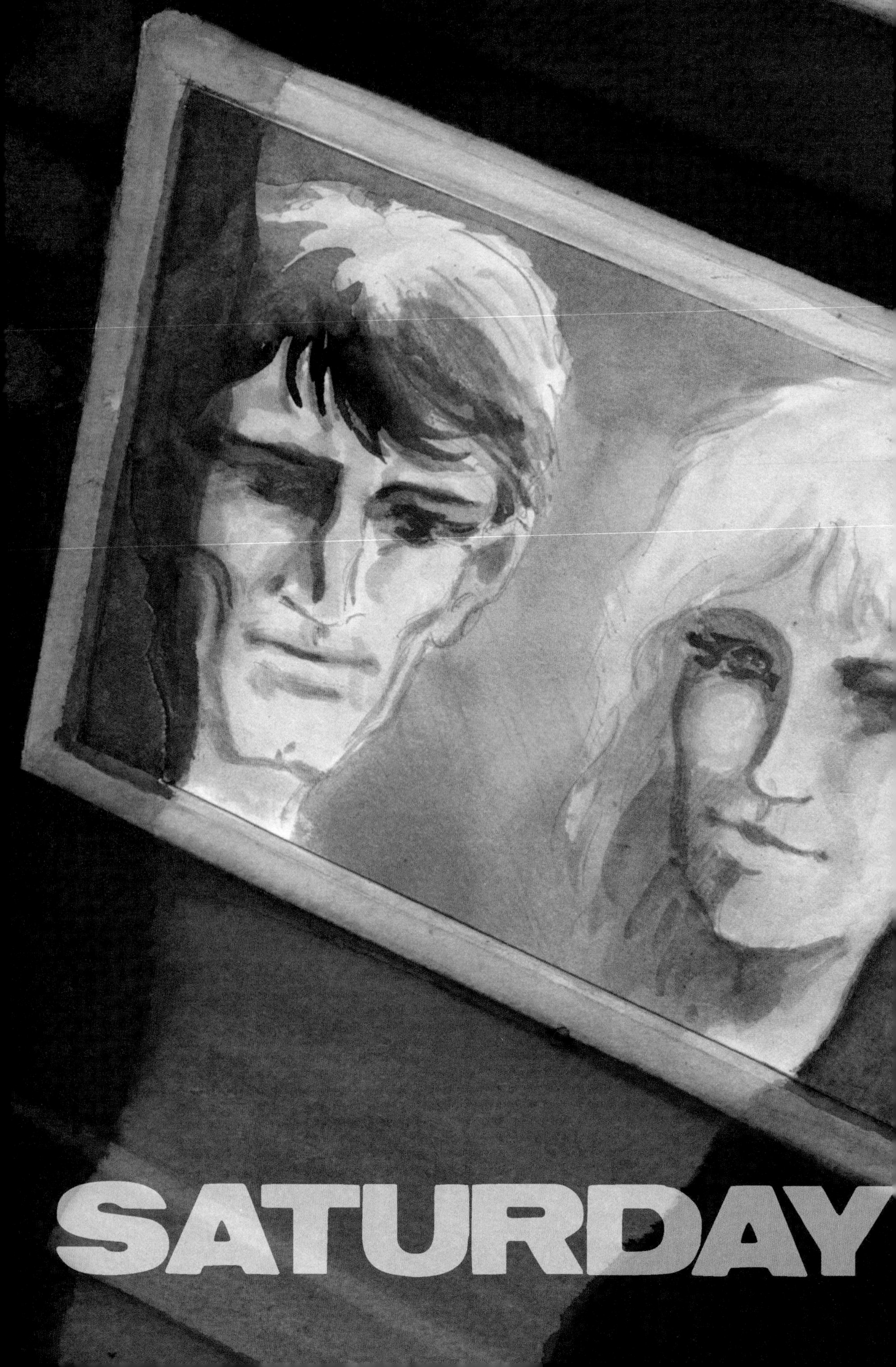

SATURDAY

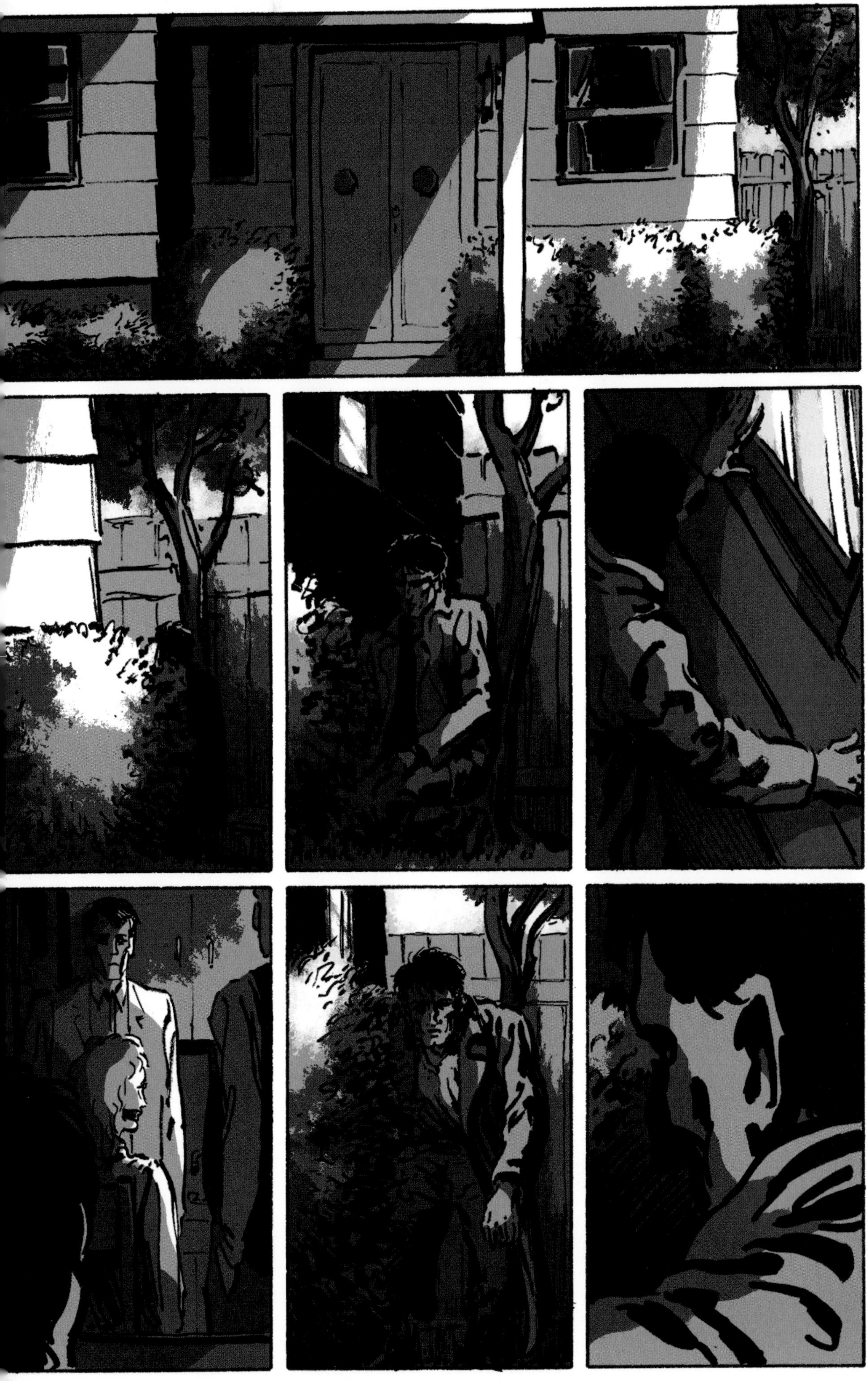

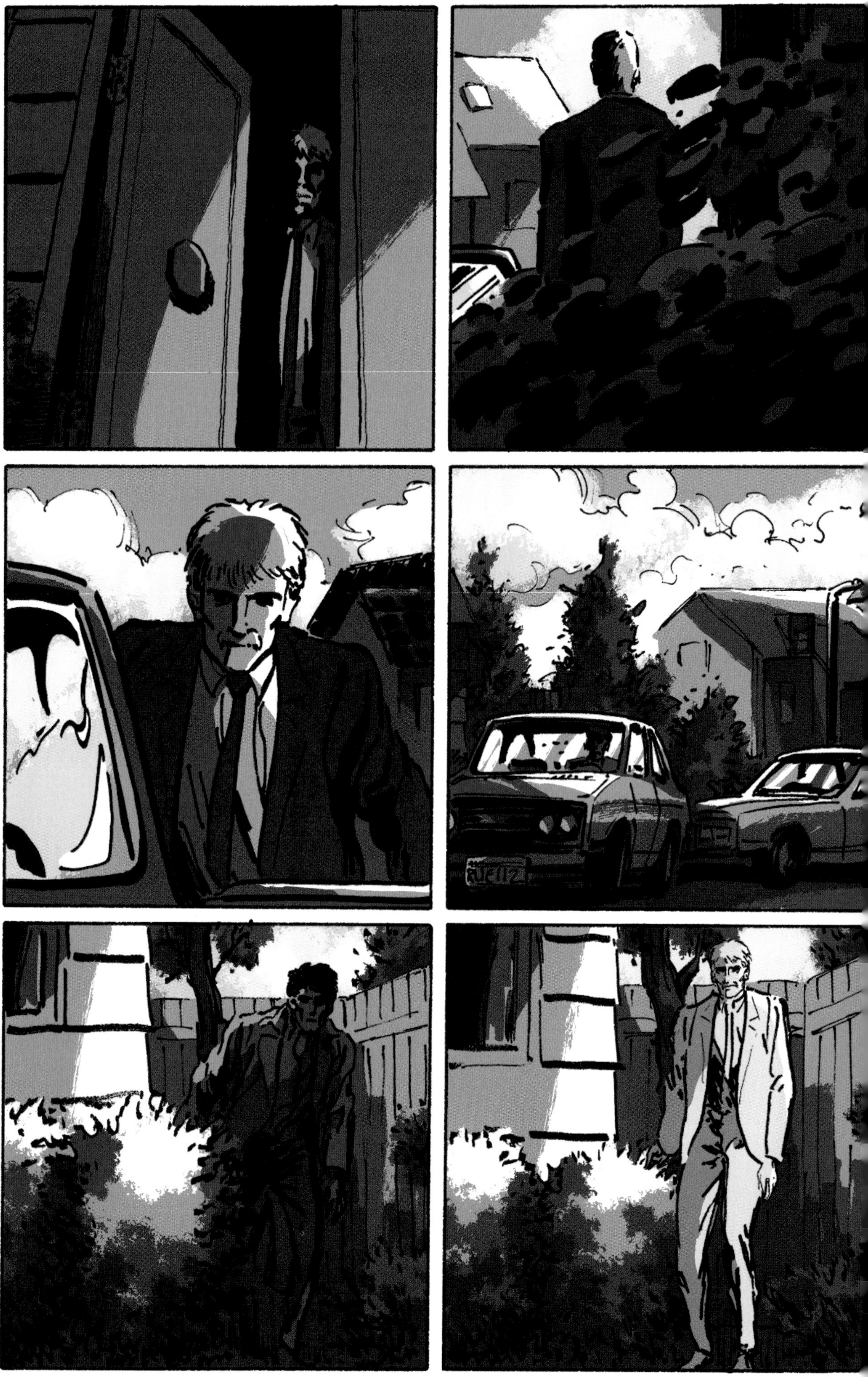
RJE112

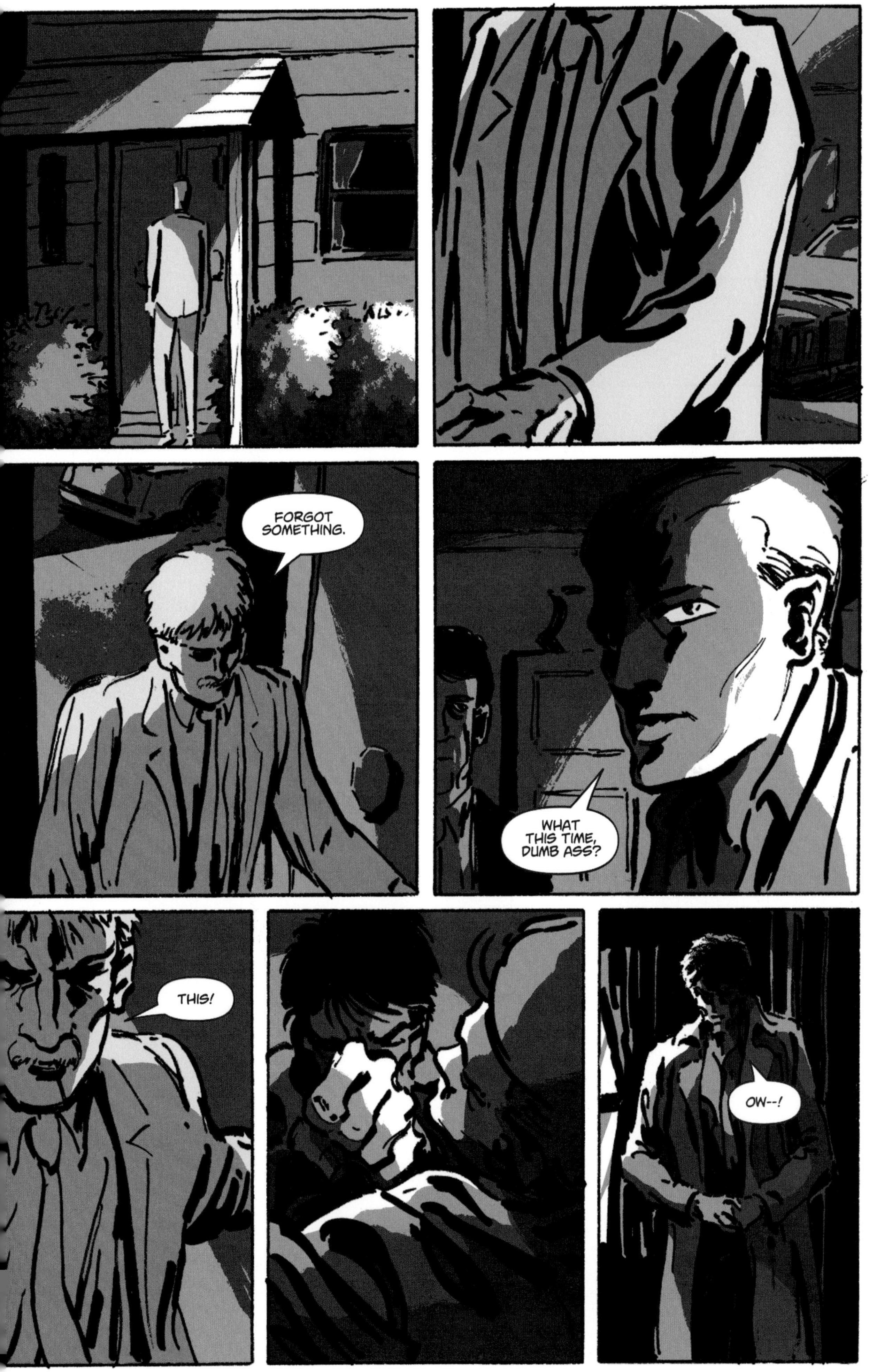
FORGOT SOMETHING.
WHAT THIS TIME, DUMB ASS?
THIS!
OW--!

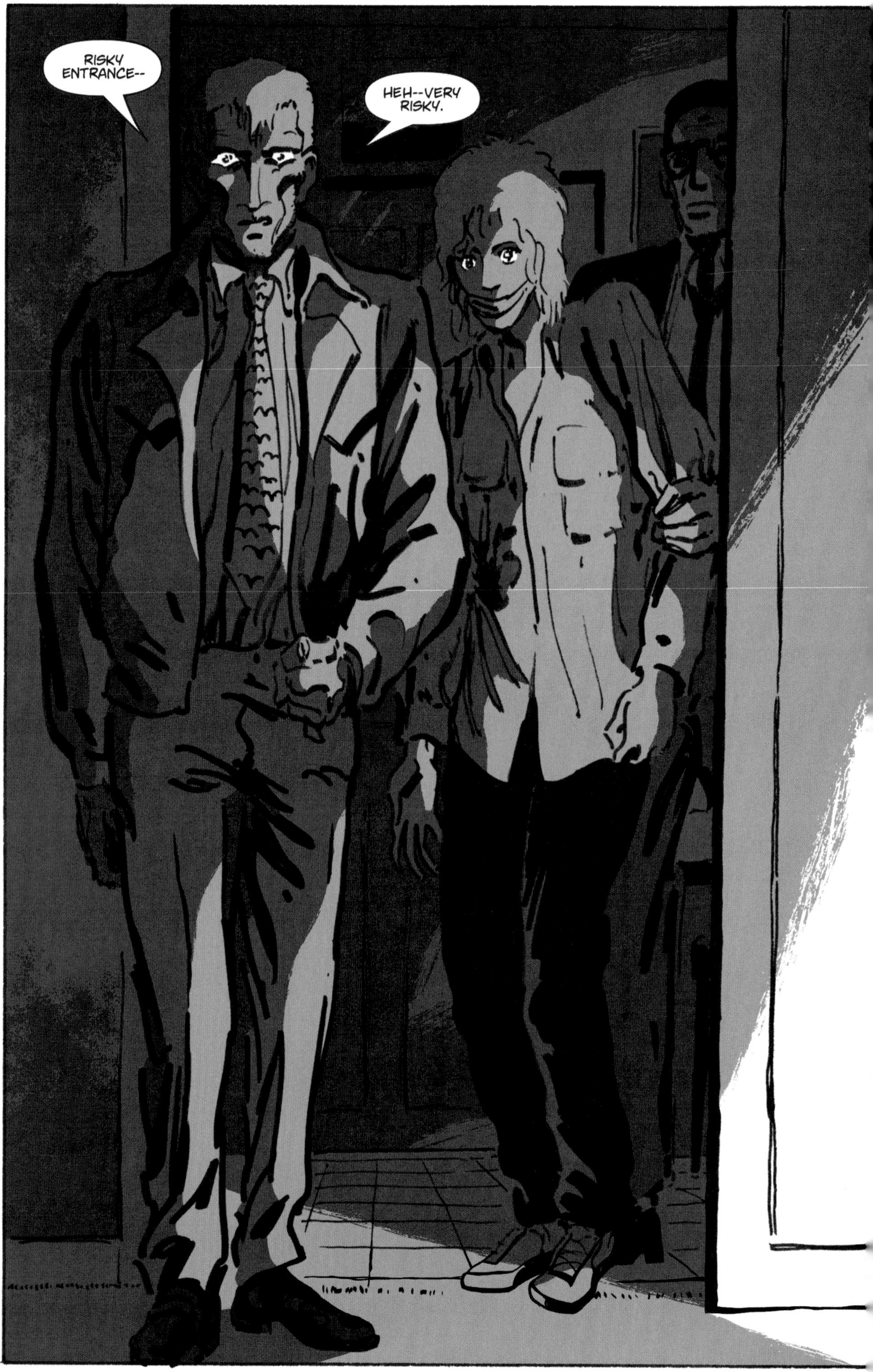
RISKY ENTRANCE--
HEH--VERY RISKY.

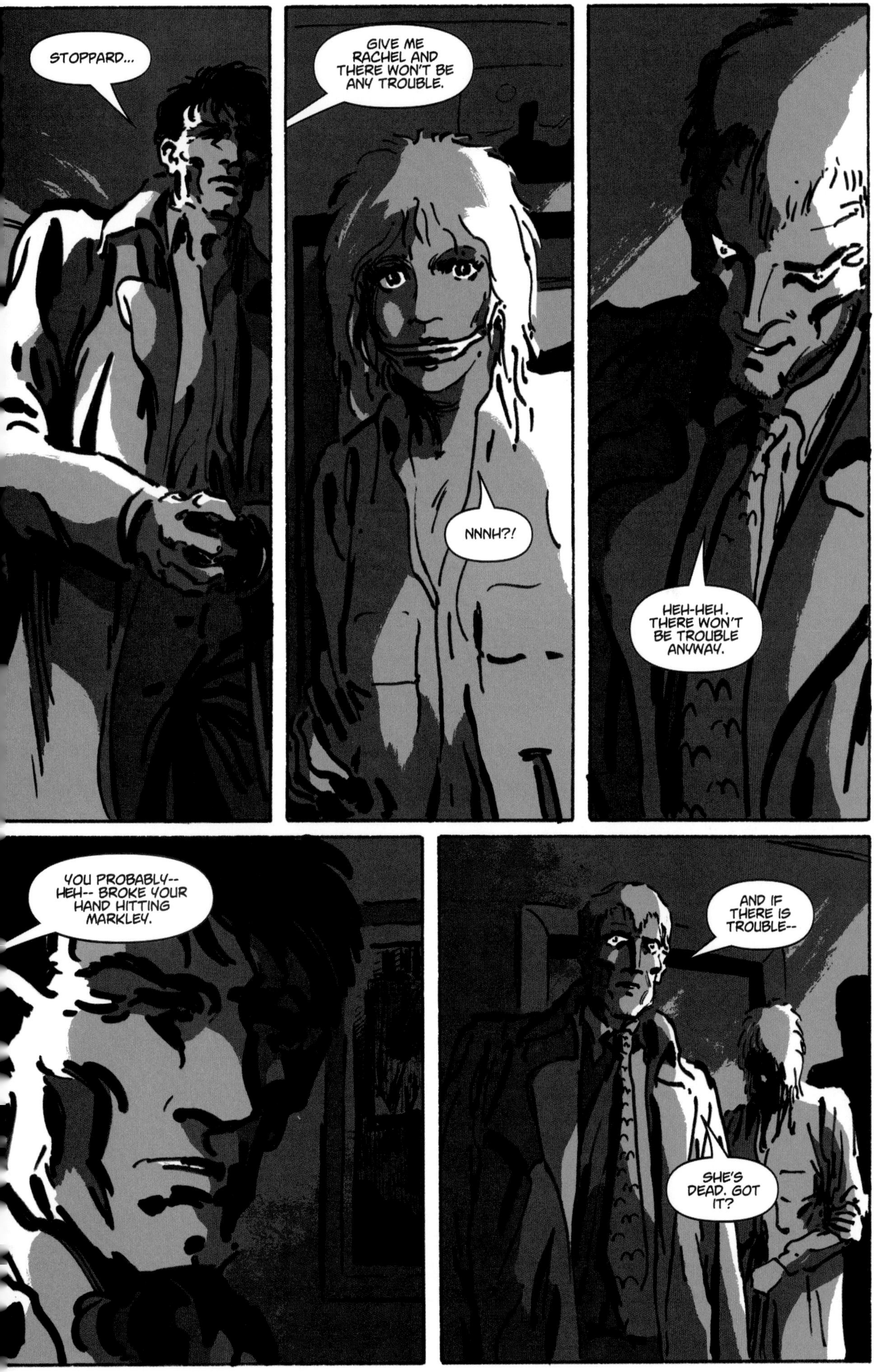
STOPPARD...
GIVE ME RACHEL AND THERE WON'T BE ANY TROUBLE.
NNNH?!
HEH-HEH. THERE WON'T BE TROUBLE ANYWAY.
YOU PROBABLY-- HEH-- BROKE YOUR HAND HITTING MARKLEY.
AND IF THERE IS TROUBLE--
SHE'S DEAD. GOT IT?

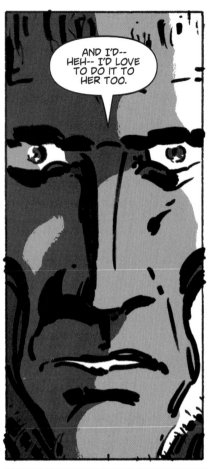

AND I'D-- HEH-- I'D LOVE TO DO IT TO HER TOO.

I MEAN, I OWE YOU ONE--

I ROTTED YEARS AWAY IN PRISON 'CAUSE OF YOU.

WHO LET YOU OUT?

OH, HEH-- GOOD STORY-- HEH-- OUR BOSS SPRUNG ME.

OUR BOSS?

WHO?

HE'LL BE HERE IN A MINUTE. ASK HIM.

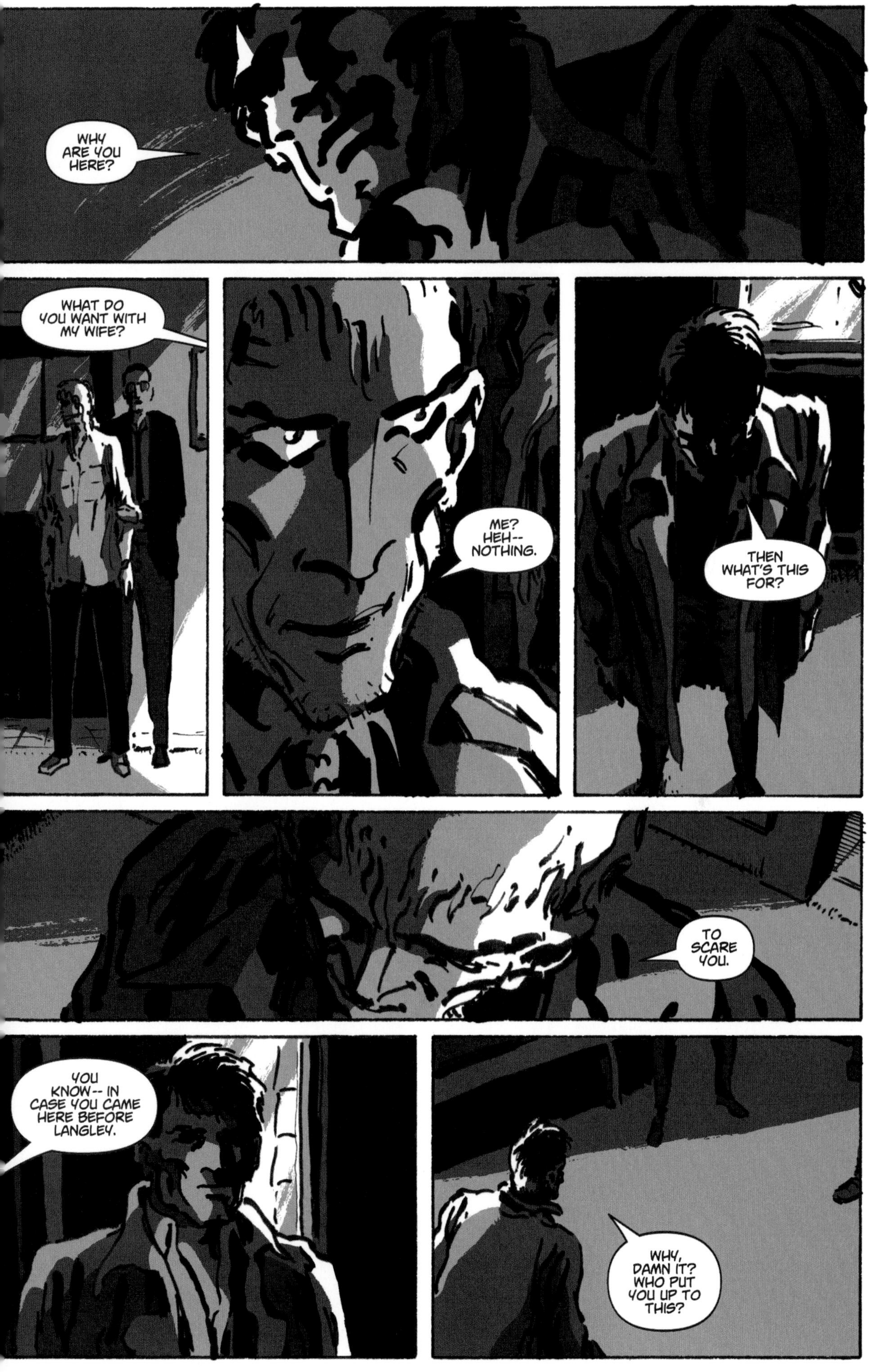
WHY ARE YOU HERE?
WHAT DO YOU WANT WITH MY WIFE?
ME? HEH-- NOTHING.
THEN WHAT'S THIS FOR?
TO SCARE YOU.
YOU KNOW-- IN CASE YOU CAME HERE BEFORE LANGLEY.
WHY, DAMN IT? WHO PUT YOU UP TO THIS?

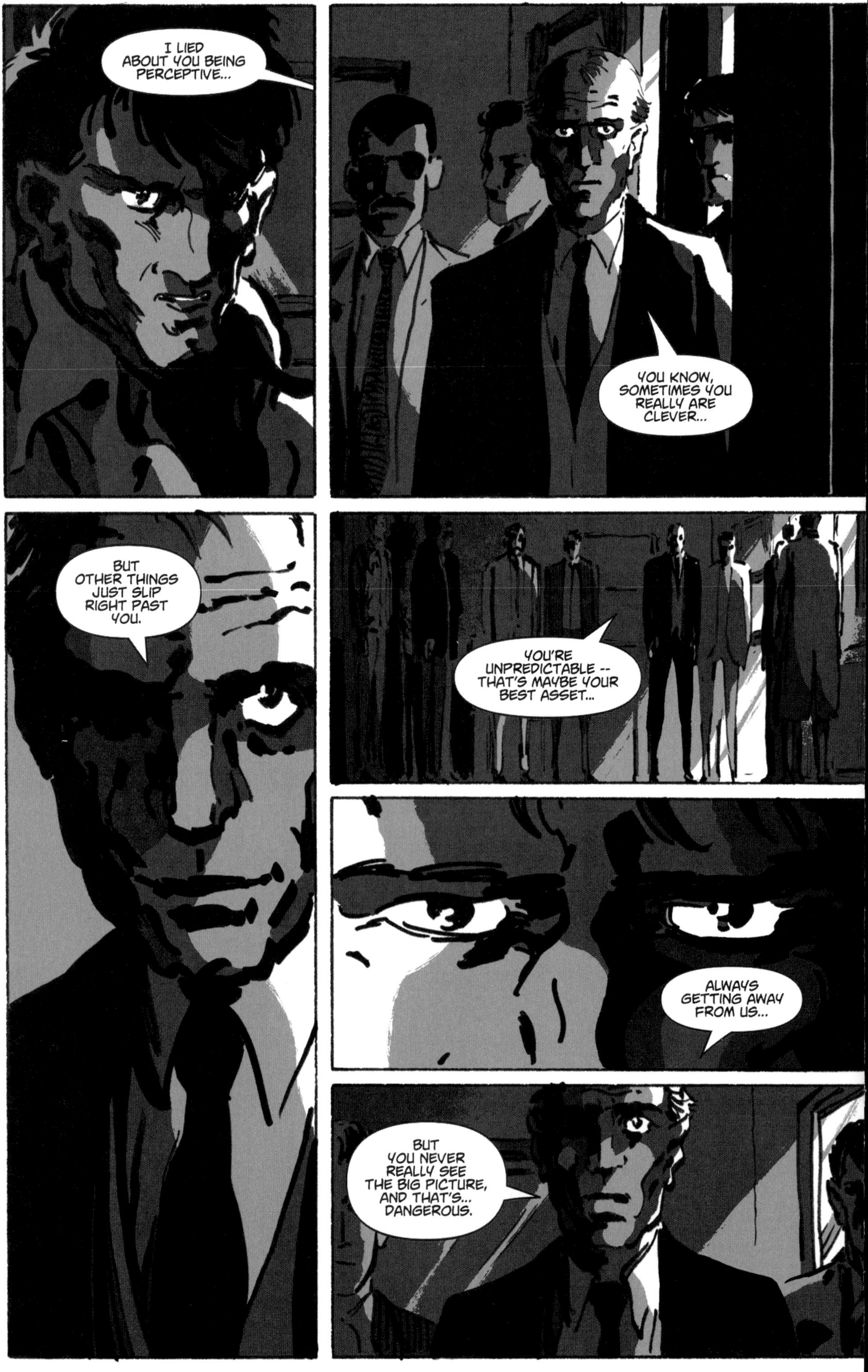
I LIED ABOUT YOU BEING PERCEPTIVE...
YOU KNOW, SOMETIMES YOU REALLY ARE CLEVER...
BUT OTHER THINGS JUST SLIP RIGHT PAST YOU.
YOU'RE UNPREDICTABLE -- THAT'S MAYBE YOUR BEST ASSET...
ALWAYS GETTING AWAY FROM US...
BUT YOU NEVER REALLY SEE THE BIG PICTURE, AND THAT'S... DANGEROUS.

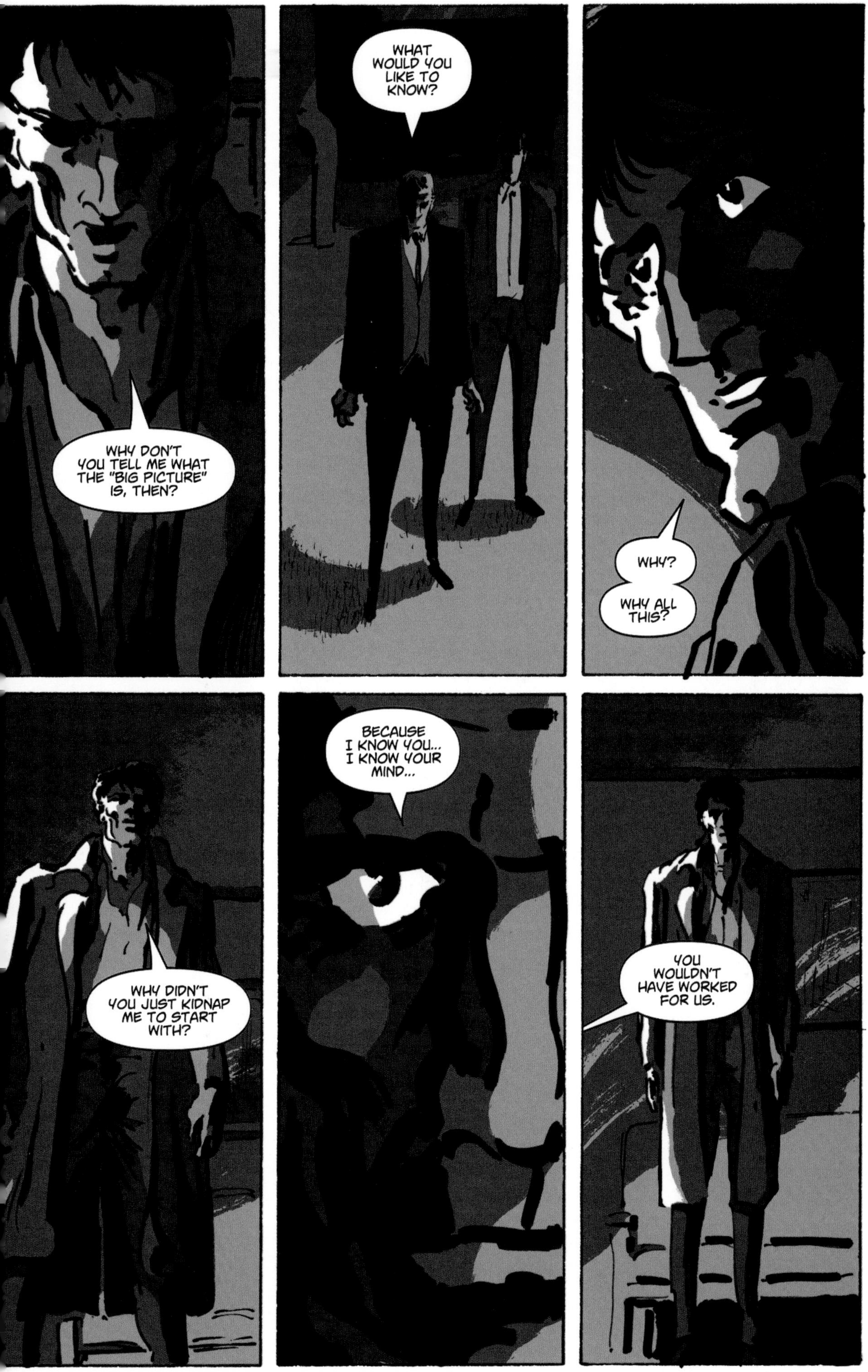
WHY DON'T YOU TELL ME WHAT THE "BIG PICTURE" IS, THEN?
WHAT WOULD YOU LIKE TO KNOW?
WHY?
WHY ALL THIS?
WHY DIDN'T YOU JUST KIDNAP ME TO START WITH?
BECAUSE I KNOW YOU... I KNOW YOUR MIND...
YOU WOULDN'T HAVE WORKED FOR US.

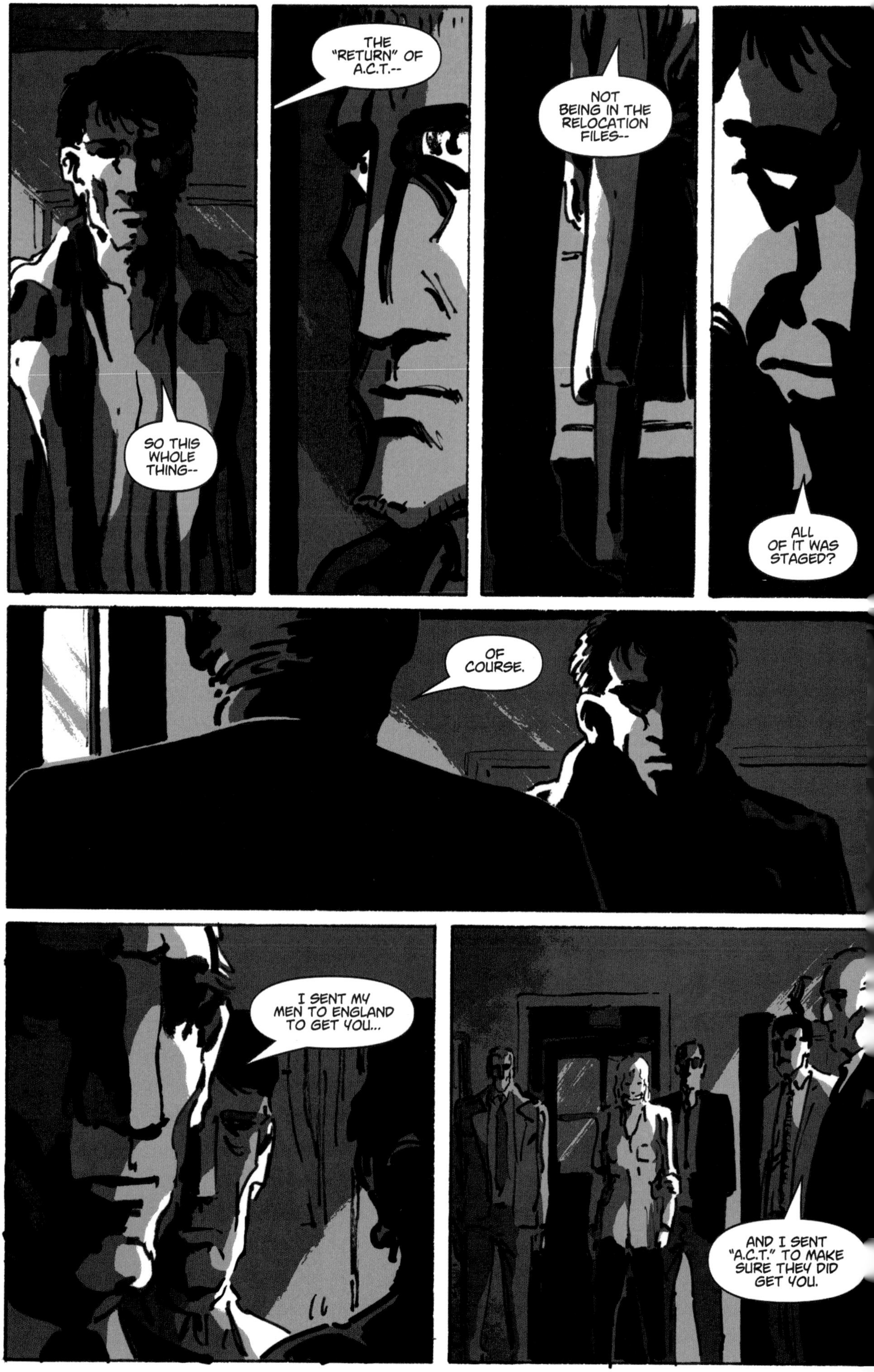
SO THIS WHOLE THING--
THE "RETURN" OF A.C.T.--
NOT BEING IN THE RELOCATION FILES--
ALL OF IT WAS STAGED?
OF COURSE.
I SENT MY MEN TO ENGLAND TO GET YOU...
AND I SENT "A.C.T." TO MAKE SURE THEY DID GET YOU.

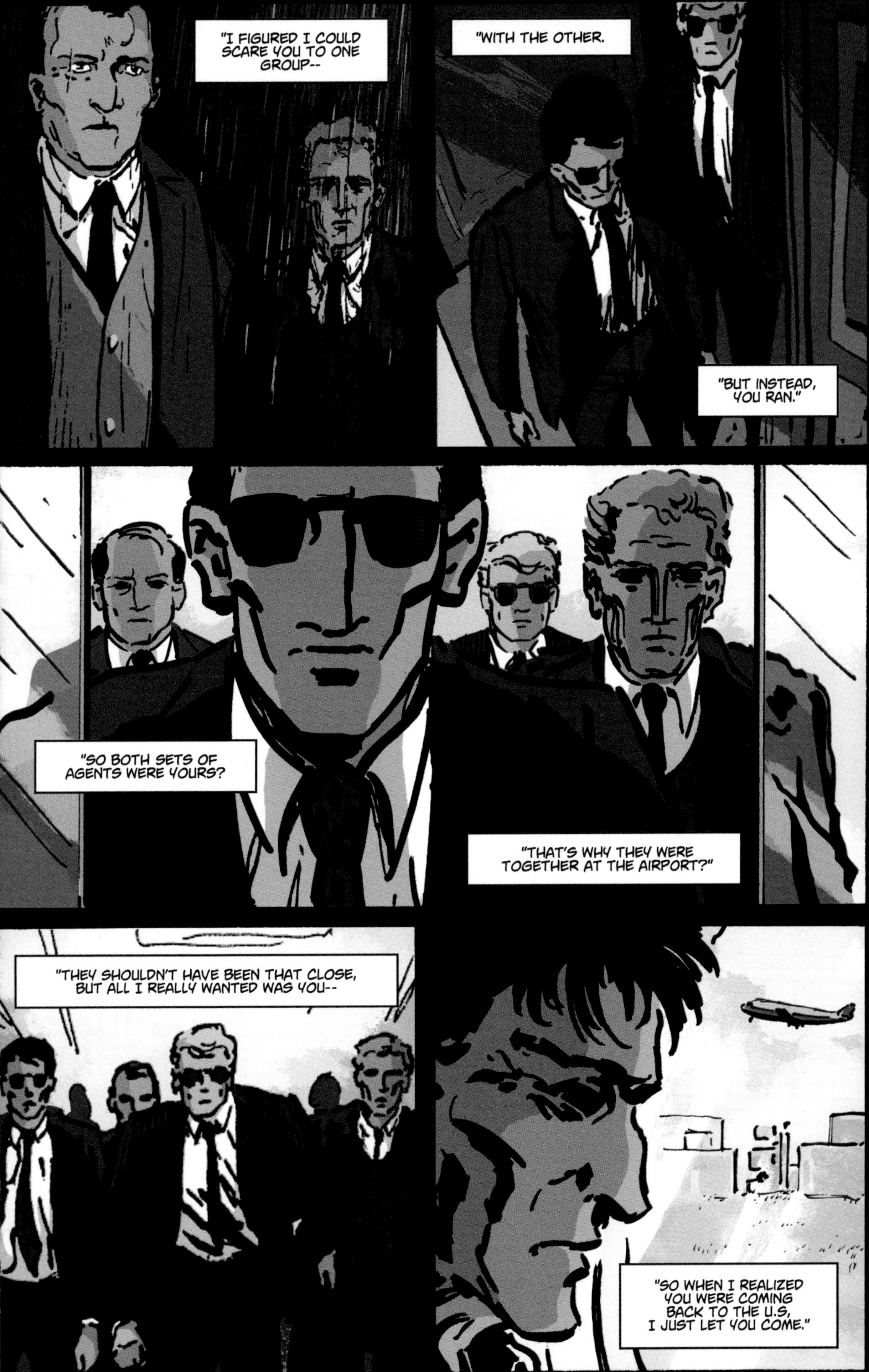
"I FIGURED I COULD SCARE YOU TO ONE GROUP--
"WITH THE OTHER.
"BUT INSTEAD, YOU RAN."
"SO BOTH SETS OF AGENTS WERE YOURS?
"THAT'S WHY THEY WERE TOGETHER AT THE AIRPORT?"
"THEY SHOULDN'T HAVE BEEN THAT CLOSE, BUT ALL I REALLY WANTED WAS YOU--
"SO WHEN I REALIZED YOU WERE COMING BACK TO THE U.S, I JUST LET YOU COME."

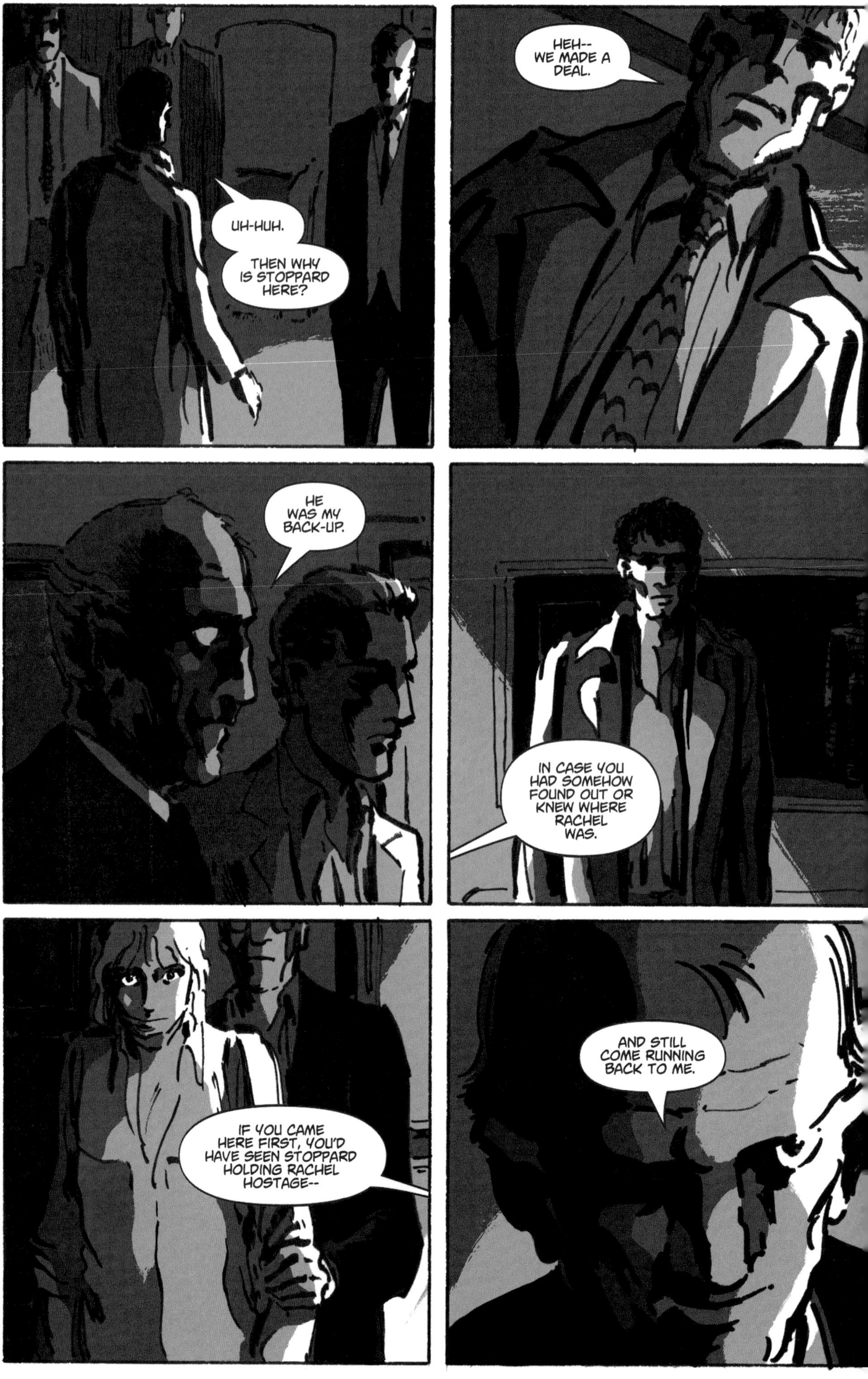
UH-HUH.
THEN WHY IS STOPPARD HERE?
HEH-- WE MADE A DEAL.
HE WAS MY BACK-UP.
IN CASE YOU HAD SOMEHOW FOUND OUT OR KNEW WHERE RACHEL WAS.
IF YOU CAME HERE FIRST, YOU'D HAVE SEEN STOPPARD HOLDING RACHEL HOSTAGE--
AND STILL COME RUNNING BACK TO ME.

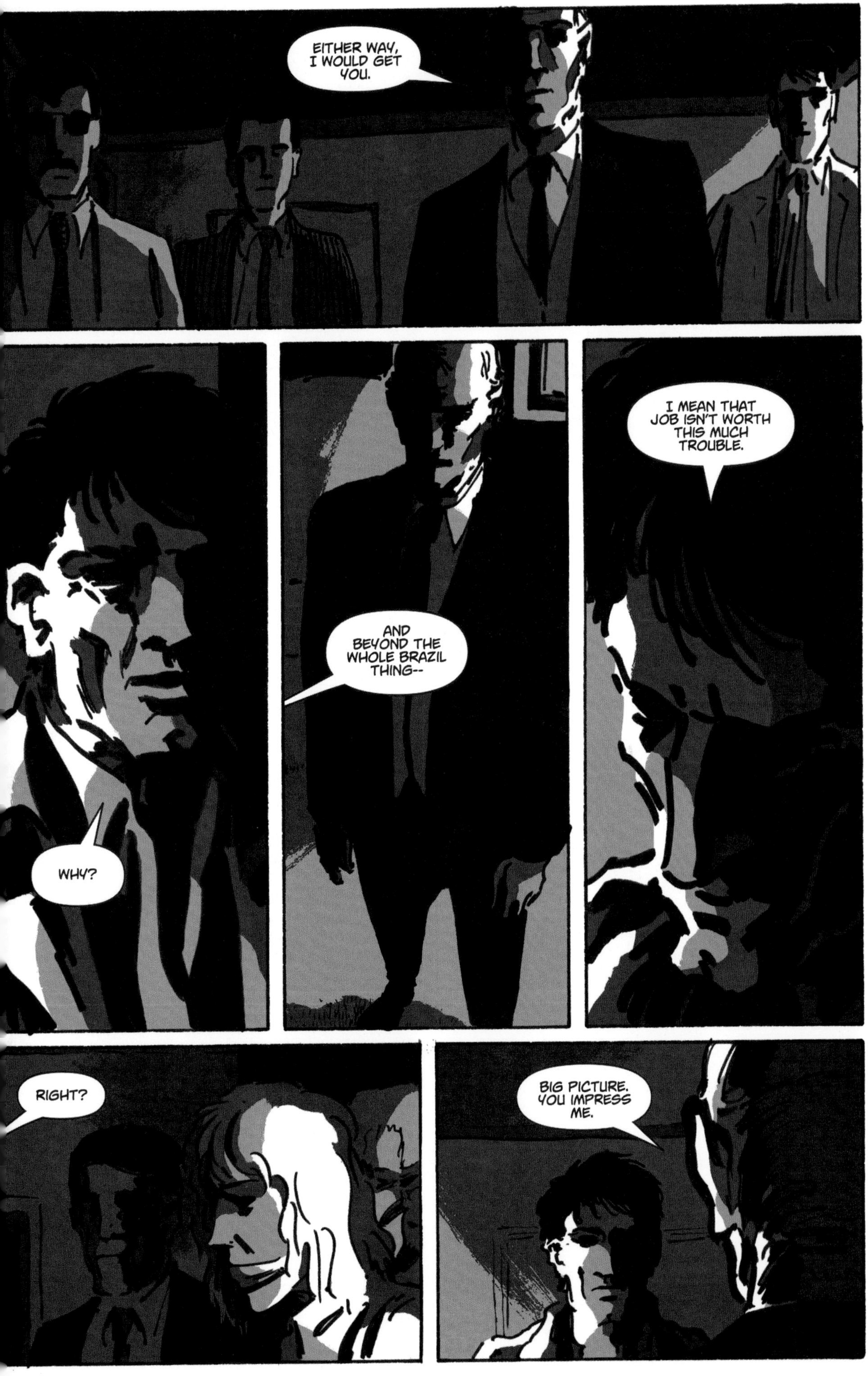
EITHER WAY, I WOULD GET YOU.
WHY?
AND BEYOND THE WHOLE BRAZIL THING--
I MEAN THAT JOB ISN'T WORTH THIS MUCH TROUBLE.
RIGHT?
BIG PICTURE. YOU IMPRESS ME.

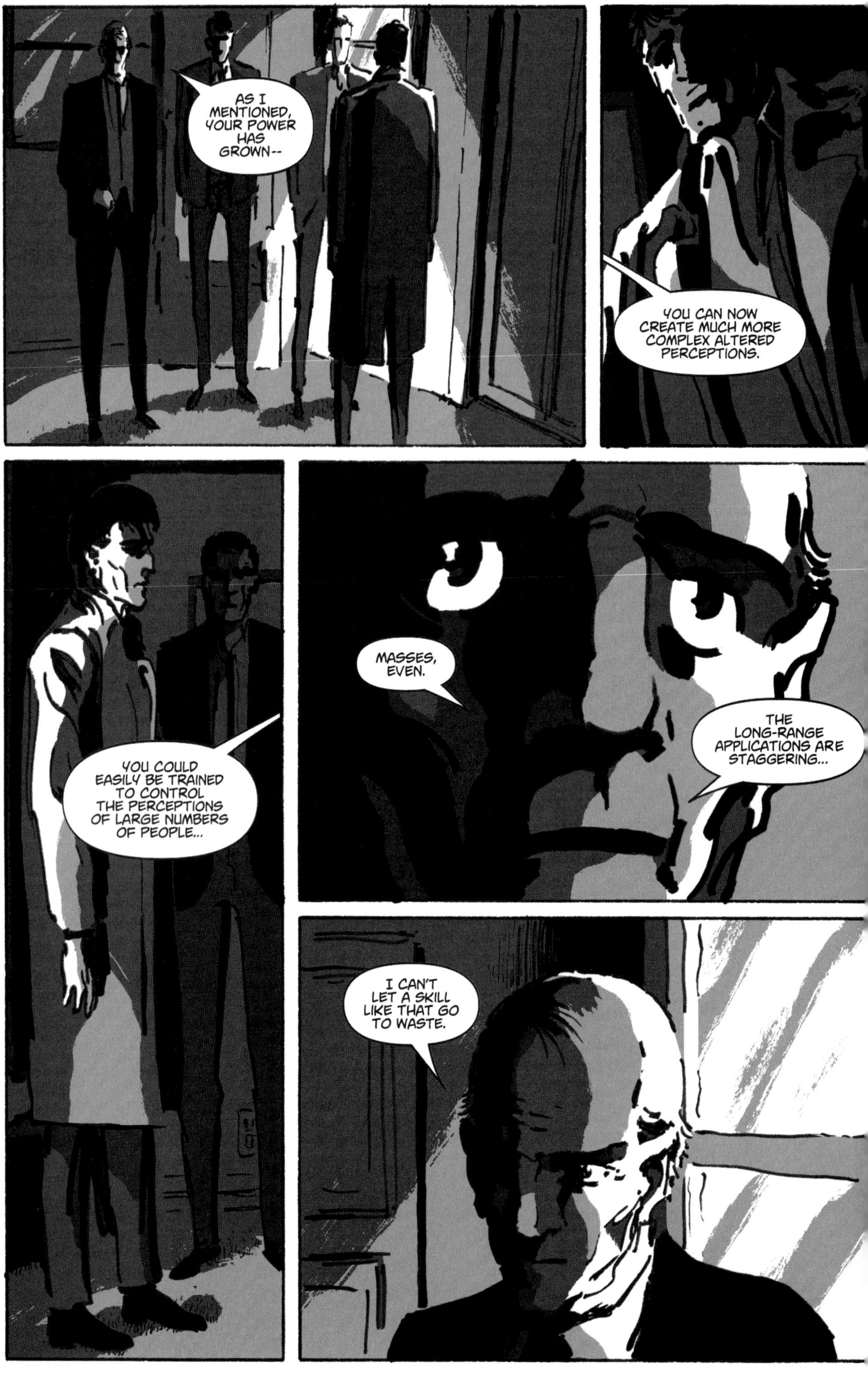
AS I MENTIONED, YOUR POWER HAS GROWN--
YOU CAN NOW CREATE MUCH MORE COMPLEX ALTERED PERCEPTIONS.
YOU COULD EASILY BE TRAINED TO CONTROL THE PERCEPTIONS OF LARGE NUMBERS OF PEOPLE...
MASSES, EVEN.
THE LONG-RANGE APPLICATIONS ARE STAGGERING...
I CAN'T LET A SKILL LIKE THAT GO TO WASTE.

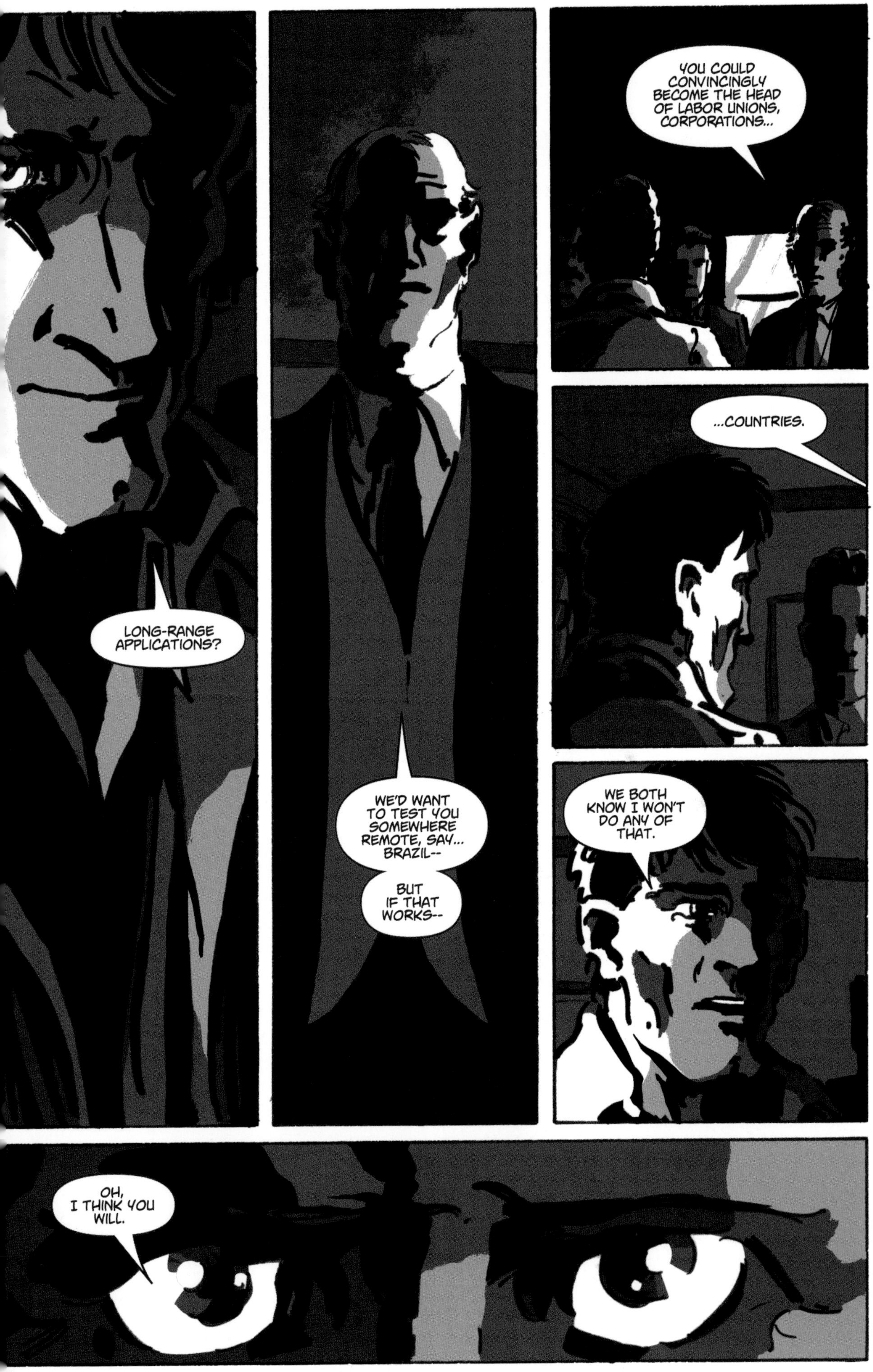
LONG-RANGE APPLICATIONS?
WE'D WANT TO TEST YOU SOMEWHERE REMOTE, SAY... BRAZIL--
BUT IF THAT WORKS--
YOU COULD CONVINCINGLY BECOME THE HEAD OF LABOR UNIONS, CORPORATIONS...
...COUNTRIES.
WE BOTH KNOW I WON'T DO ANY OF THAT.
OH, I THINK YOU WILL.

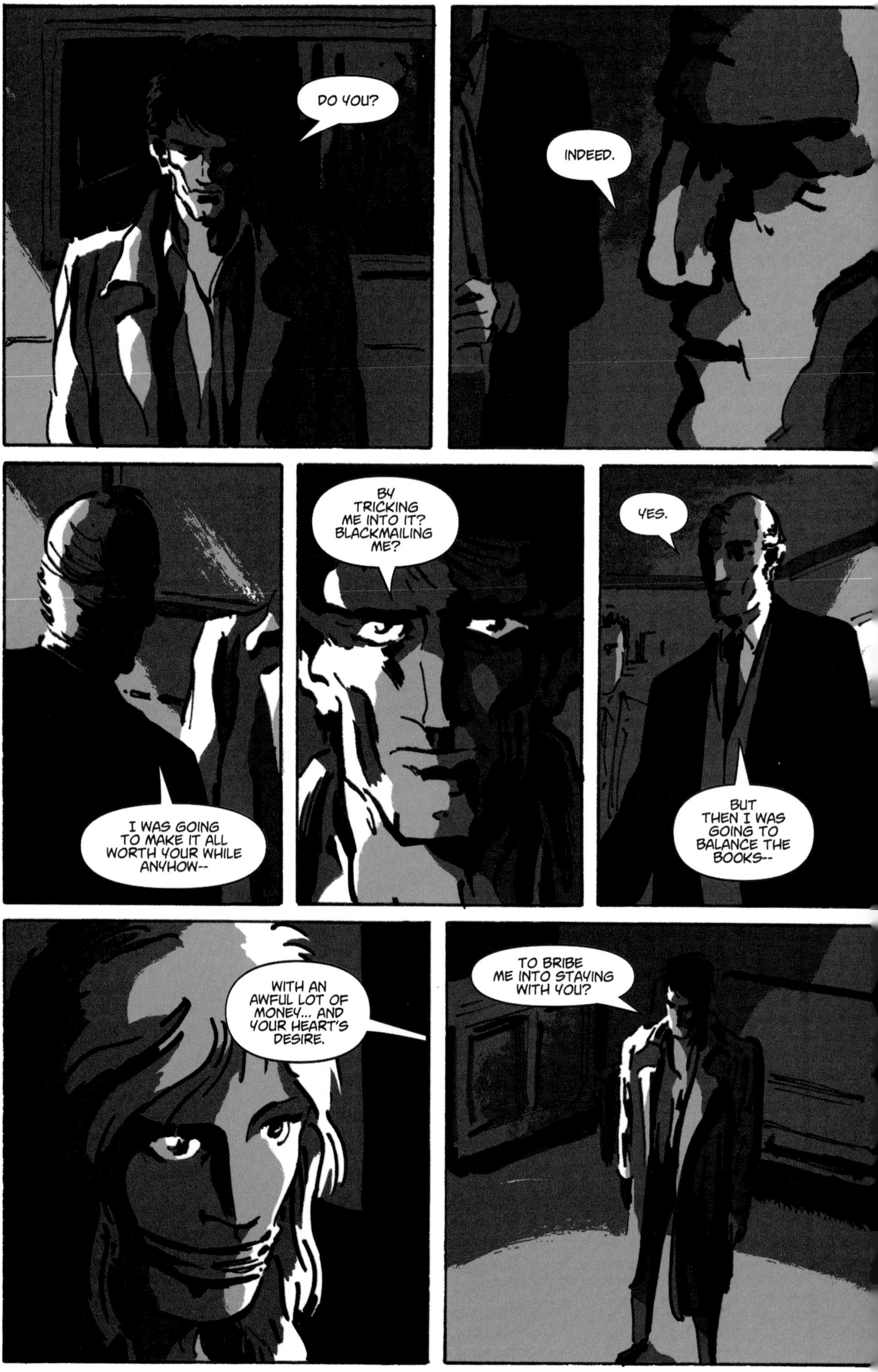
DO YOU?
INDEED.
I WAS GOING TO MAKE IT ALL WORTH YOUR WHILE ANYHOW--
BY TRICKING ME INTO IT? BLACKMAILING ME?
YES.
BUT THEN I WAS GOING TO BALANCE THE BOOKS--
WITH AN AWFUL LOT OF MONEY... AND YOUR HEART'S DESIRE.
TO BRIBE ME INTO STAYING WITH YOU?

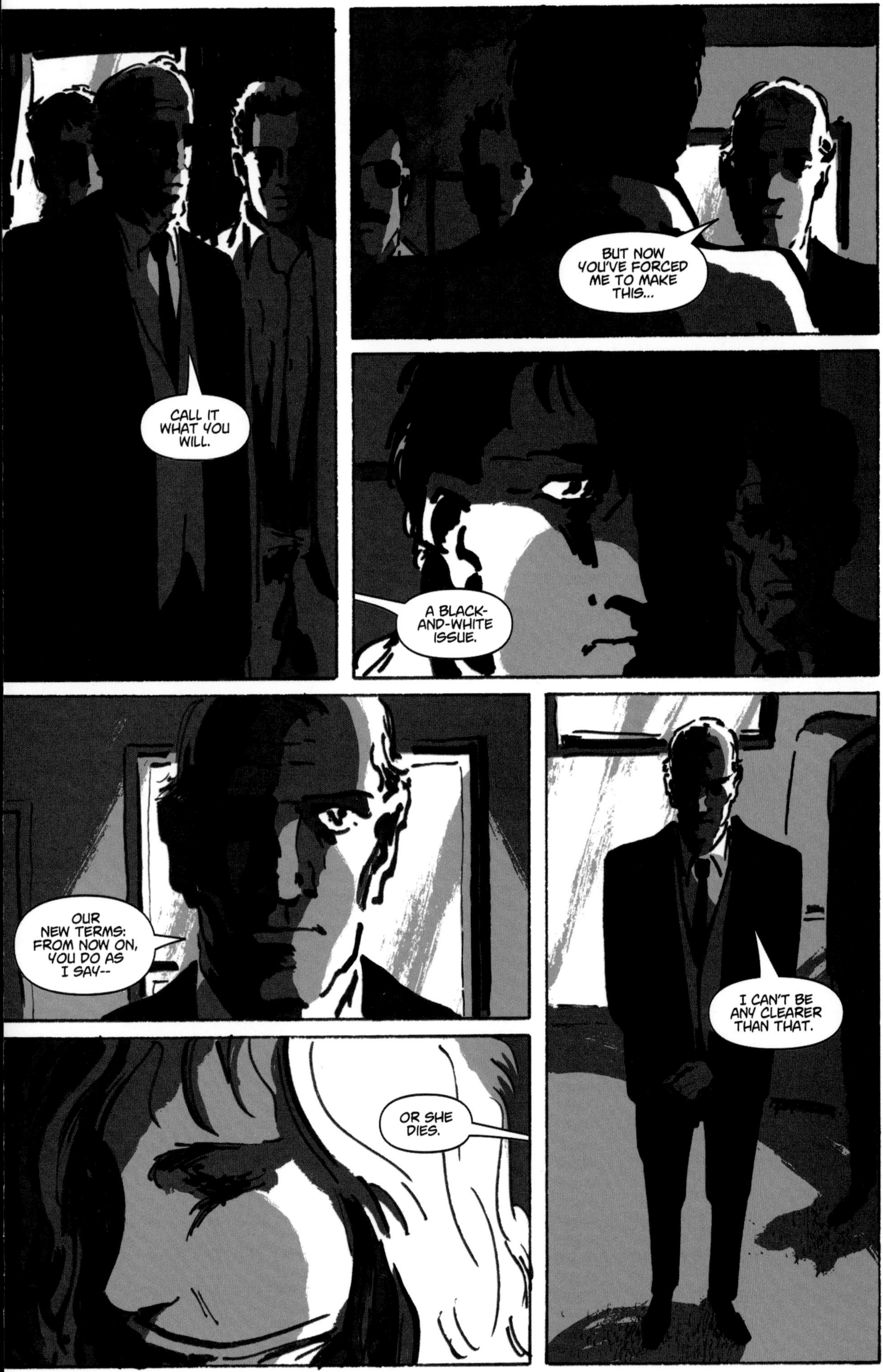
CALL IT WHAT YOU WILL.
BUT NOW YOU'VE FORCED ME TO MAKE THIS...
A BLACK-AND-WHITE ISSUE.
OUR NEW TERMS: FROM NOW ON, YOU DO AS I SAY--
OR SHE DIES.
I CAN'T BE ANY CLEARER THAN THAT.

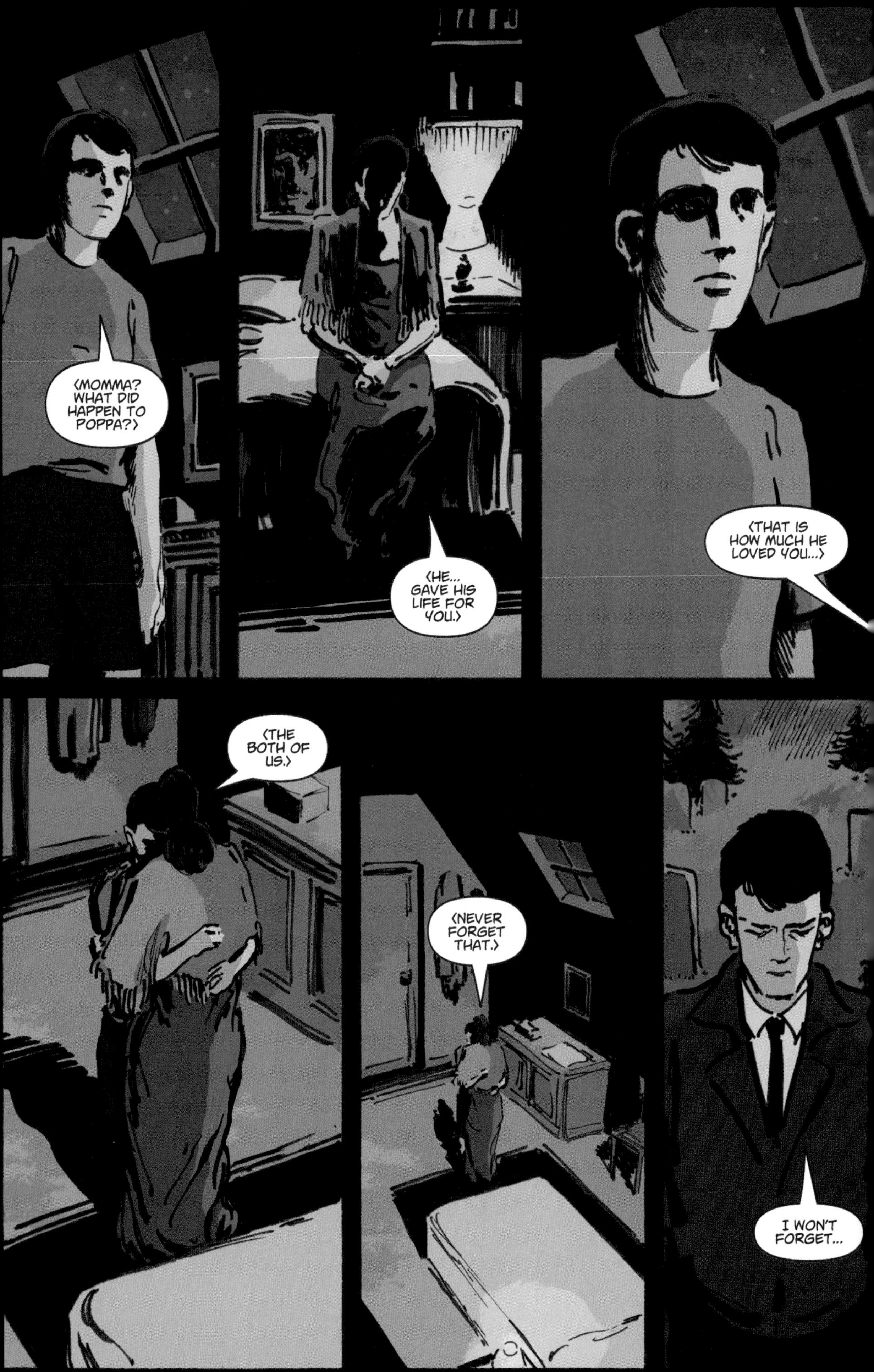

‹MOMMA? WHAT DID HAPPEN TO POPPA?›
‹HE... GAVE HIS LIFE FOR YOU.›
‹THAT IS HOW MUCH HE LOVED YOU...›
‹THE BOTH OF US.›
‹NEVER FORGET THAT.›
I WON'T FORGET...

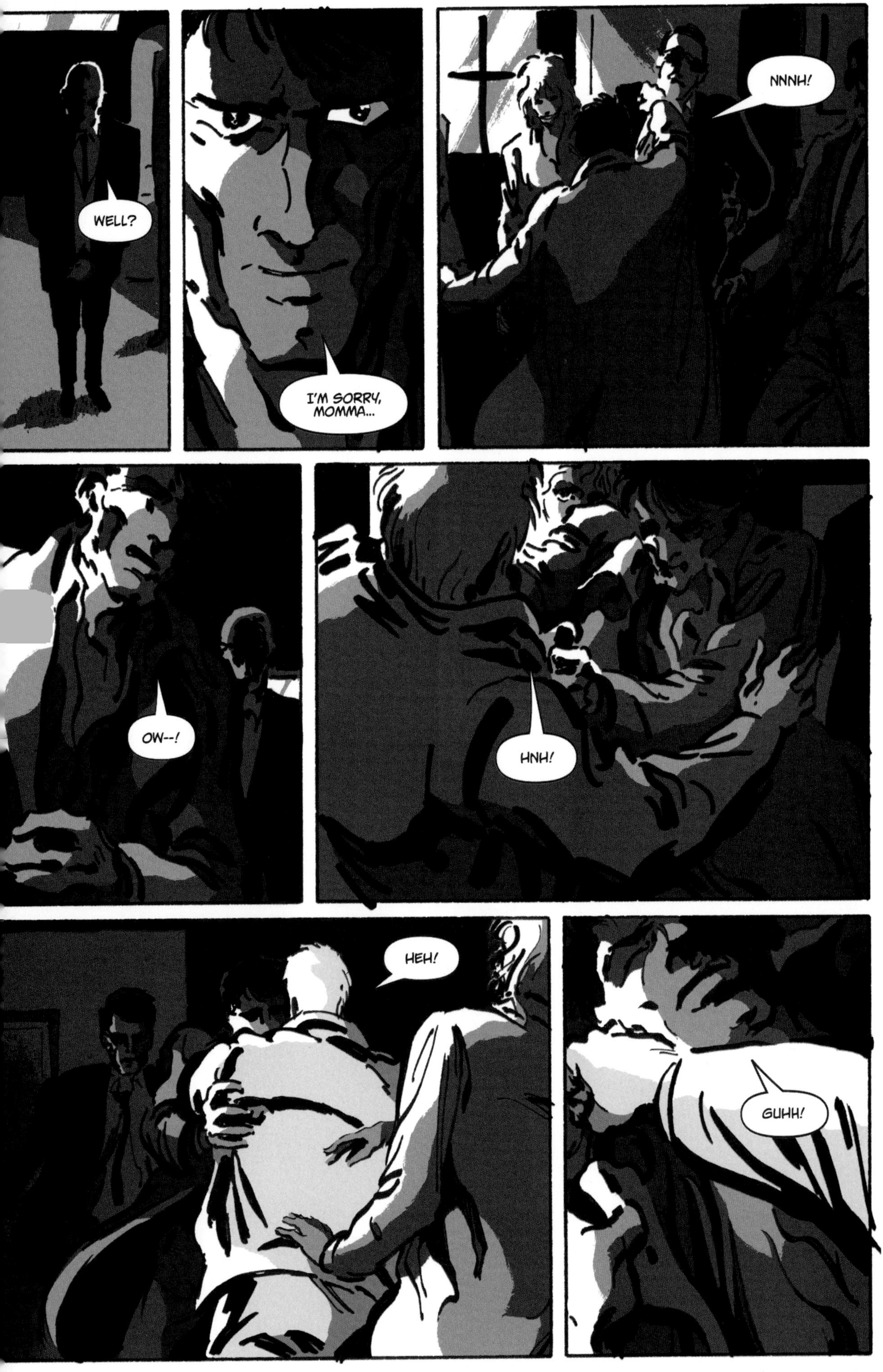
WELL?
I'M SORRY, MOMMA...
NNNH!
OW--!
HNH!
HEH!
GUHH!

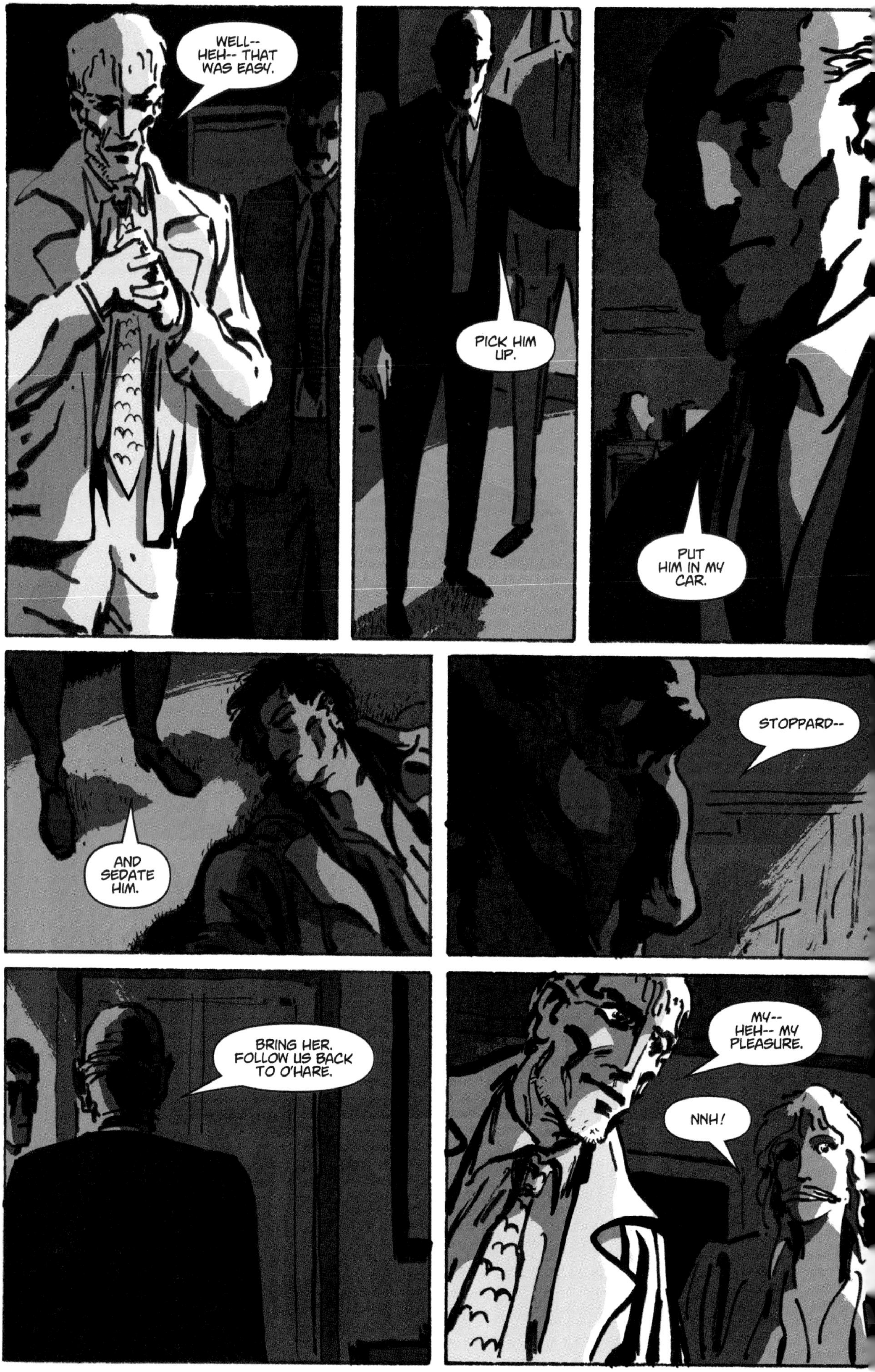
WELL-- HEH-- THAT WAS EASY.
PICK HIM UP.
PUT HIM IN MY CAR.
AND SEDATE HIM.
STOPPARD--
BRING HER. FOLLOW US BACK TO O'HARE.
MY-- HEH-- MY PLEASURE.
NNH!

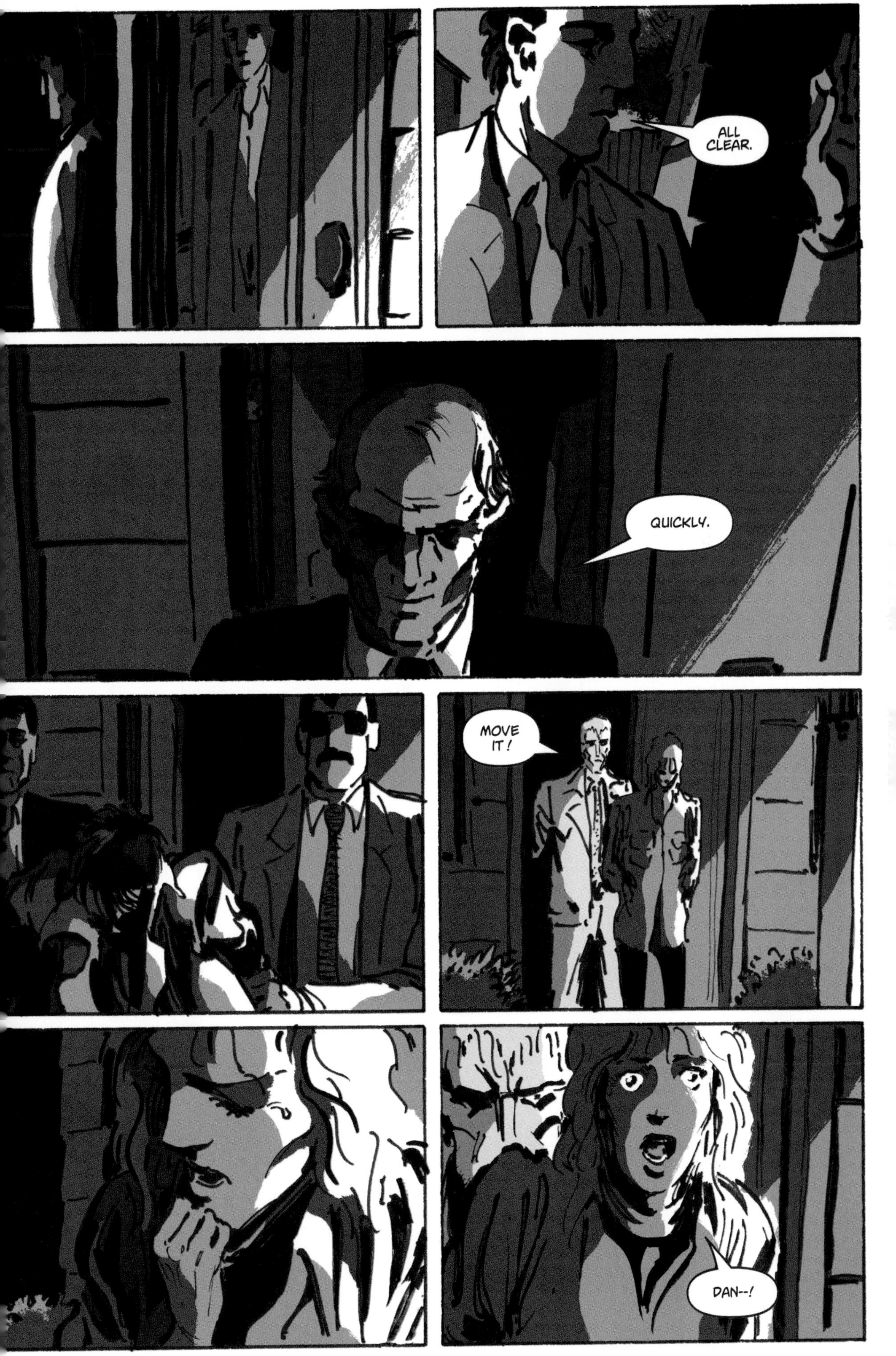
ALL CLEAR.
QUICKLY.
MOVE IT!
DAN--!

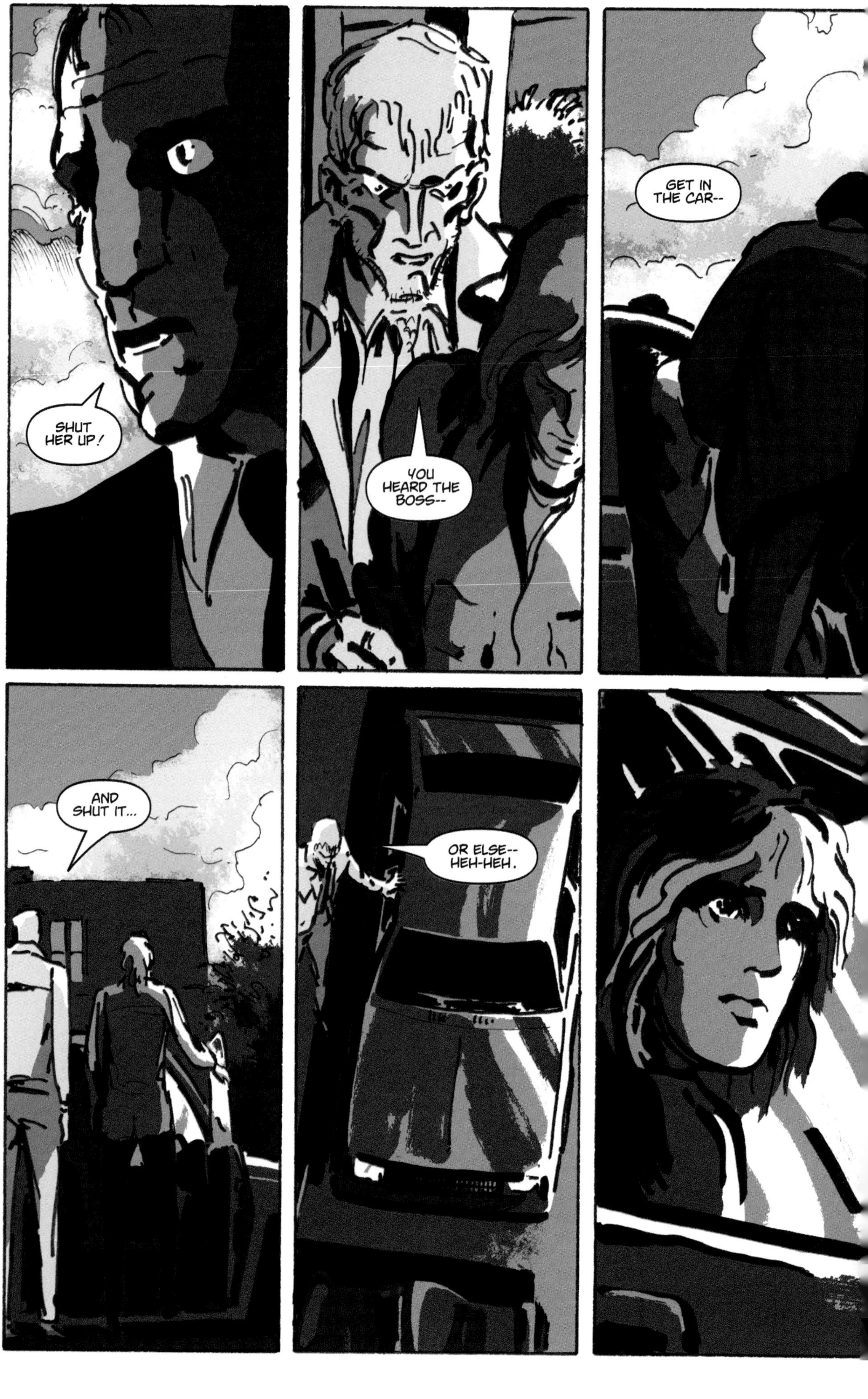
SHUT HER UP!
YOU HEARD THE BOSS--
GET IN THE CAR--
AND SHUT IT...
OR ELSE-- HEH-HEH.

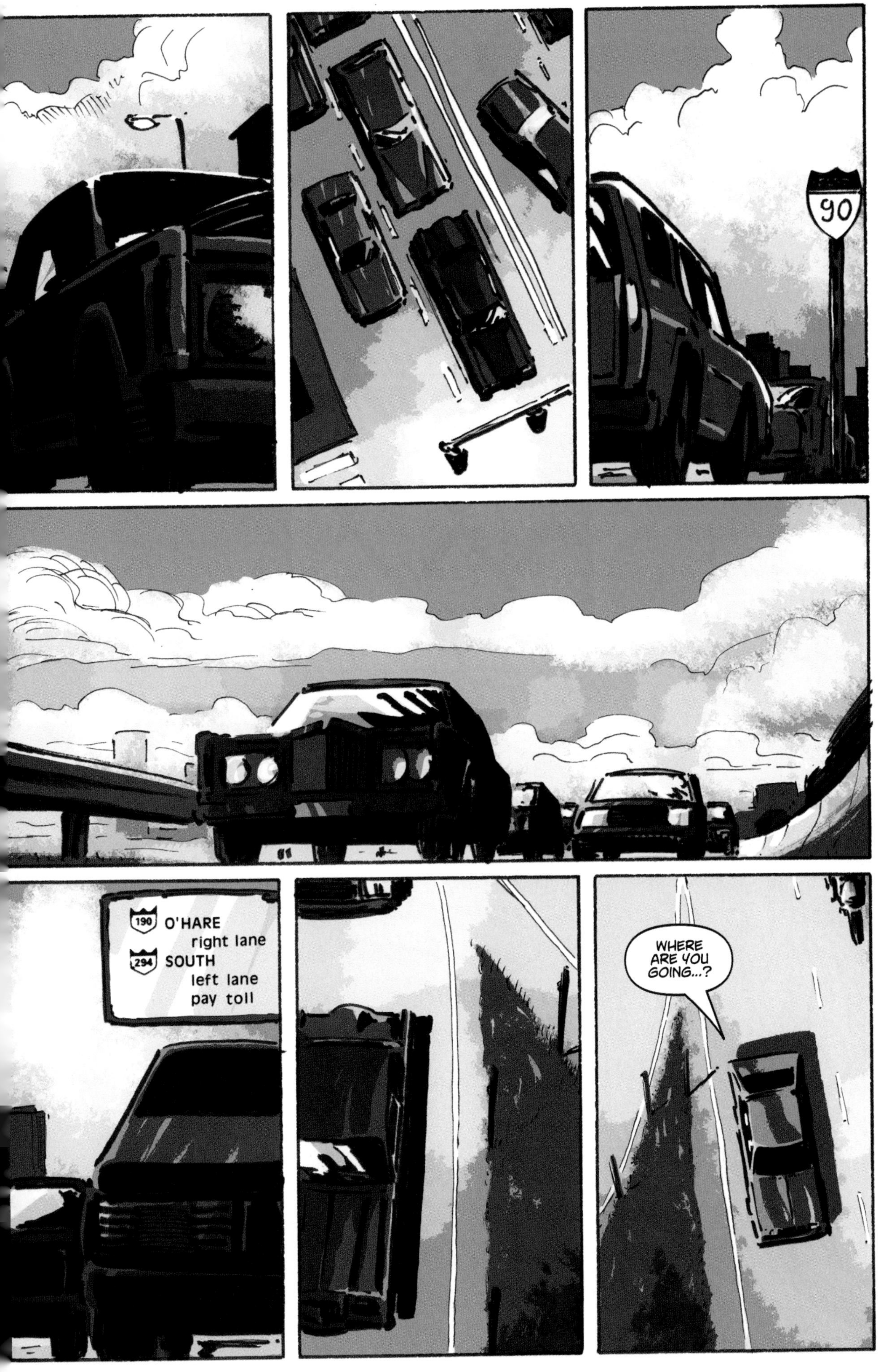
90
190 O'HARE
right lane
294 SOUTH
left lane
pay toll
WHERE ARE YOU GOING...?

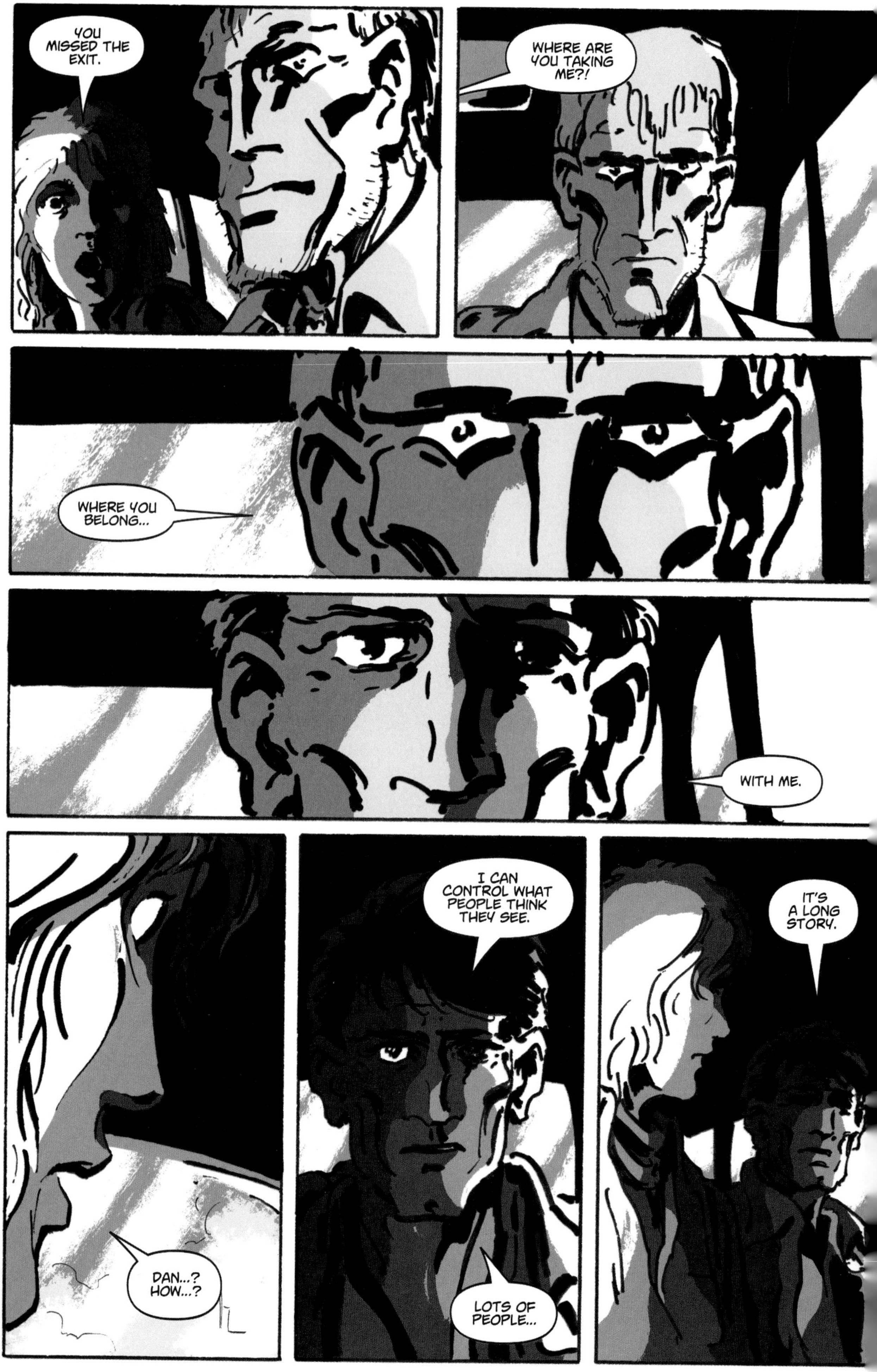
YOU MISSED THE EXIT.
WHERE ARE YOU TAKING ME?!
WHERE YOU BELONG...
WITH ME.
DAN...? HOW...?
I CAN CONTROL WHAT PEOPLE THINK THEY SEE.
LOTS OF PEOPLE...
IT'S A LONG STORY.

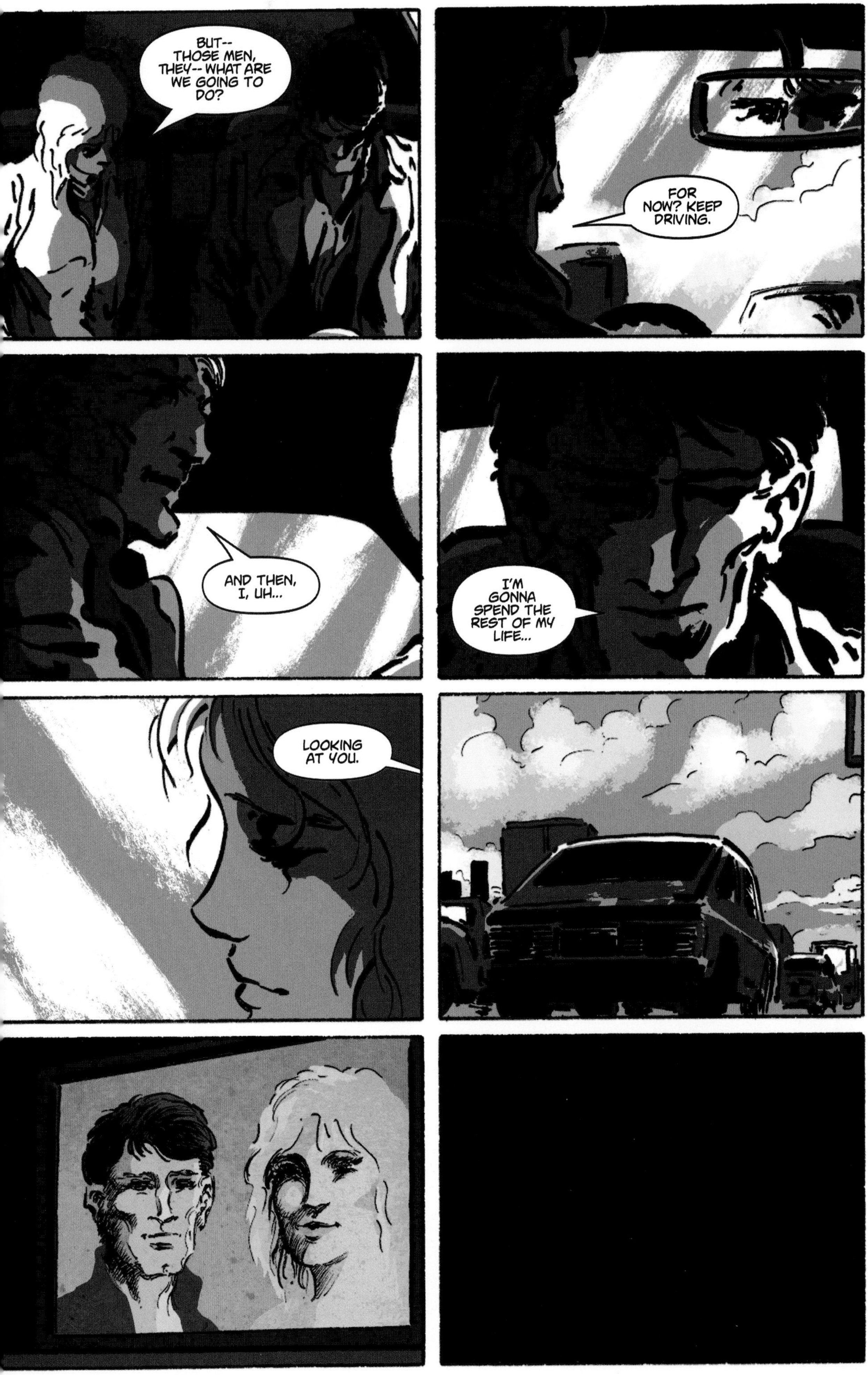
BUT-- THOSE MEN, THEY-- WHAT ARE WE GOING TO DO?
FOR NOW? KEEP DRIVING.
AND THEN, I, UH...
I'M GONNA SPEND THE REST OF MY LIFE...
LOOKING AT YOU.

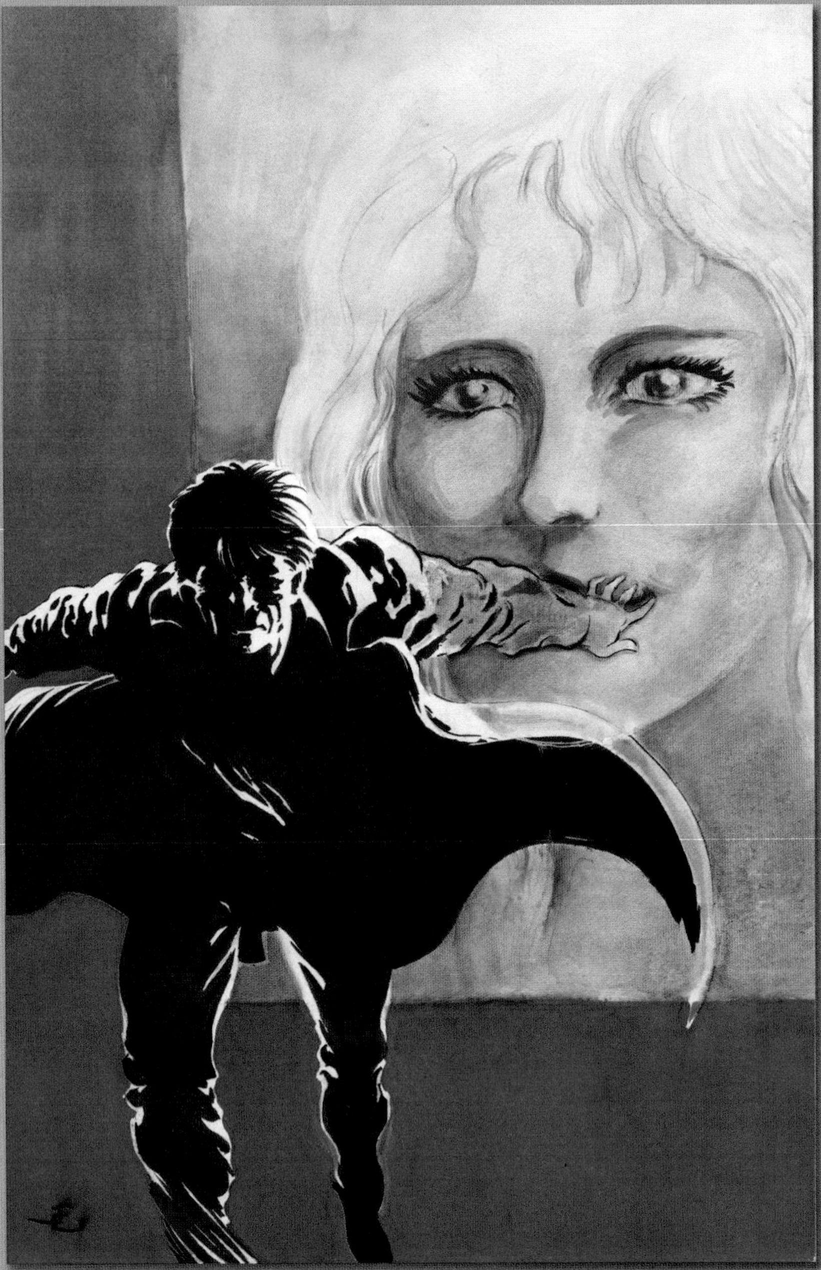

ORIGINAL FRONT COVER FOR ISSUE 1 PUBLISHED BY RENEGADE PRESS

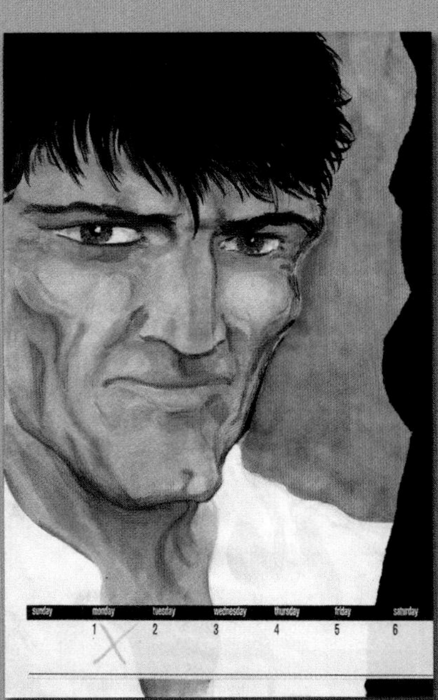
sunday
monday
tuesday
wednesday
thursday
friday
saturday
1
2
3
4
5
6

ORIGINAL BACK COVER
FOR ISSUE 1

Shades of Kafka
The Evolution of A Noir

In the shady government conspiracy-noir KAFKA, secret agent Daniel Hutton has six days to reclaim his past, his identity, his family... his home.

At the University of Colorado, Boulder, college students and aspiring comic creators, writer Steven T. Seagle [*it's a bird...*, *The Red Diary/The RE[a]D Diary*, *Sandman Mystery Theater*, *X-Men*, *House of Secrets*, *Ben 10*] and artist Stefano Gaudiano [*Daredevil, Gotham Central, Batman, Amazing Spider-Man*] had only slightly more time to get their debut mini-series KAFKA produced and published.

In the wake of critically acclaimed series like *Cerebus* and *Love and Rockets*, the black-and-white independent comics market was beginning to boom in the late 1980s. Traditional genre and artistic limits in comic books were being toppled by creators looking to push beyond the formulaic super-hero stories that dominated the American marketplace. The lower cost of producing material in black and white not only provided a safer economic threshold, but also offered a stark palette perfectly suited to the shrouded story of espionage and secret agents found in *Kafka*.

While Kafkaesque motifs wind their way through the series, the original inspiration for the story had no connection to the famous Bohemian author at all. Seagle came across the word "kafka" via his friend Erin Kelly. As fodder for their anticipated careers as renowned novelists, the two high school friends spent an afternoon thumbing through research books in search of inspiration. A thin supermarket check-out booklet listing arcane and "lost" words proved to be the spark for Seagle.

The slender volume suggested that the word "kafka" had origins as a Polish term for vanished persons. The booklet asserted that this particular usage fell away in the years following the Second World War. Though this definition was the central inspiration for the series, Seagle's later attempts to verify the reference came up empty and he has never been able to locate another copy of the booklet.
Conspiracy...?

KAFKA

SEAGLE'S ORIGINAL LOGO DESIGN

The road to publication was no less filled with intrigue and sudden twists. Seagle had interested Renegade Press in the six-issue series *Kafka* through a cold submission. The series proposal contained a synopsis of the six-day story, character descriptions, and three sample pages of art – not drawn by Gaudiano. Seagle had met artist Norm Dwyer at a Denver comic book convention and convinced him to draw sample pages in hopes of securing the series. Dwyer eventually went on to draw well-received comics like *Libby Ellis* and *Speed Racer*, but Renegade Press publisher Deni Loubert thought Dwyer's style on the samples was too slick for the story being told in *Kafka*.
She asked Seagle to keep looking for a better fit.

In the days before the Internet - when the primary comic book communities were camped out on the coasts - Colorado proved to be a challenging place to find a replacement penciler/inker. Several aspiring artists tried out for *Kafka*, but the sticking point for even the most talented illustrators proved to be panel-to-panel storytelling and continuity. The job called for someone with pre-existing comic book chops. And time was running out...

The introduction of *Kafka*'s eventual illustrator would depend on coincidence and poetry.

ORIGINAL FRONT COVER FOR ISSUE 2

sunday monday tuesday wednesday thursday friday saturday
1 2 3 4 5 6

ORIGINAL BACK COVER FOR ISSUE 2

KAFKA

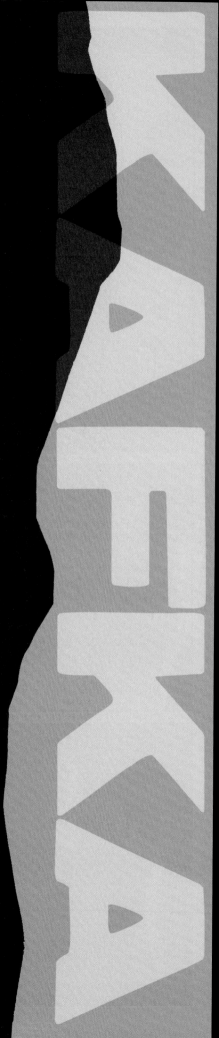

In an upper-level poetry writing class Seagle's college friend Dayton Taylor – known today as the inventor and patent holder of TIMETRACK (the camera system that produces the freeze/tracking shot popularized in the film *The Matrix*) declared he knew someone who could do the job. Taylor introduced Seagle to Italian transplant and fellow Boulder student Stefano Gaudiano.

Gaudiano had made inroads in the semi-professional comic book circuit. Having produced several short stories for the Denver-based anthology *Crimson Dreams*, Gaudiano had definitely been paying his dues in terms of practicing panel work. Seagle connected with Gaudiano who did a quick sketch of his interpretation of Dan Hutton.

GAUDIANO'S FIRST SKETCH OF DANIEL HUTTON

Loubert responded immediately to Gaudiano's loose brush style. She felt his European sensibility matched the tone of the story perfectly. With Gaudiano on board the series was approved with one remaining caveat:

The first issue had to go to press in 40 days.

Renegade Press had lost a book in their printing plan - Ted McKeever's *Transit* (which would eventually be published by Canadian publisher Vortex). As a result, Loubert needed its replacement in the printing schedule, *Kafka*, fast. Very fast. Everything from script to printable art in five weeks. And the deadlines for subsequent issues were no less daunting – complete issues every thirty days thereafter for the next five months.

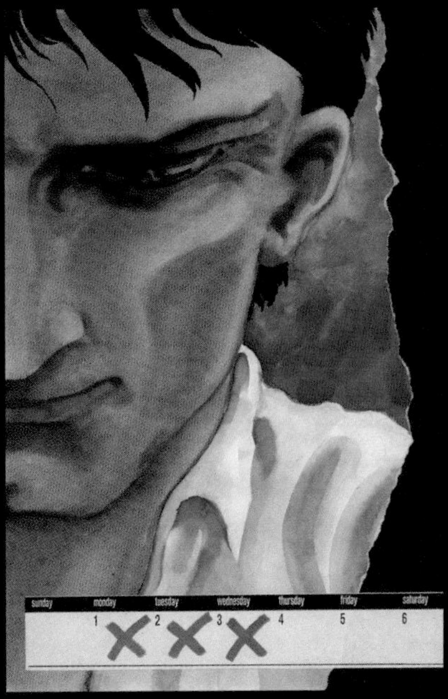
sunday monday tuesday wednesday thursday friday saturday
1 2 3 4 5 6

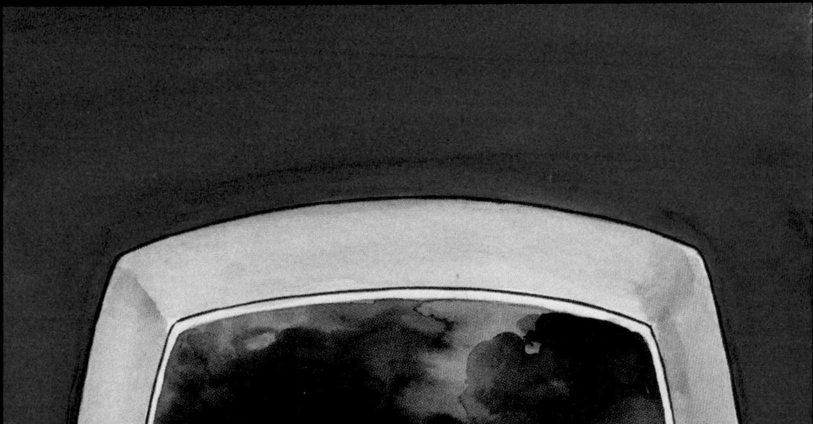

ORIGINAL FRONT COVER FOR ISSUE 3

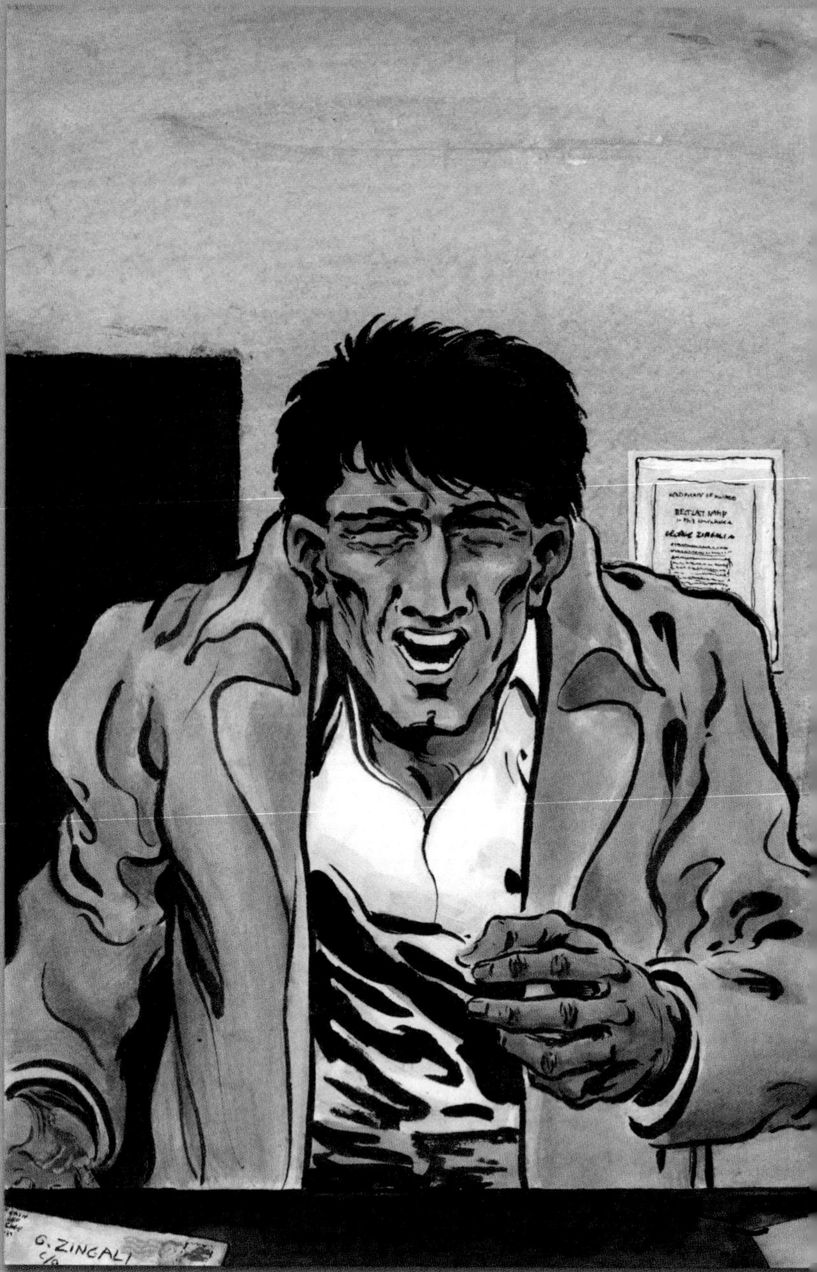
G. ZINGALI

ORIGINAL FRONT COVER FOR ISSUE 4

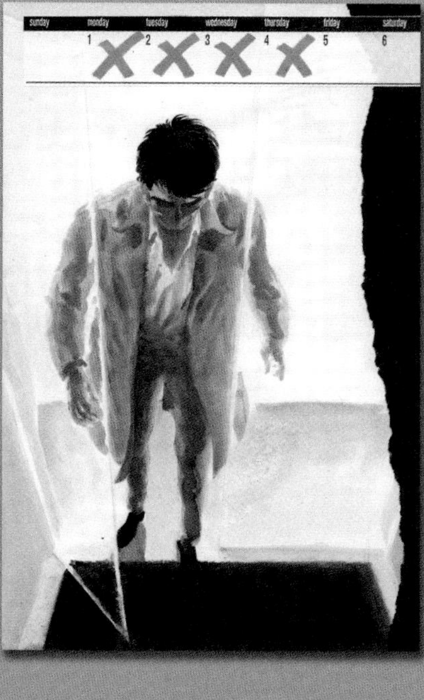
sunday monday tuesday wednesday thursday friday saturday
1 2 3 4 5 6

ORIGINAL BACK COVER
FOR ISSUE 4

In the days before personal computers and Photoshop, the tight deadlines meant Seagle and Gaudiano had to write, draw, ink and letter 25 pages of story; paint two color covers; and design and hand paste-up five text pages each and every month for six months. It would be a challenging schedule for even veteran monthly comics creators, but this "trial by deadline" proved to be a massive education for two twenty-somethings who still had classes, papers and finals by day, and full comic book production studios in their dorm rooms by night.

Seagle scripted. Gaudiano penciled. Seagle lettered. Gaudiano inked. Seagle – designed and (along with his now significant other, Liesel Reinhart) pasted up the text pages. Guadiano painted covers. Seagle designed a logo (which was cleaned and made camera-ready by Gaudiano's fellow Crimson Dreams alumnus Frank Albanese). And every thirty days from late 1987 through early 1988, one day in the life of Daniel Hutton – *Kafka* – was shipped off to Preney Print and Litho in Windsor, Ontario, Canada to become a comic book.

GAUDIANO'S ORIGINAL PENCILS FOR PAGE 144
SHOW HIS FRENETIC LINE WORK

The first issue landed in Seagle and Gaudiano's local comic shop, Boulder's Time Warp, later that same year. Sales were good, with the book making a modest profit right out of the gate. While it was no *Teenage Mutant Ninja Turtles* economically, national reaction to the work was strong. Of the title itself, an early review in *The Comics Journal* declared that naming a comic book Kafka in the super-hero dominant marketplace of the time was akin to yelling "Fire!" in a crowded theater. Whatever the perception, readers took note.

By the end of its six-issue run, the book's sparse dialogue, long stretches of silent action, lack of narration, and ethereal visuals set it apart from the standard fare of the time and critics appreciated it despite, or, perhaps, because of its rushed production. In 1989 *Kafka* received an Eisner Award nomination in the "Best Finite Series" category. It would have to be an honor just to be nominated as the Eisner was claimed by another popular mini-series of the time... *Watchmen*.

While it may have lost the award, *Kafka* did win the attention of the decision makers of the industry. Comico Comics editors Bob Schreck and Diana Schutz appreciated the book enough to commission Seagle's next work *The Amazon* – an eco-fable drawn by artist Tim Sale. Gaudiano partnered with Colorado-based writer Steve Csutoras on a project called *Harlequin* which would eventually be published by Dark Horse Comics when Schutz and Shreck transitioned to the Portland-based publisher in the early 90s.

Kafka's flirtation with a major Hollywood film director burned fast, but ended when the director's production company filed for bankruptcy. But *Kafka* continued to find new print audiences in the intervening years. Caliber Press published the first collected edition of the work in 1990 featuing a new color cover by Gaudiano and an introduction by Bob Schreck.

KAFKA
by
Steven T. Seagle
and
Stefano Gaudiano

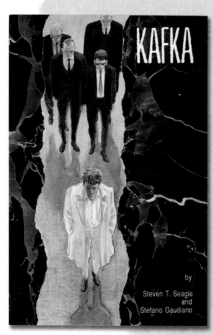

COVER FOR THE 1990 CALIBER COMICS COLLECTED EDITION – NEW ART BY GAUDIANO, DESIGN AND TYPOGRAPHY BY SEAGLE

In 2006, Twenty years after its first publication, Active Images/ Comicraft printed a new compact volume replacing Seagle's "brave" attempts at hand lettering with a cleaner computer font and balloons by Richard Starkings. The book featured a history, a round table interview between publisher Starkings and the creators, and a look at pages from Seagle and Gaudiano's never-realized Piranha Press pitch *Volcano*.

sunday monday tuesday wednesday thursday friday saturday
1 2 3 4 5 6

ORIGINAL BACK COVER
FOR ISSUE 5

ORIGINAL FRONT COVER FOR ISSUE 5

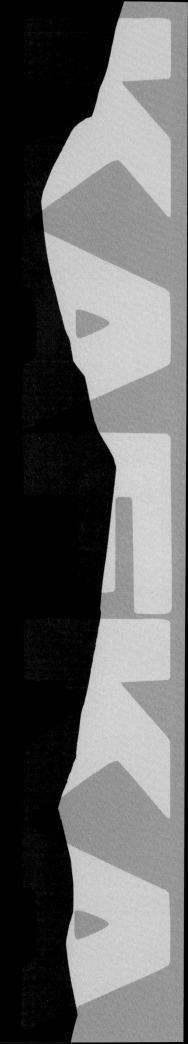

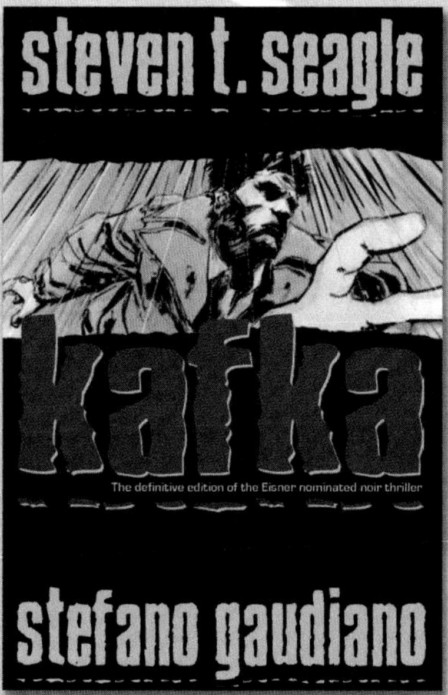
steven t. seagle
kafka
The definitive edition of the Eisner nominated noir thriller
stefano gaudiano

COVER FOR THE 2006 MAN OF ACTION/ACTIVE IMAGES COLLECTED EDITION - NEW ART BY GAUDIANO - DESIGN AND TYPOGRAPHY BY COMICRAFT & SEAGLE

The latest iteration goes somewhere new once more. Approached by lauded actor/director/writer Sir Kenneth Branagh to develop *Kafka* for television, Seagle sought to put one more polish on the work. This new volume presents the work in its largest format to date, and, most notably, in color for the first time... kind of. Seagle and Branagh envisioned a shady noir present in which Dan runs for his life counter-balanced by a vivid color past he longs to recapture. To deliver this visual metaphor, Seagle commissioned artist Marco Cinello (who previously worked with Seagle on the graphic novel *Soul Kiss* and the children's books *Frankie Stein* and *Batula*) to create a five-tone grey palette for sequences set in the present and subdued colors to define the lost past of Daniel Hutton.

In the time since *Kafka*, Seagle and Gaudiano have worked together on three other projects. The island drama *Volcano* was developed for DC Comics' experimental imprint Piranha Press but never commissioned. *My Vagabond Days* told the story of two teenage friends on opposite sides of racial and cultural lines in 1960s New York City. Originally planned for Comico, the series was delayed and eventually lost to the bankruptcy of the Philadelphia-based publisher. *My Vagabond Days* was revived at Dark Horse Comics as a planned four-issue series. The series was put on hold and eventually the first chapter was serialized in *Dark Horse Presents*. Plans were again launched to complete the series, but never fully materialized. Gaudiano also illustrated a chapter of the *Sandman Mystery Theater Annual* plotted by Matt Wagner, scripted by Seagle and published by DC/Vertigo.

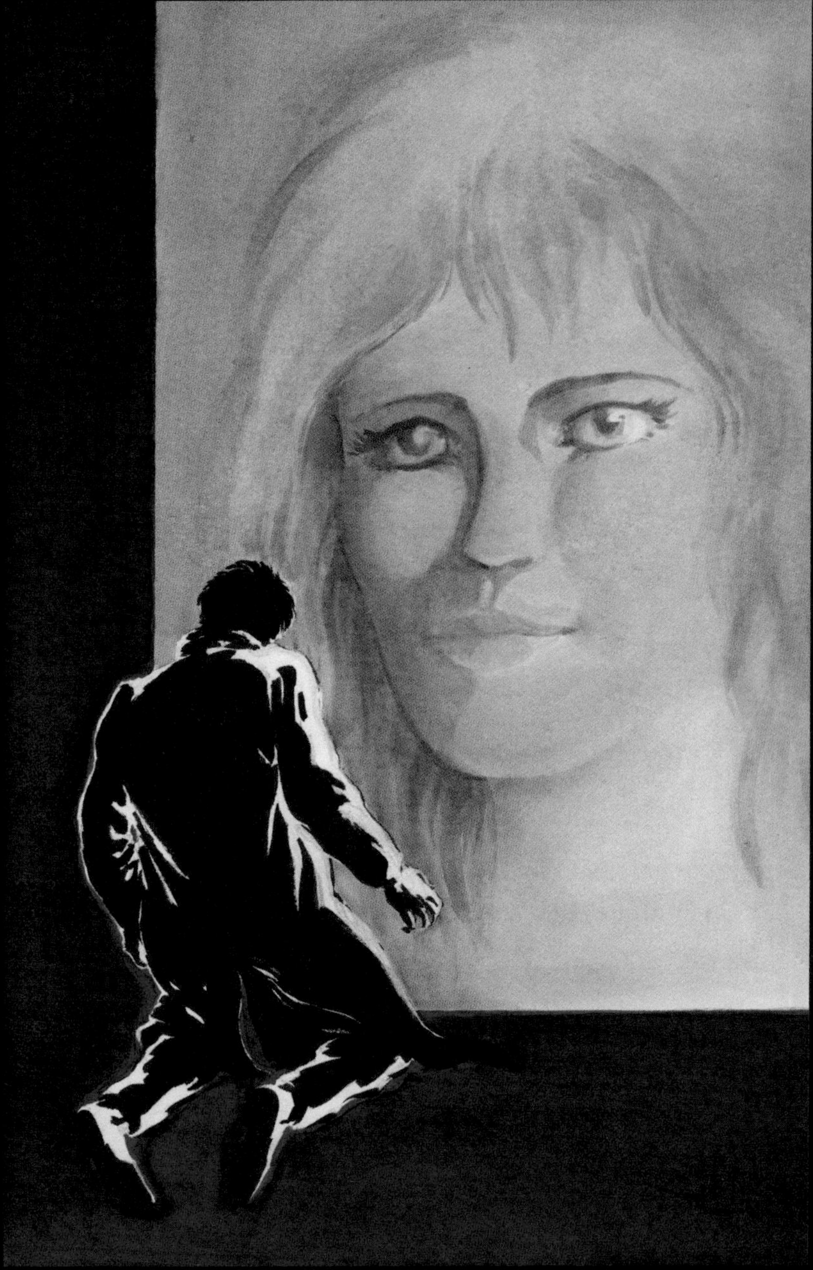

ORIGINAL FRONT COVER FOR ISSUE 6

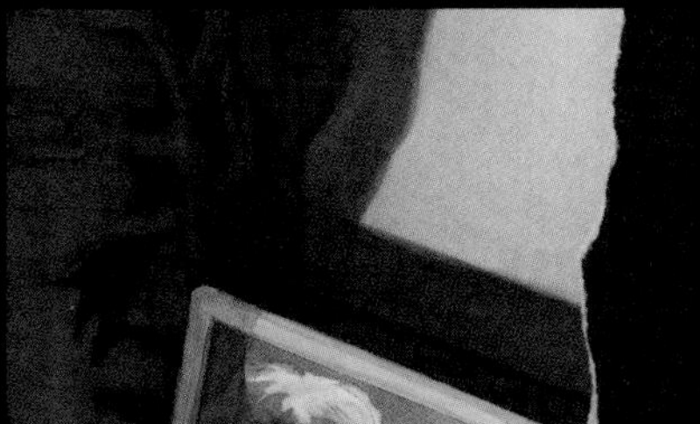
sunday monday tuesday wednesday thursday friday saturday
1 2 3 4 5 6

ORIGINAL BACK COVER FOR ISSUE 6

PROPOSAL ART

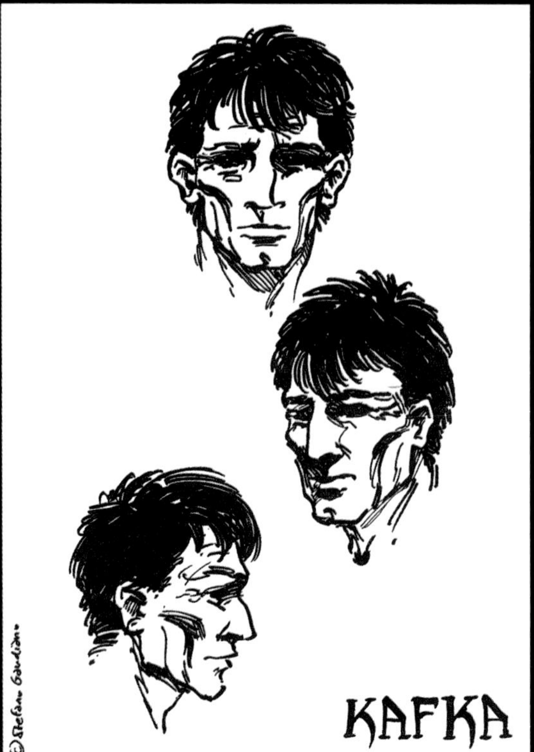
KAFKA
© Stefano Gaudiano

GAUDIANO'S ORIGINAL FACIAL STUDIES FOR DAN HUTTON WERE LATER CONVERTED INTO THE BOTTOM THREE PANELS OF PAGE 18 IN ORDER TO HELP WITH THE VERY TIGHT DELIVERY SCHEDULE.

GAUDIANO DREW THREE FULL PAGES FROM THE FIRST ISSUE AS SAMPLES. WHILE THE PANELS IN THIS PAGE ALL APPEARED IN THE FINAL BOOK (ON PAGES 22, 23, AND 24) THEY WERE ORIGINALLY ON THE SAME PAGE BEFORE A PLOT CHANGE REQUIRED THEIR SEPARATION AND RE-USE ELSEWHERE.

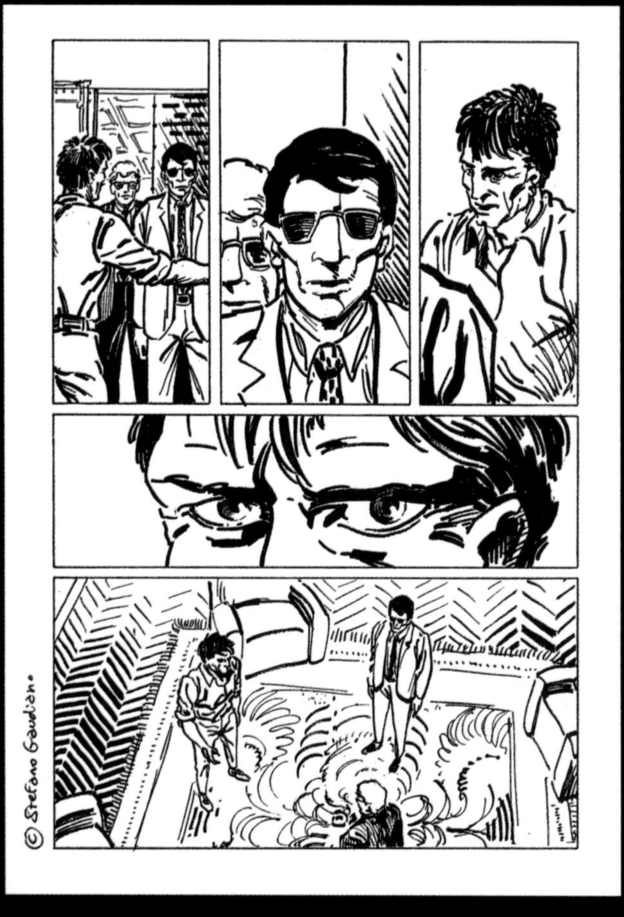
© Stefano Gaudiano

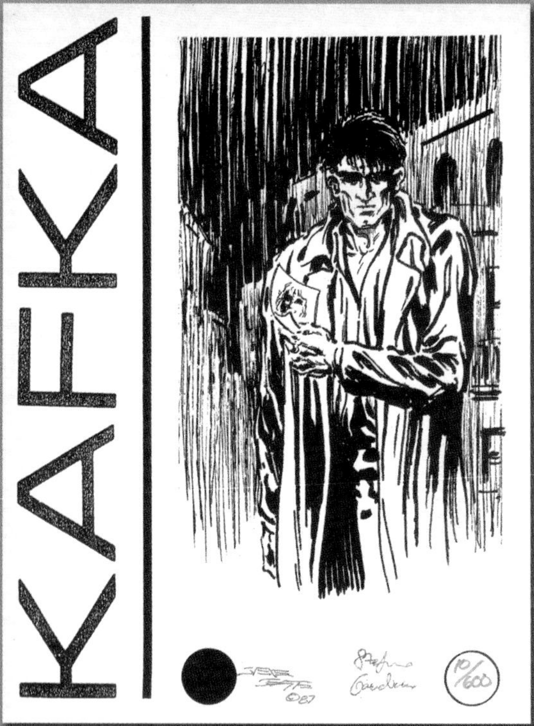
KAFKA
10/600

A PEN AND INK VERSION OF THE PROMOTIONAL POSTER WAS PRINTED ON PARCHMENT PAPER, SIGNED AND NUMBERED (FROM 600) BY SEAGLE AND GAUDIANO, AND DISTRIBUTED AT CONVENTIONS IN CHICAGO AND SAN DIEGO. IT WAS ALSO MAILED TO READERS WHOSE LETTERS WERE PUBLISHED IN THE STAND-ALONE ISSUES.

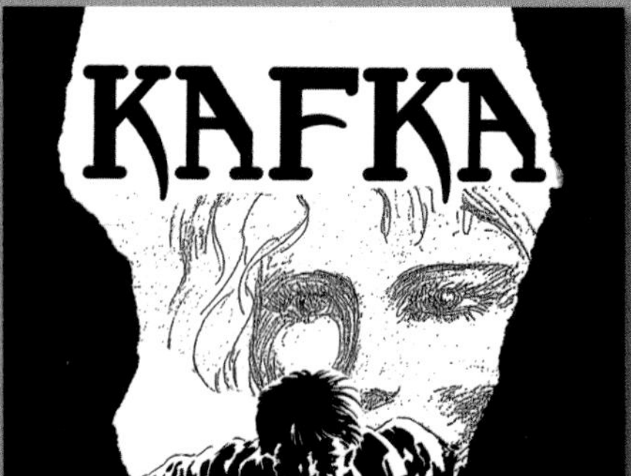
KAFKA
Renegade
ON SALE NOW

THE LACK OF LEAD TIME LED TO SOME CREATIVE RE-USE OF ART – INCLUDING THE ORIGINAL COVER SKETCHES BEING CONVERTED FOR THIS AD WHICH RAN IN THE COMICS BUYER'S GUIDE.

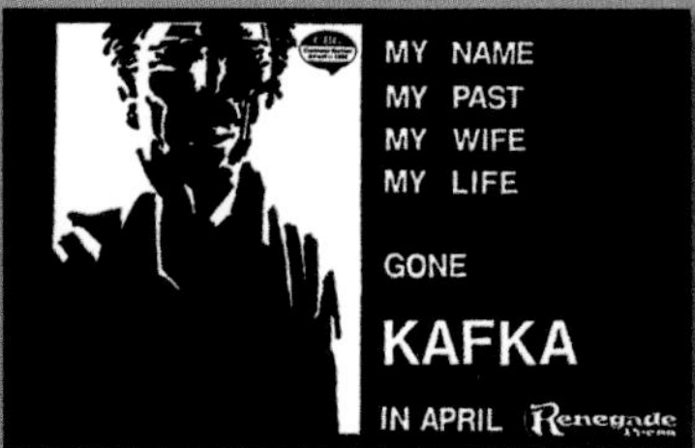
MY NAME
MY PAST
MY WIFE
MY LIFE
GONE
KAFKA
IN APRIL
Renegade Press

THE FIRST IMAGE OF KAFKA SEEN BY THE OUTSIDE WORLD WAS THIS SMALL PROMOTIONAL AD MADE FROM A PHOTOCOPY AND PRESS-ON LETTERS ADHERED TO AN INDEX CARD.

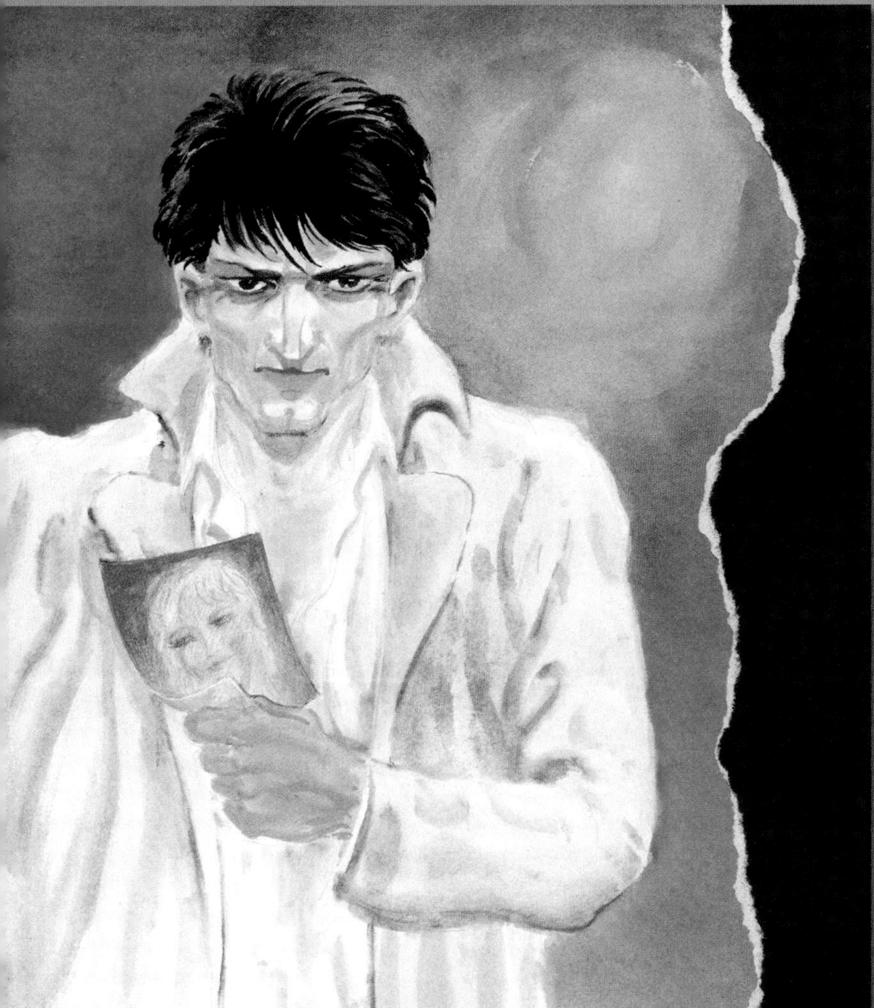
KAFKA
Renegade

A FULL COLOR PROMOTIONAL POSTER WAS PRINTED IN ADVANCE OF THE FIRST ISSUE AND DISTRIBUTED TO RETAILERS.

PROMOTIONAL PIECES

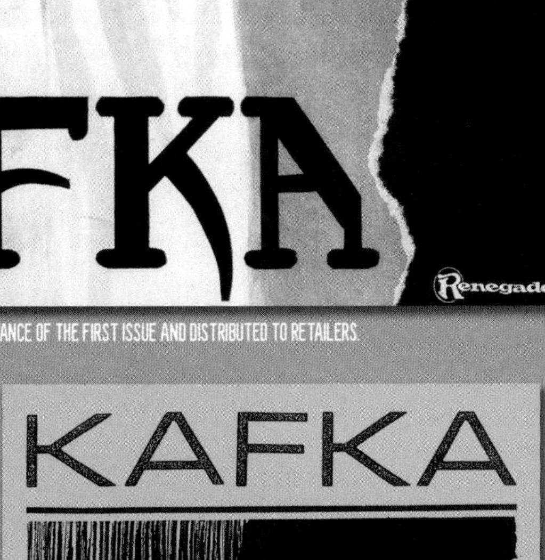
KAFKA
Renegade

SEAGLE PRODUCED A VERY LIMITED EDITION T-SHIRT FOR FRIENDS AND FAMILY USING THE PROMOTIONAL IMAGE WITH A MODIFIED TEAR MOTIF.

Steven T. Seagle

Seagle was born in a military hospital in Biloxi, Mississippi before being "relocated" to Colorado, California and other American states as part of an Air Force operation. He is best known in comics for his graphic novel memoir *it's a bird...* .

Outside of comics, Seagle is part of the mysterious creative collective MAN OF ACTION – creators of the Cartoon Network global conspiracy *BEN10*. He and his shadowy colleagues also created *Generator Rex* for Cartoon Network and serve as executive producers on MARVEL'S *Avengers Assemble* and *Ultimate Spider-Man* on Disney XD.

Seagle resides in the seemingly innocuous Pasadena area of Southern California with love-of-his-life Liesel and three cats code-named "Gaudi," "Baxter," and "Smilla." They are inches away from the nefarious Jet Propulsion Laboratories...

www.manofaction.tv

www.speaktheaterarts.com

Stefano Gaudiano

Gaudiano was born in Milan, Italy before being "disappeared" to America as part of a global information exchange conspiracy. He is best known for his work on Marvel Comics *Daredevil* series.

Gaudiano has been repeatedly abducted and forced back into comics where he co-created the original works *Harlequin*, and *My Vagabond Days* as well as doing "cover-up work" on the acclaimed titles *Gotham Central* for DC Comics, *Harbinger* for Valiant Comics, and other classified works.

Gaudiano is currently hiding out in the eerily green suburbs of Seattle, Washington with wife Kathy and adorable daughters Milena and Sabina. The family may or may not be the cause of Seattle's mysterious, low-frequency hum.

www.stefanogaudiano.blogspot.com/